Planet of Cities

Planet of Cities

SHLOMO ANGEL

LINCOLN INSTITUTE
OF LAND POLICY
CAMBRIDGE, MASSACHUSETTS

Library of Congress Cataloging-in-Publication Data
Angel, Shlomo.
    Planet of cities / Shlomo Angel
       p. cm.
    Includes bibliographical references and index.
    ISBN 978-1-55844-245-0 (pbk.) -- ISBN 978-1-55844-249-8 (e-book)
  1. Urbanization. 2. Cities and towns--Growth. I. Title.
    HT361.A537 2012
    307.76--dc23

                          2012025247

Designed and composed in Baskerville MT and ITC Franklin Gothic by
David Gerratt/DG Communications, Acton, Massachusetts

Printed and bound by Puritan Press, Inc., Hollis, New Hampshire

MANUFACTURED IN THE UNITED STATES OF AMERICA

Cover images:

Top row, left to right: Shanghai, China (p. 109, iStockphoto); Guatemala City, Guatemala
(p. 245, © Alvaro Uribe); Alexandria, Egypt (p. 234, iStockphoto); Fez, Morocco
(p. 146, Creative Commons); Hong Kong (p. 177, iStockphoto)

Map: p. 4, Angel et al. (2012 online)

Bottom row, left to right: Curitiba, Brazil (p. 35, © Gislene Pereira); Bangkok, Thailand
(p. 130, iStockphoto); U.S. sprawl (p. 109, Creative Commons); Beijing, China (p. 252, iStockphoto);
Bangkok, Thailand (p. 48, 123RF)

For Lucinda, Adam, and Daniella,
my fellow explorers

Contents

List of Illustrations

TABLES

Foreword

The science of cities is identifying and documenting common patterns of urban development across our planet, even though cities are often regarded as unique, and this volume contributes new research and illustrative evidence to this emergent discipline. Analysis of population and employment density, spatial development patterns, and travel behavior across cities has been underway for many years, but most urban empirical work has focused on the comparison of cities within individual countries because comparable data generally have been available only on a country-level basis. Such studies are normally based on census data for which national standards ensure that definitions of households, residential units, and urbanized areas are consistent across a country's cities and metropolitan areas. But national definitions, standards, and the timing of census data vary across countries, making it challenging to use such data to examine cities globally.

This volume takes on the challenge of rigorously comparing cities from a global perspective. It reports results from the analysis of a global sample of cities using data on land use obtained from satellite imagery and numerous other sources. Satellite data are defined consistently around the world, making it possible to compare land development patterns in all urban areas. Moreover, such data are accessible for all countries and for a common time period. Their availability is transforming empirical work on urban development patterns.

The analysis uses satellite imagery and other data to distinguish developed from undeveloped land, and it formulates a variety of metrics to define the extent of urbanized areas, the share of undeveloped land, and the shape and fragmentation of spatial growth experienced by a sample of 120 global cities with populations of 100,000 or more in 2000. It also combines the satellite images with census data to measure population density per unit of developed land and its change from 1990 to 2000. The analysis of satellite data is complemented by separate analyses of census tract data for 20 U.S. cities from 1910 to 2000, and of historic maps for 30 large global cities beginning as far back as 1800. The result is a compelling tour de force of empirical information about urban development patterns that reveals some striking regularities across cities and over time. In particular, all of the data sets show that cities have been decentralizing and reducing population densities as they grow.

The striking historical and global regularities in the spatial development patterns of urban areas are then used as a basis for policy recommendations that address the massive expansion of urban populations forecast to occur in developing countries—where urban populations are expected to increase from 2 billion in 2000 to 5.5 billion in 2050. Historical regularities of urban growth and expansion indicate that a doubling of urban population will be accompanied by a tripling of developed urban land. A key recommendation of this volume is that urban management regimes must make adequate plans for this expansion, particularly by reserving rights-of-way in areas of future growth for transport, other networked urban infrastructure, and public open spaces.

The Lincoln Institute of Land Policy has supported Shlomo Angel's work for several years, but this book also builds on earlier research by the author and his colleagues. This earlier work was supported in part by the World Bank, the National Science Foundation, and the National Aeronautics and Space Administration. The Lincoln Institute's support led to the development of three working papers, the policy focus report titled *Making Room for a Planet of Cities* (2011c), and the companion book, *Atlas of Urban Expansion* (2012), all of which were coauthored by Shlomo Angel, Jason Parent, Daniel L. Civco, and Alejandro M. Blei.

In addition, the complete data sets comprising the U.S. Census data for 20 cities, the historic maps for 30 global cities, and the satellite data for the sample of 120 global cities in 1990 and 2000 and for 3,646 cities with populations over 100,000 in 2000 are all available on the Lincoln Institute website at *www.lincolninst.edu/subcenters/atlas-urban-expansion*. This *Planet of Cities* volume and the accompanying *Atlas of Urban Expansion* book and website clearly demonstrate the potential of satellite data to revolutionize the analysis of the spatial dimensions of urban growth.

Gregory K. Ingram
President and CEO
Lincoln Institute of Land Policy

Introduction
and
Four Propositions

The Streets

The streets of Buenos Aires
have become my very core.
Not the ravenous streets,
bustling with crowds and commotion,
but the neglected streets of the barrio,
which hide themselves from most people,
softened by twilight and sunset
and those ones farther out
knowing nothing of kind trees
where simple little houses,
overwhelmed by infinite distances,
scarcely dare to lose themselves in the far-reaching view
of skies and plains.
For the lonely one, they are a promise
because thousands of individual souls populate them,
each one unique before God and in time
and undeniably precious.
To the West, the North, and the South
the streets—they are also my country—have been unfurled:
May their colors come through
in the lines that I pen.

Jorge Luis Borges

Translated by Benjamin Ehrlich and Daniella Gitlin in 2012 from the collection of poems, *Fervor de Buenos Aires,* by Jorge Luis Borges (1969).

CHAPTER 1

Coming to Terms with Global Urban Expansion

There are nearly 4,000 cities on the planet today with populations of 100,000 or more. Every one of these cities is different. Every one of these cities is unique and one of a kind, just like you and I are unique and one of a kind. But if you are like me, when you fall ill, you prefer to have a common rather than a rare or unique disease. Suddenly, your wish to be unique disappears and you would really prefer to be just a common person with common symptoms seeking a common cure. Cities should be in the same predicament. They would be if more common knowledge about them were available, and if those who care for them renounced their insistence on their own city remaining so unique that what happens to other cities is irrelevant.

Modern medical science is founded on the proposition that while each of us is unique, many of us share common ailments that can only be understood and addressed effectively by studying them in sufficiently large groups of people. "Science," wrote Aldous Huxley (1958, 19), "may be defined as the reduction of multiplicity to unity. It seeks to explain the endlessly diverse phenomena of nature by ignoring the uniqueness of particular events, concentrating on what they have in common and finally abstracting some kind of 'law' in terms of which they make sense and can be effectively dealt with."

This book is a modest contribution toward a science of cities, based on the study of sufficiently large numbers of cities, to help government officials, academics, activists, or interested citizens identify and address their common ailments and seek common cures. As it turns out, the only things we know about the 4,000 cities in the world today are their names, exact locations, and approximate populations (figure 1.1). There is very little common and comparable knowledge about these cities, and none of the available information can be described as scientific.

My interest in the scientific study of cities is not driven by a thirst for pure knowl-edge, but is a practical one—making realistic yet adequate preparations for future urban expansion in cities everywhere. These preparations are needed to make our cities efficient, livable, and equitable, and to keep our planet sustainable. They are needed now, when the urbanization of our planet is still in full swing, and the sooner we attend to them the more effective and the more economical they are likely to be.

A RELUCTANCE TO ENGAGE WITH URBAN EXPANSION

Much to my chagrin, I have detected great reluctance to engage with the prospects of urban expansion, for reasons that may be perfectly understandable. This reluctance tends to keep such prospects rather obscure and even somewhat frightening, and prevents us from addressing them in a clear and forthright manner. We can observe the reluctance to come to terms with urban expansion in the positions and attitudes of four groups of people: established residents of cities, municipal officials, homeowners, and environmentalists.

For many of their more vociferous established residents, cities are already threateningly large. Allowing them to become even larger is nonsensical and unacceptable. Newcomers—be they new immigrants from distant shores or new migrants from other parts of the state or country—are therefore unwelcome. They are typically seen as nuisances rather than as assets—more mouths to feed, more children to educate, threats to jobs, and more congestion on the roads. They are not seen as energetic new cadres of workers and citizens generating new demands for goods and services and enriching the diversity that fuels our creativity. If indeed these newcomers are considered nuisances, why should they be welcomed? Maybe if they are not welcomed, fewer of them will come.

FIGURE 1.1
Locations of 3,646 Cities with Populations of 100,000 or More in the Year 2000

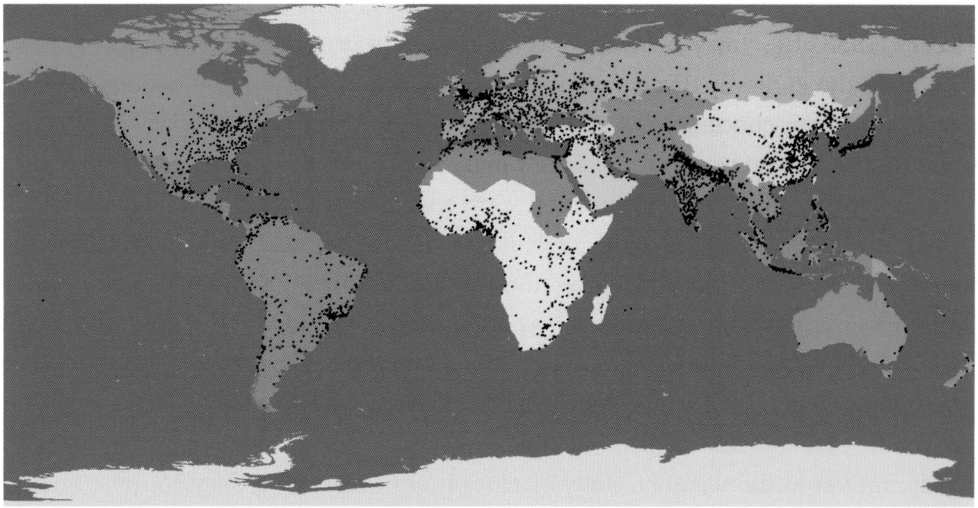

Source: City location data from Angel et al. (2012 online).

A family of immigrants disembarks at Ellis Island, New York City, in the early 1900s on its way to settling in one of America's rapidly growing cities.

Millions of rural migrants with no residence permits (hukous) have come to work in Chinese cities since 1978: Migrant workers on a lunch break outside a construction site in Beijing.

Of course, when established residents are pitted against others who have yet to arrive or are yet to be born, only those residents can have their say. If they could, the more radical among them would effectively subvert all thoughts of coming to terms with urban expansion or doing what it takes to guide and tame it. Their position may be irrational, but it is understandable. Why should they be concerned about the expansion of cities when they live in a city that is barely functional and barely livable? Why not just leave things alone, conserving and improving what they already have? Never mind that they comfortably forget that they themselves, their parents or grandparents, and definitely their ancestors, were once newcomers to the city as well.

Activists in
Portland, Oregon,
rally to support
immigrants in
2011.

In any event, what makes a city inviting is not a colorful welcome sign on the road that residents can simply remove. It is the economic opportunities the city offers and the quality of life it promises that make it attractive, and both are qualities that established residents would be unwilling to part with just to make their city unattractive to newcomers. Still, even though their reasoning may be in error, many of them may be reluctant to engage with the prospects of urban expansion.

Mayors, urban planners, city engineers, and other municipal officials are in a difficult predicament when it comes to confronting urban expansion. In some parts of the world they are accountable to current residents and must abide by their desires lest they get booted out of office. If these residents refuse to plan for expansion, they must be obeyed unless they can be persuaded otherwise. But persuading a stubborn electorate is not the only problem officials face. Making preparations for urban expansion is costly and requires the acquisition of substantial amounts of land for public use. It also requires expensive new infrastructure—the extension of roads and streets and the construction of sewer lines, sewage treatment plants, water reservoirs, and water mains. What is more worrisome, it requires thinking about the future and attending to future needs now, while other burning issues are demanding the officials' attention and meager resources.

These preparations may indeed be essential if the city is to grow and flourish and if it is to remain efficient and productive, as well as equitable and livable, for many years to come. But such farsighted considerations, important as they may be, too often give way to putting out the fires that are erupting every day. Pragmatic as it may be, succumbing to this view of managing cities is shortsighted. Some activities require municipal officials to engage in true long-term planning, while most others do not. With urban expansion, it is critically important to secure the rights-of-way for arterial roads and to protect selected open spaces before urban development takes place, preferably before rural lands even begin to be subdivided for urban use. In their report, *A Major Traffic Street Plan for Los Angeles*, for example, Olmsted, Bartholomew, and Cheney (1924) argued for acquiring the rights-of-way for roads in advance of future development. Pushing an arterial road through a built-up area is nearly impossible, and creating public open spaces in densely built neighborhoods is a pipe dream. Urban expansion must be prepared for in advance or not at all.

Homeowners, often a majority in many cities, also may perceive an economic interest in curtailing urban expansion. If land for new development on the urban periphery is easy to come by and new houses are easy and cheap to build, then housing values are likely to remain stable and affordable throughout the city. But if land is in short supply and demand for housing is strong, the value of existing houses goes up and homeowners become better off without ever having lifted a finger. The fact that the children of these homeowners will no longer be able to afford a house nearby may be of less concern since they may eventually inherit a valuable property. This is a rather cynical position on the part of homeowners, but clearly a rational one insofar as it protects their property values. William Fischel (2005, 320), who coined the term *homevoters* (homeowners who vote), noted that growth controls in American cities "seem to act more like a cartel for those already in possession of suburban homes than as a rationalizer of metropolitan development patterns."

Finally, committed environmentalists who are concerned with protecting the farmlands, forests, pastures, or sensitive wetlands on the periphery of cities from being invaded by urban development tend to see urban expansion, uniformly decried as sprawl, as anathema to global sustainability. They claim that converting farmlands to urban use destroys food supplies and exacerbates an already serious global food crisis. It also destroys forests and diminishes the diversity of flora and fauna. Moreover, the

Activists protest urban expansion in Surrey, England, in 2009.

more expansive and spread out the city is, the more energy it consumes in transport or in heating and cooling processes, exacerbating an already visible energy crisis. This energy requires the burning of fossil fuels that release carbon dioxide and other greenhouse gases into the air, trap heat, and exacerbate an undeniable global warming crisis. Denser and more compact cities encourage more walking and cycling, thereby contributing a much-needed check on an awkwardly visible obesity crisis.

It is not difficult for avid environmentalists to conclude that cities now occupy enough land and have no real need for expansion. Their idea is that cities should simply be contained and enclosed by greenbelts or impenetrable urban growth boundaries. If populations grow, some observers firmly believe, everyone can be accommodated within the existing confines of cities, through the infill of vacant lands, intensification of land use, densification and revitalization of old neighborhoods, conversion of single-family homes to multifamily dwellings, or mixed use of urban land.

When we focus attention on where most urban development is likely to take place in the coming decades—namely in the cities of developing countries—this rather purist vision of cities can be described as uninformed or utopian because it puts sustainability as an absolute end that then justifies all means to attain it. Other goals, such as full employment, the quality of urban life, the satisfaction of basic human needs, or the expression of personal or political preferences for this or that lifestyle, are readily sacrificed. This vision is also quite pessimistic when it comes to solving the global sustainability problem by other means, such as through progress in science and technology, and is quite oblivious to the cost of curbing urban expansion in comparison with the cost of other possible solutions for keeping our planet sustainable. It also

Denser and more compact cities are not always the answer: Air pollution shrouds the city of Cairo, Egypt, despite its relatively high residential densities.

assumes that existing cities can simply be densified and made more compact, despite a growing body of evidence that residents actively and effectively resist proposals that may change the character of their neighborhoods (Jenks, Burton, and Williams 1996; Vallance, Perkins, and Moore 2005).

When all of these stakeholders—established residents, municipal officials, home-owners, and environmentalists—come together, they can and often do form formidable coalitions that seek to limit urban expansion by advocating the strict containment of cities within their current footprints and incorporating all new population growth into more compact urban environments. Indeed, "since the world adoption of sustainability objectives in the early 1990s . . . promotion of the compact city—in terms of higher density development, mixed uses, and reuse of brownfield sites—is now enshrined in land use planning in many countries" (Burton 2002, 219). The costs and benefits of containment are uncertain, its potential contribution questionable, and broad political support for it may still be lacking. But despite these uncertainties, this agenda has already erected a significant barrier than can effectively block efforts to make realistic plans for urban expansion.

When a conscientious mayor of a city, large or small, is asked what she is doing to prepare for urban expansion, she may well retort that she has no desire, nor do her staff or her constituents, to allow for expansion. They believe the city consumes enough land as it is, and all future construction should take place within its current boundaries. She will oppose expansion so the planet can remain sustainable, people can walk and cycle at their leisure, municipal budgets are not unduly burdened, decaying central cities can thrive again, and precious cultivated lands on the urban fringe are not laid to waste. In other words, given the vociferous rhetoric objecting to urban expansion, she would face both criticism and ridicule if she even indulged in ideas about urban expansion, let alone committed public resources to facilitate it.

GATHERING DATA ON URBAN EXPANSION

I began to realize in 2002 that the only way for me to engage with this reluctance to confront continuing urban expansion was to assemble solid empirical data on expansion and its key attributes in cities around the world over long periods of time. Such data, I had hoped and still believe, could demonstrate the extent to which cities have expanded in the distant and recent pasts, and suggest how and by how much they are likely to grow further in the future. Coupled with theories that could explain the underlying forces that propel and shape urban expansion, the data could also provide the evidence needed to demonstrate various concerns: that it would be very difficult, if not futile, to resist expansion; that ignoring or denying it in the hope that it will not occur will simply allow it to take place unhindered and in a more costly and destructive way; that acquiring a better understanding of it will make it less formidable and more manageable; and that making minimal yet effective preparations for it is the right way, and certainly the only responsible way, to proceed.

I thus embarked on a study of global urban expansion that has taken almost a decade to complete. From a research perspective, this was a very satisfying journey, but from a practical perspective of assisting real cities to prepare for their expansion, it was more frustrating. For example, I helped organize the municipal administrations of five secondary cities in Ecuador to prepare for their expansion (figure 1.2). The project was ready to begin when it was upended by the newly elected president of Ecuador, for reasons that had nothing to do with the merits of the project. He simply canceled the project because it had financial support from the World Bank, and he wanted the bank out of the country. An attempt to revive the project two years later with funds from the Rockefeller Foundation was short-lived, too, when the foundation lost a substantial share of its portfolio in the financial crisis of 2008 and the project was removed from its budget. New efforts to engage cities in planning for their expansion are now in the making, but have not yet borne fruit.

In contrast, it was considerably easier to organize funding for research on global urban expansion. I had stumbled upon a new research frontier that, apart from a few

FIGURE 1.2
The Expansion Plan for Manta, Ecuador, 2007

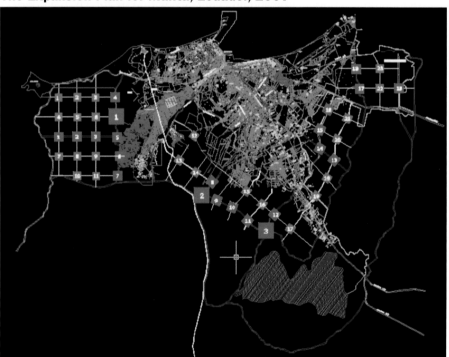

Note: The expansion plan shows the proposed arterial road grid and plots of 1 hectare each at intersections to be acquired for future public use.
Source: Provided to the author by the Department of City Planning, Municipality of Manta, Ecuador.

FIGURE 1.3
Satellite Imagery Used to Map the Expansion of Kigali, Rwanda, 1984 and 1999

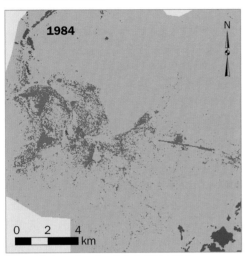
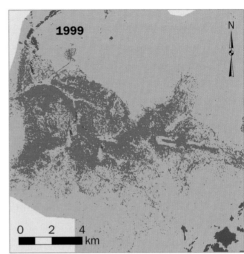

Source: Redrawn from Angel et al. (2012, 120).

empirical studies of sprawl in the United States, has been left as virgin territory for my colleagues and me to explore. Our studies of global urban expansion have been made possible by recent technological advances in global satellite imagery and the software required to analyze it (figure 1.3); by the recent creation of global databases by international organizations, academic institutions, and civil society associations; and by the accelerating ease of global communications made possible by the Internet. I consider myself fortunate to have formulated a question that these new troves of information could help answer: How and why do real cities expand?

When I embarked on the study of global urban expansion, this was the only question that occupied me. Soon thereafter, however, new questions presented themselves as I became more familiar with urban expansion and began to understand, measure, and analyze its specific attributes and manifestations. I strongly believe that coming to terms with urban expansion and its reality in cities everywhere—and especially in cities where urbanization is still occurring—will make it easier to manage in a pragmatic and responsible manner, something that denying it, rejecting it for ideological reasons, or simply neglecting it will not allow us to do.

This book provides rigorous as well as partial answers to seven sets of questions that, taken together, present a coherent view of global urban expansion.

1. What are the extents of urban areas, how fast are they expanding over time, why, and why should it matter?
2. How dense are urban areas, how are urban densities changing over time, why, and why should it matter?

3. How centralized are the residences and workplaces in cities, do they tend to disperse to the periphery over time, and if so, why, and why should it matter?
4. How fragmented are the built-up areas of cities, how are levels of fragmentation changing over time, why, and why should it matter?
5. How compact are the shapes of urban footprints, how are their levels of compactness changing over time, why, and why should it matter?
6. How much land will urban areas require in the future, why, and why should it matter?
7. How much cultivated land will be consumed by expanding urban areas, why, and why should it matter?

Seeking to use these new sources of data to answer these questions, I faced a fourfold challenge: first, to obtain the human and financial resources to assemble and organize the data into a set of digital maps of a large number of cities, preferably a global sample of cities; second, to articulate a set of simple metrics that would summarize key attributes of these maps, making it possible to compare them to each other as well as to compare their changes over time; third, to assemble a body of theory that could explain urban expansion and its attributes in a systematic and rigorous fashion; and fourth, to draw some practical policy lessons based on these various findings.

DISTINCT EXPANSION ISSUES IN DEVELOPED AND DEVELOPING COUNTRIES

My primary policy concern was, and still is, that in the absence of ample and accessible land for expansion on the urban periphery, artificial shortages of residential lands will quickly extinguish any hope that housing will remain affordable, especially for the urban poor—the majority of the future inhabitants of burgeoning cities in developing countries. Such artificial shortages and the resulting house-price inflation may be of less concern in cities in the more developed countries because they are now fully or almost fully urbanized and their expansion is rarely accompanied by urban population growth. The demand for plots on the urban periphery of these cities may be low enough to be matched by a relatively limited supply, keeping land and house prices under control. There is still a need to ensure an adequate supply of land on the fringe of these cities, of course, to keep residential prices stable, but the quantities of land are relatively modest.

Because of this modest demand for land, other more magnanimous concerns have now taken hold: the preservation of farmland, the protection of nature, the conservation of energy, the rejuvenation of town centers, or the curtailment of carbon emissions. Those concerns sometimes trump the more mundane concern with affordable housing.

The demand for land in the rapidly growing cities of developing countries—cities that are still in the midst of the urbanization process and where the bulk of urban expansion is now likely to take place—is certainly not modest, and artificial restrictions of the supply of land on the urban fringe are likely to have quite dire consequences for families struggling to meet their basic needs. To put the expected demand for plots on the urban periphery in numerical perspective, consider these statistics. Between 2010 and 2050, the urban population of the more developed countries will increase by a mere 170 million people, growing at a rate of 0.6 percent per year. During that same period, the urban population of the less developed countries will increase by 2.6 billion people, 15 times that of the more developed countries, and at a rate of 2.4 percent per year, which is 4 times faster than that of the more developed countries (United Nations Population Division 2012, file 3).

In quantitative terms, cities in the developing countries, especially those in rapidly urbanizing ones, face quite a different predicament than cities in the more developed countries. They need to create vast supplies of residential land on the urban periphery to match the vast demand for land to house their growing populations. These places cannot be expected to attend to loftier conservation and sustainability concerns before they satisfy their basic needs, including shelter.

It is therefore worrisome that most, though by no means all, prescriptions for cities in our globalized world originate in the more developed countries, especially in the United States and to a lesser extent in the European Union. This is to be expected, of course, because these countries have the best data; conduct the best cutting-edge research; publish the best journals that report on this research; welcome the best students to study abroad; have regulatory environments that can best apply the latest research findings; have private firms that are well equipped to take advantage of these findings; and have civic groups that are best organized to make use of the data in championing their causes.

The presumption, of course, is that if the best and the latest prescriptions for cities are good enough for the United States and Europe, then surely they must be good enough for the rest of the world. No one seems to mind that cities in the United States, for example, may be quite different from cities in other regions; that the extent of their sprawl and their high levels of greenhouse gas emissions may be quite unique; and that cures will tend to make them more like cities in the developing world rather than the other way around. No one seems to be complaining that American and European prescriptions for non-American and non-European cities are irrelevant or inappropriate, or if they are complaining, the complaints are not loud enough to matter.

On the contrary, the language of U.S. sprawl and its containment is now readily borrowed and applied in studies and policy prescriptions for cities in developing countries as if it were self-evident that sprawl is, indeed, a universal phenomenon requiring a universal response. An example from a recent study of Beijing, China, states (Zhao, Lu, and Roo 2010, 144):

> The empirical evaluation of containment strategies has already been widely investigated in North America and Europe, and it is now necessary that this becomes the focus of the debate in developing countries, given the emergence in these countries of sprawling urban development.

The presumption that American and European prescriptions for cities are transferable often leads to quite absurd results. The following example was related to me by Rodolfo Cordoba, a respected land developer in San Pedro Sula, the second-largest city in Honduras. One day the city planning department in the municipality decided to require environmental impact assessments for all residential land subdivisions. Environmental impact assessments, they must have figured, are "good things" because if they are good for large urban projects in the United States and Europe, they must be good for small projects like land subdivisions in San Pedro Sula as well. Faced with this new requirement, Cordoba decided to invite professional squatters to "invade" his land because, once his land was invaded, he no longer needed to comply with municipal regulations. He figured that he would make more money more quickly, thus saving himself the uncertainty, time, and expenses involved in obtaining the necessary environmental clearances for a full-fledged land subdivision. When I visited his subdivision, *Lotificadora*

Low-density sprawl has been the predominant form of urban expansion in the United States for a century or more.

***Lotificadora Monterrey*, an illegal subdivision on the fringe in San Pedro Sula, Honduras, was a well-established residential community by 2012.**

Monterrey, in 2002 he was preparing 360 small plots for sale in the informal market. Plots were provided with minimal services (unpaved roads, water, sewerage, and electricity) and measured 9 by 15 meters. A plot sold for US$2,500, with US$100 down and the rest payable in 120 monthly installments of $20, which most families in San Pedro Sula could afford.

When it comes to prescriptions, context matters. While many prescriptions are invented, tested, and applied successfully in the metropolitan centers around the world, they do not necessarily travel well, nor are they universal in their application. Prescriptions for rich megacities in industrialized countries cannot be the same as prescriptions for poor towns in developing ones, just as prescriptions for obesity cannot be the same as prescriptions for malnutrition. There are, no doubt, medical norms that apply to us all. Blood pressure, sugar levels, and body weight, for example, must remain within certain ranges to keep us in good health. When it comes to cities, we can speak of norms that apply to all cities, too. Workers must be able to get to work within a reasonable time, say, half an hour; households can spend only a certain share of their income on housing, say, one-quarter; and a significant share of urban land must be devoted to transport, say, one-fifth.

Then there are norms and standards that apply only to those who can afford them. In 1990, for example, infrastructure expenditures per capita in Helsinki, Finland, were more than 1,000 times those in Dar es Salaam, Tanzania (Angel 2000b). Helsinki now has a network of underground pipes that provides district heating to more than 90 percent of its inhabitants (Robbs 2009). What can Dar es Salaam possibly learn from Helsinki about infrastructure investment?

In another example, Portland, Oregon, adopted its much-celebrated urban growth boundary in 1979. It was designed to delimit the area where urban development was admissible in order to prevent unwanted sprawl and keep a pristine countryside in close proximity to its inhabitants (figure 1.4). Between 1980 and 2010, the population within that boundary grew from slightly less than 1 million to some 1.5 million at the average rate of 1.7 percent per year (Metro 2012a). During the same period, the population of Shenzhen, China, grew from 58,000 to 9 million, at the average rate of 16.8 percent per year (United Nations Population Division 2012, file 2), or 10 times faster than Portland. What can Shenzhen possibly learn from Portland about containing urban expansion?

ABOUT THIS BOOK

This book seeks to broaden our perspective by shifting our gaze away from a small number of cities in the developed countries and focusing it instead on a large number of cities the world over. To examine urban expansion without bias, I eliminated the artificial distinction between cities in more developed countries and cities in less developed ones, opting to study our planet of cities as a whole. To engage in this pursuit in an effective and persuasive manner, I embarked on a quest to measure urban expansion

FIGURE 1.4
Expansion to the Edge of Portland, Oregon's Urban Growth Boundary, 2011

Source: Metro (2012b).

Recent graduates look for work at a job fair in Shenzhen, China, currently one of the world's fastest-growing cities.

and its attributes everywhere, in order to understand them at a deeper level. My colleagues and I spent a number of years carefully collecting new comparative data for cities in all world regions and studying all these cities using a common analytical framework.

This book, then, is about the past, present, and future expansion of cities in the broadest and most global sense of the word. While telling numerous instructive stories about the expansion of particular cities in different parts of the world, I seek to make the study of urban expansion more scientific by moving from persuasive storytelling to the examination of large numbers of maps of the built-up areas of cities and the patterns that these maps reveal, and to the measurement of useful metrics associated with these patterns. I also want to shift from descriptive measurement of these metrics to the examination of statistical models that explain variations among them both over time and among cities in different places; from explaining past data to projecting it into the future; and from explanation and projection toward policy prescriptions that are better grounded in empirical realities.

As we move together from storytelling to measurement, from measurement to statistical modeling, from statistical modeling to prediction, and from prediction to policy prescriptions, the demands for precision increase. Reaching a global consensus that could guide our actions in the coming years—a consensus grounded in reliable measurement and solid understanding of the realities now facing cities everywhere—is likely to be very difficult. That should not surprise us, nor should it prevent us from participating in pushing the envelope further, taking chances, and laying the foundations for a robust yet exciting science of cities where all cities are studied together. This book is my invitation to join this fascinating and highly satisfying pursuit.

The core of the book has two main parts following the five introductory chapters. In part one, consisting of three chapters, I focus on what I have termed the urbanization project—the massive shift of the world population to cities—and I examine the most basic features of our planet of cities. In chapter 6, I relate urban history as a three-period narrative. The first period extends from the formation of the first cities to the onset of rapid urbanization circa 1800; the second period came to an end in 2010, when half the world population lived in cities; and the third period is expected to end late in this century, when most people who want to live in cities will have moved into them.

Chapter 7 examines the geography of world urbanization, focusing on where urban population growth has taken place in the past and where it will take place in the future. In chapter 8, I introduce the global hierarchy of cities with a view to examining why cities come in different sizes rather than having one optimal size; whether larger cities are growing at a faster or a slower rate than smaller ones; and whether cities the world over are distributed randomly or uniformly in geographic space.

In part two, I narrow the focus to the study of urban expansion and its attributes in cities of all sizes in all geographic regions and in two time periods: the last decade of the twentieth century (1990–2000) and the last two centuries of the second millennium (1800–2000). After introducing the new data sources and the metrics used to analyze them, I devote one chapter to each of the seven questions listed earlier.

The central policy prescription of this book demands a fundamental change of hearts and minds. It puts into question the main tenets of the familiar Containment Paradigm, also known as smart growth, urban growth management, or compact city, which is designed to combat boundless urban expansion. This paradigm can be traced back to the London Greenbelt Act of 1938 (figure 1.5) and the British Town and Country Planning Act of 1947 (Munton 1983). I examine this paradigm in a broader global perspective and show it to be deficient and next to useless in addressing the central questions now facing expanding cities outside the United States and Europe. In its place I propose to revive an alternative Making Room Paradigm that seeks to come to terms with the expected expansion of cities, particularly in the rapidly urbanizing countries in Asia and Africa, and to make the minimally necessary preparations for such expansion instead of seeking to contain it. I say "revive" because this paradigm guided the expansion of a number of cities in the nineteenth and early twentieth centuries: New York, Barcelona, Berlin, and Buenos Aires are a few important examples.

The Making Room Paradigm rests on four propositions that need to be introduced and discussed before delving into the core parts of the book. These propositions form

FIGURE 1.5
The Containment of Urban England: The London Greenbelt, 1973

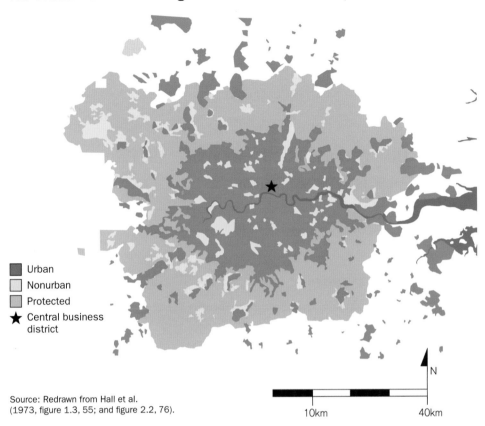

Urban
Nonurban
Protected
★ Central business
district

Source: Redrawn from Hall et al.
(1973, figure 1.3, 55; and figure 2.2, 76).

10km   40km

N

the spine of my understanding of cities. They are simple conclusions that are grounded in my studies of cities and in my personal experiences living and working in cities throughout the world.

1. The Inevitable Expansion Proposition: The expansion of cities that urban population growth entails cannot be contained. Instead we must make adequate room to accommodate it.

2. The Sustainable Densities Proposition: City densities must remain within a sustainable range. If density is too low, it must be allowed to increase, and if it is too high, it must be allowed to decline.

3. The Decent Housing Proposition: Strict containment of urban expansion destroys the homes of the poor and puts new housing out of reach for most people. Decent housing for all can be ensured only if urban land is in ample supply.

4. The Public Works Proposition: As cities expand, the necessary land for public streets, public infrastructure networks, and public open spaces must be secured in advance of development.

How Ya Gonna Keep 'em Down on the Farm,
After They've Seen Paree?

World War I song by Lewis and Young (1919)

CHAPTER 2

The Inevitable Expansion Proposition

The expansion of cities that urban population growth entails cannot be contained. Instead we must make adequate room to accommodate it.

LONDON, ENGLAND

Honest and justifiable attempts to stop people from moving to cities and to prevent construction on the urban periphery, however pitiful in retrospect, have been with us for centuries and are still with us today. The proclamation issued on 7 July 1580 by Queen Elizabeth I was one such exercise in futility:

> The Queens Majesty perceiving the State of the City of London (being anciently termed her Chamber) and the Suburbs and Confines thereof to encrease daily by Access of People to inhabit in the same . . . Her Majesty, by good and deliberate Advice of her Council . . . Doth charge and straitly command all Persons of what Quality soever they be, to desist and forbear from any new Buildings of any new House or Tenement within three Miles of any of the Gates of the said City, to serve for Habitation or Lodging for any Person, where no former House hath been known to have been in Memory of such as are now living. (Strype 1720, 34)

The official reasons for issuing the queen's proclamation are eminently sensible and not unfamiliar to the modern reader: an influx of poor and unskilled people; inconveniences caused by congestion; price inflation caused by increasing demand; the dangers to public health caused by overcrowding; unfair competition by newcomers flooding markets with cheaper goods of compromised quality; and claims "that the City could scarcely be well governed, by reason of such Multitudes flocking to live there." Official consternation with the unruly multitudes crowding into theaters to enjoy Shakespeare's plays in those years would surely have resulted in a ban on theaters as well, but for the queen's fondness for this form of entertainment and the fact that theaters were built in the suburbs outside the city's jurisdiction to make sure they were not closed down by the authorities.

The population of London in 1545 was almost 70,000 (Russell 1948). It was increasing rapidly, particularly after the destruction of Antwerp by the Spanish in 1572, which left London as the largest port in the North Atlantic at a time of rapid expansion of global trade brought about by the onset of colonization. A 1572 map of London (figure 2.1) shows that it occupied an area of 3 square kilometers (km^2). Two-thirds of the area was within the city's walls and one-third in its growing suburbs. By 1650, it was estimated that only 120,000 people lived in the city proper while 300,000 lived in the surrounding suburbs outside the city's jurisdiction (calculated from Harding 1990).

Elizabeth I, Queen of England from 1558 to 1603, forbade all new construction outside the gates of London.

John Strype (1720, 34), the chronicler of the events surrounding the queen's proclamation, notes, "This Proclamation could not hinder this strong Propension in the People towards building new Houses." Other proclamations followed, to no avail. "Between 1602 and 1630, no fewer than fourteen proclamations were enacted in attempts to limit London's growth" (Lai 1988, 28). The population of the city increased to 500,000 by 1674, to 675,000 by 1750, and to 959,000 by 1800. By 1860 the population of London was 2.76 million, by 1929 it was 8.0 million, and by 2000 the population of

FIGURE 2.1
The Braun and Hogenberg Map of London, 1572

Source: Braun and Hogenberg (1572–1617), courtesy of the Hebrew University of Jerusalem Historic Cities Research Project.

Greater London exceeded 10 million. During the 200 years between 1800 and 2000, the population of London grew more than tenfold, from 1 million to 10 million, but its built-up area grew much faster. In fact, it grew sixty-three-fold, from 3,600 hectares (36 km²) to 230,000 hectares (2,300 km²). Neither London's population growth rate nor its rate of physical expansion were atypical. Queen Elizabeth's noble attempts to contain the growth of London are now more than 400 years old, and their utter and obvious failure should have alerted us to the futility of such attempts.

Unfortunately, yet another important history lesson has gone unheeded. In early 2012, the central government of China was actively engaged in a rather nominal effort to prevent rural in-migrants from settling in its rapidly growing cities. According to its 2010 census, no fewer than 260 million villagers had migrated to China's cities without the officially required residence permits (*hukous*)—117 million of them over the last decade alone—and they now constitute almost 40 percent of the country's urban population (calculated from Hvistendahl 2011). Not only do internal migration controls fail in practice, but they are also forbidden in principle by the Universal Declaration of Human Rights to which all member states of the United Nations are signatories. Article 13.1 of the declaration states that "[e]veryone has the right to freedom of movement and residence within the borders of each State" (United Nations 1948).

The anti-urban Khmer Rouge captured Cambodia's capital city of Phnom Penh in 1975 and forced all the inhabitants—more than 2.5 million people—to leave.

There are historical examples where governments successfully prevented people from settling in cities, whether by refusing them entry, by evicting them en masse, or by denying them food, including a recent notorious example. In 1975, the Khmer Rouge evicted the entire urban population of Phnom Penh, Cambodia, and forced it to resettle in the countryside, simply because its revolutionary vision of society had no room for cities. The people returned four years later when the Khmer Rouge lost power and the population of Phnom Penh later exceeded its pre-evacuation levels. Under current international law, these cruel practices are strictly forbidden. There is little that governments can do now to prevent the growth of urban populations and, as in the case of London, there is little they can do to prevent the massive expansion of cities that the burgeoning of their population entails.

NEW YORK CITY, UNITED STATES

In stark contrast to the queen's proclamation of 1580, the 1811 New York City Commissioners' Plan for Manhattan made room for a sevenfold expansion of its built-up area at the time. Their proclamation was the exact opposite: "To some it may be a matter of surprise that the whole island has not been laid out as a city. To others it may be a subject of merriment that the commissioners have provided space for any population that is collected at any spot on this side of China" (Mackay 1987, 20).

In 1807 the Common Council of the City of New York appointed three commissioners—Gouverneur Morris, Simeon DeWitt, and John Rutherford—to prepare an expansion plan for the island of Manhattan (figure 2.2). While it is not clear whether or not the council actually sought to attract more people into the city, it certainly made active preparations for a more populous city than any that existed in the United States at the time. It specifically prepared land for a sevenfold expansion of the built-up area of the city. How many cities can claim this audacity of vision?

Wishing to overcome both the resistance to its plans by landowners and the lack of consensus among its own members, the council sought to tie its hands, so to speak, by empowering the commissioners through an official statute enacted by the State of New York. The statute, issued on 3 April 1807, applied to the entire island except for its northern tip. It gave the commissioners "exclusive power to lay out streets, roads, and public squares, of such width, extent, and direction, as to them shall seem most conducive to public good, and to shut up, or direct to be shut up, any streets or parts thereof which have been heretofore laid out . . . [but] not accepted by the Common Council" (Bridges 1811). It was also understood and agreed that the council could not deviate from the commissioners' plan "without securing specific legislative authorization" (Bridges 1811).

The commissioners settled on a simple, rigid, and rather uninspiring orthogonal grid plan because "straight-sided and right-angled houses are the most cheap to build and the most convenient to live in." They also agreed to offer reasonable compensation to landowners whose land was taken for streets after the streets were opened. "Payments could be offset in whole or in

FIGURE 2.2
The 1811 New York City Commissioners' Plan for the Island of Manhattan

Source: Bridges (1811).

part by benefit assessments, and when assessments were approved by the court and the city, payments from the assessment fund were to be made to those whose land had been taken" (Bridges 1811). In an important sense, therefore, the acquisition of the public rights-of-way for streets did not impose a burden on the public coffers. The surveying of the street grid required almost four years, and the plan was completed on 22 March 1811.

Though the commissioners' plan provided enough buildable land for a sevenfold increase in the built-up area of the island, by the end of the nineteenth century it was largely built up. Between 1810 and 1900 its built-up area did expand sevenfold, while its population grew almost twentyfold, from 96,000 to 1.85 million with a concomitant increase in overcrowding. New York City now needed more area for expansion, both to accommodate its growing population and to relieve the overcrowding in its congested tenements.

Expansion was made possible by an act of the New York State legislature (Chapter 378 of the laws of 1897) that consolidated Manhattan and the Bronx with Kings County (including Brooklyn), Queens County, and Richmond County (Staten Island) into a single City of Greater New York, later called simply New York City. The administrative area of the city was thus expanded ninefold, from 87.5 km^2 in 1810 to 790 km^2 in 1897. The Board of Public Improvements, which included all the public works commissioners and the five borough presidents, quickly endorsed a plan for the entire city prepared by Louis Risse, chief engineer of the New York City Topographical Bureau. The plan, submitted on 1 January 1900, was presented at the Paris Exposition to promote New York as a major world city. It included proposed parks as well as streets "in those parts of the city consolidated under the above act of the legislature and which had no official street plan prior to 1898" (figure 2.3). The city now had vast new lands for expansion. The total built-up area in 1900 in all five boroughs was only 102 km^2 and they had room for multiplying another sevenfold. Again we must ask ourselves: How many cities can claim this audacity of vision?

Given this new breathing room, the city expanded rapidly, and by 1930 its entire five-borough administrative area was again largely built-up and housed 6.9 million people—87 percent of its population in 2000. Subsequent growth and expansion took place largely outside the city limits, and by the year 2000 the urbanized area[1] of New York amounted to 6,215 km^2 and was home to some 16.4 million people.

When we look at the entire spectrum of the world's cities, we find great variety: cities that are neither growing in population nor overcrowded; cities that are both growing in

---

1 According to the U.S. Bureau of the Census (2002), the urbanized area consists of all census tracts within a metropolitan statistical area that have a gross population density of more than 1,000 persons per square mile (3.86 persons per hectare).

FIGURE 2.3
Planned Street Grids and Proposed Parks on the Eastern Edge of the Borough of Queens in the Board of Public Improvement's Plan of New York City, 1900

Source: Risse (1900).

population and overcrowded; cities in countries where the urbanization process has largely come to an end; and cities in countries where the urbanization process is still in full swing. The Inevitable Expansion Proposition states that first, the movement of people into cities cannot be stopped or reversed; and second, the expansion of cities that it entails cannot and will not be contained. No matter how sensible and noble the motives, rather than trying to stop people from coming to settle in cities and failing in the attempt, it makes more sense to take the necessary steps to accommodate them. In other words, when it comes to confronting the prospects of urban population growth and expansion, we would do well to heed the advice of the commissioners rather than the proclamation of the queen.

What is the sense, it is frequently asked, of further densification given that densities are already high and associated with a range of problems including infrastructure overload, overcrowding, congestion, air pollution, severe health hazards, lack of public and green space and environmental degradation? The sustainability gains from further densification will be limited under conditions where densities are already high. Under these circumstances the merits of urban densification postulated for developed country cities seem far less convincing in the context of developing countries.

Rod Burgess (2000, 15)

CHAPTER 3

The Sustainable Densities Proposition

City densities must remain within a sustainable range. If density is too low, it must be allowed to increase, and if it is too high, it must be allowed to decline.

When it comes to formulating policies to manage the expansion of cities—whether to reverse it, contain it, guide it, let it be, or encourage it—density matters. The denser the city, the less space will be required to accommodate its population. Compact cities can thus help protect and conserve the open countryside. They can also bring people closer together by sharing common walls; shortening travel times and the length of infrastructure networks; increasing the viability of walking, bicycling, and public transport; and saving energy and reducing carbon emissions. Given that climate change is now an overriding concern, it is of paramount importance to allow and encourage densities to increase over time, if they can ensure the continued sustainability of our planet.

But that is not to say that a denser city is a better city. We cannot simply assume that urban densities are too low everywhere and must now be increased. In some cities densities are too high and therefore unsustainable for a variety of reasons: overcrowding, lack of light and air, pollution, congestion, overburdened infrastructure, and unaffordable land and housing. Many other cities have densities that are sustainable: high enough to support public transport, walking, and an urban lifestyle and to conserve energy and contain carbon emissions, yet low enough to avoid overcrowding, unaffordable housing, congestion, and overburdened urban services.

Average densities in the great majority of U.S. cities may now be too low to be sustainable and should be allowed and encouraged to increase in order to reduce the distances traveled, increase the viability of public transport, reduce carbon emissions, and thus mitigate their adverse effects on climate change.

The Sustainable Densities Proposition is another version of the Goldilocks Principle. Densities should be neither too high nor too low but "just right," that is, within a tolerable or, to use a more contemporary word, sustainable range. The Goldilocks Principle itself is a version of the Confucian Doctrine of the Mean, the Buddhist Middle Way, Horace's Golden Mean, "the moral way observes the mean" of St. Thomas Aquinas, and "the right way is the mean" of Maimonides.

How do present-day densities of the built-up areas in the United States and Bangladesh compare to densities in Manhattan's Tenth Ward in 1910, for example? In the year 2000, the average densities of the built-up areas of U.S. and Bangladeshi cities with 100,000 or more people were 24 and 191 persons per hectare respectively. Urban densities in Bangladesh were, on average, 8 times higher than those in the United

The Karail Bastee in Mahakhali, Dhaka, Bangladesh, had a population density in 2005 that was more than double that of Manhattan's densest ward, the Tenth Ward, in 1910.

States. In that year, the average densities in Houston and Dhaka were 20 and 555 persons per hectare respectively. The average density in Dhaka was nearly 28 times that of Houston. In 2005, the average density in Dhaka's slums, taken as a whole, was 2,220 persons per hectare. Those densities were actually on the same order of magnitude as those of Manhattan's Tenth Ward, its densest ward, in 1910—1,440 persons per hectare. Still, in 8.3 percent of Dhaka's densest slums—409 communities packed with single-story houses like the Karail Bastee in Mahakhali—average densities in 2005 were higher than 3,750 persons per hectare (CUS 2005), or more than double that of Manhattan's Tenth Ward in 1910.

We cannot simply assume that there is an association between urban densities and carbon emissions. We must begin by asking ourselves whether lower densities are indeed associated with higher levels of carbon emissions. A growing body of evidence begins to suggest that this is the case. A study of 46 cities, for example, found that in 1990 both the per capita energy used in transport and the per capita distance traveled declined with density (Newman and Kenworthy 1999). Higher-density cities were associated with shorter travel distances and lower energy expenditures on transport than lower-density ones. We can infer that they were also associated with a lower level of carbon emissions.

Two more recent studies provide data for 2001 on the level of carbon dioxide emissions from all transport modes in the major cities in China and the United States using an identical methodology (Glaeser and Kahn 2010; Zheng et al. 2011). I used these data, in conjunction with my own 2000 data on the average built-up area densities of these cities, to compare average emissions and average densities in 64 Chinese cities and 54 U.S. cities. The differences were striking. Average population densities in the Chinese cities studied were 7 times those of the U.S. cities: 162 persons per hectare compared to 23 persons per hectare. Average annual CO_2 emissions from transport in the U.S. cities studied were 56 times those in Chinese cities: 12.8 tons per household compared to 0.27 tons per household. Except for these two new data sets, global data are not yet available to compare densities and carbon emissions in individual cities throughout the world, but it is possible to compare differences in densities and carbon emissions among countries.

Figure 3.1 illustrates the average amount of CO_2 emissions per capita from all sources and the average densities in cities with 100,000 people or more in 145 countries in the year 2000. The association between them is quite clear: the lower the density, the higher the level of CO_2 emissions per capita. The United States had an average density of 24 persons per hectare and an average annual level of 20.5 tons of CO_2 emissions per capita. Bangladesh had an average density of 191 persons per hectare and an average annual level of 0.2 tons of CO_2 emissions per capita—less than one-hundredth that of the United States.

This figure requires some further explanation. The blue dots are values for 19 selected countries. The small black dots are the values for the remaining 126 countries. (Values for countries with average densities larger than 220 persons per hectare are not shown.) The 10 larger yellow dots are the average values for each density decile (one-tenth of the countries studied). The vertical bars are confidence intervals for these decile averages (e.g., the average value of the first decile—one-tenth of the countries studied that had the lowest densities—is 12.2 tons per year), and we can assert with a 95 percent

FIGURE 3.1

A Comparison of Average Urban Densities in Large Cities and Average Carbon Dioxide Emissions per Capita from All Sources in 145 Countries, 2000

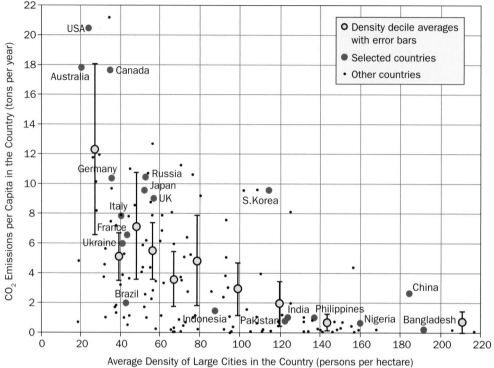

Sources: Density data from Angel et al. (2012 online); and CO_2 emissions per capita data from World Resources Institute (2012).

level of confidence that this average value is somewhere between 6.5 and 18 tons per year. Generally, therefore, if two confidence intervals do not overlap, it is clear that one average is significantly higher than the other.

The figure demonstrates that the average emission values in the first four density deciles (cities in the lower-density ranges) are significantly higher than the average emission values for the last three density deciles (cities in the higher-density ranges). In short, country comparisons show a strong association between carbon dioxide emissions and urban population densities.

This association need not imply a causal connection between the two. Why? Households in richer countries, for example, can be expected to consume more resources than households in poorer ones. They will consume both more land and more energy per capita and can be expected to have both lower densities and higher carbon emissions. Another factor, in this case income, can be the cause of both low densities and higher CO_2 emissions, rather than one causing the other. Income alone, however, does not account for the differences in carbon emissions shown in figure 3.1. In a statistical model using both average density and income to explain the variation in carbon emissions among countries, I found that income explained only half of that variation, while density explained the other half. Density appears to matter when it comes to carbon emissions. Do higher densities lead to lower carbon emissions because they require lower levels of car ownership and shorter trips? Possibly, but some will argue that the causal connection can go in the opposite direction as well. In cities with higher levels of car ownership, people can opt to live in larger houses further away, thus lowering overall densities. In other words, low densities beget more cars and more cars beget lower densities.

That said, there is some reason to believe that higher densities can indeed lead to lower carbon emissions. It has been observed that in the United States the viability of public transport, which emits less CO_2 per capita, is positively associated with residential densities in the vicinity of transit stations—the higher that density, the more people use public transport (Pushkarev and Zupan 1977). Holtzclaw (1994) found that regular bus service requires a minimum density of 30 persons per hectare to be financially viable. If these contentions are correct, then a causal link could be established between densities and carbon emissions. Simply stated, other things being equal, if densities can be increased, then transit use can increase and carbon emissions can decrease.

My colleagues and I examined the share of the total areas of U.S. cities that had "transit-sustaining" densities above 30 persons per hectare in different time periods (Angel et al. 2011a). We also examined the shares of the total populations in these cities

Decommissioned Pacific Railway trolleys in Los Angeles, California, are piled up in junkyards along with discarded World War II tanks, circa 1956.

that lived at transit-sustaining densities. In 20 cities for which we had data for the period 1910–2000, we found that both shares declined substantially over time. The average share of the area of U.S. cities that was dense enough to sustain transit declined from 38 percent in 1910 to less than 4 percent in 2000, a tenfold decline. The average share of the population that lived at transit-sustaining densities declined from 90 percent to 27 percent during that period, a threefold decline.

Examining 447 urban areas (from a total of 453) in the United States in the year 2000, we found that almost half, 46 percent, had no population living at transit-sustaining densities; only 33 percent had more than 10 percent of their population living at transit-sustaining densities; only 13 percent had more than 20 percent of their population living at these densities; and only 2 percent had more than 50 percent of their populations living at these densities. The five metropolitan areas with the highest shares were San Francisco (71.4 percent); Los Angeles (67.7); State College, Pennsylvania (65.3 percent); New York City (64.7 percent); and San Jose, California (54.7 percent). In total, 27.3 percent of the U.S. urban population lived at transit-sustaining densities in the year 2000. This finding does not mean that these percentages of the population used transit, nor that transit was even available within walking distance. It only indicates the percentage of the urban population that lived at high densities and could potentially sustain public transit.

It may be that both families living at low density and relying on their cars and families living at higher densities and using public transport instead of cars are exercising lifestyle choices by expressing cultural differences and individual aspirations. Some commentators have recently noted that cultural trends are now steering people away from low-density, car-based lifestyles—the proverbial American Dream—and toward higher-density, transit-based lifestyles (Calthorpe 2011). This may bode well for the United States, because several things are quite clear regarding present urban densities in most U.S. cities. They are too low to support public transport; too small a share of the population lives at densities that can sustain public transport; the country now produces an inordinate share of global CO_2 emissions, a share that clearly needs to be reduced to a more reasonable level that is at least on par with countries with similar per capita incomes; and higher densities may contribute to attaining that goal.

A reasonable goal for the coming decades may be to double the share of the urban population living at transit-sustaining densities from 27.3 percent to 50 percent. This goal could be accomplished through the selective densification of parts of the urban landscape—as Curitiba, Brazil, for example, densified successfully along its main transit corridors—but only if demand for higher-density, transit-based living is strong enough to support it.

More people in the United States will need to vote with their feet as well as voice their political preferences for that to become a reality. And it will not be easy. Shrill voices that insist on low-density, car-dependent development as the true American Way, and for which this new agenda is anathema, have been quick to politicize it to court suburban voters, who now form the majority of the U.S. electorate.

> They want Americans to take transit and move to the inner cities. They want Americans to move to the urban core, live in tenements, [and] take light rail to their government jobs. That's their vision for America.
> — Representative Michele Bachmann (R-MN) (Murphy 2011)

While Americans continue to debate the merits of densification, I believe that this agenda should be firmly rejected in cities that already have very high densities and need to be decongested; in cities where densities are declining but are likely to remain high enough to support public transport in coming decades; or in cities that are growing rapidly in population and need ample room for their expansion at their projected densities.

In Curitiba, Brazil, high-density apartments and office buildings line five main transit corridors serviced by a frequent and efficient bus rapid transit system.

We should not forget that at the height of the Industrial Revolution and up to the beginning of the twentieth century, there were genuine concerns that urban densities were too high and needed to be reduced to ensure that people had adequate living space and to bring more light and air into their residences. The tenements of New York City's Tenth Ward, for example, often contained 20 or more 30-square-meter (m^2) apartments with no indoor plumbing on a 7.5x30–meter lot, each containing a household of 3 to 14 persons (Dolkart 2007). Many of these units were used as a workplace as well as a residence (figure 3.2). Politicians, reformers, and scholars were seriously concerned with living conditions in the city's crowded neighborhoods.

FIGURE 3.2
New York City Tenement Floor Plan, 1864

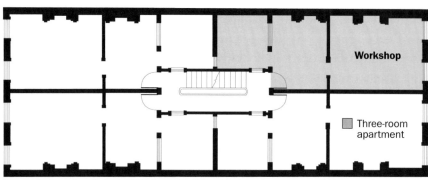

Source: Redrawn from Dolkart (2007, figure 18, 39); original drawing courtesy of Li-Saltzman Architects.

> The Tenth Ward has a population at the rate of 185,513 to the square mile [708 persons per hectare] the Seventeenth 170,006 [657 persons per hectare] and so on with others equally overcrowded. Portions of particular wards are even in worse condition. (*New York Times*, 3 December 1876)

Jacob Riis, a reformist journalist and photographer credited with exposing the overcrowding and dire living conditions in the city's tenements, was quite pessimistic in his book, *How the Other Half Lives*, about the prospects of reducing overcrowding and high densities.

> What then are the bold facts with which we have to deal in New York?
> 1. That we have a tremendous, ever swelling crowd of wage-earners which it is our business to house decently.
> 2. That it is not housed decently.
> 3. That it must be so housed here for the present, and for a long time to come, all schemes of suburban relief being at yet utopian, impracticable. (Riis 1971 [1890], 223)

Riis was wrong. Other social reformers sought to reduce overcrowding through decongestion policies made possible by the development of new transportation technologies from the early nineteenth century onward. These technologies reduced the cost of movement in cities and made it possible for large numbers of people to commute over greater distances. Adna Farrin Weber (1899, 475) in his influential *The Growth of Cities in the Nineteenth Century* had it right: "The 'rise of the suburbs' it is, which furnishes the solid basis of a hope that the evils of city life, so far as they result from overcrowding, may be in large part removed."

There is no question that suburbanization both facilitated and accelerated the decongestion of Manhattan's overcrowded neighborhoods.

> The Lower East Side contained 398,000 people in 1910, 303,000 in 1920, 182,000 in 1930, and 147,000 in 1940. To reformers who had long pressed for the depopulation of the slums, this leveling out of neighborhoods was a welcome and much celebrated relief. (Jackson 1985, 185)

Figure 3.3 shows census tract densities in Manhattan in 1910 and 2010. The column height displays densities in persons per hectare, not building heights, since buildings in 2010 were much higher, on average, than those of 1910, but they housed fewer people in smaller families that consumed much greater amounts of living space per person. As the figure clearly demonstrates, the high densities throughout the island and in the Lower East Side in particular were greatly reduced and overcrowding was largely alleviated as vast numbers of residents left Manhattan for the suburbs.

FIGURE 3.3
The Decline of Census Tract Densities in Manhattan, New York City, 1910 and 2010

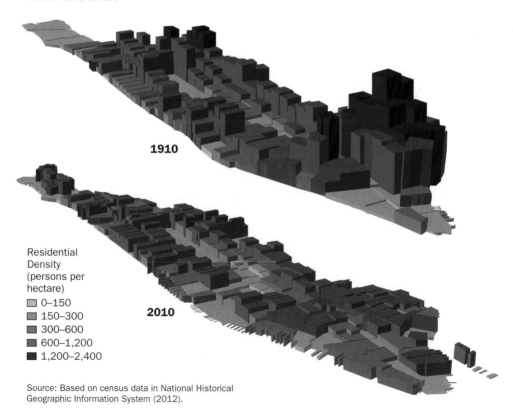

1910

Residential
Density
(persons per
hectare)
☐ 0–150
☐ 150–300
☐ 300–600
■ 600–1,200
■ 1,200–2,400

2010

Source: Based on census data in National Historical
Geographic Information System (2012).

High densities were not unique to the industrial cities of the nineteenth and early twentieth centuries. Kowloon's Walled City—a small stretch of no-man's land in Hong Kong that officially remained under Chinese rule while the British governed the colony—was demolished in 1992. It boasted much higher densities than New York's Lower East Side in 1910 and virtually no light or air. At its peak density in the mid-1980s, it may have housed as many as 35,000 people on some 2.5 hectares, at an average density of 13,000 people per hectare (Liauw 1998, 154), making it much denser than Hong Kong's high-rise residential districts of today and the world's highest-density urban neighborhood ever recorded.

The reduction of overcrowding in Chinese cities, through both suburbanization and redevelopment, has vastly increased floor space per person in recent decades. In Tianjin, for example, it increased from 6.5 m^2 in 1988 to 19.1 m^2 in 2000 and to 25.0 m^2 in 2005 (Tianjin Municipal Statistical Bureau 2006). This is welcome news, of course, and it should come as no surprise that this increase in floor area per person, coupled with the introduction of light and air into apartments, was accompanied by a corresponding decline in average densities.

There is nothing romantic about a Dhaka family of five living in a 10 m^2 room with no light and air and sharing a water tap and a toilet with six or more other families. I, for one, find it disconcerting that Stuart Brand (2010), a leading environmentalist, chooses to celebrate the greenness of slums—their very high densities, their minimum

Kowloon's Walled City in Hong Kong was the world's densest urban neighborhood, attaining a density of 13,000 persons per hectare before its demolition in 1992.

energy and material use, and the preponderance of walking, rickshaws, and shared taxis—while strictly avoiding any mention of overcrowding lest it interfere with his global densification message.

The Sustainable Densities Proposition, like the Inevitable Expansion Proposition, seeks to broaden our perspective so we can see the entire spectrum of cities—from cities that are spread out at very low densities, contribute an unfairly large share of carbon

The average density in Tianjin, China, in 2000 was only 224 persons per hectare, and it might have been denser if not for the Modernist "tower in the park" planning regulations.

emissions, and are thus unsustainable, to cities that are so dense and overcrowded they are unfit for dignified human habitation and thus unsustainable. The proposition states that no matter how sensible and noble the motives for densification may be, and despite the urgency of slowing down climate change or protecting the precious countryside, it is not the appropriate strategy for dense and overcrowded cities. On the contrary, densities in these cities need to be allowed and encouraged to decline, not to increase. This could only be done practically and economically by opening up new lands for expansion. When it comes to confronting overcrowding, we would do well to heed the advice of Weber, the detached scholar wallowing in statistics, rather than the more passionate Riis.

The affordability of housing is overwhelmingly a function of just one thing: the extent to which governments place artificial restrictions on the supply of residential land.

Donald Brash, Governor, 1988–2002
Federal Reserve Bank of New Zealand
(Demographia 2008, i)

CHAPTER 4

The Decent Housing
Proposition

Strict containment of urban expansion destroys the homes of the poor and puts new housing out of reach for most people. Decent housing for all can be ensured only if urban land is in ample supply.

The containment of urban expansion has been defined by some proponents as follows:

> Broadly speaking, urban containment programs can be distinguished from traditional approaches to land use regulation by the presence of policies that are explicitly designed to limit the development of land outside a defined urban area, while encouraging infill development and redevelopment inside the urban area. (Nelson, Dawkins, and Sanchez 2004, 425)

I use the term containment here in a more general sense to include not only greenbelts and urban growth boundaries but smart growth controls, urban consolidation, or compact city development as well. The Containment Paradigm is thus perceived as an all-encompassing paradigm that includes all strategies that prohibit development—and particularly residential development—in large areas on the urban periphery through land use controls, whether through building moratoria, rationing of building permits, requiring large minimum lot sizes, refusing to extend roads and infrastructure lines, or other restrictive practices. As noted in chapter 1, the Containment Paradigm "is now enshrined in land use planning in many countries" (Burton 2002, 219).

Urban containment, its advocates claim, is the antidote to sprawl. It can constrain the limitless expansion of cities, increase urban population densities, reduce the excessive fragmentation of urban footprints, lessen car dependency, revitalize public transport, conserve farmland, protect nature, rejuvenate central cities, decrease the cost of infrastructure, save energy, and reduce carbon emissions. There is no question that these are commendable goals, and success at attaining them may indeed be worthwhile.

Still, an accumulating body of evidence attests that successful containment results in significantly higher land and house prices—by reducing the supply of land on the urban fringe or by failing to respond to increased demand for residential land by promptly increasing land supply (Barker 2004; Cheshire 2009; Downs 1992; Eicher 2008a and 2008b; Fischel 1995; Guidry, Shilling, and Sirmans 1991; Gyourko and Summers 2006; Hall et al. 1973; Katz and Rosen 1987; Quigley and Rosenthal 2005). There is also evidence suggesting that containment leads to more volatile swings in land and housing prices (Cheshire 2009; Federal Reserve Bank of Dallas 2008; Glaeser and Gyourko 2008); to higher levels of speculation in residential land and housing (Haughwout et al. 2011; Malpezzi and Wachter 2005); and to slower rates of metropolitan job growth (Nandwa and Ogura 2010; Saks 2005; Vermuelen and Van Ommeren 2008).

Supporters of containment have argued that it does not lead to house price increases as long as developable land is plentiful, but they have conceded that land and house prices may increase when developable land is in short supply, that is, when it is successful (Burchell et al. 2002; Nelson, Dawkins, and Sanchez 2008). When containment strategies fail to constrain the supply of land on the urban periphery, we need not worry about their effects on land and house prices.

SEOUL, KOREA'S GREENBELT

The Containment Paradigm can be traced back to the London Greenbelt Act of 1938 (Munton 1983) and the British Town and Country Planning Act of 1947, but the prime example is the greenbelt of Seoul, the capital of the Republic of Korea (figure 4.1). Established in 1971, the greenbelt rigorously prohibited the conversion of land to urban use in an area of 1,482 square kilometers (km^2) around the city. The area within the greenbelt amounted to 554 km^2 while the built-up area circa 1972 amounted to 206 km^2 or only 37 percent of the area available for expansion. In other words, the greenbelt did not impose a binding constraint on urban development when it was created. It enjoyed wide public support since it "prevented urban sprawl and functioned as a source of clean air and other environmental amenities" (Lee 1999, 43–44).

But that situation was not to last. Between 1970 and 1990 Seoul experienced both a population boom and an economic boom that vastly increased the demand for housing. The population of Seoul doubled from 5.5 to 10.6 million at the same time that the average household size declined sharply from 5.0 in 1970 to 3.8 in 1990. As a result, the number of households in Seoul did not just double, but nearly tripled from 1.1 to 2.8 million (Kim and Choe 1997). GDP per capita in Korea also more than tripled—from $2,000 in 1970 to $6,900 in 1990 (measured in constant US$ in the year 2000)—while the world GDP per capita increased by a mere 40 percent. Households in Seoul,

FIGURE 4.1
Seoul, Korea's Greenbelt and Its Built-up Area, 1972 and 1989

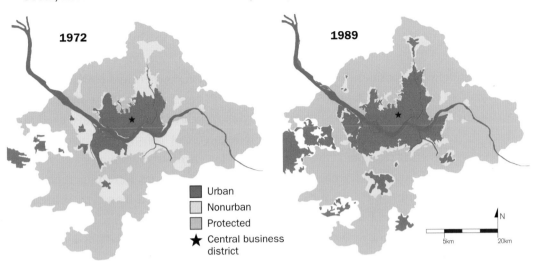

Sources: Redrawn from Kim (1990, figure 3.3, 14; figure 3.4, 16; and figure 3.5, 18).

therefore, had more resources to expend on housing, generating demand for larger homes. Between 1975 and 1990, for example, the share of dwelling units with less than 33 m² of floor area decreased from 15 percent of the housing stock to 3 percent, while the share of dwelling units with a floor area of 100 m² or more increased from 16 to 34 percent of the stock (Kim and Choe 1997).

Not surprisingly, by 1989 the built-up area of Seoul expanded to almost fill the area inside the greenbelt, resulting in "an extreme shortage of affordable land for housing and rapid land price appreciation. The nominal land price in 1989 was 23 times the 1970 price" (Lee 1999, 43, quoting Choi 1993). In other words, without adjusting for inflation, average land prices increased twenty-three-fold between 1970 and 1989. Adjusting for inflation, they had tripled. By 1990, the purchase price of an average-priced dwelling unit in Seoul required 9.3 annual incomes of an average household. That is, an average household would have to spend its entire income for almost 10 years to acquire a home. Among 53 cities in 53 countries that Stephen Mayo and I studied in 1990, this was the fifth-highest value. The average for these cities was 5.0. Rents were also unaffordable in Seoul in that year, with average monthly rents at 35 percent of monthly household incomes, the second-highest percentage and more than double the global average of 16 percent among the 53 cities studied (Angel 2000b).

The land shortage in Seoul brought about by its rigid containment had a particularly deleterious effect on its low-income population. First, it made the low-rise communities of the poorer residents the target of slum clearance efforts, typically resulting in their replacement by high-rise apartments that were not affordable to the evicted dwellers.

The 1976 Urban Redevelopment Law designated for redevelopment all residential districts that had old or substandard buildings, were overcrowded, lacked a rational land use plan, were susceptible to fire, and did not meet minimum height requirements (Kim and Choe 1997). This essentially meant that the entire low-income housing stock in the city was designated for clearance and redevelopment, with little or no thought to its devastating impact on the affected residents, both homeowners and tenants. Initial promises to resettle only homeowners in affordable new apartments onsite quickly evaporated as developers successfully claimed that, much as they would have liked to keep their original promises, the unexpectedly high cost of construction made those promises impractical (Kim and Choe 1997). Stable low-income communities with functional businesses and good access to employment opportunities were thus replaced en masse by middle- and high-income residents, as exemplified by a typical urban redevelopment project of this period in the Kumho district (figure 4.2).

So-called slum clearance and redevelopment drastically changed the physical character of the housing stock in Seoul during this period. Between 1970 and 1990, the

FIGURE 4.2
Plan for a Redevelopment Project in the Kumho District in Seoul, Korea, to Replace Informal Housing with High-Rise Apartment Blocks, 1980s

Source: Redrawn from Kim and Choe (1997, 143); original image from Seoul Metropolis (1991).

share of detached dwellings decreased to half its former amount, from 88 percent of the housing stock to 46 percent, while the share of apartment dwelling units increased ninefold, from 4 to 35 percent of the stock (Kim and Choe 1997).

The change in the composition of the housing stock was an indirect yet inevitable result of the land supply bottleneck and the resulting high price of residential land brought about by Seoul's greenbelt. The replacement of overcrowded and densely packed low-rise detached homes with generously spaced high-rise apartments did not lead to densification, however. As noted previously, low-rise communities can be much denser than high-rise districts. This transformation instead demonstrates that the ability of low-income families in Seoul to build low-cost housing was seriously diminished and made all but impossible. Why? Because low-income people generally can afford only low-rise, single-family houses that can be built progressively, one room at a time, using their meager savings and their own sweat equity rather than requiring either construction finance or mortgage finance. High-rise apartments do need that kind of financing, and, since it was in short supply in Seoul in the 1970s and 1980s, it was clearly out of reach for the urban poor.

BANGKOK, THAILAND'S AFFORDABLE HOUSING

In contrast, Bangkok, the capital of Thailand, offers a striking example of unrestricted access to land on the urban periphery that vastly expanded access to affordable housing between 1974 and 1984. Figure 4.3 shows the expansion of Bangkok over a much longer period, from 1850 to 2002, but in the mid-1970s to mid-1980s, population grew from 3.2 to 5.2 million, while the built-up area expanded from 520 to 970 km^2, converting 45 km^2 to urban use every year, on average. Housing production kept up with population growth, increasing the 1974 stock by some 60 percent by 1984.

The rapid expansion of the residential area of Bangkok was made possible by the ready availability of land on the urban periphery at that time. Bangkok is situated in a floodplain and surrounded by rice fields. There are therefore no natural limits to its expansion. A statistical study of a random sample of plots in four districts on the urban periphery in 1987 revealed that most plots belonged to their original landowners and relatively little land was being bought and sold in speculative markets or hoarded as a hedge against inflation. Plots were properly titled and registered, and there was no effective regulation to prevent the conversion of lands from rural to urban use.

Many local landowners, in collaboration with local officials, were actively engaged in negotiating road access to their plots, usually on narrow, raised, unpaved roads meandering along the edges of other plots. Local village headmen—the lowest-tier Interior Ministry officials—could and did determine the location of roads with no input from municipal planners. Typically, a landowner asked a headman to negotiate access to his land parcel from a lane already connected to a main road. The headman then

FIGURE 4.3
The Expansion of Bangkok, Thailand, 1850–2002

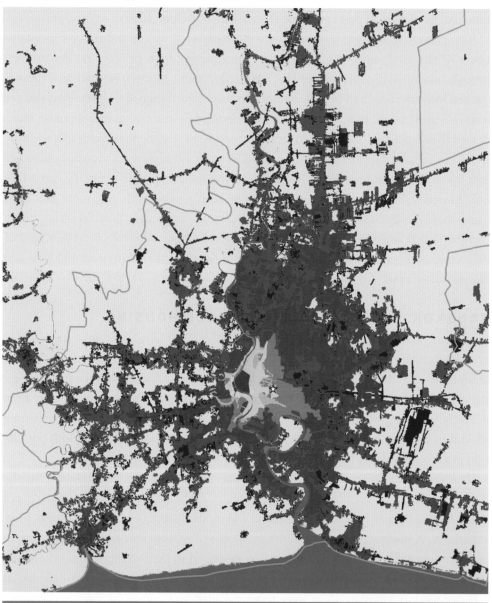

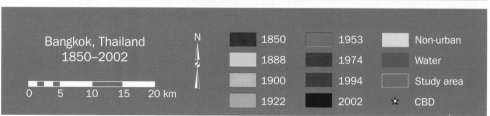

Source: Angel et al. (2012, 264).

approached pairs of landowners with adjacent parcels closer to that lane and asked them to donate (or sell in exchange for some payment) a 3-meter-wide strip along the edge of their land for a 6-meter-wide lane. If some landowners refused, the headman approached others until he managed to connect the parcel in question to a lane connected to the main road. The process was swift and efficient, and village headmen had been known to negotiate for an entire kilometer of road in six weeks. An impressive one-fifth of the plots surveyed were provided with road access between 1974 and 1984.

The composition of the housing stock in Bangkok underwent a major transformation during this period, reflecting a major increase in housing affordability.

- Public housing projects—mostly walk-up apartments and single-family homes produced with substantial subsidies—remained at 4 percent of the stock.
- Shop houses—three- to four-story row houses with shops on the ground floor and residences above, typical of East and Southeast Asia—remained at some 5 percent.
- Custom-built, single-family homes on individual plots—the traditional market for middle- and upper-income homes—decreased from 37 to 30 percent of the stock.
- Houses on plots in planned land subdivisions—both fully serviced and minimally serviced ones, but typically with relatively generous plot sizes—increased their share of the housing stock from 6 to 8 percent.
- Land-and-house packages—essentially new products made possible by the emerging availability of mortgage finance—increased their share from 4 to 13 percent of the stock.
- Most surprisingly, perhaps, the share of housing in the slums of Bangkok decreased from 25 to 18 percent of the stock (PADCO 1987, table 1, 4.6).

Three of these housing submarkets merit a closer look because they catered directly to low-income households: the land rental slums; the low-cost land-and-house projects; and the informal land subdivisions.

Land Rental Slums

By 1984, a total of 1,020 slum communities in Bangkok were home to 184,000 households, or approximately 1 million people, some 20 percent of the population of the metropolitan area at that time. They were referred to by the locals as *salaam*—a Thai pronunciation of the English word *slum*, yet without the nineteenth-century connotation of a bleak and destitute place—because they were laid out in a haphazard, ungainly, and transitory nature. Bangkok slum houses were typically built on stilts on unfilled land but were well constructed with walls and floors made of wood planks and corrugated iron roofs. They were one or two stories in height and had indoor toilets and baths with septic tanks that seeped into the low water table below and were never emptied. The houses were connected to the outside world with rickety, poorly maintained catwalks. While the houses were often spotless inside, the land under and around them was typically flooded and littered with garbage. They were relatively spacious though, typically 40–80 m^2 in area for a family of five, and the overall densities in the

Slums on rented land in Bangkok housed more than 85 percent of all slum dwellers in the city in the late 1980s.

slum communities were on the order of 300 to 600 persons per hectare, much lower than those in Dhaka, for example. These slums occupied only 2 percent of the built-up area of Bangkok in 1984, but they offered accommodation to 20 percent of its people.

Both private and public landowners willingly rented their lands to low-income families so they could form these slums. In fact, there were very few squatters, and organized invasions of land, as was typical in many Latin American countries, were unknown. Slum households had informal arrangements with their landlords to construct homes in exchange for minimal land rents, typically on the order of US$3 per month. Landlords often overcharged for water and electricity as a form of additional rent, but those charges were not considered excessive.

In 1984, some two-thirds of the communities were on private lands and one-third on lands belonging to temples and mosques or public agencies. Private landlords typically rented their lands for decades, but expected renters to leave when they, or more typically their heirs, decided to sell the land. When landowners wanted the land cleared, they gave people ample notice, often stopping the collection of rents for a year, and helped move the homes to new locations. People always obliged. Public agencies had more difficulty evacuating their lands and often agreed to proposed infrastructure upgrading by the National Housing Authority, which allowed people to stay or to enter land-sharing arrangements, whereby people cleared one-third of the better located land and resettled permanently in the remaining two-thirds (Angel and Boonyabancha 1988).

Slum communities in Bangkok were located throughout the metropolitan area and had good access to employment opportunities (figure 4.4). The better located slums were gradually evicted to make way for new development, and residents moved to new communities further away. A 1987 slum eviction survey found that some 3 percent of the households in the communities identified in 1984 were evicted; an additional 4 percent received eviction notices; and there were rumors of or plans for eviction in 10 percent of the communities. In the remaining 83 percent of the communities, there

FIGURE 4.4
The Locations of Slums in Bangkok, Thailand, 1984

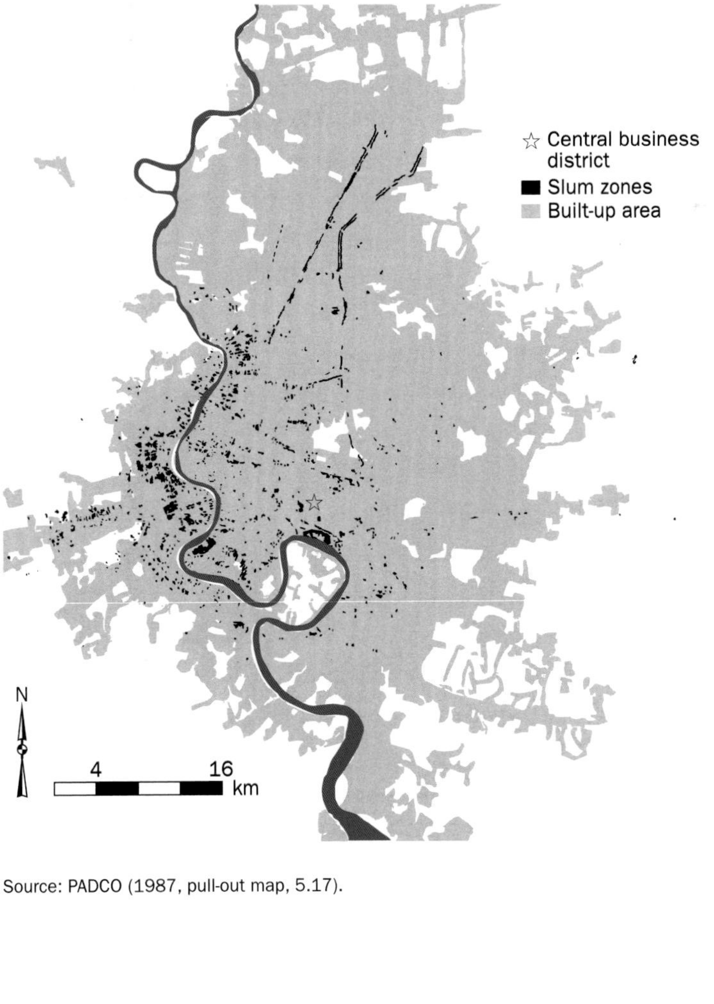

☆ Central business
  district
■ Slum zones
▨ Built-up area

N

4   16
     km

Source: PADCO (1987, pull-out map, 5.17).

In the late 1980s, the Tab Kaew housing estate in Bangkok sold land-and-house packages for $6,000. These properties were affordable for more than one-third of Bangkok's slum households: A view of the estate in 2012.

was no sign of eviction or pending eviction. In other words, unlike the situation in Seoul, there was little pressure to destroy slums because developers had a sufficient supply of alternative locations where they could build.

Land-and-House Packages

Between 1974 and 1984, the market in new land-and-house packages with access to mortgage finance expanded almost sixfold. In 1974, some 200 housing projects built 20,000 units, mostly townhouses and single-family homes. By 1986, the number of projects passed 800, with some 120,000 units (PADCO 1987). Most important, land-and-house packages became more affordable in the intervening period. Whereas only 5 percent were priced below $10,000 in 1980, for example, more than 10 percent were priced below that value in 1986. Developers looking for new profit opportunities were not shy to reach further down the economic ladder. In 1987, we found 37 projects that were selling land-and-house packages for less than $10,000, thus competing directly with the highly subsidized houses produced by the National Housing Authority.

The reduction in prices between 1980 and 1986 was made possible despite a modest increase in land prices during the intervening period for several reasons: The floor areas of the newer units were smaller, averaging 50 m^2 in 1986; houses were almost exclusively row houses; plots were smaller, averaging 80 m²; projects were located further away, averaging 22 km from the city center; developers' access to operating capital was improved; there was a marked reduction in mortgage interest rates, from 16 to 12 percent per annum; paying for the down payment in installments became more prevalent; and household incomes increased in real terms.

As a result, while 80 percent of households in Bangkok could not afford to buy a house in 1980, only 40 percent could not afford to do so in 1986, if they were willing to spend a quarter of their household income on housing. This was an extraordinary development, since one-third of slum households could now afford a land-and-house package in one of those projects. However, most chose not to do so. They preferred the greater accessibility to income opportunities, the low monthly housing expenditures, and neighbors they could trust to a modest privately owned house in a new, remote, and possibly insulated community on the urban periphery.

Informal Land Subdivisions

Low-income households in Bangkok were also offered increasingly affordable plots of land in informal residential subdivisions on the urban periphery. This housing arrangement was often seen as preferable to a land-and-house package because it offered a considerably larger plot of land. These subdivisions typically used a loophole in the land subdivision law that allowed an exemption for subdivisions of nine or fewer plots from the need to provide a full complement of services. This arrangement also allowed for larger tracts of land to be subdivided again and again, as long as they were subdivided into no more than nine segments. Plots in such subdivisions were on unfilled land and provided with road access, an unpaved road on landfill, water from an onsite well, and an electrical connection. No sewers and no storm drainage were provided, however.

An estimated 100 land subdivision projects in Bangkok in 1987 sold 10,000 to 15,000 plots per year. More than one-third of the plots sold for $3,000 to $4,000. The average plot size was 240 m². Payments were typically made in 60 installments, often at a zero interest rate, directly to the landowner for the first 18 months and then to a local bank. These plots were also affordable by at least one-third of slum families at that time, and it was not uncommon to see former slum dwellers relocate their old wooden houses on stilts in a new informal land subdivision before gradually starting to build their new homes.

In short, the open land market on Bangkok's periphery in the 1980s provided unrestricted access to residential land for large numbers of low-income households, leading to a substantial increase in housing affordability and to a marked improvement in housing conditions. In the ensuing decades, the land and housing markets of Bangkok underwent several more transformations, including a major new market in high-rise condominiums that attracted large numbers of local and international investors; a speculative bubble in real estate in the 1990s fueled by the ready access to international capital; a collapse of the bubble that led to the collapse of the Thai financial sector; and a realigning of land and house prices in the early years of the new millennium. All in all, however, while there were substantial increases in land prices during these years, they have kept in line with the substantial increases in household incomes. What has clearly worsened, however, is accessibility as Bangkok became more congested and travel times increased markedly.

CONCLUSIONS

The experiences of Seoul and Bangkok demonstrate that as long as urban populations and household incomes are growing rapidly, the containment of urban expansion through artificial restrictions on the conversion of peripheral land to urban use results in unnecessary land and house price inflation that reduces the ability of urban dwellers, especially low-income or newly formed families, to house themselves. Conversely, when peripheral land is in ample supply, housing becomes more plentiful and more affordable.

The Decent Housing Proposition has been my primary reason for writing this book and my original motivation for engaging in the research that preceded it. My earlier studies of the housing problem in developing countries have convinced me that the affordable housing problem is, in essence, a land problem (Angel et al. 1983). Like many other observers, such as John Turner (1967) in Latin America, I found that wherever the urban poor could obtain affordable access to minimally serviced land, they could build their own homes and create vibrant communities with little if any support from the government. When free of government harassment and the threat of eviction, their houses would quickly improve over time with their investment of their savings and sweat equity. People could house themselves at the required scale and create many millions of decent homes, while leaving very few people homeless, something that all governments (save that of modern-day Singapore, an outlier on every possible scale) have consistently failed to do. Admittedly, the expanding settlements of the poor did not conform to building codes, land subdivision regulations, land use and zoning re-quirements, or even property rights regimes. In that sense, they were firmly entrenched in the informal sector—a substantial part of the economy of many developing coun-tries that still remains outside the laws that were typically formulated without due regard to meeting their citizens' basic needs.

It is a clear sign of progress, then, that in the past three decades official attitudes toward these informal settlements have changed gradually yet decisively. Most of those now concerned with the housing problem in developing countries have focused on improving living conditions in informal settlements. Local and central governments in many countries are engaged in a variety of improvements to provide these settlements legitimacy and legality by upgrading their roads, sewers, and water supplies and connecting them to the infrastructure grid of the city; engaging them in the political process; increasing public safety; and occasionally providing access to finance, typically micro-finance, to help residents improve their homes gradually over time. But this focus on settlement upgrading, commendable as it is, addresses only one-half of the housing problem, the half that includes the existing housing stock. The other half has to do with enabling and facilitating the creation of additional housing stock in order to provide shelter for the millions of new households that are being formed every year.

The key to a viable national housing policy, then, is a viable urban land supply. A viable housing policy is always a two-pronged policy. One prong involves stabilizing the occupation of land in existing communities and transforming them into thriving urban neighborhoods, while the other involves opening up new lands—in adequate quantities and with good access to job opportunities—to accommodate newly formed families and newcomers to the city. That second prong of a viable housing policy thus stands in direct conflict with the Containment Paradigm and brings it into question. If we are not proactive about creating the conditions for the formation of the new housing stock, we will always remain in the settlement upgrading mode, which is less satisfactory than enabling new settlements to form in a more organized and better-planned way. As it turns out, infrastructure upgrading in informal settlements is also considerably more expensive than the provision of new infrastructure of the same standard in planned land subdivisions prior to their occupation.

A detailed engineering study that estimated the costs of providing residential infrastructure—water, sewerage, drainage, paved roads and pathways, retaining walls, electricity, street lighting, garbage collection, and landscaping—in three major slum upgrading programs in Brazil in 2003 found them to be between two and three times more expensive than their provision, at similar standards, in new land subdivisions (Abiko et al. 2007). Similar cost multipliers were reported in Bogotá, Colombia (Fernandes 2011).

In comparing average slums to new subdivisions, Abiko et al. (2007) contributed additional expenditures to several factors: demolishing and relocating 6 percent or more of the houses, on average, to make way for roads; working while residents continued with their normal lives; working with smaller equipment; lengthier and more complex management and coordination; the irregular alignment of roads; and incomplete plans that required frequent revision. An earlier study of upgrading costs in Brazil found that in one-third of the slums considered to be complex—very large sites or those located on difficult terrain, on stilts in shallow water, or at long distance from infrastructure lines—the upgrading costs were more than triple those of average slums (COBRAPE 2000, cited in Abiko et al. 2007).

The cost of providing residential infrastructure in the Matinha favela in Rio de Janeiro, Brazil, in 2007 was three times the cost of its provision in new residential subdivisions.

Efforts by the World Bank in the 1970s to address the need for new housing by promoting sites-and-services projects—publicly managed land subdivisions where people could build their own homes—have long been abandoned. Contrary to earlier claims that such projects could recover their costs in full, they required large subsidies (Mayo and Gross 1987). Premised on giving mortgages to households with irregular incomes, they suffered from high levels of default. And, contrary to expectations, they did not serve as demonstration projects for the private sector, because no private developers were interested in emulating them. In contrast, many developers are still willing and able to create minimally serviced land subdivisions that would be affordable by the large majority of the urban populace (Baross and van der Linden 1990). Such projects come into being only if the developer can obtain access to inexpensive land on the urban fringe with reasonable access to the main infrastructure grid, and that can happen on a large scale only if land on the urban fringe is in ample supply. Such access to land, in turn, can happen only if local and central governments are proactive about keeping land affordable and are willing to engage in facilitating and guiding urban expansion rather than reluctant to address it.

The Decent Housing Proposition focuses our attention on the possibility that the protection of our planet as a whole and of our natural environment in particular could come at the expense of multitudes of poor people, mostly in developing countries, who have come or are now coming to cities in search of better livelihoods. I worry that strict measures to protect the natural environment by blocking urban expansion or by making it more difficult to develop new settlements will limit the ability of ordinary people to house themselves in a decent and affordable manner. Writing of Darwin's reaction to the natives he met in his travels in Patagonia, Chatwin (1977, 128) says that he "lapsed into that common failing of naturalists: to marvel at the intricate perfection of other creatures and recoil from the squalor of man." Our fellow human beings, especially those still living in squalor in our cities and towns, deserve close observation, and in my own experience, their nesting abilities can elicit our sense of wonder no less than any other precious species building its intricate nest on the urban periphery.

When we faced the matter of subdivisions in the
County of Los Angeles . . . we reached the conclusion
that it would be absolutely necessary to go out and try
to beat the subdividers to it by laying out adequate
systems of primary and secondary highways at least,
thus obtaining the necessary areas for highways
and boulevards.

Gordon Whitnall, Los Angeles Planner, 1924
(Foster 1980, 470)

CHAPTER 5

The Public Works Proposition

As cities expand, the necessary land for public streets, public infrastructure networks, and public open spaces must be secured in advance of development.

The same Goldilocks Principle that applies to urban densities also applies to the balance between the shares of public and private lands in cities. The Public Works Proposition requires that there be sufficient land for public use for cities to be sustainable—essentially land for public works identified and secured throughout the city in a planned fashion by a public authority or authorities, rather than allocated by market forces.

MOSCOW, U.S.S.R.

This proposition applies to some land in the city, typically no less than one-third of its area, not to all land. When all urban land for all land uses is in public ownership and all lands are allocated by a planning authority—as was the case in Moscow between 1917 and 1989—decisions about what to build on a given plot of land are often made without reference to competing demands that seek to realize a parcel's full potential or, to use the language of urban economics, to put it to its highest and best use.

The all-powerful Moscow Construction Committee—which in the late 1980s during the last years of the U.S.S.R. employed no fewer than 350,000 people—did not allocate building sites for its construction projects on the basis of their market value, because there was no market in land and no reliable information about relative land prices. At best, it allocated land with the objective of minimizing the bureaucratic costs and the out-of-pocket costs of developing it. As a result, there was little incentive to recycle unused or underused land in central locations and a preference for greenfield projects on the urban fringe. The committee sought to economize on the conversion of land to urban use in order to reduce the cost of providing services. That desire to economize became more pronounced over the years, with the strange result that residential densities in Moscow by the end of Communist rule increased with distance from the city center rather than decreased as they do in most cities with properly functioning land markets. This pattern reduced overall access in the city, unnecessarily increasing the average length of trips with a concomitant energy loss and increased pollution (Bertaud and Renaud 1995). There were also no market signals to determine how much land was needed for industrial use and how much for residential use. As a result, too much land was typically allocated for industrial use, including land that remained idle when factories closed, and too little for residential use.

Similar distortions occur when municipalities do not own all the land but exercise strong powers over its designated use, as is currently the case in Israel, for example. Israeli planning law mandates that as much as 40 percent of any land to be converted to urban use must be transferred to the municipality for public use, free of charge. This percentage is now considered to be a baseline to which municipalities and other government ministries, such as the Education Ministry or the Interior Ministry, add additional requirements for schools and parks, resulting in a much higher share of land claimed necessary for public use.

The Israel Lands Authority, which owns many large parcels of land required for urban expansion, now refuses to allow the share of lands for public use to exceed 65 percent. Strange as it may seem, were it not for the authority's oversight, other public entities would try to seize more than 70 percent of the land for public use, often

Defying the urban patterns common in most cities, the Kremlin at the center of Moscow is surrounded by low-rise rather than high-rise buildings.

The Moscow Construction Committee preferred to locate its high-rise buildings on greenfields at the urban fringe, rather than recycle land in central locations.

holding it in reserve for future use, or possibly for sale or lease to private enterprises.[1] This practice is no doubt excessive, reflecting a rather bureaucratic approach to city planning that is out of touch with the way successful cities develop and thrive. The wealth of cities is generated on lands in private use. An ample supply of private land, therefore, must be available for production, commerce, civic activities, and residences for a city to grow and flourish. And it is in the public interest to ensure that ample land remains in productive private use to generate the surplus that can be taxed and used for investing in and operating a full complement of public services.

BANGKOK, THAILAND

Bangkok in the 1980s, in sharp contrast to Moscow during that period, represented an unfettered, laissez-faire land market that ensured an ample supply of land for urban expansion and an ample supply of affordable housing. That said, Bangkok failed miserably when it came to allocating adequate lands for public works, specifically for its arterial road network that carries public transport as well as the primary infrastructure grid for water, sewer, and storm drainage lines.

1 Conversation with architects Amir and Ofer Kolker, who recently completed the
  master plan for Rishon LeZion in Israel, January 2012.

The road network in every country typically forms a three-tier hierarchy of primary, secondary, and tertiary roads. Central or state governments usually plan, acquire land, finance, construct, and maintain the primary intercity road network that connects the country. Municipalities typically plan, acquire land, finance, construct, and maintain the secondary or arterial road network within their jurisdictions. In many cases, private developers of residential neighborhoods or commercial, office, and industrial projects typically plan, acquire land, finance, and construct the tertiary roads that serve buildings within their projects. In other cases, as we saw in the 1811 New York City Commissioners' Plan for Manhattan, the municipality plans and builds the tertiary road network as well.

The primary concern here is with the secondary network of arterial roads, because these roads are classic public goods and users cannot be excluded from using them. Since they are public goods, there is no market mechanism that can ensure an adequate supply in appropriate locations. In other words, a shortage of arterial roads is a form of market failure. And, because the market typically fails to supply roads in adequate quantities, they must be financed by municipal budgets rather than from tolls or revenues from the sale of plots abutting them. Given the strained budgets of most municipalities, especially in developing countries, and their limited ability to borrow funds, it is no wonder that their arterial road networks are typically undersupplied. Such artificial shortages cannot and will not be remedied through the interaction of supply and demand in land markets on the urban periphery, nor are they likely to be remedied correctly through the actions of dysfunctional or myopic public authorities either. It is important that we understand why.

In recent decades, public authorities have often been characterized as rife with inefficiency and corruption, beholden to powerful private interests, and perceived by the general public as no longer acting in its interest. Frustration with these practices has led a number of intellectuals, opinion leaders, and political movements to champion the free market as the only workable system for modern postindustrial societies.

There have been repeated calls for the privatization of public services, be they water supply and sewerage companies, transportation lines, or power networks, and for weakening the regulation of businesses to make them more efficient and more creative. There have been calls for lowering local tax rates and sometimes national tax rates that would compromise the ability of local governments to invest in and maintain public facilities and essential services. And, most relevant for this discussion of making the necessary preparations for urban expansion, there have even been calls for weakening the ability of public authorities to acquire private property for public use through the power of eminent domain. This is a worrisome development because this power is essential for laying out both the primary intercity roads and the secondary arterial roads that connect locations within metropolitan areas to each other.

Some of these calls resonate with many of us. There is no question that the private sector has played a very useful role in building cities and extending development into the urban periphery, while the public sector has utterly failed to supply affordable housing or services at the required scale. Through the actions of formal and informal developers, firms, and households, and through harnessing the financial resources of international capital as well as those of neighborhoods and families, the private sector has managed to build millions of houses in thousands of cities, with the surprising result that only 3 households per 1,000 in any city, on average, remain homeless (Angel 2000b).

Unfortunately, when it comes to preparing for urban expansion, our fervent hopes that the private sector can ensure an efficient, let alone an equitable or sustainable, development of the metropolitan fringe by relying entirely on free market transactions are entirely misplaced. The urban periphery must contain a network of arterial roads, but there is simply no market mechanism that can bring such a network into existence. If a private entrepreneur wanted to build a long road from A to B, for example, she would be correct in wanting to make it as straight as possible. Such a design would reduce the costs of its right-of-way and construction, as well as the time that its users would require to traverse it. But, once she decides on the alignment of the road, she has lost her ability to bargain with those who own the lands on which it must be built. Each one of them now has a monopoly on a stretch of land, and each one can set a price many times higher than the price of nearby properties.

Only public authorities can plan roads that traverse through the lands of multiple owners, and only public authorities can acquire such lands using the power of eminent domain—a power that allows them to acquire lands in exchange for a price equal to the prevailing price in adjacent properties outside the road's right-of-way. That public power of eminent domain, enshrined in most national constitutions, is needed not only for roads but for railway lines, airports, harbors, power lines, water reservoirs, and canals, as well as for water, sewer, and drainage lines. In short, it is needed wherever the public needs to assemble land *for public use* from a large number of landowners, each of whom can refuse to sell. That power must remain in the public realm. It cannot be privatized. And because it cannot be privatized, the market cannot be counted on to plan and prepare for urban expansion in an efficient manner.

That is not to say that the public sector, given its power of eminent domain and other resources, can be relied upon to plan and prepare for urban expansion in a more efficient manner. It, too, is likely to fail, especially if it refuses to address urban expansion with the seriousness it deserves. The public sector may choose to underinvest in planning a network of arterial roads on the urban periphery, for example, or to insist on preventing the conversion of lands to urban use, which in turn makes it harder for the private sector to supply enough plots to meet demand, and increases the price of

Arterial roads in Bangkok are in short supply, making the city one of the most congested in the world.

land and housing. An unresponsive public sector may also choose to plan and invest in arterial roads in locations that do not match the needs of the private sector, or to underinvest in water reservoirs and water and sewer trunk lines, making it difficult, if not impossible, for the private sector to supply plots with adequate services.

In other words, urban expansion in the real world comes about through the merging of two spheres—the essential public actions that make cities habitable and the essential private actions that make them productive and livable. Neither the public nor the private sphere can survive or thrive on its own. Public goods such as arterial roads and water and sewer systems need the cooperation of all citizens *acting as a public*, rather than as private individuals. To be of any use to those who inhabit and thrive in cities, private goods—such as serviced plots of land for homes and businesses—need these underlying public goods to be installed in a well-planned and timely manner.

The hands-off, laissez-faire approach to urban development that characterizes Bangkok illustrates how the absence of arterial roads creates large efficiency losses and stymies organized urban expansion. Much of the built-up area on its urban fringe consists of thin ribbons along arterial roads, and much of the area between arterial roads remains undeveloped (see figure 4.3). At a smaller scale, figure 5.1 shows the pattern of narrow lanes in a large area of a northeastern inner suburb of Bangkok that was developed during the 1960s, 1970s, and early 1980s. This example underscores one of the drawbacks of laissez-faire, market-led urban expansion because it ignores the substantial land needs of public works. The arterial roads are spaced no less than

8 kilometers (km) apart, and the local roads are not connected to each other to facilitate through traffic. Congestion increases as longer intracity trips are crowded into a small number of arterial roads, resulting in more air pollution and energy use and reduced labor productivity.

The absence of an arterial road grid in Bangkok makes it very difficult to extend the primary grid of key infrastructure services: water supply, sewerage, and storm drainage. Indeed, most Bangkok districts do not have a piped water supply and must continue to rely on water pumped from increasingly deeper wells. The city is located on the delta of the Chao Phraya River, a flat plain only slightly above sea level that consists of many layers of clay and sand. Fresh water accumulates in the sand layers and can be pumped out by digging wells into these layers. As the upper layers become polluted from sewage or the incursion of saline seawater, wells have to reach into deeper layers of sand. In the Lad Phrao district shown in figure 5.1, drilling had to go down some 100 meters to find fresh water in the 1970s.

FIGURE 5.1
The Absence of Arterial Roads in a 60 km² Section of Northwest Bangkok, Thailand, 1984

Source: PADCO (1987, figure 10, 3.10).

Sand does not change in volume when water is pumped out of it because water occupies the small spaces between its grains. But when the sand dries up, water gradually seeps into it from the layers of clay above and below it. When clay dries up, it shrinks in volume. When an entire layer of clay shrinks, the land above it subsides. The Lad Phrao district, for example, subsided by several centimeters every year during the late 1970s. Since most of Bangkok is already at or below sea level, the more it subsides, the more difficult it is to manage flooding during the monsoon season.

The absence of an arterial road network also makes it much more difficult for the city to collect and treat its storm water and sewer water before pumping it out or recycling it. Indeed, Bangkok does not have either a piped drainage system or a piped sewerage system. In the old days it was a city of canals, called the Venice of the East, and the tides drained both its sewage and its storm water into the Chao Phraya River, but those days are long gone. Most of the canals have been filled to make way for streets. Most modern homes are built on a meter or more of landfill, rather than on stilts as in the past, to stay above the flood level. They are fitted with septic tanks that are too close together and rarely emptied, so that sewage simply seeps into the wet ground around it, polluting deeper and deeper levels of groundwater. Finally, in the absence of any public pressure or appropriate and binding legislation, the newly developed areas outside Bangkok's traditional center have little public open space. Their entire land area is used up by buildings of all types.

In short, for Bangkok, one of the world's largest and fastest-growing cities, the absence of adequate lands for public works has been devastating. It is expanding rapidly without

An unfazed *tuk-tuk* driver in Bangkok makes his way down a street during the monsoon floods of 2009.

an arterial road network; without a primary infrastructure network that can carry water, sewage, or storm water; without a system of dikes to manage its storm water; and without a hierarchy of public open spaces. As a result, it suffers from acute traffic congestion and air pollution, water pollution, a chronic inability to take care of its sewage, a dire absence of parks and playgrounds, and land subsidence that makes its flooding problems ever more severe.

The solutions to this self-inflicted environmental crisis require massive investments in public works, but in the absence of the rights-of-way for an arterial road network, a dike system, and the lands for a hierarchy of public parks and playgrounds protected from development, such investments are now exorbitant and quite possibly unaffordable. Necessary as they may be, the amount of destruction of private property that they could entail renders them next to impossible. Public lands for these public works should have been acquired or reserved before the city's expansion ever took place or, at the very least, hand-in-hand with the earlier phases of urban development. In fact, a 25-meter-wide arterial road grid, spaced 1 km apart, would have taken up only 5 percent of the land in areas of expansion. Lands for a hierarchy of open spaces would have required, at a minimum, 5 percent more of the city's surface area. It is too late to acquire them now.

Public works are those common goods that no individual property owner can do without and no individual property owner can create alone in the right amount and in the right places. Converting a rural area, whether large or small, to urban use requires the timely provision of public works to serve the individual properties. This, in turn, requires that a share of this area, typically no less than one-third of it, be allocated for public works, most of it for a hierarchy of streets that can also serve as rights-of-way for other public works, and some of it for a hierarchy of public open spaces. In addition, land is required for other public facilities, such as schools, hospitals, and other public buildings, and sometimes for airports, harbors, and rail terminals. I am particularly concerned about roads and a select hierarchy of open spaces because these are the lands that need to be identified in specific locations and acquired before urban development takes place. The land for most public facilities (other than large transportation terminals) does not usually require specific locations and can be identified and acquired gradually as urban development takes place, and sometimes only after most urban development has taken place.

LIMA, PERU

Planning and acquiring the land for public works requires organization. While Bangkok illustrates a state of anarchy and hardly any organization, the creation of Pampa de Comas, a large squatter settlement on public land on the desert outskirts of Lima, did require serious planning and coordination.

The El Carmen settlement in the Comas district of Lima, Peru, was laid out in a block pattern by squatters prior to their occupation of the site in the late 1960s. By 2012, it was an established suburban neighborhood.

Comas was formed by a series of organized invasions that were carefully thought out and far from spontaneous. People came together in the city, often organized by zealous priests, to plan and prepare for them. Civil engineering students from a local university were called upon to help with site planning and, using their school's instruments, they clandestinely surveyed the land in advance of its occupation. Then, on a carefully selected date, usually at night, dozens of families occupied a large site in Comas. Often joined by hundreds of settled squatters from nearby communities, they confronted the police the next day, and usually succeeded in fending them off, in part because the revolutionary military government at that time saw itself as working for the people, not against them. Each invading family occupied one building site that had been surveyed and selected in advance. The sites were relatively large, measuring 10x20 meters. There were 20 sites to a block and 10-meter-wide roads between blocks. Some blocks were intentionally left open for markets, schools, and public open spaces.

The occupants initially built a shack made of woven bamboo mats at the center of their plot. They then dug a deep trench around the plot, and gradually, as they accumulated enough bricks, they built a 3-meter-high wall around it and slowly began to build rooms within their walled compound. Comas is now a fully built urban neighborhood, indistinguishable from any other neighborhood in the city. Squatters were eventually awarded title documents, and the houses in the district are now part of Lima's formal housing market. Given its small blocks and wide streets, no less than 27 percent of the land area in Comas was devoted to local streets and an additional 3 percent to public open spaces. By comparison, the planned street grid in New York City devotes only 21 percent of the city area to streets.

Planning and the reservation of rights-of-way for street grids at the block level are essential. In his book, *La Grille y El Parque*, Adrian Gorelik (2010) equates the 1898 street grid in Buenos Aires—shown in its 1904 plan as covering the entire territory of the Federal Capital District—with the homogenization of its territory in the spirit of social reform by obliterating the differentiation between rich and poor and formal and informal, and equalizing the distribution of public services, including streets and public open spaces. In the same way, it stands to reason that the Comas street grid and its open spaces accelerated its incorporation into metropolitan Lima as a district among equals. By making all plots similar to each other and facing a broad street, the Comas plan also reduced the difference in real estate values among the houses in the neighborhood and increased the value of real estate in the metropolitan area as a whole. This important lesson has been learned by other developers of minimally serviced informal land

A house in the Comas district of Lima, Peru, was sold for $38,000 in 2012. It had a floor area of 150 m² on a standard squatter plot of 200 m².

subdivisions catering to the urban poor by laying out streets and plots to create future neighborhoods that will be indistinguishable from higher-income areas (Baross and van der Linden 1990).

The basic street grid with its myriad variations at the neighborhood level has an important social and economic value for neighborhood residents, and it is in the interest of landowners, developers, and local residents to cooperate in making it happen. It requires a degree of local organization higher than the anarchy of suburban Bangkok, but relatively low levels of expertise. Similarly, laying out an arterial road grid on the urban periphery of a city does not require a high level of professional expertise, at least not until it reaches the detailed engineering stage.

TORONTO, CANADA

Toronto has an enviable grid of arterial roads that are spaced sufficiently close to each other that public transport is within walking distance of most of the built-up area. This network was made possible by the grid of 20-meter-wide (one chain) concession roads that were surveyed and put in place throughout rural Canada by the British colonial administration in the late nineteenth century with the object of organizing and facilitating agricultural development. Concession roads were typically spaced 2 km apart, enclosing 4 km^2. The enclosed area was usually divided into five 0.8 km^2 lots for cultivation. Concession roads occupied only 1 percent of the land (figure 5.2).

FIGURE 5.2
Concession Roads Spaced 2 Kilometers Apart in York County Surrounding Toronto, Canada, 1878

Source: Miles and Company (1878).

A similar grid of rural roads, spaced 1.6 km (1 mile) apart, was laid out in the area west of the Appalachian Mountains by the 1785 Land Ordinance in the United States to facilitate the agricultural colonization of the newly formed states. Initiated by Thomas Jefferson, the ordinance divided the territory into square-mile segments, with a rural road grid running between them. Both the Canadian concessions and the U.S. Land Ordinance of 1785 have a historical precedence: the centuriation of lands in the Roman Empire that facilitated the agricultural colonization of newly conquered territories. Centuriation involved dividing the land into a grid, with each square consisting of one *centuria* of land, measuring some 700x700 meters and surrounded on all four sides by a road, and then dividing this square into smaller agricultural plots. This grid is still visible in some parts of Italy (figure 5.3).

While the absence of an arterial grid may prevent the introduction of an effective public transport system that extends far into the urban fringe, putting in place an arterial road grid is not a guarantee, in and of itself, that the grid will be used effectively to carry public transport. Unless strong and enduring political alliances take effective steps to introduce and strengthen public transport alternatives to the use of individual automobiles, the appropriation of the arterial grid by cars and trucks—to the exclusion of buses, bicycles, or other environmentally friendly forms of transport—should come as

FIGURE 5.3
Remnants of the 700x700–meter Roman Centuriation Grid near Imola, Bologna, Italy

Source: Benevolo (1980, 215; original map published by Instituto Geographico Militare, n.d.).

FIGURE 5.4
Toronto, Canada's Bus and Streetcar Network, Located Largely on its Arterial Road Grid, 2010

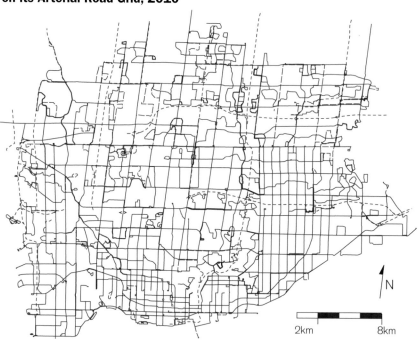

Source: Redrawn from Toronto Transit Commission (2012).

no surprise. Toronto is one city that has been able to build and maintain an effective public transport system that extends along an arterial road grid far into the suburbs, and it now boasts the third-largest transit system in North America (figure 5.4). To the extent that a good public urban transport system can free us from our dependence on the private automobile, the arterial grid can provide an essential building block in meeting the global objective of reducing our carbon footprint.

In addition to an arterial road grid that carries the bulk of its public transport, Toronto has an enviable park system (figure 5.5). The City of Toronto's Parks, Forestry and Recreation division is responsible for the stewardship of 7,393 hectares of green space (11.5 percent of the city's total area) and 1,473 named parks, in addition to 854 playgrounds, 839 sports fields, 130 public swimming pools, 89 ice skating rinks, and 124 community gardens. The division's vision is that Toronto will be known by the world as the "'City within a Park,' a rich fabric of parks, open spaces, rivers and streams that will connect our neighbourhoods and join us with our clean, vibrant lakefront" (City of Toronto 2012).

Such a park system is entirely missing in the metropolitan area of São Paulo, Brazil, (figure 5.6). Its enormous built-up area of 1,548 km² was home to some 15.5 million people in the year 2000, yet it contained few if any open spaces. While Toronto's

FIGURE 5.5
**The Hierarchy of Public Open
Spaces, Toronto, Canada,
2011**

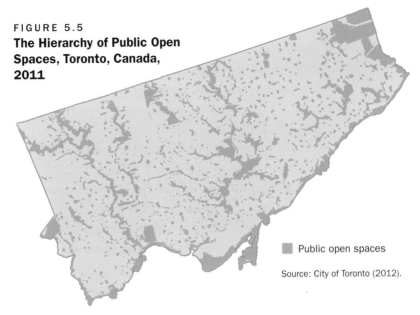

Public open spaces

Source: City of Toronto (2012).

FIGURE 5.6
**The Built-up Area and Near Absence of Public Open Spaces,
São Paulo, Brazil, 2000**

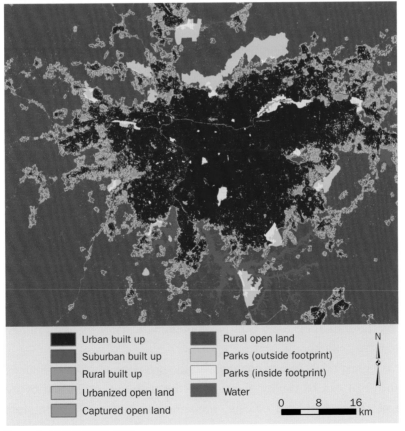

Urban built up
Suburban built up
Rural built up
Urbanized open land
Captured open land

Rural open land
Parks (outside footprint)
Parks (inside footprint)
Water

N

0   8   16
km

Source: Angel et al. (2012, 200).

open space system remains a lofty objective for most cities to aspire to, it is clear that São Paulo has failed to supply even a modicum of public open space to its inhabitants, subjecting them to tiresome vistas of endless rows of buildings, with no chance of escaping into an occasional patch of green for a rest, a game, or a stroll.

CONCLUSION

The Public Works Proposition requires that an adequate amount of land on the urban fringe—where expansion is most likely to take place—be allocated for public works, typically on the order of one-third or more of the land, before urban development takes place. About 5 percent should consist of the rights-of-way for a grid of arterial roads, preferably spaced 1 km apart and within walking distance from the interior of the areas they enclose. This grid can carry public transport and trunk infrastructure as well as facilitate drainage. Another share of 5 percent should consist of a select hierarchy of public open spaces where development, whether by formal developers, informal developers, or squatters, can be repulsed effectively.

The laissez-faire operations of the urban land market may be relied upon in most, but not all, cases to provide public works at the block level or at the subdivision level. But they cannot be relied upon to allocate sufficient lands for two essential forms of public works—arterial roads and a hierarchy of public open spaces. This is a serious market failure with serious consequences for the environmental sustainability of cities. The allocation of lands for public works at the municipal and metropolitan levels calls for organized public action that cannot come about simply by market transactions among individuals and firms acting in their own self-interest. In New York City, the pinnacle of global capitalism and free market ideology, no less that 48 percent of the land is devoted to public works (roads, utilities, and public open spaces) and an additional 5 percent to public facilities and institutions. In the final analysis, public works are part and parcel of the free market, for they enable it to work.

FINAL COMMENTARY ON THE INTRODUCTION AND FOUR PROPOSITIONS

This chapter ends the introductory part of this book. I have presented the realities of urban expansion so you as a reader can understand the issues. I have asked you to engage in a rather uncomfortable intellectual discourse, considering that most of the rhetoric on this important topic calls for containing urban expansion rather than on coming to terms with it.

There is a great reluctance to engage with the prospects of global urban expansion, a reluctance that can be clearly observed in the positions articulated by established residents of cities, municipal officials, homeowners, and environmentalists, among others. When all of these stakeholders come together, they can and do form formidable coalitions that seek to limit urban expansion once and for all by advocating the strict containment of cities within their current footprints and incorporating all new population growth into more compact urban environments. Indeed, the Containment Paradigm, which I associate with smart growth, urban growth management, and the compact city, is designed to combat boundless urban expansion and has been enshrined in urban planning legislation in many countries. This paradigm has been of special importance in developed countries, mostly in the United States and the European Union, and I am afraid that it is now being exported, rather aggressively sometimes, to developing countries where cities are growing rapidly, but where it may be quite irrelevant and indeed harmful.

In its place I propose an alternative paradigm—the Making Room Paradigm—that seeks to come to terms with the expected expansion of cities, particularly in the rapidly urbanizing countries in Asia and Africa, and to a lesser extent in Latin America as well, and to make the minimally necessary preparations for such expansion instead of seeking to contain it. The Making Room Paradigm rests on four propositions that together make up the basic policy framework for engaging with urban expansion in a sensible and realistic manner:

1. The Inevitable Expansion Proposition: The expansion of cities that urban population growth entails cannot be contained. Instead we must make adequate room to accommodate it.
2. The Sustainable Densities Proposition: City densities must remain within a sustainable range. If density is too low, it must be allowed to increase, and if it is too high, it must be allowed to decline.
3. The Decent Housing Proposition: Strict containment of urban expansion destroys the homes of the poor and puts new housing out of reach for most people. Decent housing for all can be ensured only if urban land is in ample supply.
4. The Public Works Proposition: As cities expand, the necessary land for public streets, public infrastructure networks, and public open spaces must be secured in advance of development.

The next part of the book shifts our focus from these pragmatic policy concerns to the study of urban expansion in a global and historical perspective in order to deepen our understanding of the possible relevance of these concerns today. A book that calls itself *Planet of Cities* must fulfill its promise. It must provide a new and deeper understanding of cities in the world at large.

Part One:
The Urbanization Project

This ex-rural population, I found, was creating strikingly similar urban spaces all over the world. . . . These transitional spaces—arrival cities—are the places where the next great economic and cultural boom will be born or where the next great explosion of violence will occur. The difference depends on our ability to notice and our willingness to engage.

Doug Saunders (2011, 3)

CHAPTER 6

Urbanization in Historical Perspective

The occupation of more and more lands by cities everywhere today is the direct result of urbanization, simply defined as the gradual concentration of the human population in towns, cities, and metropolitan areas.

THE THREE-PERIODS NARRATIVE

The relevant history of urbanization for the study of global urban expansion can be usefully divided into three main periods. The first period started with the earliest cities that were founded at the advent of settled agriculture and the domestication of plants and animals circa 10,000 BC, and it continued until about 1800. The second period began around 1800, when urban growth rates began to accelerate, and continued until 2010, when 50 percent of the world's population lived in cities and urban population growth rates were already declining in all world regions.

A third period has already begun in some countries, where the urban share of the total population is no longer increasing, and it will last until the urbanization project slows to its end, possibly by the end of this century. By that time, some 75–80 percent of the world's population is projected to live in urban areas as the world population stabilizes at some 9–11 billion people. Barring major catastrophes, that percentage is expected to remain relatively stable over time. This recognition that the urbanization project—the settlement of the human population in urban areas—has a beginning, middle, and end lends urgency to engage with it now, before it is too late to intervene in the shaping of cities in a meaningful manner.

During the first period, most people lived in villages and farms. Cities as a whole rarely, if ever, contained more than 10 percent of the world's population at any time (Bairoch 1988). Any individual city accommodated very few people, typically not more than tens of thousands, and most of them lived within its defensive walls at

During the first urbanization period, all cities were walking cities, as illustrated in the painting, "Fight Between Carnival and Lent," by Pieter Bruegel the Elder, 1559.

near-subsistence levels in crowded quarters within walking distance of each other. A few cities that could command large empires—Babylon in 300 BC, Rome in 200 AD, Chang'an in 700 AD, or Baghdad in 900 AD—grew to accommodate much larger populations for a while, but they were the exception rather than the rule.

The transition into the second period began at the end of the eighteenth century. A sharp break with the past, often referred to as a scientific and technological revolution, set in motion a series of persistent, irreversible, mutually supportive, and lasting transformations. During this period, a consistent increase in real incomes was coupled with a consistent increase in the world's population. More and more people came to inhabit the planet, and in many countries a greater share of the population came to live in cities. City walls were finally dismantled as the burden of their defense shifted to their emerging nation states. The dangers to public health and the spread of epidemics were ameliorated as people lived longer and had fewer children. The commuting range—initially by the omnibus, horsecar on rails, cable car, and electric trolley, and later by the automobile, bus, and fast train—was extended tenfold and more, resulting in cities that were no longer walking cities. In parallel, the range for obtaining food supplies was also extended several-fold. As a result, many cities could now contain millions of people and take up a lot more land than they did before.

No grand historical narrative has yet explained why these parallel and mutually supporting transformations started in earnest at the end of the eighteenth century, or which one, if any, was the primary cause of all others. However, the year 1800 was a critical turning point in the history of urbanization and in five parallel histories: economic development; world population as a whole; public health; city walls; and transport. Becoming familiar with what happened in 1800 will lead us to a simple yet profound understanding of urbanization in historical perspective, make it easier to come to terms with it, and help prepare for it effectively in the years to come.

FROM MALTHUSIAN TO MODERN ECONOMICS

Students of economic history characterize the first period before 1800 as largely governed by Malthusian economics, or the economics of subsistence. During this period, incomes were largely stagnant because the innovations and the science-based industrial organizations that would lead to increases in productivity and higher incomes had not yet occurred. Income gains during this period, if there were any, were typically translated into having more children, and income per capita remained stagnant. In addition, "the returns to education were low in the mostly agricultural Malthusian economies, and hence parents preferred to invest in child quantity," rather than quality, namely in having more children with lesser education and skills rather than fewer children with better education and skills (Pereira n.d., 7).

The second period was governed by modern economics. It was characterized by science-based technological advances and new forms of knowledge-rich industrial organization that led to major and regular increases in productivity and hence in real

Rapid urbanization went hand-in-hand with industrialization at the onset of the second urbanization period: Copper works in Swansea Harbor, Wales, late 1800s.

FIGURE 6.1
Two Estimates of Average World GDP per Capita, 0–2000

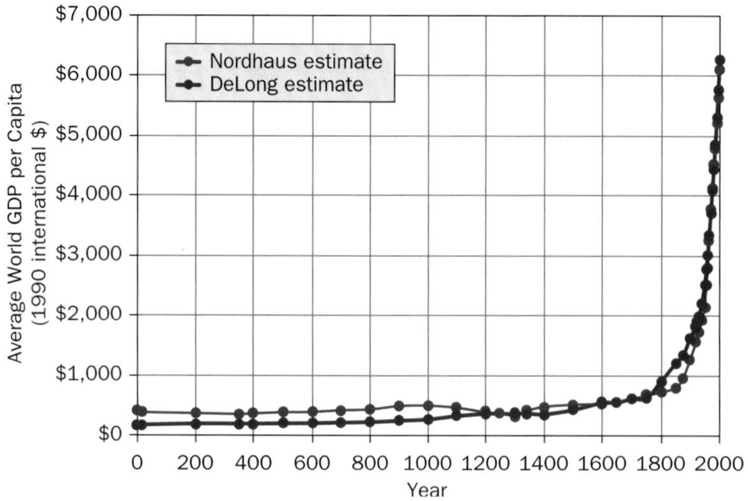

Sources: DeLong (1998) and Nordhaus (1997).

incomes, as well as by increasing returns to education and skills, and by increasing specialization and trade. Occasional episodes of modern economic growth occurred in earlier centuries, such as the Dutch Golden Age in the seventeenth century (De Vries 2001), but consistent growth in average real incomes occurred dramatically from the early nineteenth century onward (figure 6.1).

Global economic development since 1800 has led to a significant enrichment of all segments of the global population and a shift away from subsistence economics for the great majority of people.

> In effect, world economic growth, though strongly inegalitarian, contributed to a steady decline in the headcount measure of poverty throughout the period under analysis. Over the 172 years considered here [1820–1992], the mean income of world inhabitants increased by a factor of 7.6. The mean income of the bottom 20 percent increased only by a factor of slightly more than 3, that of the bottom 60 percent by about 4, and that of the top decile by almost 10. (Bourguignon and Morrison 2002, 733)

RAPID POPULATION GROWTH AND URBANIZATION

Before the advent of settled agriculture, around 10,000 BC, the world's population is estimated at no more than 1 million people. It grew extremely slowly, at an average growth rate of 5.4 percent per century to reach 200 million by 1 AD. It then took some 1,200 years to double, reaching 400 million by the year 1200. It doubled again in 550 years, reaching 800 million in the year 1750. In the second part of the eighteenth century, world population growth started to accelerate, when it doubled in only 150 years, reaching 1.6 billion in 1900, and then again in 63 years, reaching 3.2 million in 1963. By the mid-1960s, the world population reached its fastest-ever annual growth rate, 2 percent per annum. That rate then began to decline and by the mid-1980s it was declining in all world regions. By the year 2010, marking the end of the second period, the world's population was 6.9 billion, and half of it was accommodated in cities (figure 6.2).

The third period started with a slower world population growth rate of only 1.2 percent per year, and that rate is now expected to decline gradually to less than 0.1 percent by 2100. The world population is projected to grow to 8.2 billion by 2025, 9.7 billion by 2050, 10.5 billion by 2075, and 10.9 billion by 2100 (United Nations Population Division 2012). In other words, it is no longer expected to double again. Between 2010 and 2100, it is forecast to grow only by slightly more than half. Considering that in the first two millennia the world population grew thirty-two-fold and that between 1800 and 2000 alone it grew more than sixfold, we must conclude that world population growth is slowing to a halt and will reach a steady state by the end of the twenty-first century.

The historical growth of the world population has paralleled the growth in real per capita incomes, but with a difference. It started to grow earlier, albeit rather slowly. The colonization of the Americas, Africa, and Asia, the increase in world trade, and the onset of commercial agriculture all led to increases in wages and incomes. These

FIGURE 6.2
World Population and Urban Population Growth Trends, 0–2010

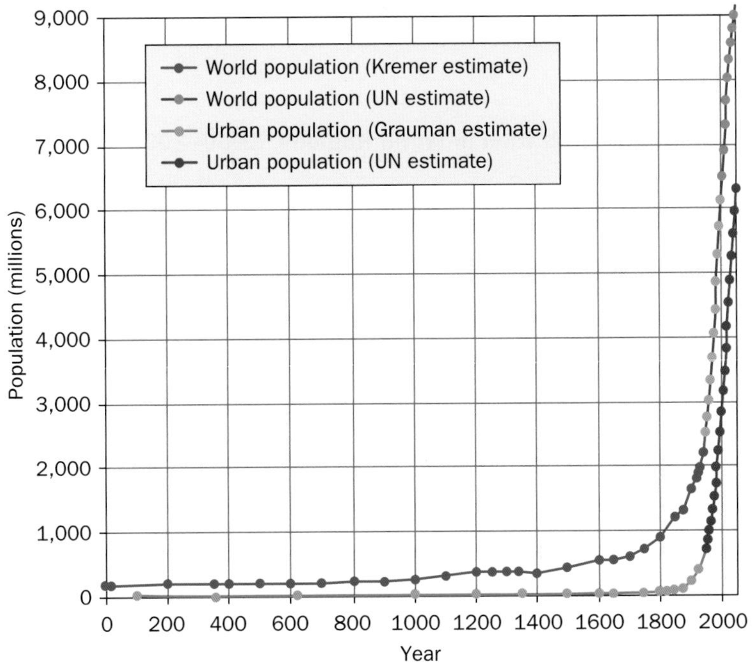

Sources: World population data to 1950 from Kremer (1993); urban population data to 1950 from Grauman (1976); and remaining data from United Nations Population Division (2012).

increases allowed more children to be born and more people to survive, but only at subsistence or near-subsistence levels without any real improvement in their lives. Only when the world population reached 1 billion around the year 1800 did it start to grow at a much faster rate and with parallel increases in the standard of living.

By the year 2010, as we entered the third period in the history of urbanization, population growth slowed everywhere, and Europe was already experiencing negative population growth. Still, the world population as a whole was growing by very substantial absolute numbers. In 2010, 220,000 people were added to the world's population every day, an estimated 80 million per year. These numbers are already lower than they were in 1990, however, when the population added annually to the world total reached a peak of 90 million people, most of whom are now accommodated in cities.

Early urbanization went hand-in-hand with the domestication of plants and animals and the beginning of settled agriculture. Cities provided protection, technological innovations, and opportunities for trade with the countryside and, in turn, appropriated the agricultural surplus whether by force or through cultural and commercial exchange. As the world population increased, the urban population increased as well, and at a faster rate in the nineteenth century as people began to move from villages into towns and cities. Figure 6.3 shows the parallel increases in urbanization and GDP per capita in seven world regions. In all regions except Sub-Saharan Africa, economic development and the share of the population residing in cities have increased together since 1960.

Economic historians focus on a number of factors that empowered this shift: technological innovations that relied on the exchange of new science-based ideas; economies of scale in manufacturing; organized specialization; easy access to large product and labor markets in the cities; and expanded trade with improved access between cities.

FIGURE 6.3
Economic Development and Urbanization in World Regions, 1960–2008

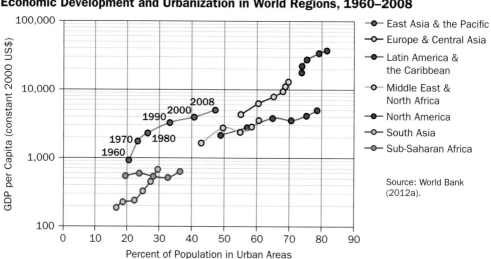

These factors increased urban productivity and wages, creating a wage differential with the countryside and attracting villagers into cities. These economic changes went hand-in-hand with changes in outlook, improvements in public health, a conscious decline in fertility, and greater emphasis on education and training that led to higher incomes per capita. Technological innovations in the countryside, on the other hand, increased farm productivity and released some agricultural workers, often forcing them to move to cities in search of work. Other agricultural workers sought temporary work in cities to reduce the risk to the subsistence of their households when sufficient income from crop cultivation could not be assured.

Social explanations of rural-urban migration focus on escaping from the strong social bonds in the village to a more open and anonymous urban society with more possibilities for individual achievement and upward mobility. Political explanations focus on the attractiveness of cities as concentrations of money and influence and as gateways to global power and capital, where one could get closer to the sources of subsidies or participate in political activities that aimed to gain a larger share of resources.

In 1750, when 800 million people inhabited the planet, only some 40 million people —slightly more than the current population of Greater Tokyo—lived in cities. Today, half the population of the planet lives in cities. The urban population of the world thus increased eightyfold since 1750, from 40 million to 3.2 billion, while its population as a whole increased only eightfold, from 800 million to 6.4 billion. Since 1950, when 730 million people lived in cities, the world's urban population has more than quadrupled. At the 2010 growth rate of 2 percent, 190,000 people are added to the world's urban population every day and an estimated 69 million are added every year. In other words, out of every eight people added to the planet today, seven are added to cities and only one to the countryside. The number of people added to cities every year will continue to grow until 2030, when an estimated 79 million people will be added annually to the world's urban population, and it will then start to decline.

IMPROVEMENTS IN URBAN PUBLIC HEALTH

The three periods in the global history of urbanization are associated with three corresponding periods in the global history of public health. The theory of epidemiologic transition distinguishes three main ages: pestilence and famine; receding pandemics; and degenerative and man-made diseases (Omran 2005).

In the first age, infectious diseases, malnutrition, maternity complications, and recurring epidemics kept the world population in check. This age corresponds to the first urbanization period up to 1800, when average life expectancy at birth remained between 20 and 30 years.

In the second age, improvements in nutrition and personal hygiene associated with higher incomes and the (largely unexplained) disappearance of disease-carrying hosts, particularly in late eighteenth and early nineteenth centuries, led to higher rates of survival and therefore to net population growth in both cities and rural areas. Overcrowding, filthy water, and the absence of water-borne sanitation, storm drainage, and regular garbage collection in nineteenth-century industrial cities were still associated with higher mortality rates in cities than in rural areas. The populations of cities grew only because of rapid rural-urban migration.

In June of 1798, Edward Jenner published a pamphlet detailing his scientific investigations into the protective effects of cowpox as a vaccine against smallpox (*vaca* being Latin for cow).

> In 1799, vaccination was begun on a large scale in Vienna. The same year, Benjamin Waterhouse introduced it in America, actively supported by President Jefferson, who had himself, his family, and his slaves vaccinated, writing Jenner that he had 'erased from the calendar of human afflictions one of its greatest'. Napoleon had his army vaccinated in 1805 and so revered Jenner that he would liberate English prisoners if shown a petition for their freedom from Jenner. 'Ah Jenner,' the emperor was quoted as saying, 'I cannot refuse Jenner anything'. (Roses 1996, 33)

In the first urbanization period, pestilence and famine limited population growth, as illustrated in the painting, "The Marketplace in Naples During the Plague of 1656," by Carlo Coppola.

Only in the second half of the nineteenth century was the connection between filthy water and cholera understood, and only then did a massive expansion of water, sanitation, and drainage works begin in earnest in European and North American cities. Improvements in medicine and vaccination came into their own in the twentieth century, much accelerated by the discovery of penicillin in 1928. The reduction in mortality, especially among infants and mothers, as well as the demand for skilled labor and its associated costs of child rearing, gradually led to decreases in fertility. Average life expectancy at birth during this age increased rapidly from less than 30 years to more than 50.

The third age in the epidemiologic transition accompanied the reduction in the rates of infectious disease and the increase in life expectancy. It was associated with the advent of degenerative diseases of old age, such as cancer, stroke, heart disease, and dementia, as well as man-made diseases caused by smoking, radiation, pollution, or unhealthy diets. Although many infectious diseases became a thing of the past, expanded trade and tourism posed a significant risk of global outbreaks of infectious diseases by new vectors or by new mutations of old ones. During this third age, average life expectancy at birth continued to increase above 50 years of age with advances in both public works and medical care. Different world regions have experienced these public health transitions at different times. As with urbanization, the second age started earlier in Europe and North America, somewhat later in Latin America, and most recently in Asia and Africa. It is important to note that once the benefits of public works and later of vaccination and active medical care were understood, these improvements were quickly imported to other regions. As a result, the duration of the second age of receding pandemics was shortened in the late-developing regions.

While cities at the advent of the age of receding pandemics were associated with higher health risks than rural areas, they became associated with lower health risks than rural areas in the third age. Urbanization did not necessarily bring about improvements in public health, at least not initially, nor did those improvements make urbanization possible. They do share common historical patterns, however, that are quite evident in the data for seven world regions over the last 50 years (figures 6.4, 6.5, and 6.6).

An important feature of these three figures is that within each of the seven world regions, there was a significant change in the public health metrics as they became more urbanized: infant mortality declined, life expectancy increased, and the fertility rate declined. That said, in recent decades the regional or country level of urbanization itself is no longer a good predictor of its relative level of public health among regions and countries. The three less-urbanized regions—East Asia and the Pacific, South Asia, and Sub-Saharan Africa—exhibit high levels of public health that are not commensurate with their relatively low levels of urbanization. This can be attributed to the global spread of innovative public health practices that has led to a significant and rapid reduction in the spread of epidemics and infectious diseases the world over.

FIGURE 6.4
Decline in the Infant Mortality Rate with Urbanization, 1960–2008

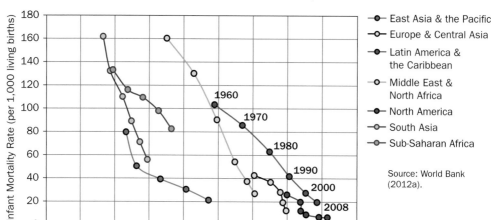

FIGURE 6.5
Increase in Life Expectancy at Birth with Urbanization, 1960–2008

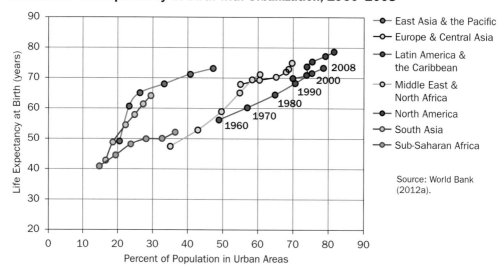

In three other world regions—Europe and Central Asia, North America, and East Asia and the Pacific—the fertility rate in recent years was either at or below the rate necessary to keep their populations from declining, but their fertility rates were no longer in decline. Some countries in these regions, especially in Europe, are now beginning to experience negative population growth. Any future growth in population in these countries will likely be due to international migration.

An important implication for this study of urban expansion is that the global decline in the fertility rate was translated into a decline in household size, which was

FIGURE 6.6
Decline in the Fertility Rate with Urbanization, 1960–2008

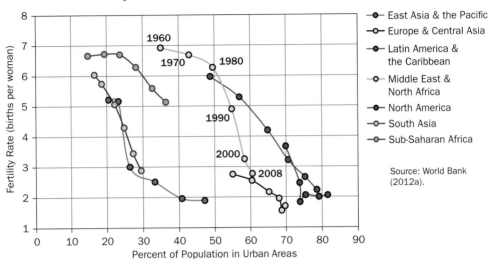

Source: World Bank (2012a).

then translated into an increase in the number of dwelling units for a given population and an increase in the amount of land necessary to accommodate that population. There is no doubt that two three-person households living in two separate dwelling units take up more floor area and therefore, other things being equal, more land area than one six-person household.

"AND THE WALLS CAME TUMBLING DOWN"

Throughout the first period and up until the early 1800s almost all cities—with the important exception of cities in Britain and North America—were surrounded by defensive walls. Their primary function was strategic: to control the surrounding territory by frustrating all efforts to overrun the city, whether by invading armies, marauders, or rebels. "A clever military leader," observed the Prussian General von Moltke, "will succeed in many cases in choosing defensive positions of such an offensive nature from the strategic point of view that the enemy is compelled to attack us in them" (Liddell Hart 1967, xiii). Well-located walled cities complied with his dictum. And as Sun Tsu observed in *The Art of War*, from the perspective of military strategy "the worst policy of all is to besiege walled cities" (Liddell Hart 1967, xi).

The defense of cities required a heavy investment in their fortifications, including elaborate systems of towers, walls, bastions, moats, and gatehouses designed to repel raids and withstand a prolonged siege. A city wall had to be complete to be of any use and was only as good as its most vulnerable section. It was no doubt the city's most important public works project, as the wall had to be planned, properly budgeted, efficiently executed, and regularly maintained. Beyond its strategic value, the wall also

During the first urbanization period, almost all cities were surrounded by defensive walls, such as the walls in Xian, China, built between 1347 and 1378.

served a control and symbolic function that often outlasted its defensive role: to distinguish city residents from nonresidents by regulating the entry and exit of people and goods through a small number of gates that were usually closed at night. Historical perceptions of the city as an entity are closely associated with walls, which clearly distinguish it from the surrounding countryside. In classical Chinese, for example, the character *Chéng* (城) denoted both city and defensive wall. The symbolic act of entering a walled city through one of its gates gave residents a sense of having arrived, of coming home, of crossing to safety.

The history of city walls is as old as the history of urbanization. The town of Jericho in the Jordan Valley, for example, one of the earliest human settlements on record, was surrounded by a massive wall 3.6 meters high and 1.8 meters wide at its base as early as 9,400 BC, when it housed some 1,000 people. The city of Ur on the Euphrates River in Mesopotamia had a wall surrounding it in 3,000 BC, and Chinese cities were surrounded by walls from 2,000 BC onward.

This history is important for understanding contemporary urban expansion for three reasons. First, a walled city almost always had a fringe area outside its walls, the *suburbium* or *faubourg*, that was at least functionally an integral and inevitable part of that city. In contrast with our romantic notion of the wall as making the city distinct from the open countryside, urban settlements taken as a whole have always had fuzzy boundaries. Second, city walls did not necessarily block or contain urban expansion. In fact, walled areas were enlarged from time to time to encompass established urban functions on the fringe, new residences built by accretion, extramural institutions, or planned extensions. Third, although generations of defensive walls outlasted the introduction of cannons by several centuries, their strategic value was eventually lost and they were gradually dismantled during the early part of the nineteenth century. The end of the Napoleonic Wars in 1815 is associated with a fundamental change in the physical character of the city: the loss, or at the very least the downfall, of its defensive walls.

The first two of these three historic aspects of city walls are illustrated in Koblenz, Germany, in the Middle Ages (von der Dollen 1990). Koblenz was situated at the entrance of the Mosel River into the Rhein River (figure 6.7). Before the construction of its outer wall in 1276–1289, the city was surrounded by a late Roman wall, a semicircular barricade punctuated by towers connected to a straight wall along the Mosel. It contained the archbishop's palace and castle, the town hall, a market, a guild hall, residences, churches, and a cemetery. The area outside the wall contained a fringe area of endogenous urban land uses that could not be accommodated within the walls, several exogenous spontaneous ribbon developments along roads leading out of the walled town, and a number of institutions, such as monasteries, nunneries, and hospitals, that catered to the poor and destitute.

Endogenous land uses on the urban fringe were those expelled from the walled city: noxious trades such as tanners; trades posing a fire risk such as blacksmiths, salt makers,

FIGURE 6.7

Suburban Expansion Outside the Late Roman Walls in Koblenz, Germany, in the Middle Ages

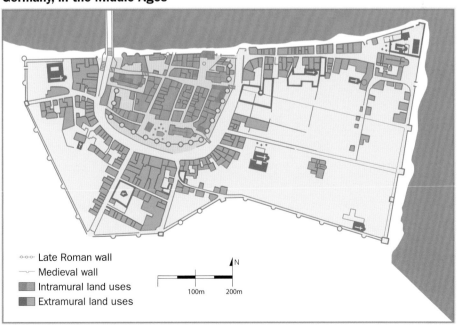

Late Roman wall
Medieval wall
Intramural land uses
Extramural land uses

100m   200m

N

Source: Redrawn from von der Dollen (1990, figure 15.1, 330).

and brick kilns; weavers, because of their need for bleaching greens; marketplaces; quarries; cemeteries; and garbage dumps. Exogenous uses were those propelled toward the walled city: inns for late visitors; the homes and businesses of out-of-town merchants and free traders; and the homes of laborers and migrants who together formed mixed-income neighborhoods along the roads leading into the city. The location of monasteries of the mendicant orders on the urban fringe "acted as a magnet for both migrants generally and the poor social groups in particular" (von der Dollen 1990, 331).

Like Koblenz, many other walled medieval cities in Europe and elsewhere enlarged their walled areas several times to accommodate their fringe belts and to prepare room for additional expansion. The city of Florence in Italy, for example, expanded its walled area at least five times. Its 1300 wall encompassed such a generous area that it was not fully built up until the middle of the nineteenth century (Kostof 1992, 50).

With the advent of gunpowder, city walls became more vulnerable. Although artillery was introduced into the battlefield in China as early as the twelfth century AD, cannons that could bring down city walls were perfected only in the fifteenth century. The battle of Constantinople in 1453 was won and the Byzantine Empire was brought to an end when the army of Mehmet II breached the defensive walls of the city with a 40-day

FIGURE 6.8
The Land-Intensive Star Fortifications of Geneva, Switzerland, 1832

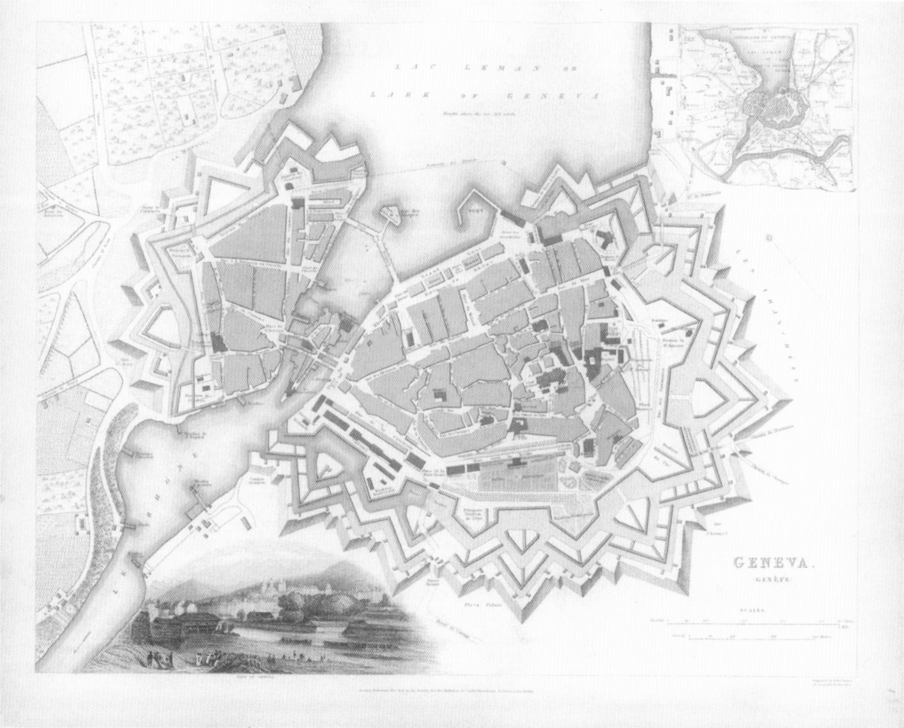

Source: Society for the Diffusion of Useful Knowledge (1844, 180).

barrage of artillery fire. That battle marked the end of vertical defensive walls, but it did not mean that the age of reliable urban fortifications was over.

A new generation of urban fortifications—the star fort or *trace italienne*—was developed by Italian military architects in the fifteenth century and perfected by the French military engineer Vauban in the sixteenth century. These fortifications involved lower walls, ditches, and a series of zigzagging bastions, typically sloping at generous angles rather than being vertical, and requiring an area often larger than the built-up area of the city they protected (figure 6.8). They also required keeping all this area free of settlement to ensure open lines of fire in all directions from the city's own cannons, a requirement that often involved the demolition of any settlements already built there. These complex fortifications required an enormous expense and a vast land area, and they made urban expansion much more difficult and considerably more expensive, but not impossible, as the case of Turin demonstrates (figure 6.9).

Star fortifications provided an excellent defense for European cities for more than 200 years and until the end of the Napoleonic Wars in 1815, when it became clear that single cities could not defend themselves independently against large modern armies. City walls

FIGURE 6.9

Expansion of the Walled City of Turin, Italy: 1600, 1620, 1673, and 1714

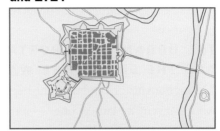

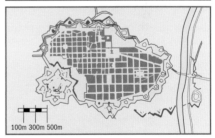

100m 300m 500m

Source: Redrawn from Benevelo (1980, figures 990-993, 693).

lost their defensive function, their main *raison d'être*, but only a few cities, such as Turin, Frankfurt, and Brussels, were forced by Napoleon to pull down their walls (Kostof 1992). In many cities the walls remained important as customs barriers, divisions to facilitate law and order, and symbols of past grandeur and status, but these uses were not adequate to justify the investment in new fortifications. Throughout the nineteenth century some 100 walled border cities in Germany and France served as state fortresses that helped defend the country, not only the single city. After 1815, the defense of the state was the only reason to keep a place militarily fortified (Mintzker 2006).

To conclude, by the beginning of the nineteenth century, the modern city embarked on its transformation into an open rather than a closed city. It was now defined by its administrative boundaries or by the limits of its built-up area—what Pliny called the *extrema tectorum*—rather than by its walls.

THE URBAN TRANSPORTATION REVOLUTION AND THE END OF THE WALKING CITY

Throughout history and until the beginning of the nineteenth century, all the cities in the world—even the largest ones—were walking cities. Their physical size was generally limited to an area small enough for people to walk from one place to another. Goods were moved by pack animals or carts and a small minority of people could travel on horseback or by carriage, but the great majority walked. Rome in the third century AD, during the time of the Emperor Aurelian, was the largest city in the world. It had a population of around 1 million people within the 19 kilometers (km) of walls built by Aurelian in 270–275 AD that encompassed an area of 13.7 km^2 (figure 6.10). The maximum distance from the wall to the center of Rome—*Forum Romanum*—was only 2 km, easily walkable in less than half an hour.

In the last decades of the eighteenth century, long before the introduction of automobiles, a series of technological innovations in transportation and communication, and their commercialization, made it possible for cities to expand beyond their walkable range. These innovations began with several forms of public transport—the horse-drawn omnibus, the horsecar on rails, the steam-propelled ferry and train, the electric trolley, the elevated and underground train, and later, in the early decades of the twentieth century, the private automobile, truck, and bus, all propelled by internal

Omnibuses, such as this one in Paris, France in 1900, facilitated the expansion of cities beyond their earlier walking city limits.

FIGURE 6.10
Rome as a Walking City Within the Aurelian Walls, 270–275 AD

Forum Romanum ☆
2 km radius
City area
Servian wall
Aurelian wall
Aqueducts
Roads

N

200m 600m 1km

Source: Base map redrawn from Benevolo (1980, figure 236, 150).

combustion engines. At the same time, important innovations in communications that began with the telegraph soon included the telephone, the facsimile machine, and eventually the cellular phone and the Internet.

The commercialization of these technological innovations, coupled with increasing personal incomes that have made them widely affordable, meant that urban dwellers

The horsecar on rails expanded cities beyond the range of the omnibus in the late nineteenth century: One of the last horsecars in New York City, 1917.

no longer had to live in close proximity to each other in order to walk from place to place. Some urban dwellers now had the choice to move further away in physical space and still be close enough to conduct their affairs.

Governments and markets responded differently to the demand for these choices, and every city offered or made possible different choices to its inhabitants. A common attribute of the availability of all these choices was the possibility of increasing the size of the city beyond walking distance range. Newman and Kenworthy (1999, 27) point out an important relationship between the length of the journey to work and urban extent.

> One characteristic people have shown that has been important in shaping the nature of our cities is that they do not like to commute, on average, more than half an hour to major urban destinations. In the United Kingdom, a government study found that travel time for work trips has been stable for six centuries.

The transportation developments of the past two centuries have made it possible for city populations to grow beyond the limits of the walking cities of the past, which had restricted urban populations to around 1 million people. By the beginning of the nineteenth century transportation developments also made trade easier. Cheaper and more reliable trade by steamships, steam-powered trains, and later gasoline-powered trucks allowed food, clothing, building materials, energy supplies, and other necessities to be brought from further away. The largest cities in the world began to pass the 1 million mark, and by the end of the twentieth century there were cities of 10 million or more on all continents (figure 6.11).

Individual cities and metropolitan areas now contain greater numbers of people than ever before. In 1950, for example, there were only 2 urban agglomerations in the world with more than 10 million people, 6 with more than 5 million, and 75 with more than 1 million. Twenty-four percent of the world's urban population of 730 million in that year lived in cities with more than 1 million people. By 2010, there were 21 urban agglomerations in the world with more than 10 million people, 54 with more than 5 million, and 442 with more than 1 million. Thirty-eight percent of the world's urban population of 3.5 billion in that year lived in cities with more than 1 million people (United Nations Population Division 2012, file 2).

In all of these urban agglomerations, given contemporary population densities, residents had come to rely on vehicles of one kind or another—bicycle, motorcycle, car, bus, trolley, or train—to reach many more desirable destinations than those that could be reached by foot in a given time period. It should not be surprising, therefore, that nostalgic urban dwellers, longing for the not-so-distant past when every desirable

FIGURE 6.11
Population of the Largest City by Continent, 800–2000

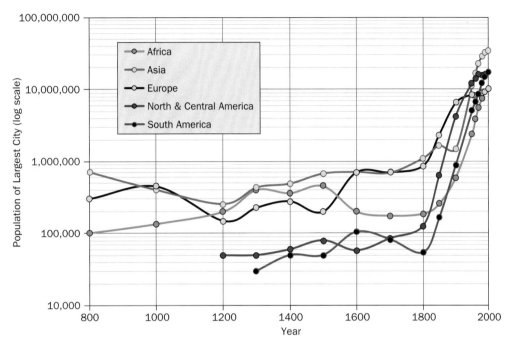

Sources: Data for the years 800–1950 from Chandler (1987, 528–534); and data for the years 1950–2000, from United Nations Population Division (2005, table A.11, 258–260).

destination in the city was within walking distance of their homes, perceive the new metropolitan landscape as limitless or endless sprawl.

We are now in the midst of the third and, quite possibly, final period in the history of urbanization, with one-half of the world's population living in a global network of cities spanning the entire planet. Barring a major catastrophe that will make cities unlivable, we can expect that toward the end of this century an even larger share of the world's population will live in cities, and that net migration from rural areas to cities will have largely come to an end. The urbanization project, arguably the most ambitious and momentous one that humanity has ever undertaken, will have lasted a mere 300 years, a modest total of 12 generations.

The cities and towns of Africa, Asia and Latin America are central to the demographic, economic and environmental challenges of the 21st century. The urban centres of low- and middle-income countries represent the new global frontier.

Martin, McGranahan, Montgomery, and Fernandez-Castilla (2008, 1)

CHAPTER 7

The Geography
of World Urbanization

The historical pattern of world urbanization presented in chapter 6 pertains to global trends and composite patterns established by bringing together the unique historical trajectories of many countries and regions. The central question addressed in this chapter revolves around examining these trajectories in greater detail. When have different countries and regions urbanized in the past, and where is urbanization likely to take place in the twenty-first century?

To answer this question I look at the history and the future of urbanization by examining the United Nations population data for 1950–2050 for all countries and associating projected urban growth rates in different countries with their levels of economic development, present levels of urbanization, and levels of governance, as well as their urban densities, consumption of energy, and carbon emissions. In coming to terms with global urban expansion, we must first identify where it is likely to take place and then select the appropriate strategies for managing it there, rather than importing strategies that may only be appropriate elsewhere. In other words, there are no one-size-fits-all strategies for managing global urban expansion. In rapidly urbanizing countries with a weak rule of law, for example, we must be wary of urban expansion strategies that rely for their success on the rule of law; and in rapidly growing high-density cities with low-carbon emissions, we must be wary of urban expansion strategies designed to lower carbon emissions in cities with low-density sprawl.

HISTORICAL FOCUS ON DEVELOPED COUNTRIES

We begin our investigation with a look at the different urbanization trajectories in eight developed or industrialized countries between the years 1300 and 2050 (figure 7.1). Several aspects of these data merit attention. While the average global level of urbanization before 1800 never exceeded 10 percent, this was not true of individual countries.

FIGURE 7.1
Urbanization Trajectories in Eight Countries, 1300–2050

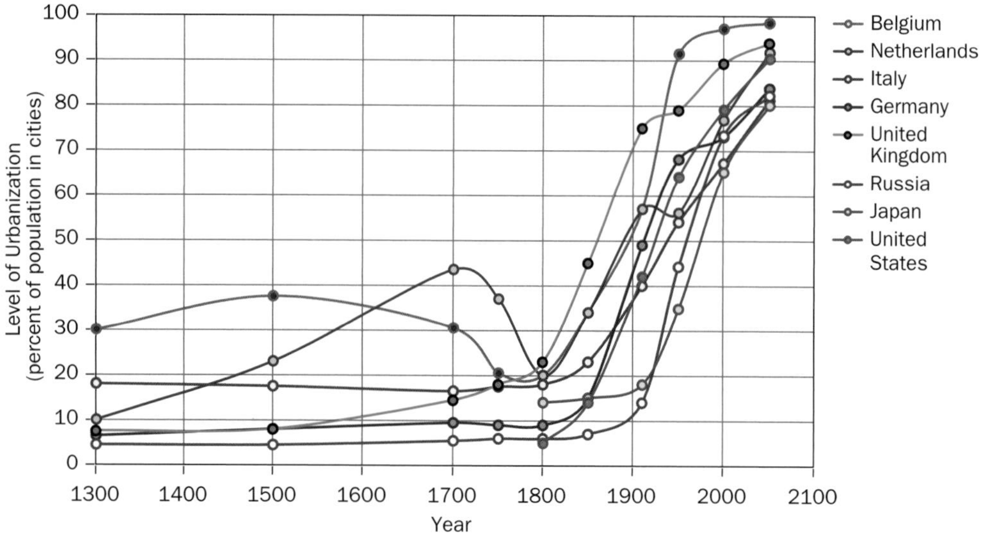

Sources: Data from Bairoch (1988, table 11.2, 179; table 13.1, 215; and table 13.4, 221); and from United Nations Population Division (2012, file 2).

Belgium, whose cities specialized in textile manufacturing and exporting prior to the Industrial Revolution, was highly urbanized during the late Middle Ages. The Netherlands in 1700 was by far the most urbanized country in the world "as intermediary for Europe at large, carrying out a substantial portion of the Continent's foreign trade, though it had only one-sixtieth of its population" (Bairoch 1988, 179). Italy had its own trading network and a level of urbanization twice that of the world at large from the late Middle Ages until 1800.

England (later a part of the United Kingdom) had quite a low level of urbanization before the Industrial Revolution began there in the eighteenth century. It then started to urbanize rapidly, becoming the world's most urbanized country by 1850. Other countries, notably the United States and Germany, started their industrialization and rapid urbanization later than England, after the beginning of the nineteenth century, while Russia and Japan started to industrialize and urbanize rapidly in the twentieth century.

Over time, levels of urbanization taper off eventually. In small countries such as Belgium that import most of their foods, the levels are now expected to stabilize at close to 100 percent by 2050, when almost all Belgians will live in cities. In large countries that export food, such as the United States, the levels are expected to taper off at almost 90 percent by 2050. More generally we may expect mature levels of urbanization to stabilize in a broad range from 75 to 100 percent. To get a more accurate sense of where and when future urbanization is likely to take place, we must look at the historical trajectories of specific countries and regions.

Some countries urbanized rapidly before 1800, including the Netherlands: Untitled painting of Amsterdam Harbor by Abraham Storck (1644–1708).

Other countries are becoming more urbanized and industrialized in the twenty-first century: An electronics factory in Cicarang, Indonesia.

Some countries urbanized and industrialized rapidly in the early twentieth century: A silk factory in Japan.

The rapid urbanization that started in the latter part of the eighteenth century in Europe and later in North America accompanied the development of their modern industrial economies. These regions urbanized rapidly in the nineteenth and early twentieth centuries, and the majority of their populations resided in urban areas by 1950. Latin America began to urbanize later but at a faster rate, and its share of the population residing in cities surpassed Europe's share by 1990. In North America and Latin America more than 80 percent now live in cities; in Europe, 72 percent; and in Western Asia, 66 percent. Urbanization in these regions is still noticeable, often influenced by international migration rather than by internal migration from rural areas. In other world regions, notably parts of Asia and Sub-Saharan Africa, one-half or less of the population now resides in cities, and the urbanization project there is ongoing.

FUTURE GROWTH PRIMARILY IN DEVELOPING COUNTRIES

By 2050, the share of the population living in urban areas in all regions will surpass the 50 percent mark, and in the world as a whole it will almost reach 70 percent (figure 7.2). An overview of the geography of world urbanization at the country level shows the percent of urban population by country in 1950, 2010, and 2050 (figure 7.3). The level of urbanization in every single country on the planet increases substantially over time. While these maps show the shares of the total population living in cities, figure 7.4 focuses on the actual numbers of urban dwellers in 22 countries that had more than 35 million people living in cities in 2010. Only six countries had urban populations in excess of 100 million people in that year: China, India, the United States, Brazil, Indonesia, and Russia. Altogether the 22 countries shown in figure 7.4 had a total

FIGURE 7.2
The Growing Share of Population in Urban Areas by World Region, 1950–2050

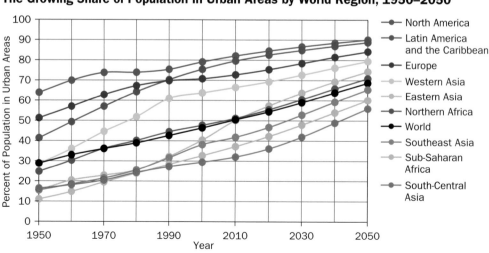

Source: United Nations Population Division (2012, file 2).

FIGURE 7.3
Levels of Urbanization in All Countries: 1950, 2010, and 2050

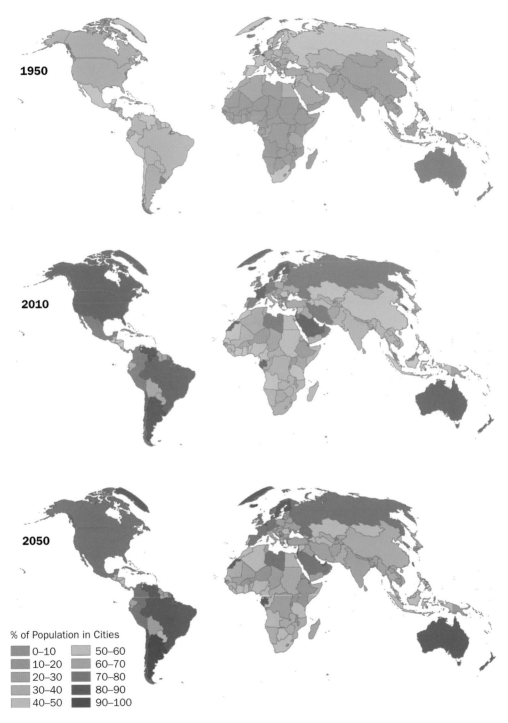

Source: Drawn from data in United Nations Population Division (2012, file 2).

FIGURE 7.4

Urban Populations in 22 Countries with 35 Million or More Urban Residents, 2010

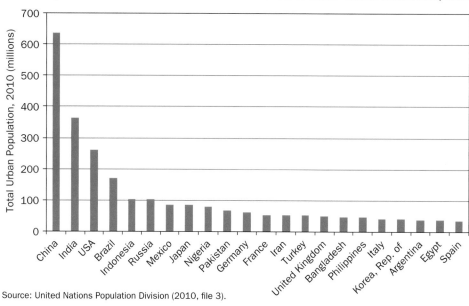

Source: United Nations Population Division (2010, file 3).

urban population of some 2.5 billion in 2010, more than 70 percent of the total world urban population of 3.5 billion in that year. More than half of these countries are developing countries.

In 1950 the urban population of the world amounted to 730 million, of which some 300 million (42 percent) lived in developing countries. By 2010 it was 3.5 billion, of which 2.6 billion (73 percent) lived in developing countries. By 2050 the world's urban population is projected to grow to 7.3 billion, of which 5.2 billion (83 percent) will live in developing countries. In other words, between 2010 and 2050, the urban population of developed countries will grow by some 160 million—100 million in the United States alone—while the urban population of developing countries will grow by 2.6 billion, or 15 times that of the developed countries.

Where in the developing countries will that dramatic growth take place? Figures 7.5 and 7.6 summarize the expected increase in the urban population between 2010 and 2050 by geographic regions and subregions. Figure 7.5 shows the expected increase in millions of people, while figure 7.6 shows the share of the total expected increase in percentage terms. The two figures also show the total urban population in each region in 1950, the increase in that population between 1950 and 2010, and the expected total urban population in 2050.

The largest shares of all the expected urban population growth on the planet between 2010 and 2050, at 25 percent each, will be in Sub-Saharan Africa and the Indian Subcontinent. Another 15 percent will be in China. Western Asia and North

FIGURE 7.5

Relative Shares of the World Urban Population by Geographic Regions (in millions), 1950–2050

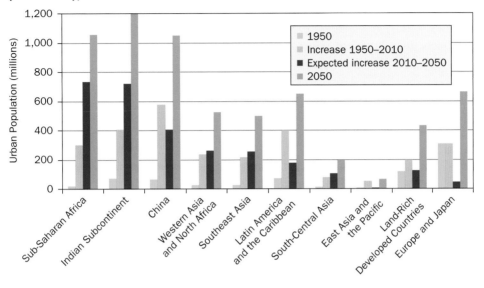

Notes: The Indian Subcontinent includes India, Pakistan, and Bangladesh. South-Central Asia excludes the Indian Subcontinent. East Asia and the Pacific excludes China.
Source: Calculated from United Nations Population Division (2010, file 3).

FIGURE 7.6

Relative Shares of the World Urban Population by Geographic Regions (in percentages), 1950–2050

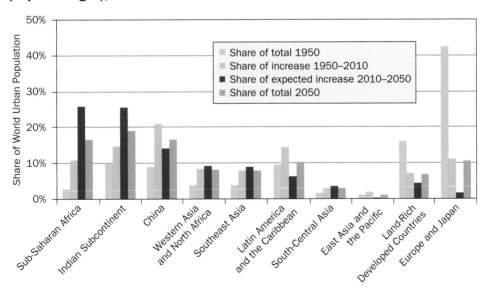

Notes: The Indian Subcontinent includes India, Pakistan, and Bangladesh. South-Central Asia excludes the Indian Subcontinent. East Asia and the Pacific excludes China.
Source: Calculated from United Nations Population Division (2010, file 3).

Africa together will absorb some 9 percent of the expected growth, while Southeast Asia will absorb a similar share. Latin America can expect to absorb only 6 percent of the expected growth, while land-rich developed countries (the United States, Canada, Australia, and New Zealand) will absorb less than 5 percent. Europe and Japan will absorb less than 2 percent. Twenty-two countries will absorb the bulk of the expected urban population growth between 2010 and 2050 (figure 7.7). Only five countries will add 100 million people or more to their urban population between 2010 and 2050: India, China, Nigeria, Pakistan, and the United States. These 22 countries will increase

FIGURE 7.7
Urban Population Increases in 22 Countries Expected to Add 25 Million or More People, 2010–2050

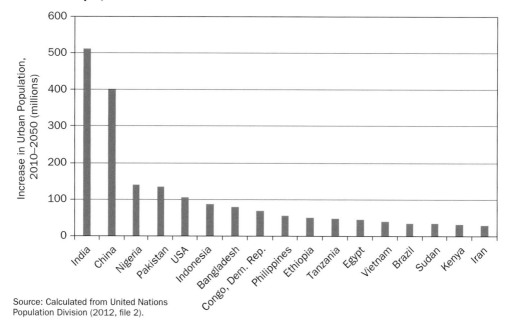

Source: Calculated from United Nations
Population Division (2012, file 2).

their total urban population by some 2.0 billion, more than 70 percent of the total 2.8 billion that will be added to the world urban population during that period. While only half of the countries with the highest urban populations in 2010 were developing countries (figure 7.4), 21 of the 22 countries in figure 7.7 are developing countries.

Is there anything more specific about the countries that will experience rapid urban population growth in the coming decades, beyond the fact that most of them will be developing countries? To answer this question, I calculated the expected average annual growth rate of the urban population between 2010 and 2050 in 153 countries that had 1 million people or more in the year 2000 using the United Nations population projections. I then compared it with several economic, political, and geographic characteristics of these countries to see whether projected urban growth rates were significantly correlated (at the 99.9 percent confidence level) with these characteristics.[1]

A clear picture emerged from this analysis (figure 7.8 and table 7.1). We can now assert with a high level of statistical confidence that the rate of urban population growth in coming decades will be significantly higher in tropical countries; in less urbanized and poorer countries; in countries with lower government expenditures; in more isolated countries with weaker air travel links to the world at large; in countries with higher urban densities, lower energy consumption, and lower carbon emissions; and in countries with weaker and less effective governance.

More specifically, urban population growth will be significantly higher in countries with the following characteristics compared to other slower-growing countries.

- The distance to the equator is shorter.
- The level of urbanization (the percentage of the population living in cities) in 2010 was lower.
- GDP per capita in 2010 was lower.
- The value added from agriculture as a percent of GDP in 2009 was higher.
- Agricultural employment as a percent of total employment in 1999–2009 was higher.
- The value added in manufacturing as a percent of GDP in 2008 was lower.
- Net overseas development assistance as a percent of gross national income in 2009 was higher.
- General government expenditures as a percent of GDP in 2008 were lower.
- The built-up area density in cities with 100,000 people or more in 2000 was higher.
- Energy use in kilograms of oil equivalents per capita in 2008 was lower.
- CO_2 emissions in metric tons per capita in 2007 were lower.
- The number of airline passengers per capita in 2009 was lower.
- The rule of law in 2010 was less effective.
- There was less opportunity to voice complaints and less accountability in 2010.
- There was less political stability and more violence in 2010.
- Government was less effective in 2010.
- There was lower regulatory quality in 2010.
- There was less effective control of corruption in 2010.

---

1 Data on country demographic characteristics were obtained from the United Nations Population Division (2010); data on country economic characteristics were obtained from the World Bank (2012a); data on governance indicators were obtained from the World Bank (2012b); and data on the built-up area densities in large cities were obtained from the *Atlas of Urban Expansion* (Angel et al. 2012; *www.lincolninst.edu/subcenters/atlas-urban-expansion/google-earth-data.aspx*).

FIGURE 7.8

Projected 2010–2050 Annual Urban Population Growth Rates in 153 Countries with 1 Million or More People in 2000: Selected Characteristics

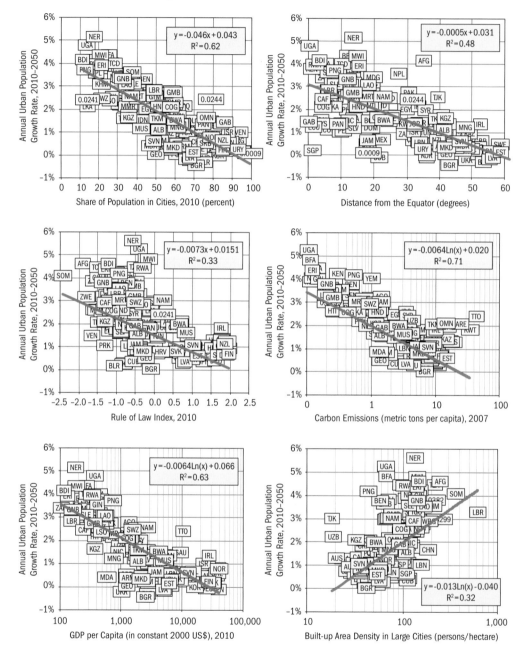

Sources: Population growth rates calculated from United Nations Population Division (2010 file 3); economic characteristics and carbon emissions data from World Bank (2012a); and governance data from World Bank (2012b).

TABLE 7.1
Three-Letter Labels for Countries in Figure 7.8

Label	Country	Label	Country	Label	Country	Label	Country
AFG	Afghanistan	ESP	Spain	LBY	Libya	RWA	Rwanda
AGO	Angola	EST	Estonia	LKA	Sri Lanka	SAU	Saudi Arabia
ALB	Albania	ETH	Ethiopia	LSO	Lesotho	SDN	Sudan
ARE	United Arab Emirates	FIN	Finland	LTU	Lithuania	SEN	Senegal
ARG	Argentina	FRA	France	LVA	Latvia	SGP	Singapore
ARM	Armenia	GAB	Gabon	MAR	Morocco	SLE	Sierra Leone
AUS	Australia	GBR	United Kingdom	MDA	Moldova	SLV	El Salvador
AUT	Austria	GEO	Georgia	MDG	Madagascar	SOM	Somalia
AZE	Azerbaijan	GHA	Ghana	MEX	Mexico	SRB	Serbia
BDI	Burundi	GIN	Guinea	MKD	Macedonia	SVK	Slovak Republic
BEL	Belgium	GMB	Gambia, The	MLI	Mali	SVN	Slovenia
BEN	Benin	GNB	Guinea-Bissau	MMR	Myanmar	SWE	Sweden
BFA	Burkina Faso	GRC	Greece	MNG	Mongolia	SWZ	Swaziland
BGD	Bangladesh	GTM	Guatemala	MOZ	Mozambique	SYR	Syrian Arab Republic
BGR	Bulgaria	HKG	Hong Kong	MRT	Mauritania	TCD	Chad
BIH	Bosnia & Herzegovina	HND	Honduras	MUS	Mauritius	TGO	Togo
BLR	Belarus	HRV	Croatia	MWI	Malawi	THA	Thailand
BOL	Bolivia	HTI	Haiti	MYS	Malaysia	TJK	Tajikistan
BRA	Brazil	HUN	Hungary	NAM	Namibia	TKM	Turkmenistan
BWA	Botswana	IDN	Indonesia	NER	Niger	TTO	Trinidad and Tobago
CAF	Central African Rep.	IND	India	NGA	Nigeria	TUN	Tunisia
CAN	Canada	IRL	Ireland	NIC	Nicaragua	TUR	Turkey
CHE	Switzerland	IRN	Iran	NLD	Netherlands	TZA	Tanzania
CHL	Chile	IRQ	Iraq	NOR	Norway	UGA	Uganda
CHN	China	ISR	Israel	NPL	Nepal	UKR	Ukraine
CIV	Cote d'Ivoire	ITA	Italy	NZL	New Zealand	URY	Uruguay
CMR	Cameroon	JAM	Jamaica	OMN	Oman	USA	United States
COG	Congo, Republic of	JOR	Jordan	PAK	Pakistan	UZB	Uzbekistan
COL	Colombia	JPN	Japan	PAN	Panama	VEN	Venezuela
CRI	Costa Rica	KAZ	Kazakhstan	PER	Peru	VNM	Vietnam
CUB	Cuba	KEN	Kenya	PHL	Philippines	WBG	West Bank & Gaza
CZE	Czech Republic	KGZ	Kyrgyz Republic	PNG	Papua New Guinea	YEM	Yemen, Republic of
DEU	Germany	KHM	Cambodia	POL	Poland	ZAF	South Africa
DNK	Denmark	KOR	Korea, Republic of	PRI	Puerto Rico	ZAR	Congo, Dem. Rep.
DOM	Dominican Republic	KSV	Kosovo	PRK	Korea, Dem. Rep.	ZMB	Zambia
DZA	Algeria	KWT	Kuwait	PRT	Portugal	ZWE	Zimbabwe
ECU	Ecuador	LAO	Laos	PRY	Paraguay		
EGY	Egypt	LBN	Lebanon	ROM	Romania		
ERI	Eritrea	LBR	Liberia	RUS	Russian Federation		

Source: International Standards Organization (ISO 1974).

CONCLUSION

Urban population growth and its concomitant urban expansion in the coming decades will take place in many countries that are poor and have relatively weak governance structures. Unlike previous waves of urbanization that were often accompanied by vigorous economic growth, future urbanization may occur with few public resources to support and sustain it. On the positive side, however, cities in these countries may continue to have higher densities, consume less energy, and emit lower quantities of CO_2.

Rapid urban expansion will take place in countries that are poor and have weak regulatory environments: Street scene in Lagos, Nigeria.

The only industrialized country that can expect a significant wave of new urbanization is the United States, which is expected to grow by more than 100 million people between 2010 and 2050, increasing its urban population by 40 percent. U.S. cities have among the lowest built-up area densities in the world, and both energy consumption and CO_2 emissions are very high in global terms. The level of governance is much higher in comparison with other rapidly urbanizing countries, and cities tend to expand in accordance with the rule of law. In short, the United States is a clear outlier among rapidly urbanizing countries, and it stands to reason that the strategies formulated in the United States for managing urban expansion—notably containment strategies such as growth management, smart growth, densification, or urban growth boundaries—may not be applicable in most cities in rapidly urbanizing countries that are now growing under very different circumstances.

The United States is an outlier among countries undergoing rapid urban expansion because of its extremely low suburban densities.

China is also an outlier among countries undergoing rapid urban expansion, in part because of its extensive urban infrastructure investments, such as this bridge approach in Shanghai.

China, another rapidly urbanizing country, may also be an outlier because its urban expansion has been accompanied by rapid economic growth, strong intervention by the central government in the urban expansion process, and massive investment in public infrastructure.

In coming to terms with global urban expansion, we must keep in mind that less than one-fifth of the total growth of the global urban population in the coming decades will take place in the United States and China. Virtually no population growth at all will occur in either Europe or Japan. Most of it will take place in developing countries that may be less equipped to prepare for and guide urban expansion, be it through effective regulation or through the timely provision of basic public works.

Are there laws which determine the number, size and distribution of towns?

Walter Christaller (1966 [1933], 1)

CHAPTER 8

The Global Hierarchy of Cities

Are there more people now living in larger cities than in smaller ones? Are large cities now growing faster than smaller ones? Are we moving toward a world where most people will live in large cities? Answers to these questions can provide a broad perspective on our planet of cities. They also may be of practical use because they can help forecast the populations of individual cities and metropolitan areas correctly and better prepare them to accommodate their expected population growth. While the previous chapter focused on the global distribution of the urban population among different countries and regions, this chapter focuses on the distribution of the urban population among cities of different population sizes within countries and regions and in the world at large.

THE SIZE DISTRIBUTION OF CITIES

Across the world in 2000, 3,646 large cities had 100,000 or more people, and they were home to a total of 2.01 billion people. A dozen of them had 12.8 million or more people and could be referred to as megacities (in size order): Tokyo, New York City, Mexico City, Seoul, São Paulo, the Rhein-Ruhr conurbation, Los Angeles, Mumbai, Delhi, Shanghai, Kolkata, and Osaka. Their average size was 17.7 million, and they were home to 213 million people, or 10.6 percent of the total population in large cities in that year. At the other end of the spectrum, 1,745 cities had populations between 100,000 and 200,000 people. Their average size was 138,000, and they were home to 240 million people, or 12 percent of the total population in large cities in the year 2000.

The average city population for this universe of large cities was 550,000 people, but that average tells us very little about the distribution of city population sizes. Averages are informative metrics when most observations hover about the average—some are larger and some are smaller, but most are average. There are many examples of this pattern, such as the weight of airline passengers. Some are heavy and some are light,

Greater Tokyo, Japan, is the world's largest metropolitan area with a population in 2000 almost as large as the total world urban population in 1750.

but most hover about an average that can be used in calculating the dimensions of aircraft engines, for example. In these cases, it is not uncommon for individual observations to conform to the normal distribution, commonly known as the bell curve because of its shape.

But the distribution of city sizes does not conform to a bell curve at all. It contains a very large number of small cities, relatively few average-sized cities, and a long tail of cities with larger and larger populations. In figure 8.1, the actual distribution of city population sizes in the universe of cities is shown in dark blue, and a theoretical normal distribution with the same average population size of 550,000 people is shown in red. When comparing the two distributions for the year 2000, 131 cities had 2.5 million people or more, but no city had a population of 2.5 million or more in the theoretical normal distribution. Only 191 cities were in the average range—500,000–600,000 people—compared to 650 cities expected in the theoretical normal distribution.

The distribution of city populations in large countries and regions can be better approximated by a power law than by the normal distribution (Blank and Solomon 2000; Carroll 1982). In other words, the distribution of city populations is more like the distribution of wealth—a very large number of poor people with little or no wealth, relatively few with average wealth, and a long tail of fewer and fewer people with more and more wealth.

FIGURE 8.1
Distribution of City Population Sizes in the Universe of 3,646 Cities, 2000

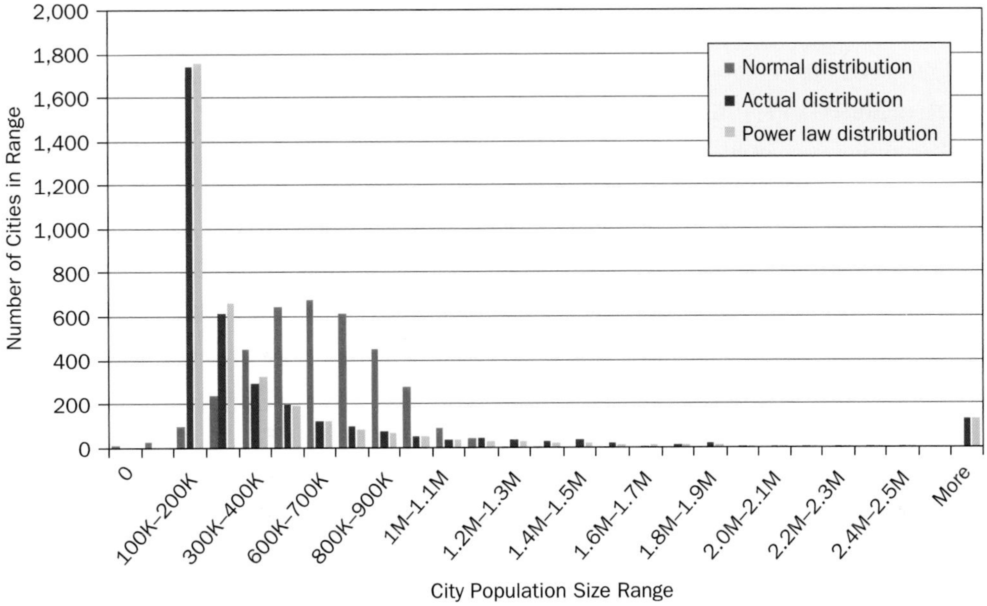

Source: City population data from Angel et al. (2012 online).

A simplified version of a power law for cities is Zipf's Law, which states that "if cities are ranked in decreasing population size, then the rank of a given city will be inversely proportional to its population" (Zipf 1949, 5).[1] I used a more general power law function that closely approximates Zipf's Law to construct the predicted distribution of city populations according to the power law (shown in light blue in figure 8.1), and it is an almost perfect fit to the actual distribution.

As a practical observation, the realization that the distribution of city population sizes obeys a power law and not a normal distribution holds great value. It tells us, first, that in the absence of constraints on urban size—such as the walking-city constraint discussed in chapter 6—cities can become very large. Second, there is no reason to expect—as Richardson (1972) rightly pointed out—that cities should converge to an optimal size or to some expected average size. There is, therefore, little meaning in

---

1 A more general version of Zipf's Law states that if cities are ranked in decreasing population size, then the rank of a given city will be inversely proportional to its population raised to some power with an exponent close to 1. In the United States, for example, the estimate of that exponent for 1900 was found to be 1.044, and it declined to 0.949 in 1990 (Dobkins and Ioannides 2000). Rosen and Resnick (1980) suggest that a power law with an exponent not too far from 1 fits the city population size distributions for other countries as well. There has been no estimate for the exponent of the power law in the entire universe of cities. I have calculated that exponent for all 3,646 cities and metropolitan areas in the world that had more than 100,000 people in the year 2000. The earlier findings were indeed confirmed. I found it to be 1.053, very close to but still significantly larger than 1 at the 95 percent confidence level.

proclaiming that some cities are too large while some are not large enough if they do not conform to some utopian, optimal, or most efficient population size. Many have tried: 32,000 as suggested by Howard (1902); 50,000–100,000 as suggested by Hirsch (1959); 100,000–200,000 as suggested by Clark (1945); 250,000–1,000,000 as suggested by Redcliffe-Maud (1969); or as much as 18 million as suggested by Zheng (2007).

In a typical urban hierarchy, at the high end we should expect to find a few cities that are very large, in the middle a large number of cities of lesser size, and at the low end a very large number of cities that are small or very small. We would do well to accept this situation rather than try to reorganize it forcefully to conform to some preconceived utopian order of optimal size cities. The recurrence of the power law in different countries, in different historical periods (Dittmar 2011), and in the world at large suggests that it is a powerful pattern that cannot be manipulated easily to meet some idealized scheme for redistributing the urban population in geographic space. It is no wonder, therefore, that the most repressive efforts on the part of governments to redistribute the urban population away from the large cities—the Soviet *propiska* system (Hojdestrand 2003), Mao's rustification efforts (Li, Rosenzweig, and Zhang 2009), and the Khmer Rouge's evacuation of Phnom Penh (Fletcher 2009), to take a few radical examples—have utterly failed. Needless to say, the more benign efforts of all other governments have utterly failed as well.

There also should be no doubt that city population size in and of itself is no indication that a place is too large. The Tokyo metropolitan area, the largest in the world, is better managed and more efficient than the great majority of smaller cities anywhere. It stands to reason, then, that the only real limits to the population size of cities are organizational constraints that can affect the benefits of increased size or the absence of a large enough source of potential native or international migrants.

Economists have long tried to construct theories that would explain why city populations should arrange themselves with such amazing regularity in accordance with a power law (e.g., Córdoba 2001; Duranton 2002; Gabaix 1999; Henderson 1974; Krugman 1996; Rosen and Resnick 1980; Simon 1955). These efforts have not yet yielded satisfactory results, so the detailed distribution of city population sizes in accordance with Zipf's Law or a more general power law must remain unexplained in formal economic terms. That said, some more general patterns that are inherent in that detailed distribution may be more amenable to a less formal yet still intellectually satisfying explanation.

DISTRIBUTION OF THE URBAN POPULATION BY SIZE CLASSES

Kingsley Davis (1972), who studied world urbanization from 1950 to 1970, observed that if cities are divided into classes so that the average population in one class is double that of the previous class, then the number of cities in this class will be half that of the previous class. He did not relate his findings to Zipf's Law or to a more general power law, but it is not difficult to prove that if the distribution of city population sizes obeys Zipf's Law, then this would indeed be the case.

The result is even more general. If cities whose populations obeyed Zipf's Law are divided into classes so that the average population in one class is three times that of the previous class, then the number of cities in this class will be one-third that of the previous class. The same would hold true for any other factor. The implication of this finding also means that if cities are divided into classes so that the average population in one class is some multiple of the previous class, then the total urban population in each class will be the same. These observations are useful because, rather than focusing on the detailed ranks of individual cities, they shift our attention to city size classes. We thus ignore minor differences in city population sizes that may arise because of a host of particular circumstances that are of little importance in understanding overall patterns and instead focus on population size ranges.

The data on the universe of large cities in the year 2000 confirm Davis's (1972) original insight. Those 3,646 cities were divided into size ranges: 100,000–200,000, 200,000–400,000, and so on, so that the upper limit of a range was twice that of its lower limit. Altogether there were 8 such ranges or classes, with the highest one containing the 12 megacities that had 12.8 million people or more. Figure 8.2 shows the average population size in each of these eight ranges, as well as the number of cities in each size range. It is clear that the average city population is nearly doubled at each higher range, while the number of cities in the higher range is nearly halved.

If Davis's (1972) original observation is true, and the evidence from the universe of 3,646 cities appears to confirm it, then we should expect the total population in cities in each range to be roughly equal to the total urban population in every other range. Figure 8.3 shows that the urban population in every range is quite close to the average value of 251 million, varying by only 11 percent on average from that value.

This is an important finding, and it immediately suggests its converse, too. If we ranked all cities by their population size and divided them into a specific number of ranges so there is an equal urban population in each range, then the average city population size and the number of cities in each range will vary in a regular fashion. There will be a factor associated with this specific number of ranges, so that the average city population in one range will be equal to the average city population of the previous range multiplied by that factor, while the number of cities in this range will be equal to the number of cities in the previous range divided by that factor.

This proposition is also confirmed by our evidence. If we divide the total population of 2.01 billion in large cities in 2000 into four population size ranges, for example, that factor turns out to be 3.9. That is, the average population in a given range is

FIGURE 8.2

Regularities in the Average City Population (top) and Average Number of Cities (bottom) in Different City Population Size Ranges in the Universe of 3,646 Cities, 2000

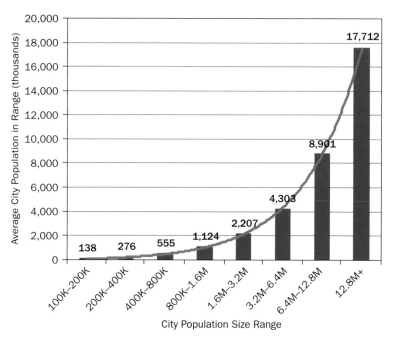

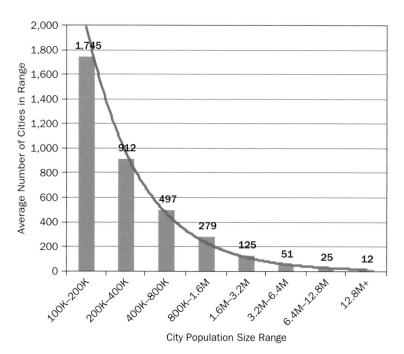

Source: City population data from Angel et al. (2012 online).

approximately four times that of the previous range, while the number of cities in that range is approximately one-quarter the number of cities in the previous range.

With these findings we can answer the first question posed at the beginning of this chapter: Are there more people now living in larger cities than in smaller ones? The answer is a resounding no. An approximately equal number of people live in cities of all size ranges, and together they form a global hierarchy of cities. In this hierarchy, people and firms are distributed approximately evenly in all city population size ranges. There are very few large cities in the world today, and their total population is not very different from the total population in all intermediate-sized cities, or from the total population in all small cities. This suggests that, as far as attracting people and businesses to cities, there may be no inherent advantages to city population size, and hence, as already noted, cities would have no optimal size.

These findings also suggest that cities of all size classes can now be expected to grow at the same average rate, and that in general we should not expect larger cities to grow any faster than smaller ones, and vice versa. This implies, among other things, that once megacities have taken their place in the global hierarchy of cities, they should not command our undivided attention. Insofar as we are concerned with urban growth and expansion, our attention should instead be divided among cities in all size classes.

FIGURE 8.3

The Relatively Equal Total Urban Population in Different City Size Ranges in the Universe of 3,646 Cities, 2000

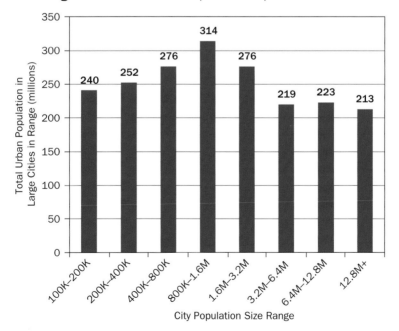

Source: City population data from Angel et al. (2012 online).

THE GLOBAL DISTRIBUTION OF CITIES
IN GEOGRAPHIC SPACE

Christaller's (1966 [1933]) own response to the question he posed, quoted at the beginning of this chapter, was his central place theory. It predicts that cities of different size classes would be dispersed relatively uniformly across the countryside. A large number of small towns would produce and provide essential goods and services to their surrounding countryside. They would be dispersed uniformly and rather densely across cultivated lands to be readily accessible to their rural hinterlands, thus forming an array of central places as the lowest tier of the urban hierarchy.

> [T]here wasn't much to Bridger's Wells: Arthur Davies' general store, the land and mining claims office, Canby's saloon, the long, sagging Bridger Inn, with its double-decker porch, and the Union Church, square and bare as a New England meeting house, and set out on the west edge of town, as if it wanted to get as far from the other church as it could without being left alone. (Van Tilburg Clark 1940, 6–7)

Larger cities in the central place hierarchy would be fewer in number. They would produce and provide a higher order of goods and services to the population of rural areas and to the population of smaller cities and towns. They, too, would be relatively uniformly yet less densely distributed as central places to be as readily accessible to their hinterlands as possible. Tiers of larger and larger cities would form a spatial hierarchy of central places in which smaller towns would be more immediately accessible to the countryside and to still smaller villages and hamlets than larger cities. But they would not be able to offer what the larger cities could offer because of the advantages inherent in the varieties of goods and services they would provide and in their economies of scale. Krugman (1996, 409), for example, describes the location of industries.

> [N]ew cities will form first for industries with high transport costs or low fixed costs . . . lower transport cost or higher fixed cost industries will concentrate in fewer cities . . . the result will be the formation of a hierarchy of central places with a number of levels.

Central place theory and the empirical evidence supporting it could thus tell us something important about the underlying rationale for the existence of cities of different sizes and about the distribution of cities of different sizes in geographic space. The theory has a normative content as well. If cities of every population size class are uniformly located throughout inhabited regions, then both the access of households to a hierarchy of goods and services and the access of the firms producing these goods and services to their markets would be maximized. Conversely, overall transport costs would be minimized by the interdependent location decisions of households and firms.

To further explain central place theory before seeking to confirm its empirical validity given our data on the universe of cities, figure 8.4 introduces a simple and rather formalized example of Christaller's hierarchy.

- There are three tiers of cities in a settled rural area on a featureless plane.
- The rural population has equal spending power and is uniformly distributed.
- The cities in every tier are located uniformly on a triangular grid.
- Travel can take place in all directions with equal ease.
- The rural population travels to the nearest city for goods and services.
- The rural population travels to larger cities for higher-order goods and services.

Given this set of assumptions, it is possible to determine the market area of every city in every level of the hierarchy. It is the area in which the homes of all the rural people who will travel to that particular city, and only to that particular city, are located. Since the rural population always travels to the nearest city in a given tier to obtain goods and services, the market areas of cities located on a triangular grid will take the shape of hexagons. All points within a given hexagon will be closer to the city at its center than to any other city in the same tier of the urban hierarchy. Larger cities are located

FIGURE 8.4
A Theoretical Three-Tier Hierarchy of Central Places and Their Associated Market Areas

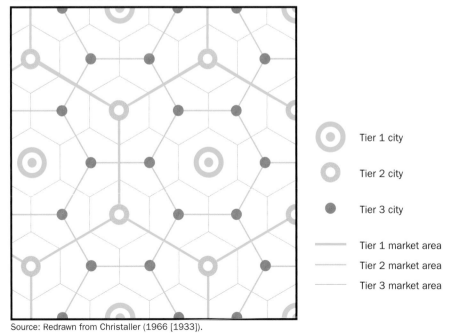

Source: Redrawn from Christaller (1966 [1933]).

further apart and are sustained by larger market areas than smaller cities. Central place theory thus provides a ready explanation for the emergence of tiers of cities of different population sizes.

We can now ask whether the spatial distribution of the universe of 3,646 large cities formed a central place hierarchy: Were the cities dispersed uniformly across inhabited regions, rather than clustered in a few places, or simply distributed at random here and there? Following Christaller, we can safely assume that most cities will be located in populated rural areas or, more generally, in inhabited regions. We can also safely assume that to serve the same number of people, cities will be more spaced out in sparsely inhabited regions and closer together in densely inhabited regions.

Inhabited regions were identified by their population density in a global map of the *Gridded Population of the World* (SEDAC 2011) that shows the distribution of the world population in 5x5 kilometer (km) pixels in 2000.[2] We divided these inhabited regions into four population density zones (figure 8.5). We also divided the universe of 3,646 cities into a four-tier hierarchy, with the largest cities in the first tier and the smallest in the fourth one, so that one-quarter of the total population of 2.01 billion in this universe of cities was in every tier. We then examined whether cities in every one of these four tiers were uniformly dispersed or not. More specifically, we tested whether cities in a given tier in a given density zone were dispersed in a more uniform pattern than a random distribution of cities in that zone would be.

The central place hierarchy in the northern region of the Indian Subcontinent is shown in figure 8.6. Cities in all four tiers appear to be relatively uniformly distributed throughout this highly populated region. The exceptions in being closer together than expected are Kolkata, India, and Dhaka, Bangladesh, located across a once-contentious border and home to large numbers of refugees after the partition of India in 1947.

Preliminary statistical results provide some, but not unequivocal, confirmation of central place theory for the universe of 3,646 cities at the global level. The distances among cities in a given tier were found to be roughly double the distances among cities in a lower tier, and the distances among cities in the same tiers in higher-density zones were clearly shorter than those in lower-density zones. These observations confirm that, despite a progressive decline in transport costs, distances still matter, and cities in many areas of the world are more uniformly distributed than would be expected if transport costs mattered less.

---

2 The map was simplified to form four density zones. The density zone ranges were determined informally so that: (1) range limits were approximately multiples of each other, i.e., $35/5 \approx 200/35$; and (2) there was a similar number of cities in each density zone. Areas of less than 20,000 km^2 in a higher-density zone were incorporated into the next lower-density zone.

FIGURE 8.5
Population Density Zones, 2005, and the Spatial Distribution of the Universe of 3,646 Cities with Populations of 100,000 or More, 2000

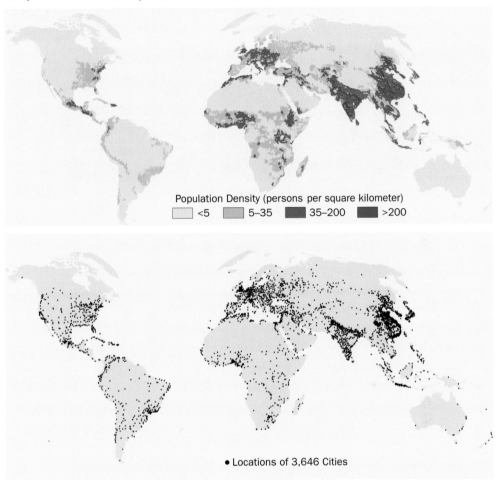

Population Density (persons per square kilometer)
<5   5–35   35–200   >200

● Locations of 3,646 Cities

Sources: Density ranges calculated from SEDAC (2011); and city location data from Angel et al. (2012 online).

The initial results we obtained for the statistical uniformity in the spatial dispersion of cities were mixed.

- In the high-density zone, for example, cities in three of four tiers were more uniformly dispersed than a random distribution would be, in conformity with central place theory.
- In the medium-density zone, cities in the two middle tiers were dispersed more uniformly than expected. Cities in the lowest tier were randomly distributed, while cities in the highest tier were clustered.
- In the two lower-density zones, most cities were clustered or randomly distributed, possibly because these zones were only sparsely inhabited and in many places contained no cities with 100,000 people or more.

FIGURE 8.6

The Relatively Uniform Dispersion of Central Places in the Northern Part of the Indian Subcontinent, 2000

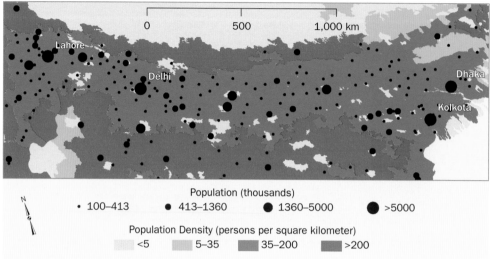

Sources: Density ranges calculated from SEDAC (2011); and city location data from Angel et al. (2012 online).

The empirical evidence begins to suggest that many cities around the world are dispersed in a more uniform pattern than would be expected if they were randomly distributed, in conformance with the predictions of central place theory. In our planet of cities there is a ready rationale for the existence of cities in different size classes because tiers of larger and larger cities form a spatial hierarchy of central places. These central places are located to maximize their access to local as well as global markets. Their population sizes reflect trade-offs between production and marketing economies on the one hand and congestion costs and high land prices on the other, as well as trade-offs between production economies and access to their local markets. Very few central places are large, widely dispersed, and reliant on access to global markets. Many of them are small, densely dispersed, and reliant on access to local markets.

POPULATION GROWTH RATES IN CITIES OF DIFFERENT SIZES

If different tiers in an urban hierarchy have the same share of the urban population, it stands to reason that the population of cities in every tier would grow, on average, at the same rate. It has been observed, in fact, that cities in different population size classes in relatively large regions grow at the same average rate (Eaton and Eckstein 1997; Eeckhout 2004; Ioannides and Overman 2003). Given the information now available for cities on a global scale, we can ask: Is this similarity in growth rates true for cities in the world as a whole and, if so, is it true for recent decades as well as for previous periods? We can now answer both questions affirmatively.

Davis (1972) investigated the question of whether or not size affects a city's growth for the world at large for two periods, 1950–1960 and 1960–1970. He concluded that in most population size ranges it does not and that the largest cities (too few to draw statistical conclusions) grew at a slower rate. Global data on city population growth rates have been assembled from two data sources: (1) population growth rates for 1997–2006 for some 7,000 cities with populations of 50,000 or more in some 100 countries (Brinkhoff 2012); and (2) population growth rates for four decades, 1960–2000, for some 2,720 cities that had 100,000 people or more in the year 2000 in some 140 countries.[3]

The first data set contained population data from circa February 1997 to circa October 2006 for 6,457 cities in 48 countries that had more than 20 cities with 50,000 people or more at the beginning of 1997.[4] Together these cities had a total population of 1.42 billion people. To obtain the net population growth rates of individual cities, I subtracted the average population growth rate of cities with 50,000 or more people in the country as a whole from the growth rate of individual cities. I then arranged the cities in ascending order of their populations circa 1997 and divided them into four size classes, each containing the same number of people: (1) 4,470 small cities with an average population of 83,000; (2) 1,409 medium-sized cities with an average population of 243,000 people; (3) 482 larger cities with an average population of 793,000 people; and (4) 98 very large cities with an average population of 3.6 million people. Figure 8.7 displays the net population growth rates as a function of city population size for all cities, as well as the averages for the four city population size classes.

In the world at large, we can say with 99.9 percent confidence that in recent years cities in all four population size classes grew at the same average rate, and that this rate was not significantly different from zero.[5] We can conclude, therefore, that while actual city population growth rates vary considerably from place to place, in the absence of additional information, cities of all sizes in a given country can be expected to grow at the same average rate. In particular, large cities are not growing at a faster rate than smaller ones.

---

3 Unpublished data provided to the author by Professor Vernon Henderson, Brown University.
4 The data were obtained from www.citypopulation.de for the latest two census periods that are one decade apart. The only large countries for which census data for two time periods were not available were Angola, Libya, Myanmar, Nigeria, North Korea, and Thailand. The data are for the administrative boundaries of named cities, not for urban agglomerations or metropolitan areas, and therefore the largest cities are typically smaller than their associated urban agglomerations.
5 The variances of these averages were also quite similar, varying between 0.03 and 0.04 percent. At a lower level of confidence, say that of 95 percent, it appears that small cities grew at a positive rate of 0.8 percent per annum, while larger cities in the remaining three size classes had negative growth rates of –0.14 percent, –0.23 percent, and –0.36 percent per annum respectively, and that all rates were significantly different from zero.

FIGURE 8.7

Net Annual Population Growth Rates in 7,059 Cities with 1997 Populations of 50,000 or More, 1997–2006

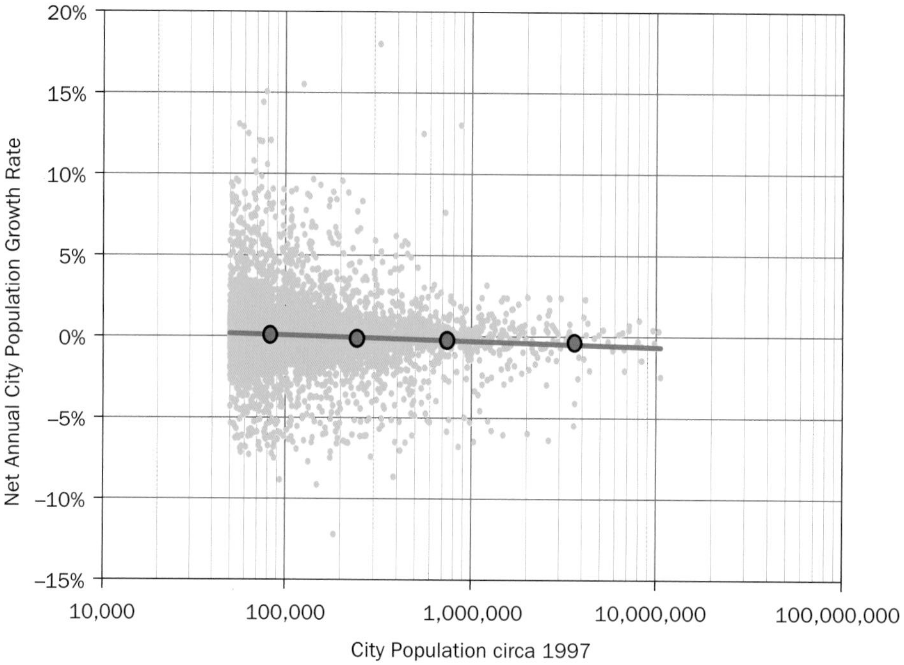

City Population circa 1997

Source: Calculated from Brinkhoff (2012).

Given a set of points on a graph, we can draw a regression line associated with these points (the red line in figure 8.7) that is calculated to have the smallest overall vertical distance to all points in the graph. If that line is horizontal, it can be said to have a slope of 0; if vertical, a slope of 1; if sloping upward, a slope between 0 and 1; and if sloping downward, a slope between 0 and –1. The slope of the regression line for all cities in figure 8.7 is sloping downward and is therefore slightly negative. We can ascertain that it is significantly different from zero at the 95 percent confidence level, suggesting that the annual population growth rate of cities declined by 0.1 percent when their populations doubled—that is, larger cities grew at slightly slower rates than smaller ones, but certainly not any faster.

We next examined the graphs for the 48 individual countries with more than 20 cities of 50,000 people or more circa 1997. This sample included enough cities for the slopes of their regression lines to be of statistical significance. Constructing a regression line for each of the 48 countries and comparing them to see whether the slopes varied systematically revealed the following results.

- In 34 of these countries (71 percent of the total), the slopes were flat, i.e., not different from zero at the 95 percent confidence level.

- In 7 countries (15 percent of the total)—Bulgaria, Belarus, the Czech Republic, India, Ukraine, Japan, and Germany—the slopes were positive and significantly different from zero at the 95 percent confidence level.
- In 7 countries (another 15 percent of the total)—Brazil, Venezuela, Mexico, Spain, China, Algeria, and Malaysia—the slopes were negative and significantly different from zero at the 95 percent confidence level.
- In Bulgaria, for example—the country with the steepest positive slope—a doubling of the city population was associated with an increase of 0.4 percent in the annual city population growth rate, while in the 7 countries with a positive slope taken as a whole, it was associated with an average increase of only 0.2 percent.
- In Malaysia—the country with the steepest negative slope—a doubling of the city population was associated with a decline of 1.3 percent in the annual city population growth rate, while in the 7 countries with a negative slope taken as a whole, it was associated with an average decline of only 0.5 percent.
- In rapidly urbanizing India, large cities were growing at a significantly faster rate than smaller ones, while in rapidly urbanizing China, they were growing at a significantly slower rate. We have no ready explanation for this result.
- Five of the 7 countries where large cities were growing at a significantly faster rate than smaller ones were in Eastern Europe, if we include Germany among them (now that it includes the former East Germany).
- Cities of all sizes in North America and Western Europe, except in Spain and Germany, grew at the same average rate.
- Among the 27 countries in Asia, Africa, and Latin America and the Caribbean, growth rates in large and small cities were the same in 20 countries, lower in large cities than in small ones in 6 countries, and higher in large cities than in small ones in only one country—India.

The data for the world as a whole generally confirm that recently small, medium, and large cities were growing at the same rate in most countries. Neither the size of the urban population of a country, nor its urban population growth rate, nor its level of economic development appears to matter in explaining the variation of the average rates of population growth in cities of different sizes in the world at large.[6]

---

6 The empirical evidence on equal growth rates for cities of different sizes presented here may help explain why cities arrange themselves in accordance with a power law. One of the more intriguing theories describing a statistical process that can generate a city population distribution that obeyed a power law was given by Gabaix (1999), building on an early insight by Gibrat (1931). He showed that cities with populations above a certain minimum size growing at different rates, yet at the same overall average rate, will arrange themselves over time in accordance with a power law.

Next I examined the Henderson data set for annual population growth rates in four decades (1960–1970, 1970–1980, 1980–1990, and 1990–2000) in countries that had more than 20 cities with populations of 100,000 or more by the end of the decade. Instead of subtracting the overall urban population growth rate in individual countries to obtain a net growth rate for cities of different sizes in that country, I simply subtracted the average growth rate of all cities in all countries during a given decade (figure 8.8).

The slopes of the regression lines were not different from 0 (at the 99 percent confidence level) in all decades except in 1970–1980, when the slope was negative and significantly different from 0. The net growth rates of the four city population size classes were not different from 0 (at the 99 percent confidence level) in all decades

FIGURE 8.8

Net Annual Population Growth Rates in Cities with Populations of 100,000 or More at the End of Each Decade, 1960–2000

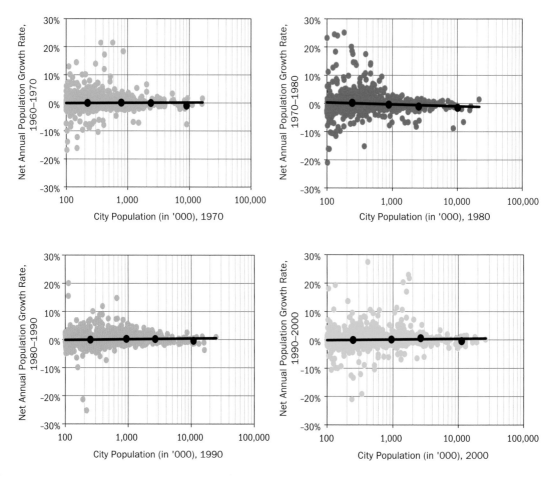

Source: Calculated from unpublished data courtesy of Professor Vernon Henderson, Brown University.

except in 1970–1980, when rates were significantly negative for the second, third, and fourth population size classes.

On the whole, then, a city's population size does not seem to matter in explaining its rate of growth. In the world at large, cities of all sizes are now growing at the same average rate, and we can safely conclude that in most countries, larger cities are not growing at a faster rate than smaller ones. If we were to see large cities on the order of 100 million people in the future, they would not likely be the result of rapid population growth, but rather the result of the coming together of cities that were formerly separated. The Tokaido corridor in Japan, for example, which includes Tokyo, Nagoya, Osaka, and Fukuoka, already runs for almost 1,200 km, with a total population of 82.9 million. The Northeast Corridor in the United States, which includes Boston, New York, Philadelphia, Baltimore, and Washington, DC, runs for almost 700 km with a population of some 49.7 million.

The findings summarized in this section imply that there are no inherent economic advantages to city population size as such that would attract more people, more firms, and more resources to larger cities at the expense of smaller ones. Any size advantages appear to be canceled by higher costs of living, production, or transport. Therefore, on average, cities of all sizes are likely to grow at the same rate and to form a hierarchy of cities—possibly a spatial hierarchy of central places as well—where urban population growth is rather evenly distributed among cities of all population size classes.

PRIMATE CITIES

The largest city in a country is its primate city. Primacy in a country's urban hierarchy has been defined as the share of the total urban population in the primate city, or the ratio of the population of the primate city to the next largest city (e.g., Moomaw and Alwosabi 2004; Vapñarsky 1975). In this discussion we use the first definition. Singapore has only one city and therefore its level of primacy is 100 percent. India had an urban population of 188 million in 2000 and its primate city, Mumbai, contained only 16 million people. India's primacy is thus quite low, on the order of 6 percent. It has often been observed that the primate city is an outlier in the sense that if a power law curve were fitted to the rank and population data for all cities in the country, the point for the primate city would not lie on the curve, but rather above or below it.

In most countries, and especially in smaller countries with a small number of cities, the population of the primate city is typically larger than expected by Zipf's Law. In contrast, it is smaller than expected by Zipf's Law in large countries with very large urban populations, such as China, India, Russia, or the United States. Because primate cities are typically exceptions to Zipf's Law, they require special attention when we seek to understand the overall dimensions of urban growth and expansion.

The urban hierarchy in Thailand in 2000, for example, appears on first impression to exhibit a relatively high degree of primacy. The population of Bangkok, its capital, comprised 34 percent of the nation's urban population in that year. It was 29 times larger than Udon Thani, the largest city outside the Bangkok metropolitan region. One might conclude that in Thailand the primate city is larger than expected, and the secondary cities like Udon Thani are smaller than expected. But Thailand's primacy as the share of the urban population in the primate city is, in fact, quite close to the global average. In 2007, for example, United Nations data show that the average primacy in 118 countries that had cities larger than 750,000 in that year was 30 ± 3 percent, and that percentage did not change significantly between 1950 and 2010 (United Nations Population Division 2008, file 2).

Figure 8.9 shows clearly that countries with larger urban populations (and hence a large number of cities) have smaller shares of the urban population in their largest city. The regression line summarizing the data has a significantly negative slope. That is to be expected even if city populations, including the primate city, obeyed Zipf's Law, which posits that the larger the number of cities in the country, the smaller the share of their total population in the primate city.

FIGURE 8.9
Primacy as a Function of the Total Urban Population in 158 Countries, 2000

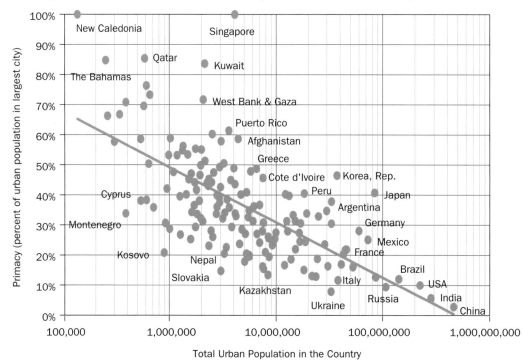

Source: Urban population data from United Nations Population Division (2010, file 3).

FIGURE 8.10

Observed versus Expected Primacy According to Zipf's Law in 158 Countries, 2000

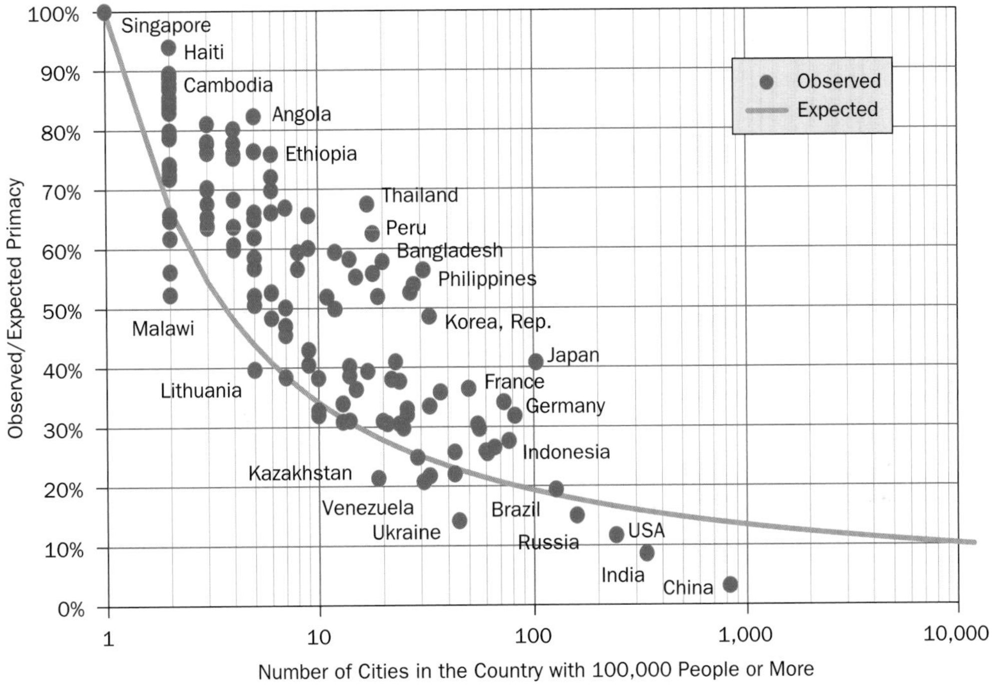

Source: Urban population data from United Nations Population Division (2010, file 3).

The expected primacy as a function of the number of cities in the country (not the total urban population) is shown in figure 8.10 as a continuous line. Also shown are the observed levels of primacy as a function of the number of cities in the country with 100,000 people or more in 2000. Primacy is thus defined here in another way, as the population of the largest city divided by the population of all cities with 100,000 people or more.[7] This graph makes clear that most primate cities have larger populations than expected by the power law. Most observations in figure 8.10, except those for countries with very large numbers of cities, are clearly above the line showing their expected value. In the large countries, primacy is below the expected value. As noted earlier, the largest cities in these countries are not as large as expected by Zipf's Law.

A number of economists have tried to explain high values for primacy or the existence of "urban giants" as termed by Ades and Glaeser (2001). Rosen and Resnick (1980) and Wheaton and Shishido (1981) showed that more populated countries have lower levels of primacy. Krugman and Livas (1996) showed that the larger the share of

---

7 Primacy levels for countries are not the same in figures 8.9 and 8.10. First, the urban population in cities with 100,000 people or more is smaller than the total urban population. Second, there is no fixed ratio between the total population of large cities and the total urban population in a country.

Bangkok, Thailand's primate city, had 29 times the population of Udon Thani, the second largest city in the country, in 2000.

external trade in the GNP, the higher the level of primacy. Ades and Glaeser (2001) further showed that the less democratic a country is and the less dense its road network, the higher the level of primacy.

I tried to repeat their calculations with more recent data for a larger number of countries and could not reproduce their results. In my models, external trade and agriculture as shares of the GDP were indeed associated with greater primacy, and road density (total road length per country land area) was associated with lower primacy, but all of them were significant at only the 90 percent confidence level. In other words, the effect of these factors was rather weak and statistically insignificant. The only relationship that I could establish beyond dispute is the one shown in figure 8.9 confirming the early findings of Wheaton and Shishido (1981)—that is, the larger the urban population of the country, the smaller the share of this population residing in its primate city. Other things being equal, even capital cities, where power and influence were concentrated, were not necessarily larger than expected by Zipf's Law.

The most satisfactory explanation for high levels of primacy in most countries is simply the abundance of small nation states that have too small an urban population to have both a mature hierarchy of cities and a large enough single city. To be a part of the world at large, citizens and firms, government agencies, and civic groups must necessarily aggregate their efforts into building at least one large city that is their country's gateway to the world, that projects their country into the world, and that makes it possible for their country to compete globally.

In other words, a higher than expected level of primacy is not an anomaly. It is intimately associated with the modest urban populations of most nation states and with the impenetrable borders between states that prevent the free movement of people among them. In large countries and in the world at large, primacy is very low. Large cities are not large enough, and there are too few of them. Primate cities in the rest of the countries in the world are large and must be large, in other words, because the urban populations in these countries are small. Yet, even though most primate cities in the world are larger than expected, they did not grow any faster or slower, on average, than nonprimate cities during the past decade.

CONCLUSIONS

When we shift our focus from a few megacities to all cities above a certain size and examine our planet as a whole, we can see that (1) the distribution of their population sizes conforms to Zipf's Law or to a more general power law rather than to the normal distribution; (2) different city size classes each contain a roughly equal share of the urban population; (3) megacities do not contain a larger share of the world's urban population than smaller or intermediate-size cities; (4) cities are arranged in a spatial hierarchy, dispersed in a nonrandom and a more uniform pattern in the inhabited regions of the world; (5) on average, cities everywhere grow at the same rate (net of the overall urban population growth rate in the country or region) regardless of their population size; (6) the planet's megacities are not growing any faster than other cities; and (7) the primate cities in small and medium-sized countries have larger populations than those expected by Zipf's Law, while also growing at the same rate, on average, as other cities.

With the global and historical perspective on the urbanization project as a preparatory background, the next part of the book turns attention to the detailed study of global urban expansion—the study of the key attributes of the spatial organization of cities, their changes over time, what these changes mean, and what we can and cannot do about them.

Part Two:
The Study of Global
Urban Expansion

When you can measure what you are speaking about, and express it in numbers, you know something about it; when you cannot express it in numbers, your knowledge is of a meager and unsatisfactory kind.

William Thomson, Lord Kelvin (1883)

Although the [monocentric city] model is oversimplified, it remains a useful analytical tool, requiring only modest modifications to be remarkably accurate.

Daniel P. McMillen (2006, 129)

CHAPTER 9

The Evidence:
New Maps, New Metrics,
Old Theory

Coming to terms with urban expansion and its reality in cities everywhere—and especially in cities where urbanization is still in full swing—will make it easier to manage and guide in a pragmatic and responsible manner. Denying urban expansion, rejecting it for ideological reasons, or simply neglecting it will not allow us to shape the future. Accepting it, on the other hand, will require the creation of new knowledge that will make urban expansion more familiar and better understood, and hence less threatening. This knowledge will be particularly important in those parts of the world where we know the least about urban expansion, but it would be better if this knowledge were of a more general nature, pertaining to all countries. Then we could explore the broadest spectrum of this phenomenon in all its varieties and manifestations, rather than being limited to one or another part of it.

I thus embarked on an inclusive study of global urban expansion that could bring together information on cities and metropolitan areas of all sizes, income ranges, and world regions at different points in time. Originally, I posed only one question to myself and to my colleagues: What are the extents of urban areas, how fast are they expanding over time, and why?

The search for an answer to this question called for three interdependent activities: (1) identifying and exploiting sources of reliable data to create accurate maps of urban expansion; (2) articulating metrics that could effectively summarize these maps into single numbers in order to make comparison among them possible; and (3) assembling a body of theory that could shed light on these comparisons and explain them.

As I became more familiar with maps of urban expansion and began to understand and then to measure and analyze them by highlighting their common attributes and by sorting out the variations among them, other questions concerning urban expansion presented themselves. In this second part of the book I devote one chapter to each of these questions.

1. What are the extents of urban areas, how fast are they expanding over time, why, and why should it matter?
2. How dense are urban areas, how are urban densities changing over time, why, and why should it matter?
3. How centralized are the residences and workplaces in cities, do they tend to disperse to the periphery over time, and if so, why, and why should it matter?
4. How fragmented are the built-up areas of cities, how are levels of fragmentation changing over time, why, and why should it matter?
5. How compact are the shapes of urban footprints, how are their levels of compactness changing over time, why, and why should it matter?
6. How much land will urban areas require in the future, why, and why should it matter?
7. How much cultivated land will be consumed by expanding urban areas, why, and why should it matter?

Rigorous as well as partial and exploratory answers to these seven questions, taken together, begin to offer a coherent and comprehensive view of global urban expansion today—a view that should contribute to understanding it, coming to terms with it, and preparing for it. These answers will highlight questions that were left unanswered and raise new questions for interested scholars to explore and take our understanding of urban expansion further in the coming years.

NEW GLOBAL MAPS FOR STUDYING URBAN EXPANSION

Four complementary sets of maps and their associated data, three of them newly created during this study, were used to examine urban expansion and calculate various metrics characterizing it on a global and historical scale.

The Global Sample of 120 Cities, 1990–2000

This data set of digital maps is based on satellite images of 120 cities and metropolitan areas in two time periods, circa 1990 and 2000. In an earlier study (Angel et al. 2005), we identified a total of 3,945 large cities with populations of 100,000 or more that were home to a total of 2.12 billion people or three-quarters of the world's urban population in the year 2000. The global sample of 120 cities is a stratified 3 percent sample from this universe including cities from nine geographic regions, four population size classes, and four per capita income classes (figure 9.1). The nine-region classification approximates that of UN-Habitat, except that developed countries were regrouped into two

FIGURE 9.1
Nine Regions with the Global Sample of 120 Cities and the Representative Sample of 30 Cities, 2000

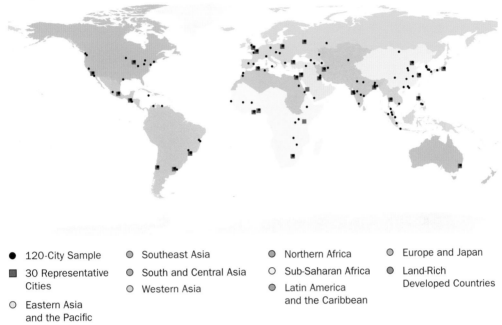

- ● 120-City Sample
- ■ 30 Representative Cities
- ○ Eastern Asia and the Pacific
- ○ Southeast Asia
- ○ South and Central Asia
- ○ Western Asia
- ○ Northern Africa
- ○ Sub-Saharan Africa
- ○ Latin America and the Caribbean
- ○ Europe and Japan
- ○ Land-Rich Developed Countries

Source: Drawn from data on sample cities in Angel et al. (2005, table II-4, 24–26).

regions: land-rich developed countries (United States, Canada, and Australia) that had more than 0.6 hectares of arable land per capita in 2000 (13 cities in the sample); and Europe and Japan (19 cities in the sample).

For each sample city we obtained two medium-resolution Landsat satellite images, one for each time period. These images were classified into built-up and nonbuilt-up 30x30–meter pixels, using a thematic extraction algorithm (Angel et al. 2005). The resulting classifications for Ho Chi Minh City, Vietnam, in 1989 and 1999 are shown in figure 9.2 as an example. Using 10,000 Google Earth validation sites, Potere et al. (2009) reported that pixels identified as built-up in our sample were found to be built-up in Google Earth 91 percent of the time, and those identified in Google Earth as built-up were identified in our sample as built-up 89 percent of the time, confirming a high level of accuracy in our classifications.

We obtained population figures for the 1990 and 2000 census periods, as well as maps for the administrative districts of each city encompassing its built-up area. We interpolated the population in these districts for the dates corresponding to the satellite images, assuming a constant rate of population growth between census periods. Using ArcGIS software, we then calculated the values for a set of metrics characterizing urban expansion within the relevant administrative districts for all 120 cities in this sample.

FIGURE 9.2
The Built-up Area of Ho Chi Minh City, Vietnam, 1989 and 1999

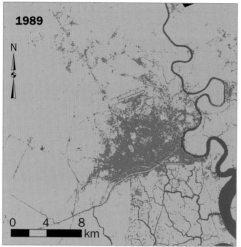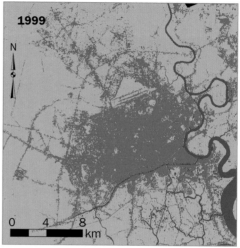

Source: Redrawn from Angel et al. (2012, 92).

The Set of 20 U.S. Cities, 1910–2000

Historical population density data at the census tract level for U.S. cities and metropolitan areas are now readily available in digital maps that can be analyzed using ArcGIS software (National Historical Geographic Information System 2012). Seven of the 20 cities chosen for this analysis have census tract digital maps and population data

FIGURE 9.3
Historical Census Data Showing the Expansion of the New York Metropolitan Area, 1910–2000

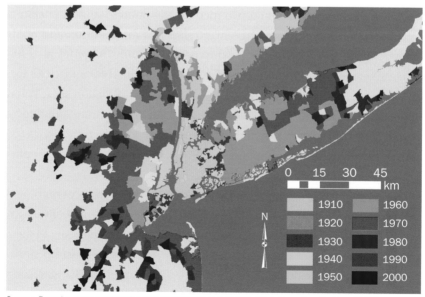

Source: Based on census data from National Historical Geographic Information System (2012).

extending back to 1910; only 3 cities have maps for 1920 because of data loss; 11 additional cities have tract density maps from 1930 onward, and the remaining 2 cities have maps from 1940 onward. Figure 9.3 shows the expansion of the New York metropolitan area. Census tracts were added to the urbanized area of metropolitan New York once their density reached 1,000 persons per mile (3.86 persons per hectare), which is the U.S. census definition for an urbanized area.

The Global Representative Sample of 30 Cities, 1800–2000

A global historical subsample of 30 cities was created to explore long-term changes in urban extent and in urban population density from 1800 to 2000. The selection of cities for historical analysis was guided by three factors: their inclusion in the global sample of 120 cities; their regional distribution; and the availability of historic maps depicting their built-up area at 20- or 25-year intervals.

The selected historic maps depict the totality of the built-up area of the metropolitan agglomeration at a given date and contain sufficient reference points that could be identified on Google Earth so they could be stretched to fit a geographically accurate representation of space such as Google Earth. This process, known as *georeferencing*, ensured that maps of different sizes and scales could be compared accurately to one another.

Arriving at an estimate of population density required historical population data in addition to built-up area data, and two publications proved invaluable to our investigation (Chandler 1987; United Nations Population Division 2008). At earlier dates the correspondence between population figures and the built-up area was clear, but for later dates it became more difficult to discern whether the reported population matched the extent of the built-up area. For 1990 and 2000 we again had accurate data from the global sample of 120 cities.

We created digitized maps of the built-up area for each city for each date, and the area of each built-up area map was calculated using ArcGIS software. The population associated with each map was interpolated from available historical population data, assuming a constant population growth rate in the intervening period. My colleague Alejandro Blei meticulously identified, digitized, and analyzed a total of 261 such maps, an average of 8.7 maps per city approximately 19 ± 1 years apart (figures 9.4 and 9.5). Using these digitized maps, we were able to calculate the urban extent and the average population density in each city and their changes over time. It was also possible to calculate the rate of density change over the decades on a global historical scale.

The Universe of 3,646 Large Cities, 2000

We created a new global digital map of the urban land cover of 3,646 large cities that accommodated 100,000 or more people in the year 2000. The map was prepared on a Google Earth platform based on Mod500 satellite imagery with a 463x463–meter

FIGURE 9.4
The Built-up Area of Paris, France, 1832

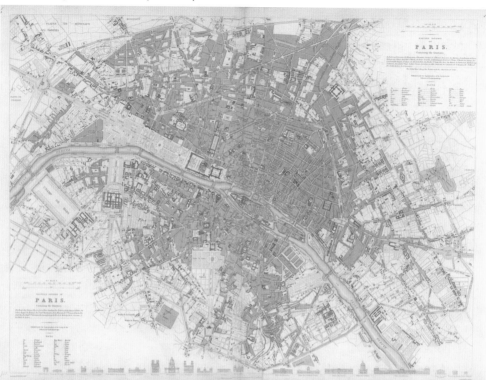

Source: Society for the Diffusion of Useful Knowledge (1844, 198).

pixel size (Schneider, Friedl, and Potere 2009). Potere and his colleagues tested the accuracy of eight global urban land cover maps and concluded: "Among the eight maps examined for accuracy, the Mod500 map was found to be the most accurate by all three accuracy measures employed" (Potere et al. 2009, 6553). Figure 9.6 compares two classifications of satellite images of Paris, France, one obtained from Landsat with a 30x30–meter pixel resolution and one from Mod500 with a 463x463–meter pixel resolution. It shows that while the higher-resolution map has fuzzier edges, the overall shapes of their areas are not substantially different from one another.

The global Mod500 urban land cover map allowed us to estimate and explain the extent of urban land cover, as well as average built-up area densities, in all large cities, in all countries, and in all world regions at one point in time, in the year 2000. Given the United Nations urban population projections and realistic assumptions about long-term density change, it also made possible the projection of urban land cover for all countries for every decade between 2010 and 2050. In addition, since the Mod500 global land cover map includes information on the location of cultivated lands in 2000, this map also allowed us to estimate their projected losses due to urban expansion in every decade from 2010 to 2050.

FIGURE 9.5
The Expansion of Paris, France, 1800–2000

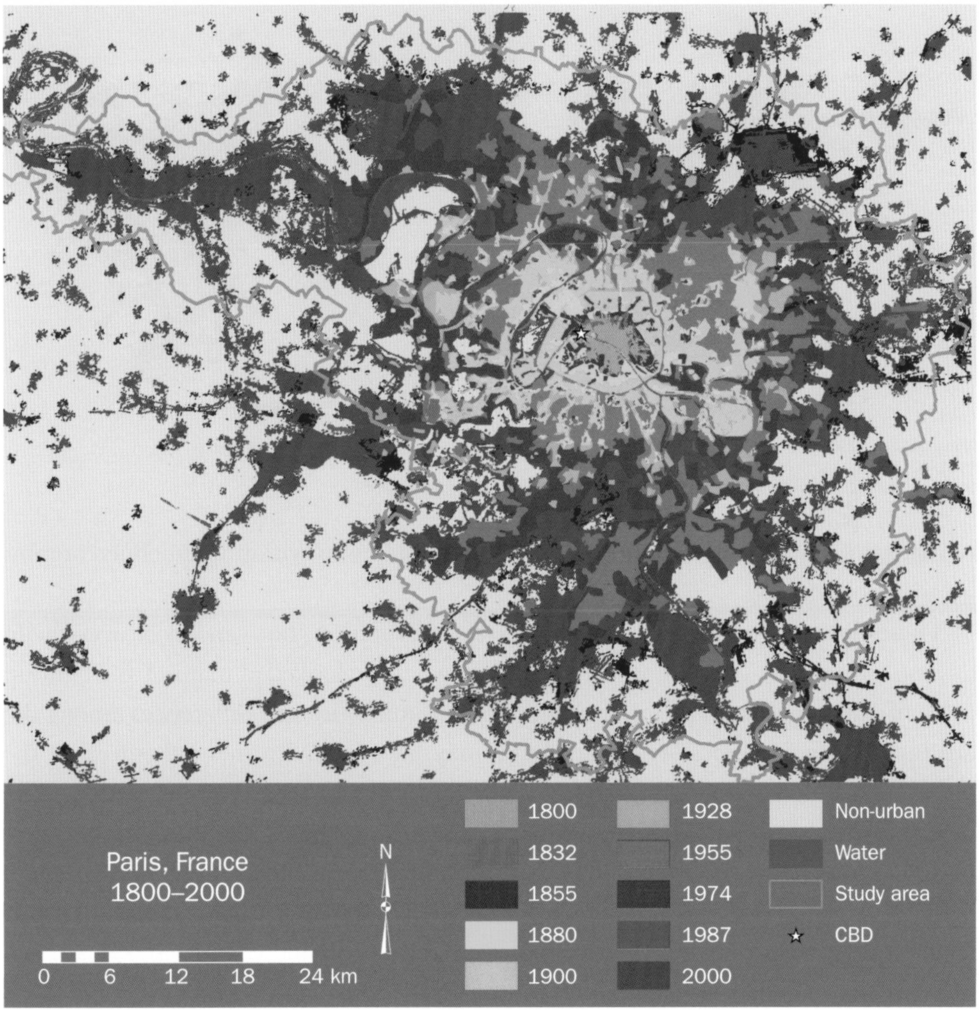

		Non-urban
1800	1928	
1832	1955	Water
1855	1974	Study area
1880	1987	☆ CBD
1900	2000	

Paris, France
1800–2000

N

0   6   12   18   24 km

Source: Angel et al. (2012, 302).

We refined the original Mod500 map to include 311 new urban clusters for large cities that had no corresponding clusters in the original Schneider, Friedl, and Potere (2009) map, but we did not change the extent of any of their Mod500 clusters because that would have compromised the overall accuracy of the map (Angel et al. 2011b). We then created a map of urban clusters with a 463x463–meter pixel size that were associated with a total of 3,646 named large cities and metropolitan areas in all countries (see figure 1.1). These cities accommodated a total population of 2.01 billion people in 2000 (Angel et al. 2012 online). However, since we did not have maps of the administrative boundaries of all cities in this data set, as we did for the global sample of 120 cities, the population estimates were associated only with the name of the city

FIGURE 9.6

Two Satellite-Based Maps of the Built-up Area of Paris, France, 2000

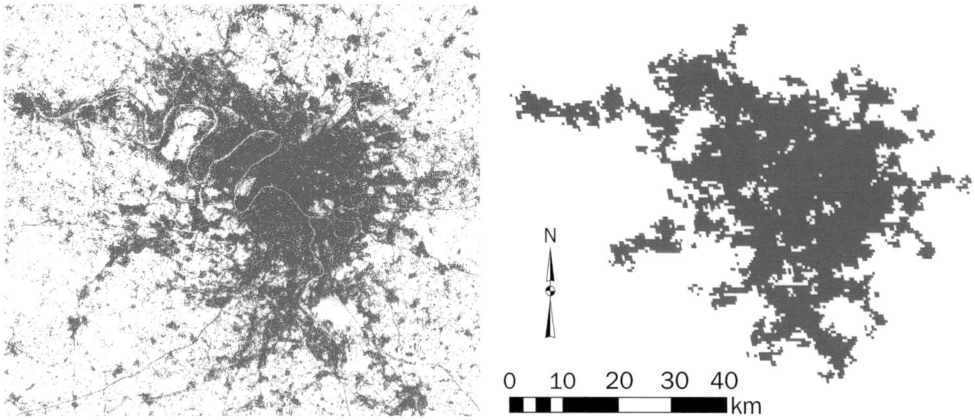

Note: 30x30–meter pixel resolution from Landsat imagery (left) and 463x463–meter pixel resolution from MOD500 imagery (right).
Sources: Left: NASA (multiple dates); Right: Schneider, Friedl, and Potere (2009).

or metropolitan agglomeration; they were not populations within well-defined administrative boundaries.

These data sets contain vast quantities of information that can easily overwhelm anyone trying to make any sense of them. Yet, when we looked at maps of the built-up areas of cities again and again, we began to see similarities and differences among the attributes of their shapes. These attributes may have looked rather ephemeral at the outset but seemed to hint at something systematic and, in a real sense, "objective." The next challenge was twofold. First, we had to discover attributes that exposed meaningful differences between cities, differences that mattered in the sense of making them better or worse in one way or another. Second, we had to construct and test appropriate metrics that correctly captured and measured those attributes with single numbers, one number per map, so cities could be compared to each other or to themselves in different time periods.

Understanding the Spatial Structure of Cities

In *The Dynamics of Global Urban Expansion* (Angel et al. 2005), we focused mainly on the first question posed in this chapter regarding the extent of urban areas and its change over time. We began to explore densities and wanted to uncover something about the overall shape of urban areas as well. In particular, we wanted to incorporate a measure of their compactness—the extent to which the overall shape of cities approximated a circle rather than a tentacle-like form or a long, serpentine one. We intuitively sensed that the more circular a city is, the more accessible it is to its inhabitants, because all urban locations would be, on average, closer to each other. We therefore looked for a compactness metric that could differentiate less circular cities from more circular ones.

After a quick survey of the literature, we settled on a measure that proved to be wrong: the ratio of the built-up area of the city to the area of the circle fully encompassing it. This measure is inappropriate for measuring the compactness of urban footprints because it focuses attention on the distance between the furthest edges of the city, and is therefore subject to the undue influence of small built-up patches that are part of the city but far away from the bulk of it. This measure, we realized later, is a natural metric for measuring the extent to which straying parts of the shape have ventured away in different directions, but not for overall accessibility in a city.

The realization that different compactness metrics measure different compactness properties of shapes led us to an exploration of all the possible ways of measuring shape compactness in geography. This intermittent exploration took several years to complete and resulted in the publication of "Ten Compactness Properties of Circles: Measuring Shape in Geography" in *Canadian Geographer* (Angel, Parent, and Civco 2010). The key insight in this paper was that while the circle is indeed the most compact of shapes, it has at least 10 distinct compactness properties. Medieval cities needed a perimeter approximating a circle to reduce the overall length of their walls, their most expensive public works. Circus tents need to be circular to get everyone as close to the action as possible. Election districts need to approximate circles to avoid gerrymandering. Contemporary cities, where employment is highly decentralized, need to approximate a circle to maximize everyone's access from every place in the city to every other place.

The choice of the appropriate metric for measuring the compactness of a given shape thus depends on what that shape is trying to do. We now know that the metrics appropriate for measuring election district compactness are not the same as those required for measuring city footprints, because election districts and cities have different functions (Angel and Parent 2011). The selected metrics described later in this chapter capture particular spatial attributes of the form of the built-up areas of cities that can become meaningful only when we understand their function, the underlying forces that bring them into being, and their possible contributions to human welfare.

FIVE KEY ATTRIBUTES OF URBAN SPATIAL STRUCTURE

Our empirical study of urban expansion has benefited from previous efforts to measure urban sprawl, while ignoring the negative connotations of that term. The academic literature includes numerous attempts to define and measure sprawl, and there is almost universal consensus on its key manifestations: endless cities, low densities, fuzzy boundaries between city and countryside, a polycentric urban structure, decentralized employment, single-use rather than mixed-use urban expanses, ribbons and commercial strips, scattered development, leapfrogging development, and the fragmentation of open space. Many of these attributes can be used to characterize urban expansion everywhere, and quite a few of them can be measured precisely so we can compare them among cities or in a given city in two periods of time.

Following Galster et al. (2001), we defined and measured both urban extent and its attributes as *patterns* of urban land use—spatial configurations of a metropolitan area at a point in time—and urban expansion and its attributes as *processes*—changes in the spatial structure of cities over time. Patterns and processes are to be distinguished from the causes of spatial patterns, or from the consequences of such patterns.

"Sprawl" in the 1940s in the Lakewood suburb of Los Angeles, California contrasts sharply with "sprawl" in the 2000s in the large-lot subdivision in Franklin Township, New Jersey.

We also took these spatial attributes of cities to be a relative rather than an absolute characterization of an urban landscape. In historical terms, the suburban densities of yesteryear—epitomized by the endless suburbs built in the 1940s in and around Los Angeles—may no longer be considered low densities in comparison with the newer subdivisions with large-lot mansions now springing up in many U.S. metropolitan regions.

We have identified five discrete attributes of urban spatial structure that can now be measured and analyzed systematically in all cities and countries. Measured over time they provide a relatively comprehensive characterization of urban expansion worldwide.

1. Urban land cover, or urban extent, is typically measured by the total built-up area (or impervious surface) of cities, sometimes including the open spaces captured by their built-up areas and the open spaces on the urban fringe affected by urban development. Over several decades, Sinclair (1967), Brueckner and Fansler (1983), Lowry (1988), and Hasse and Lathrop (2003) have defined and measured sprawl as the quantity of land converted to urban use. The data sets used in this study allowed for the calculation of urban land cover.

2. *Density*, or more precisely average urban population density, is typically measured as the ratio of the total population of the city and the total built-up area it occupies. Brueckner and Fansler (1983), Brueckner (2000), Civco et al. (2000), El Nasser and Overberg (2001), Fulton et al. (2001), Ewing, Pendall, and Chen (2002), and Bruegmann (2005), for example, define and measure sprawl as low density or density decline. All four data sets used in this study allowed for the calculation of average densities.

3. *Centrality* concerns the relative proportion of the city population that lives in close proximity to its center rather than in its suburban periphery. It is typically measured by both parameters of the density curve defined by Clark (1951)—the maximum densities at the urban center (the intercept of the curve) and the rate of decline in density as distance from the city center increases (the gradient of the curve). Self (1961), Gottmann and Harper (1967), Jackson (1975), Kasarda and Redfearn (1975), and Hall (1997), for example, define and measure sprawl as the increasing share of the urban population living in suburbs or, alternatively, as the flattening of the density curve. Centrality, in a more general sense, can also refer to the decentralization of employment away from the central business district (CBD) (Glaeser and Kahn 2004), and to the emergence of polycentric cities with several employment centers scattered throughout the urban area (Anas, Arnott, and Small 1998; Clawson and Hall 1973). The calculation of centrality requires data at the census tract level, which is considerably more difficult to obtain on a global scale. This lack of data restricted our analysis to the few cities and countries where such data were readily available.

4. *Fragmentation*, or scattered development, is typically measured by the relative amount and the spatial structure of the open spaces that are fragmented by the noncontiguous expansion of cities into the surrounding countryside. Clawson (1962), Peiser (1989), Weitz and Moore (1998), Carruthers and Ulfarsson (2001), Heim (2001), Bruegmann (2005), and Burchfield et al. (2006), for example, define and measure sprawl as noncontiguous, fragmented development. Only the data set for the global sample of 120 cities for the 1990–2000 period allowed for the calculation of fragmentation.

5. *Compactness*, or the degree to which the city footprint approximates a circle rather than a tentacle-like shape, is typically measured by a set of compactness metrics (Angel, Parent, and Civco 2010). To our knowledge no one else has proposed measuring the shape compactness of urban footprints, even though it does have an effect on overall accessibility—the more circular the city, the closer its locations are to its center and to one another. The compact-city literature (e.g., Burton 2002) typically refers to compactness as a form of high density rather than as shape compactness. All four data sets used in this study allowed for the calculation of compactness.

These five attributes include most, yet not all, aspects of urban spatial structure that are mentioned in the sprawl literature. One aspect that could not be studied with the data we compiled is the preponderance of large areas of single-use rather than mixed-use development (Nelson et al. 1995). Nor could we distinguish properly between open spaces in public and private ownership to determine whether urban expansion allowed for the creation of adequate public open spaces. Given these limitations, however, these five attributes can and do provide a rather comprehensive perspective on the manner in which cities occupy geographic space.

These attributes are only weakly correlated with each other because they measure different phenomena. The correlations between the key metrics used to measure density, fragmentation, and compactness, for example, all have absolute values of less than

High density and low fragmentation in the medinah in Fez, Morocco, in 2010 contrasts with high density and high fragmentation in Le Corbusier's 1925 *Plan Voisin* for Paris, France.

0.2 and are statistically insignificant at the 95 percent confidence level. The density of the built-up areas of cities may be high or low regardless of its level of fragmentation. The medinah in Fez, Morocco, illustrates high built-up area density and low fragmentation, whereas Le Corbusier's *Plan Voisin* for Paris proposes high built-up area densities and high fragmentation. A city footprint may have a compact shape whether the city is fragmented or not and whether its average density is high or low.

METRICS

The unit of investigation in this study is the metropolitan area—typically a central city surrounded by suburbs and secondary cities that form a relatively contiguous whole. Urban land is occupied by urban uses that include all land in residential, commercial, industrial, and office use; land used for transport, parks, and public facilities; protected land; and vacant land. Land in urban use does not include cultivated lands, pasture lands, forests, farms, rural villages, intercity roads, or nature areas. The terms *city* and *metropolitan area* are used interchangeably. Rather than choosing to put a wedge between central cities and their surrounding suburbs, both are treated as interdependent parts of a single whole.

A central problem involved in measuring the attributes of urban spatial structure correctly concerns a precise and consistent definition of what constitutes the area of the city (Parr 2007; Wolman et al. 2005). Using the administrative area of a city is typically inadequate, because it can be changed from one day to the next by decree and because it may include large rural areas. For example, in 1999 the administrative area of Beijing (measured in square kilometers as 16,801 km²) was 11 times larger than its built-up area (1,576 km²) (figure 9.7).

The built-up area of the city is a much more precise, consistent, and comparable measure of its area, and the analysis of satellite images now allows us to identify built-up areas by

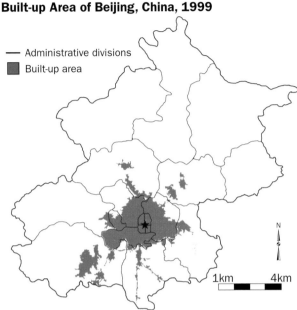

FIGURE 9.7

The Administrative Divisions and the Built-up Area of Beijing, China, 1999

Sources: Divisions redrawn from a base map in Wikipedia; and built-up area map adapted from Angel et al. (2012, 48).

impervious surfaces (pavements, rooftops, and compacted soils). We used Landsat imagery with a 30x30–meter pixel resolution and Mod500 imagery with 463x463–meter pixel resolution to map the built-up pixels and the open pixels in and around cities. We then used these digital maps, in combination with population data for the administrative districts encompassing these cities whenever possible, to calculate most spatial metrics in a consistent manner across cities and countries using geographic information systems (GIS) software.

Area, Extent, and Expansion Metrics

The key data used for measuring urban spatial structure are built-up and open space pixels of several types. To define these pixels, we first define the *walking distance circle* as a circle 1 km² in area around any given pixel.

- *Urban built-up pixels* have more than 50 percent of built-up pixels within their walking distance circle.
- *Suburban built-up pixels* have 10 to 50 percent of built-up pixels within their walking distance circle.
- *Rural built-up pixels* have less than 10 percent of built-up pixels within their walking distance circle.

Landscape ecology studies maintain that settlements developed near a forest or prairie affect vegetation and wildlife along their edges, often in a belt up to 100 meters in width (Brand and George 2001; Chen, Franklin, and Spies 1992; Winter, Johnson, and Faaborg 2000). Four open space metrics are used to characterize density, fragmentation, and compactness.

- *Fringe open space* consists of all open space pixels within 100 meters of urban or suburban pixels.
- *Captured open space* consists of all open space clusters that are fully surrounded by built-up and fringe open space pixels and are less than 200 hectares in area.
- *Exterior open space* consists of all fringe open space pixels, which are less than 100 meters from the open countryside.
- *Urbanized open space* consists of all open space pixels that have a majority of built-up pixels within their walking distance circle.

In the cases where population data can be obtained at the census tract level, we can also define the urban tract area as the set of tracts within the administrative area of the city that have a population density above a certain threshold. The U.S. Census Bureau, for example, defines urban census tracts as those with more than 1,000 persons per square mile (3.86 persons per hectare). Based on these preliminary definitions, we use four area metrics to measure various attributes of urban spatial structure.

- The *built-up area* is the set of built-up pixels within the administrative boundary of the city or metropolitan area.
- The *urbanized area* is the set of built-up pixels and urbanized open space pixels.
- The *city footprint* is the set of urban and suburban pixels, their fringe open space pixels, and the captured open spaces these pixels surround.
- The *urban tract area* is the set of census tracts within the administrative area of the city with a population density greater than 3.86 persons per hectare.

Density Metrics

Three measures of average density are based on the area metrics listed above.

- *Built-up area density* is the ratio of the population within the administrative area of the city and the area of its built-up pixels.
- *Urbanized area density* is the ratio of the population within the administrative area of the city and its urbanized area.
- *Urban tract density* is the ratio of the total population and the total area of urban census tracts.

These three different definitions of density yield different values, of course, and therefore cannot be compared directly. In general, built-up area densities are higher than urbanized area densities, which in turn are higher than tract area densities. Urban census tracts contain large amounts of vacant land and, in general, urban tract densities are lower than built-up area densities. Because the main focus in this report is on comparing densities among cities or on density change over time, the choice of any particular metric for measuring density is not important. These metrics will be used interchangeably, but values obtained by different metrics will not be compared to each other.

The choice of metric used to measure densities depended largely on the available data. Built-up area densities were used when maps generated from classifying satellite images were available. Urbanized area densities obtained from satellite imagery were used only for the years 1990 to 2000. In earlier periods going back to 1800, they were calculated by digitizing historical maps.[1] Tract densities were used mostly in analyzing U.S. cities where such data are available from 1910 onward.

Centrality Metrics

Centrality can be analyzed when detailed maps of census tracts and their associated residential populations are available. Clark (1951) postulated and showed that residential population densities decline at a constant rate as distance from the city center increases. Figure 9.8 shows that, in the case of Paris, central density is low because of

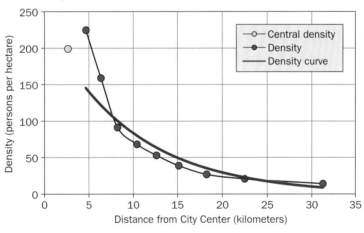

FIGURE 9.8
The Density Curve for Paris, France, 1999

Source: Institut National de la Statistique et des Etudes Economiques (INSEE 1999).

---

1 The historical maps that we digitized and analyzed to determine the built-up areas of cities were often at a very coarse scale that did not distinguish built-up segments from open space segments in their interiors. We therefore chose to include urbanized open space in determining their extent. In order to combine the maps generated from historical maps with the maps generated from satellite data from 1990 to 2000, we used the urbanized area in the latter maps as the closest approximation to built-up areas of cities and their urbanized open space identified in the historical maps.

the proliferation of public, office, and commercial buildings in the city center, and that value was not included in estimating the overall density curve. Two metrics are of interest in studying centrality and its change over time.

- The *tract density gradient* is defined as the slope of the residential density curve.[2]
- The *tract density intercept* is defined as the value of the residential density curve at the city center.

For Paris in 2000, the gradient of the residential density curve was 0.092; that is, residential density declined by 9.2 percent, on average, as distance from the center increased by 1 kilometer. The theoretical density at the center (the density intercept) was 226 persons per hectare. If residences disperse to the suburbs over time, the density curve may become both flatter and shallower. Its gradient may decline, signaling a more even density throughout the urban area, and its intercept may become smaller as well, signaling a relative decline in residential densities in locations closer to the city center. For example, the average density gradient in 20 U.S. cities declined from 0.22 to 0.05 between 1910 and 2000, and the average density intercept declined from 318 to 44 during that same period (see figure 12.6).

The dispersal of residences to the suburbs in the United States during the early decades of the twentieth century was followed by the decentralization of workplaces into the urban periphery in later decades. The same density metrics used to measure the centrality and dispersal of residences can be used for workplaces. In addition, it is possible to study commuting patterns that link both residences and workplaces, and thus shed more light on the spatial structure of urban areas. For every circular cordon about the city center, for example, it is possible to determine what share of commuting trips remains inside the cordon, what share remains outside, what share crosses the cordon inward, and what share crosses it outward. Clearly, the more dispersed residences and workplaces are, the smaller the share of trips that enter the CBD and the larger the share of suburb-to-suburb trips. Comparable data for studying the spatial structure of workplaces and commuting patterns and its change over time at the global scale are sorely lacking. Data are now available, however, for all U.S. metropolitan areas for the year 2000. In chapter 12, we shall employ these metrics in analyzing these patterns in a sample of 40 U.S. metropolitan areas for that year.

---

2 The residential density curve is typically defined in mathematical terms as $D(r) = D(0) \cdot e^{\beta \cdot r}$, where r is the distance from the city center, $D(r)$ is the average density in a ring with distance r from the center, β is the gradient or slope of the density curve, and $D(0)$ is the theoretical density at the center, commonly referred to as the density curve intercept. The parameters $D(0)$ and β can be estimated from data on densities at different distances from the city center by taking the logarithms of both sides, fitting a linear equation to the data points i in $LnD(r_i) = LnD(0) - \beta \cdot r_i$, and finding the best estimates for $D(0)$ and β.

Fragmentation Metrics

Five metrics were used in this study to measure different aspects of fragmentation.

- The *openness index* is the average share of open space in the walking distance circle around each built-up pixel in the city.
- The *city footprint ratio* is the ratio of the city footprint and the built-up area in the city.
- *Infill* is defined as all new development that occurred between two time periods within all the open spaces in the city footprint of the earlier period excluding exterior open space.
- *Extension* is all new development that occurred between two time periods in contiguous clusters that contained exterior open space in the earlier period and that were not infill.
- *Leapfrog* development is all new construction that occurred between two time periods and is entirely outside the exterior open space of the earlier period.

Compactness Metrics

Finally, three metrics were used to measure shape compactness. To calculate these metrics we first define the *equal area circle* as a circle with an area equal to that of the city footprint centered at the city's center, identified as the location of its city hall.

- The *proximity index* is the ratio of the average distance from all points in the equal area circle to its center and the average distance to the city center from all points in the city footprint.
- The *cohesion index* is the ratio of the average distance among all points in an equal area circle and the average distance among all points in the city footprint.
- The *depth index* is the ratio of the average distance from points in the city (including all its fully contained open spaces) to its outer periphery and the average distance to the periphery in a circle of the same area.

We measured the shape compactness of different areas in two different data sets: the city footprint areas in the global sample of 120 cities for the years 1990–2000, and the urbanized areas in the representative sample of 30 cities for the years 1800–2000. As in the case of densities, the urbanized area was found to be the more appropriate areal extent for comparing maps generated from satellite imagery and those obtained by digitizing the boundaries of historical maps of cities.

The Metrics Applied to Bandung, Indonesia

The city footprints of Bandung, Indonesia, in 1991 and 2001 are shown in figure 9.9. In 1991 Bandung had a built-up area of 108 km^2, of which 64 percent was urban, 34 percent was suburban, and 2 percent was rural. Fringe open space added 103.2 km^2

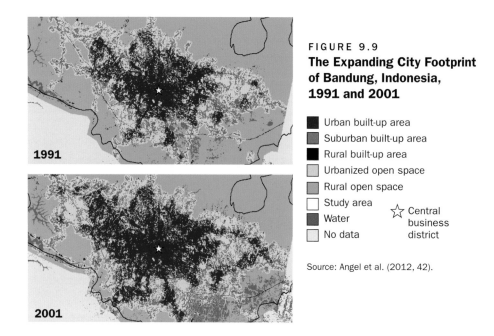

FIGURE 9.9

The Expanding City Footprint of Bandung, Indonesia, 1991 and 2001

■ Urban built-up area
■ Suburban built-up area
■ Rural built-up area
□ Urbanized open space
■ Rural open space
□ Study area
■ Water
□ No data

☆ Central business district

Source: Angel et al. (2012, 42).

and captured open space added 5.1 km² respectively to its built-up area. The city footprint area thus amounted to 217.0 km², roughly double its built-up area. In 1991, the built-up area density in Bandung was 274 persons per hectare and its urbanized area density was 216 persons per hectare. The openness index was 0.41 and the city footprint ratio was 2.0. The proximity index was 0.84 and the cohesion index was 0.82.

The area of new development in Bandung between 1991 and 2001 amounted to 45.1 km², of which 23 percent was infill, 60 percent was extension, and 17 percent was leapfrog. By 2001, the built-up area density in Bandung declined to 239 persons per hectare at an annual rate of decline of 1.4 percent, and its urbanized area density declined to 187 persons per hectare at an annual rate of decline of 1.4 percent as well. Bandung became less dense. Its openness index declined to 0.37 and its city footprint ratio declined to 1.85, as it became less fragmented. And its proximity index increased to 0.87 and its cohesion index increased to 0.86 as it became more compact.

URBAN EXPANSION: THE CONCEPTUAL FRAMEWORK

The theoretical foundation for the economic analysis of urban spatial structure was laid out by Alonso (1960; 1964), Mills (1967), and Muth (1961; 1969) and later refined by Wheaton (1974; 1976), Brueckner (1987), and others. The evidence presented in this study validates the key results of their theoretical insights and confirms the observation of Mills and Tan (1980, 314) that "[t]here are few cases in economics in which such a simple theory leads to so many testable implications."

The following paragraphs introduce the basic elements of this theory and the set of testable hypotheses derived from it. In general, the classical theory predicts that variations in urban land cover, density, and centrality among cities and countries, as well as their rates of change, can be explained largely by variations in city population, household income, the availability of buildable land for expansion (i.e., relatively flat dry land), the cost of agricultural land on the urban periphery, and the cost of urban transport.

The empirical evidence supports most of these predictions. All in all, the statistical models we examined are robust. They are able to explain a substantial amount of the variations in urban spatial structure among cities by variations in population, income, buildable land, the cost of transport, and the cost of agricultural land on the urban periphery. These results suggest that variations in the climate, cultural traditions, or policy environments in different cities may matter less than fundamental economic forces in giving shape to their spatial structure.

The stylized city in the classical economic model of urban spatial structure is circular, with a single CBD surrounded by concentric rings of residences. The households have homogeneous incomes and preferences, and their breadwinners all commute to the CBD, where all jobs are concentrated. The theory confirms that, in equilibrium, the price of land will decline with distance from the city center while the quantity of land and housing consumed by individual households will increase. In other words, both land price and population density will decline with distance from the CBD. Much empirical evidence supports these predictions (figure 9.10).

FIGURE 9.10
The Decline in Land Prices and Population Density with Distance from the City Center of Bangkok, Thailand, 2000

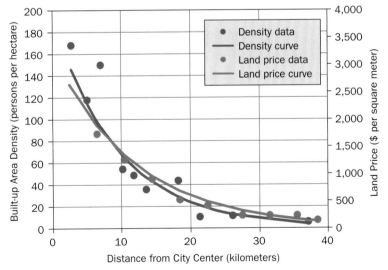

Source: Data provided by Dr. Sopon Pornchokchai, Agency for Real Estate Affairs, Bangkok, Thailand.

Furthermore, on the urban periphery housing producers must compete with agricultural users to convert land to urban use, and in equilibrium the urban land price at the edge of the city must therefore equal the price of land in agricultural use. Finally, the entire population of the city must be accommodated in the buildable area inside a circle of a finite radius. Given these simplifying assumptions, as well as data on the city population and its income, the cost of transport, the share of buildable land in every ring, and the prevailing agricultural land price on the urban periphery, the classical theory can provide a mathematical answer as to the radius of the area that the city will occupy as well as its average density.

In addition, the solution of a set of equilibrium equations in this theoretical model of the city yields a number of mathematical inequalities that can be translated into a set of hypotheses and tested with empirical data (Brueckner 1987).

- The area of the city will increase when its population increases, when household incomes increase, when transport costs decrease, when the share of buildable land increases, and when agricultural rents on the urban periphery decrease.
- Average density will increase when the population increases, when household incomes decrease, when transport costs increase, when the share of buildable land decreases, and when agricultural rents on the urban periphery increase.

An extension of the classical theory by Wheaton (1976) suggests that cities with higher levels of income inequality will occupy more land and have lower densities. He shows that when the rich do not obtain housing in the same land market as the poor, then "[t]his reduced competition in turn allows the poor to bid somewhat less, expand their land consumption, and improve their situation" (Wheaton 1976, 43). This condition exists in cities where a substantial share of the urban population lives in informal settlements with minimal infrastructure services and other locations that are not desired by higher-income people. This insight leads to another hypothesis.

- The area of the city will increase and its density will decrease if income inequality is more pronounced and if a larger share of the population inhabits informal settlements.

The classical theory does not allow us to predict why certain cities will be more fragmented than others, so we formulated several hypotheses.

- Fragmentation will decrease when the city population increases, when household incomes decrease, and when agricultural rents increase.
- Since cars make it possible to reach all locations at low cost, the higher the level of car ownership, the lower the level of fragmentation.
- Since the presence of groundwater makes it possible to locate anywhere, the larger the share of households obtaining water from wells, the higher the level of fragmentation.

- Since informal settlements typically occupy undesirable lands, the higher the share of informal settlements, the lower the level of fragmentation.

The classical theory assumes that all jobs are concentrated in the CBD and that all commuters travel on radial routes to the center. It does not allow for jobs to decentralize in order to reduce traffic congestion and become more accessible to commuters or shoppers or to reduce land costs. The decentralization of employment can be explained by the ubiquity of trucking and the availability of a dense network of roads throughout urban areas, eliminating the location advantages of the city center. This would naturally lead to the decentralization of residences as well, commonly known as suburbanization, leading to further job decentralization in a so-called positive feedback loop. The key hypothesis regarding centralization follows.

- Trucking and the decentralization of jobs will lower the location advantages of the city center and will result in lower intercepts and lower gradients of population density curves.

Finally, the classical theory assumes that the abstract city is circular, but does not shed any light on why cities should be circular. There are good reasons for cities to attain a circular shape, and they have changed over time. Ancient walled cities had a ready rationale for being circular or near circular in shape to minimize the cost of wall construction while encompassing as large an area as possible. In the early phases of industrialization, when most jobs were concentrated in the CBD, the circular shape minimized the average distance to its center. In the postindustrial age, when jobs are distributed throughout the metropolitan area, a third reason is that the circular shape maximizes access from every place to every other place. A key hypothesis can be formulated regarding compactness.

- Transportation corridors that lower travel time and costs along them tend to make cities less circular and more tentacle-like. As transport cost differentials decline over time, cities tend to become more circular again, only to become more tentacle-like again with the introduction of new transport technology.

The remaining seven chapters in this part of the book use the databases, the metrics, and the theoretical foundation introduced here to answer the seven questions posed at the beginning of this chapter.

[R]ather than being determined by a process which indiscriminately consumes agricultural land, urban sizes are the result of an orderly market equilibrium where competing claims to the land are appropriately balanced.

Brueckner and Fansler (1983, 479)

CHAPTER 10

Global Urban Land Cover and Its Expansion

What are the extents of urban areas, how fast are they expanding over time, why, and why should it matter?

Accra, the capital of Ghana, offers a startling example of recent urban expansion. Between 1985 and 2000, the city's population grew from 1.8 to 2.7 million, a 50 percent increase, while its urban land cover expanded from 13,000 to 33,000 hectares, a 153 percent increase. Urban land cover in Accra grew at an annual rate more than twice as fast as its population. This expansion was accelerated by population growth, but the faster rate of expansion requires further explanation.

The late twentieth century in Ghana coincided with the resumption of stable economic growth after a period of stagnation and negative growth rates. Per capita income (measured in purchasing power parities to account for its buying power) doubled between 1984 and 2000, from US$484 to US$946 (World Bank 2012a). In Accra, increased household incomes provided more financial resources to purchase land for housing. Higher incomes also triggered a boom in car ownership in Ghana, mostly centered in Accra, allowing households to purchase accessible residential plots at further distances from the city center (Grant 2009; Yankson, Kofie, and Moller-Jensen 2004; Yeboah 2000). Both of these developments facilitated a steady shift from extended-family, compound-type housing to single-family, bungalow-style housing.

> Whereas only a decade ago peri-urban Accra consisted of dispersed rural settlements where subsistence agriculture was widely practiced, today these settlements are surrounded by construction and little farmland remains. Richer households are moving into newly completed houses, whereas poor households seek rooms to rent, often within indigenous settlements. (Gough and Yankson 2006, 198)

157

The rapid suburbanization of Accra in only 15 years was facilitated by the continued dominance of the customary ownership of tribal lands on its urban periphery (figure 10.1). These lands cannot be bought and sold freely and are subject to little regulation by the authorities beyond the requirement to register transactions with a Lands Commission. Tribal lands are administered by village chiefs or elders, who subdivide land and then assign plots to their villagers and lease plots to outsiders, usually for 99 years. The plots are typically quite large, most measuring 750–900 square meters (m²). In 1996, they were selling for 2.5–3 million cedis (US$1,600–$1,900), paid to village chiefs as "drink money" and typically used at their discretion for various village development projects (Gough and Yankson 2000).

The government of Ghana procures large tracts of land on the urban fringe for various uses, and although compensation is required, it is typically not paid. Fear of government seizure of land without due compensation serves as an incentive for village chiefs to dispose of their lands to private individuals faster than they would in the absence of this threat, possibly depressing land prices on the urban periphery and increasing affordability. In the words of the chief and elders of Agbogba, a village on the northern fringe of Accra, "When government sees an idle area of land then we are in trouble; they will take it without any compensation. . . . So we have decided to lease land to individuals to enable us to get money for the development of our community" (Gough and Yankson 2000, 2494).

While the particular circumstances of the recent expansion of Accra are unique, the rate of its expansion is not very different from the rates in other cities and countries.

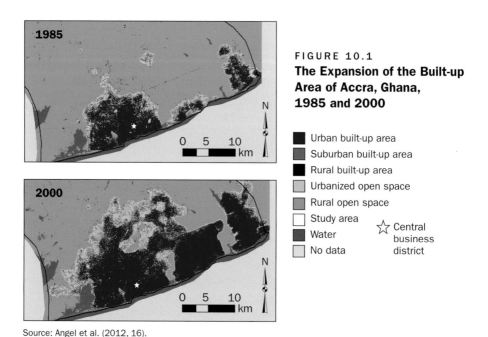

FIGURE 10.1
The Expansion of the Built-up Area of Accra, Ghana, 1985 and 2000

■ Urban built-up area
■ Suburban built-up area
■ Rural built-up area
□ Urbanized open space
■ Rural open space
□ Study area
■ Water
□ No data
☆ Central business district

Source: Angel et al. (2012, 16).

Village chiefs subdivided customary lands for low-density suburban development on the fringe of Accra, Ghana, in 2008.

When we examined the growth rates of the urban population and the urban land cover in the global sample of 120 cities between 1990 and 2000, we found that population growth averaged 1.60 percent per annum, and land cover growth averaged 3.66 percent per annum. The difference between them was 2.06 percent. Thus, as in Accra, urban land cover in all 120 cities grew on average at more than double the rate of growth of the urban population. At the growth rate of 3.66 percent per year prevailing in the 1990s, the world's urban land cover will double in only 19 years.

The rapid growth of urban land cover is by no means a recent phenomenon, as shown in the historical expansion of Cairo, the capital of Egypt, during the past 200 years (figure 10.2). While growing rather slowly during the nineteenth century, Cairo increased its urbanized area more than thirty-two-fold in the twentieth century. By 1911, it occupied 2,073 hectares. It doubled its area in 27 years (1911–1938), then doubled it again in 25 years (1938–1963), doubled it in 9 years (1963–1972), doubled it in 8 years (1972–1980), and doubled it in 20 years (1980–2000). Between 1938 and 2000, the urbanized area of Cairo thus increased sixteenfold, at an average annual growth rate of 4.67 percent. The rapid population growth in Cairo began in earnest after World War II with waves of migrations from rural areas to the city to take advantage of the new economic opportunities created by industrialization and by the emergence of large service and government sectors. Population growth naturally led to rapid urban expansion.

Cairo is situated on the fertile banks of the Nile River and fans out into an agriculturally productive delta to its north. The banks of the Nile and its delta contained 35,000 square kilometers (km²) of cultivated land in 2005, more than 97 percent of the total cultivated land area in Egypt. But cultivated lands in the country amounted to

FIGURE 10.2
The Expansion of Cairo, Egypt, 1800–2000

Source: Angel et al. (2012, 270).

only 3.5 percent of its total area in 2005 (Hereher 2009), and most of Egypt's population, totaling 74 million in that year, lived in close proximity to these lands. To protect the country's food supplies, the government of Egypt issued a law in 1966 (Law 59-1966) forbidding construction on agricultural lands. The law has been amended many times and supplemented with strict military decrees that impose heavy fines and even imprisonment (Sejourné 2009).

These restrictions limit the expansion of Cairo to highly regulated new towns on desert lands to its east and west, usually in public ownership, that require a full complement of infrastructure services. The towns typically include limited amounts of new dwelling units and cannot meet the vast demands for housing in the rapidly growing metropolis. The total population of new towns in 2006 amounted to 600,000 people or 3.7 percent of the population of Greater Cairo—well below government expectations (Piffero 2009).

Rent control laws promulgated in the 1940s and rescinded in 1996 discouraged apartment owners from renting them, first because they could not get market rents, and second because of the risk of failure to evict tenants who did not pay their rents. This policy has exacerbated housing shortages and led to the absurd result that as many as 2 million dwelling units in Greater Cairo were vacant in 2006 (Piffero 2009).

The combination of these three government policies—the containment of expansion into agricultural lands, planned new towns, and rent control—proved unrealistic in meeting the demand for housing in Cairo. Despite the high productivity of lands under cultivation, their subdivision and sale to private developers for the construction of walk-up apartments proved much more lucrative to the owners. Demand for such apartments was high because they were less regimented than the planned new towns in the desert, more accessible, more affordable, and more sensitive to people's diverse needs.

Faced with housing shortages as well as pressures and inducements from landowners and developers, Egypt's public authorities turned a blind eye to residential development on agricultural lands, while continuing to disparage and condemn it in public. As a result, "at the end of the 1990s informal areas represented approximately 53% of the built residential surface of Greater Cairo and hosted 62% of its inhabitants" (Piffero 2009, 21, referencing Sims 2000 and Sejourné 2006).

Cairo had a population of 13 million in 2000, 20 percent of Egypt's total population, and occupied a total land area of 663 km^2. Approximately 350 km^2 of that total was agricultural lands, an equivalent of 1 percent of Egypt's total cultivated land area at that time. As of 2006, informal settlements on agricultural lands already contained 65 percent of the population of the metropolis, or 10.5 million out of a total of 16.2 million (Sims and Sejourné 2008).

Unlike in Accra, the expansion of Cairo did not take the form of low-density, single-family suburban homes, but higher-density, multifamily structures that conserved much more agricultural land. By comparison, the average density in Cairo in 2000 was almost triple that of Accra. Nevertheless, the new buildings on the urban fringe of Cairo were constructed at lower densities than those in the older central areas, and overall densities in the metropolitan areas declined over time. The city thus expanded its area at a faster rate than the growth of its population. Between 1938 and 2000, the city's population increased nearly sixfold while its area increased sixteenfold.

Most urban population growth in Cairo today entails the rapid expansion of an informal market in agricultural land on the urban fringe. This responsive market is capable of meeting the vast demand for housing that accompanies population and income growth. It provides both rental and owner-occupied housing to all segments of the urban population—from garbage pickers to blue-collar workers to white-collar professionals—in mixed-use communities with well-built structures accommodating shops and businesses as well as residences. It is common for the owner of a building to occupy one apartment while renting the rest of the units.

The deliberate absence of regulatory involvement by the authorities in the formation of these settlements—even though they failed to conform to government prohibitions—vastly reduced the amount of land allocated to public works, particularly to arterial roads and public open spaces. This lack of oversight also made the provision of municipal infrastructure more difficult and cumbersome, and has prevented the authorities from enforcing the building code regarding structural safety. An urban development policy based on coming to terms with the expansion of Cairo into cultivated lands and preparing for it properly, rather than delegitimizing it and failing to contain it, would have been a more efficient, equitable, and sustainable approach.

When we examined the growth rates of urban populations and their associated urban land covers in the representative global sample of 30 cities between 1800 and 2000, we found that the rates of expansion in Cairo were not atypical: 28 of the 30 cities studied increased their areas more than sixteenfold during the twentieth century. The only exceptions were London and Paris, the two largest cities in the sample in 1900, which had increased their areas sixteenfold since 1874 and 1887 respectively (figure 10.3).

On average, the 30 cities in the representative global sample doubled their urbanized area in 16 years (1930–1946), doubled it again in 15 years (1946–1961), doubled it again in 15 years (1961–1976), and doubled it yet again in 23 years (1976–2000). The total urban land cover of these cities grew at an average long-term rate of 3.3 percent per annum. The advocates of containment must come to terms with these facts. How can anyone contain a metropolitan area that expands its land area sixteenfold, or even eightfold for that matter, in 70 years?

Informal residential development can be seen expanding into agricultural lands on the fringe of Cairo, Egypt between 2002 (top) and 2010 (bottom).

FIGURE 10.3
Urban Expansion in 30 Cities in 6 World Regions since 1800

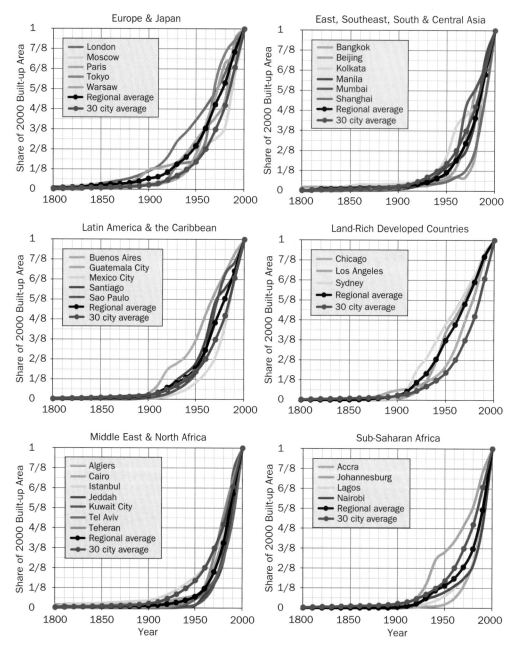

Source: Calculated from Angel et al. (2012, 260–319).

URBAN LAND COVER IN LARGE AND SMALL CITIES

We have defined large cities as those with populations of 100,000 or more. They are to be distinguished from megacities that may contain 10 million people or more. In the year 2000, there were only 16 megacities in the world, compared to 3,646 cities that contained 100,000 people or more (United Nations Population Division 2008, file 11a).

These large cities contained some 2 billion people in the year 2000 and occupied a land area of 340,000 km² (table 10.1). Both 70 percent of large cities and 70 percent of the total population of large cities were in developing countries, but these cities occupied less than one-half of the total land cover of all large cities. The shares of the total urban population in large cities in different regions ranged from 52 to 89 percent, with an average of 69 ± 4 percent. Worldwide, large cities accounted for 71 percent of the urban population. We should expect the respective shares of the urban population in small and large cities in all regions to be quite similar, but this is apparently not the case. This quandary is left for further investigation by other researchers.

The Mod500 global land cover map could not be relied upon for calculating urban land cover in smaller cities and towns with populations of fewer than 100,000 people that could not be easily distinguished from villages. To estimate total urban land cover in small cities in each country, we first computed the total urban population in small cities and towns as the difference between the country's total urban population (as estimated by the United Nations) and our calculated total population of large cities, both

TABLE 10.1

Regional Data on the Number, Population, and Built-up Areas of Large Cities, 2000

Region	Large Cities			
	Number of Cities	Total Population (millions)	Share of Urban Population (percent)	Total Land Cover (km²)
Eastern Asia & the Pacific	891	458.1	89.2	42,218
Southeast Asia	196	107.3	52.2	12,883
South & Central Asia	539	287.0	65.9	29,705
Western Asia	157	89.6	73.6	12,999
Northern Africa	115	53.1	61.1	5,342
Sub-Saharan Africa	256	131.6	63.4	12,778
Latin America & the Caribbean	403	258.9	66.3	43,280
Europe & Japan	799	400.9	66.5	85,871
Land-Rich Developed Countries	293	226.9	84.8	94,759
All Developing Countries	2,557	1,385.5	70.7	159,206
All Developed Countries	1,092	627.8	72.1	180,630
World Total	3,646	2,013.3	71.1	339,836

Source: Angel et al. (2012 online).

in the year 2000. Because these estimates come from different data sources, subtracting them from one another is problematic.

In a regression model using data on 3,646 large cities, we found that a doubling of the city population was associated with a 16 percent increase in density. We used this density-population factor in generating our estimates of the land area consumed by small cities. Total urban land cover in small cities was calculated as the ratio of the total population to the overall density in small cities. We estimated the overall density in small cities in every region from information on the overall density in large cities, the median city population in large cities, the median city population in small cities, and the density-population factor in that region. According to our calculations, overall densities in small cities were roughly half those in large cities, and urban land cover in small cities added 266,000 km² to total global urban land cover in the year 2000.

URBAN LAND COVER IN ALL COUNTRIES, 2000

We combined our estimates of urban land cover in large and small cities to calculate the total in all countries and world regions in the year 2000 (Angel et al. 2012, table 5.3). Table 10.2 summarizes our estimates for total urban land cover in each region, as well as urban land cover as a share of the total land area in each region.

Worldwide, urban land cover occupied 0.47 percent of the total land area of countries in the year 2000, ranging from 0.62 percent of the land area of all developed

TABLE 10.2
Estimated Urban Land Cover in All Regions, 2000

Region	Total Urban Population (Millions)	Urban Land Cover in Large Cities (km²)	Urban Land Cover in Small Cities (km²)	Total Urban Land Cover (km²)	Urban Land Cover as Percent of Total Land Area
Eastern Asia & the Pacific	514	42,218	10,760	52,978	0.45
Southeast Asia	206	12,883	21,565	34,448	0.85
South & Central Asia	435	29,705	30,166	59,872	0.58
Western Asia	121	12,999	9,714	22,714	0.49
Northern Africa	87	5,342	6,775	12,104	0.15
Sub-Saharan Africa	208	12,778	13,721	26,500	0.12
Latin America & the Caribbean	390	43,280	47,952	91,233	0.45
Europe & Japan	602	85,871	88,755	174,581	0.76
Land-Rich Developed Countries	268	94,759	36,688	131,447	0.50
All Developing Countries	1,960	159,206	140,655	299,847	0.37
All Developed Countries	870	180,630	125,444	306,028	0.62
World Total	2,830	339,836	266,099	605,875	0.47

Source: Angel et al. (2011b, 70–78).

countries, but only 0.37 percent of the land area of developing countries. For example, urban areas occupied 0.85 percent of the land area of the countries of Southeast Asia, but only 0.12 percent of the land in the countries of Sub-Saharan Africa.

Among the 20 countries with the largest areas of urban land cover, 5 of them—the United States, China, Brazil, India, and the Russian Federation—had more than 25,000 km^2 of urban land cover in the year 2000 (figure 10.4). The United States contained 112,220 km^2 of urban land cover, or 18.5 percent of the global total, while its urban population in 2000 comprised only 8 percent of the total. Its urban land cover was more than double the 47,169 km^2 of urban land cover in the next highest country, China, while its urban population was only half that of China at that time.

Figure 10.5 shows urban land cover as a share of the total land area of countries that had large cities in 2000.

- Ten countries had more than 5 percent of their total land area occupied by cities, among them Singapore, Bahrain, the United Kingdom, Italy, and Germany.
- Twenty-two countries had 2 to 5 percent, among them Japan, France, and the Philippines.
- Twenty-two additional countries had between 1 and 2 percent, among them the United States, Bangladesh, Turkey, and India.

FIGURE 10.4
Twenty Countries with the Largest Areas of Urban Land Cover, 2000

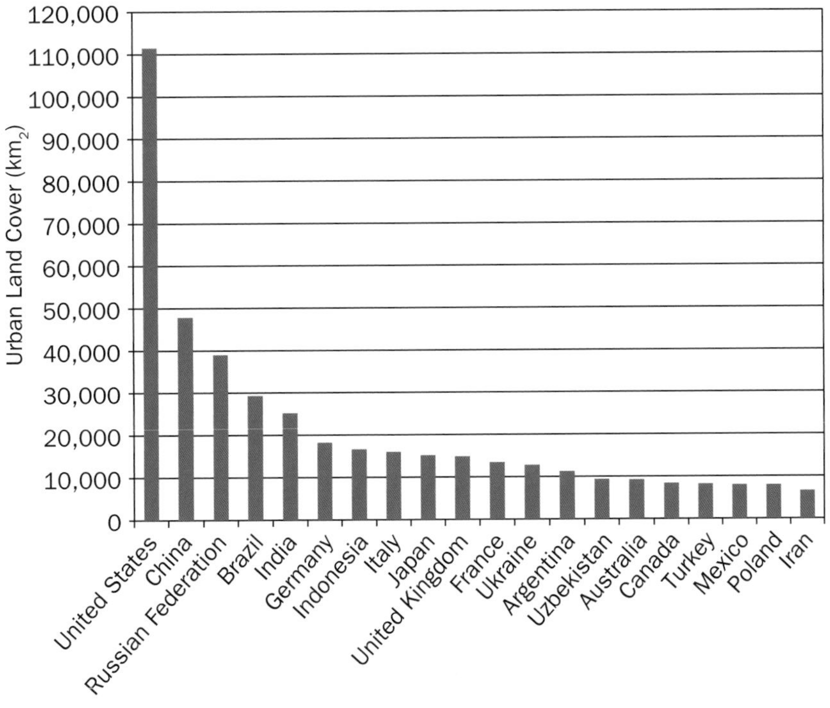

Source: Angel et al. (2012 online).

FIGURE 10.5

Urban Land Cover as a Share of Total Land Area in All Countries, 2000

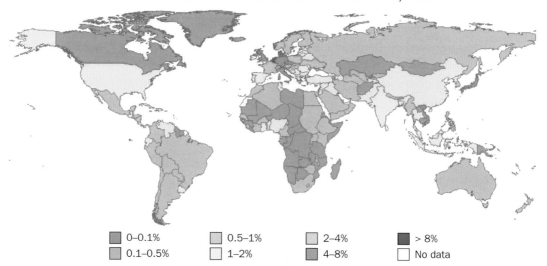

■ 0–0.1%	■ 0.5–1%	■ 2–4%	■ > 8%
■ 0.1–0.5%	■ 1–2%	■ 4–8%	☐ No data

Sources: Urban land cover data from Angel et al. (2012, table 5.4, 362–380); and country land area
data from World Bank (2012a).

- Twenty-eight more countries had between 0.5 and 1 percent of their total area occupied by cities, among them Indonesia, Pakistan, Venezuela, and China.
- Twenty-seven countries had between 0.2 and 0.5 percent, among them Brazil, Mexico, and Egypt.
- Eighteen additional countries had between 0.1 and 0.2 percent, among them the Russian Federation, Saudi Arabia, and Australia.
- The remaining 28 countries had less than 0.1 percent of their land in urban use, among them Canada, the Democratic Republic of Congo, Libya, and Mongolia.

EXPLAINING THE VARIATIONS IN URBAN LAND COVER

Multiple regression models were able to explain 93 to 95 percent of the variations in urban land cover among countries (Angel et al. 2011b).

- A 10 percent increase in the urban population is associated with a 10.3 ± 0.1 percent increase in urban land cover.
- A 10 percent increase in GNP per capita is associated with a 1.8 ± 0.3 percent increase in urban land cover.
- A 10 percent increase in arable land per capita is associated with a 2.0 ± 0.0 percent increase in urban land cover.
- A 10 percent increase in gasoline prices is associated with a 2.5 ± 0.4 percent decrease in urban land cover.
- A 10 percent increase in informal settlements is associated with a 0.08 percent decrease in urban land cover.

In a second set of models, we obtained similar results using only the total land area in large cities in the country in the year 2000 as the dependent variable. In a third set of models, we used the urban land cover in individual cities in the year 2000 as the dependent variable. These latter models were able to explain almost 70 percent of the variations in urban land cover in the universe of 3,646 large cities. City population, GNP per capita, and arable land were found to have similar effects on urban land cover in individual cities as those identified for countries. However, the coefficient for gasoline prices was not significantly different from 0 at the 95 percent confidence level.

Increased levels of GNP per capita generate increased land consumption by households, businesses, and public authorities in parallel with increased consumption of all resources. They also lead to higher land consumption by decreasing average household size, thus increasing the number of units required to house a given population, as well as the floor area of dwelling units and hence the land required to accommodate those dwellings.

All in all, the statistical models were found to be robust and were able to explain a large amount of the variation in urban land cover among cities and countries. Variations in climate, cultural traditions, or the policy environment among countries may matter less than the fundamental forces giving shape to the spatial extent of cities: population, income, low-cost land on the urban periphery, and inexpensive transport.

CONCLUSION

We now have answers to the question posed at the beginning of this chapter. During the past two centuries, urban land cover has been growing very rapidly compared to earlier periods, yet by the year 2000—when half of the world's population lived in cities—urban areas worldwide occupied less than one-half of 1 percent of the total land area of all countries. In a representative global sample of 30 cities, urban land cover grew sixteenfold, on average, between 1930 and 2000. It grew at a global average rate of 3.3 per year. At these longer-term growth rates, global urban land cover will double in 21 years.

In a global sample of 120 cities, urban land cover expanded at a rate of 3.7 percent per year in the final decade of the twentieth century, while the population of cities grew at an average rate of only 1.6 percent per year. At these shorter-term growth rates, global urban land cover will double in 19 years. Urban expansion is driven by urban population growth; increasing household incomes leading to higher land consumption by households, which become smaller while occupying larger homes; expanding businesses and public facilities accompanying higher household incomes; and inexpensive transport.

European cities were more compact and less sprawled in the 1950s than they are today, and urban sprawl is now a common phenomenon throughout Europe.

European Environment Agency (2006, 5)

CHAPTER 11

The Persistent Decline in Urban Densities

How dense are urban areas, how are urban densities changing over time, why, and why should it matter?

Any cursory survey of the literature on urban sprawl, from the purely abstract treatise to the purely polemical tract, would reveal that low population density or density decline is its most salient characteristic (Brueckner 2000; Bruegmann 2005; Hayden 2004; Torrens and Alberti 2000). The empirical evidence presented and explained in this chapter shows that average urban population densities in different world regions vary by more than a decimal order of magnitude, that they are now in decline practically everywhere, and that they have been in decline for a century or more. In other words, to amplify what we observed in Accra, Ghana, in chapter 10, urban land cover has been growing at a faster rate than the urban population.

The decline in the average population density of the United States going back to 1920 and earlier has been observed, recorded, and explained by Mills (1972). Fulton et al. (2001) and Overman, Puga, and Turner (2008) provided empirical evidence on its further decline in recent years. Density decline has now been detected in Europe as well. What has not been so evident is that this phenomenon is global in scope and also includes cities in developing countries.

The statistical evidence presented here contradicts the early claims of Berry, Simmons, and Tennant (1963, 401) that "non-Western cities experience increasing overcrowding, constant compactness, and a lower degree of expansion at the periphery than in the West." It also contradicts the more recent claims of Acioly (2000, 127) that "there was evidence that a general process of change was leading to more compact cities" in developing countries. Moreover, it contradicts the claims of Richardson, Bae, and Baxamusa (2000, 25) that cities in developing countries "are not becoming significantly less compact in spite of decelerating population growth and the beginnings of decentralization."

This is important because most urban population growth (and most urban expansion) in the coming decades will take place in developing countries. Their urban population will grow at a rate five times faster than that in more developed countries. And while the urban population of the developed countries will stabilize at around 1 billion people, that of developing countries is projected to increase from 2 billion in 2000 to 4 billion in 2030 and to 5.5 billion in 2050 (United Nations Population Division 2008, file 3). In addressing urban expansion as a global phenomenon, we must pay special attention to cities in developing countries, yet without sacrificing our global perspective.

HISTORICAL EVIDENCE OF LONG-TERM DENSITY DECLINE

Fine-grained census tract data in digital form are now available for some U.S. cities from 1910 onward. These data allow us to measure average urban tract density in U.S. cities as the ratio of the total population living in urban tracts to their total area. Urban tracts are census tracts that contain more than 1,000 persons per square mile (3.86 persons per hectare). The urban tract population of Baltimore, Maryland, for example, increased from 554,000 in 1910 to 1.89 million in 2000, while its urban tract area increased from 5,640 to 128,000 hectares. Its urban tract density, therefore, declined from

FIGURE 11.1
The General Decline in Average Tract Densities in 20 U.S. Cities, 1910–2000

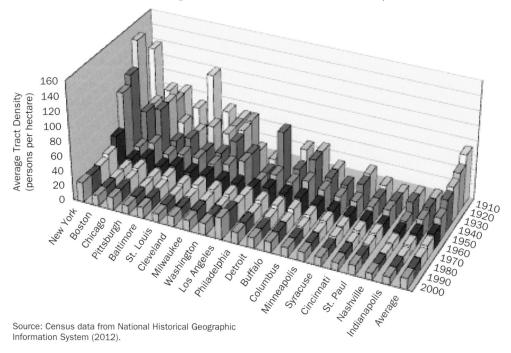

Source: Census data from National Historical Geographic
Information System (2012).

98 to 15 persons per hectare during this period. We investigated the changes in average urban tract densities in 20 U.S. cities in every decade between 1910 and 2000 (figure 11.1). For 7 of these cities, tract density maps were available from 1910 onward; for 11, from 1930 onward; and for 2, from 1940 onward.

This investigation yielded quite robust results. The average tract density of all these cities taken together declined in every decade since 1910, from 69.6 persons per hectare in 1910 to 14.6 persons per hectare in 2000, almost a fivefold decline. Fitting an exponential curve to this average density in every decade from 1910 to 2000, we found that the average annual rate of decline for the entire period, assuming a constant rate, was 1.92 percent. Declines in average tract density between any two consecutive censuses were registered in 124 of the 153 observations, or 81 percent of the time. Subjecting these 153 individual observations to a single-sample statistical test, we found that the average decline between consecutive censuses was significantly different from zero, and that it averaged 1.55 percent per annum.

Short-term rates of decline in the average tract density of U.S. cities, based on two data points 10 years apart, appear to have peaked in 1940s and 1950s, when they averaged 3 percent per annum, and are now on the decrease, averaging only 0.3 percent per annum in the 1990s (figure 11.2). In fact, between 1990 and 2000, six cities in this group registered an increase in average tract density: New York, Washington, Los Angeles, St. Paul, Syracuse, and Nashville. Hence, while average densities in U.S. cities have been in general decline for almost a century, they may now be reaching a plateau and even gradually increasing.

The data shown in red in figure 11.2 are for the 20 U.S. cities for which we have data from 1910 to 2000. The data shown in blue are for a larger set of 65 metropolitan areas that had populations in excess of 50,000 in 1950. The pattern of decline is the same for both sets of cities. The rate of decline began to slow down rapidly during the 1950s, reversed itself in the 1960s, and then continued to decline from the 1970s onward, indicating that average tract densities in U.S. cities have now

FIGURE 11.2

Average Rate of Annual Tract Density Change in Two Sets of U.S. Cities, 1910–2000

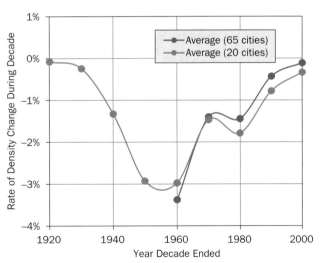

Source: Census data from National Historical Geographic Information System (2012).

been in decline for almost a century. Was this decline particular to the United States or was it a global phenomenon?

We used our global representative sample of 30 cities, for which we have data from 1800 to 2000 in roughly 20-year intervals, to calculate the average built-up area density of each city as the ratio of its historical population to its built-up area at a given map date. We calculated the built-up area density in each city in this representative sample at each map date and at the end of each decade. Because of the lack of administrative district maps that corresponded to the population estimates, it was not possible to ensure that populations strictly matched the built-up areas identified in the maps. Thus, we could not ensure consistency in the measurement of built-up areas from one period to another, nor could we make sure that city populations corresponded exactly to their built-up areas in every time period. We could only use this representative sample to explore whether the long-term decline in average density observed in the set of 20 U.S. cities was due to American exceptionalism or whether it was part of a global historical trend.

Our analysis of the composite built-up area maps of the global representative sample of 30 cities allowed us to observe that, on the whole, cities experienced both increasing and declining densities in the nineteenth century—before the emergence of inexpensive urban transport and the acceleration of economic development—and mostly declining densities in the twentieth century. Figure 11.3 illustrates the change in built-up area density in Mexico City, Mexico, from 1807 to 2000. The figure identifies the highest density peak of 674 persons per hectare in 1910 and shows the density decline in later periods. The city's densities increased in a regular fashion in the nineteenth century and declined in a regular fashion in the twentieth century. If we fit an exponential curve to the declining densities from their peak in 1910 to the year 2000, the average rate of

FIGURE 11.3
Density Change in Mexico City, Mexico, 1807–2000

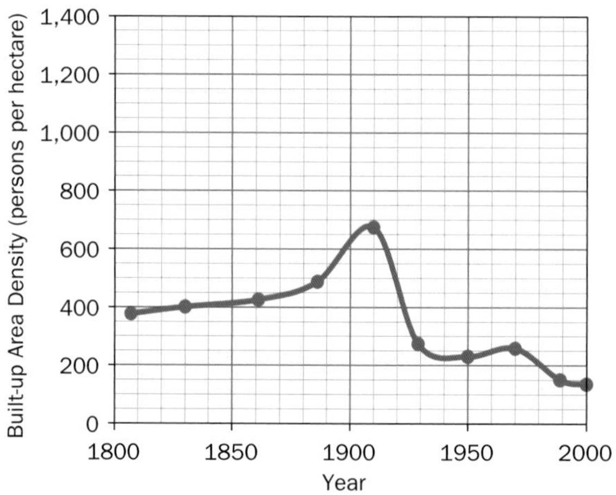

Source: Based on data from Angel et al. (2012, 295).

density decline during this period was 1.49 percent per annum. Overall, there was a fivefold decline from peak density in Mexico City between 1910 and 2000.

Similar graphs, drawn for all 30 cities in the representative sample, showed that built-up area densities peaked, on average, in 1894 ± 15 years and then began to decline (figure 11.4). The density decline generally started in the last two decades of the

FIGURE 11.4
Changes in the Built-up Area Density of 30 Cities in 6 World Regions, 1800–2000

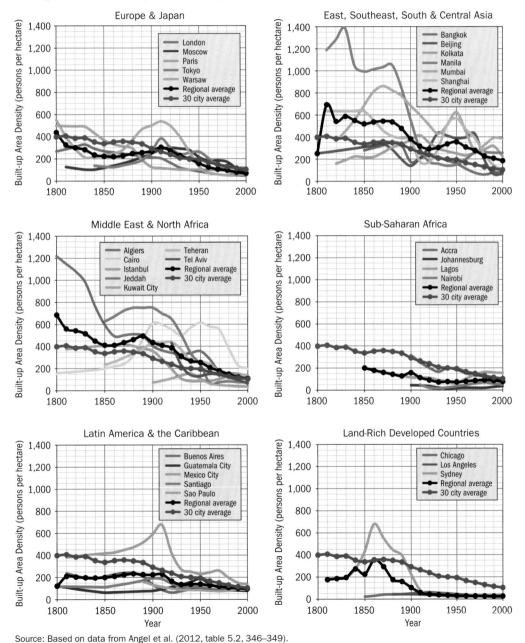

Source: Based on data from Angel et al. (2012, table 5.2, 346–349).

nineteenth century, several decades before the advent of the automobile, although Guatemala City, the latest city in this group to attain a density peak, did not reach that point until 1950 (figure 11.5). For the 25 cities shown, densities declined fourfold from their peak, from an average of 397 persons per hectare to an average of 102 persons per hectare circa 2000, at an average annual rate of 1.5 percent. At this rate of density decline, when the population of cities in developing countries doubles, from 2 to 4 billion between 2000 and 2030, as expected, the land occupied by these cities will triple. When the urban population in these countries increases from 2 to 5.5 billion between 2000 and 2050, as expected, the urban land it will occupy will increase sixfold.

FIGURE 11.5
Density Decline in 25 Cities from the Peak Density Year to circa 2000

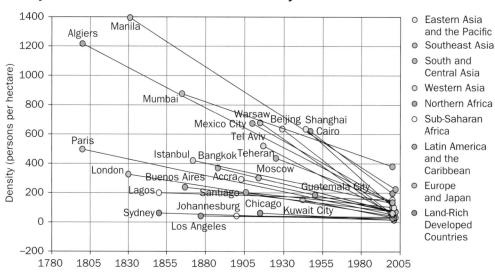

Source: Based on data from Angel et al. (2012, table 5.2, 346–349).

These data suggest that density decline is both a long-term historical phenomenon and a global phenomenon. More recent data for 1990–2000, collected for a global sample of cities in a rigorous manner that allowed for global intercity comparisons, made it possible to compare densities among cities worldwide, to test whether density decline is indeed a global phenomenon, and to estimate recent regional and global rates of density decline.

DIFFERENCES IN DENSITIES AND RATES OF DENSITY DECLINE IN THE GLOBAL SAMPLE OF 120 CITIES, 1990–2000

The empirical investigation of densities in the global sample of 120 cities revealed several interesting patterns that, as far as we could tell, were not detected in earlier studies.

First, there was a surprisingly wide variation in average population densities in the global sample. In 2000, for example, the ratio between the highest observed density in

Downtown Hong Kong, China, and downtown Tacoma, Washington, illustrate striking contrasts in density.

Hong Kong, China (550 persons per hectare) and the lowest observed density in St. Catharines, Canada, or Tacoma, Washington (15.7 persons per hectare) was 35.

Second, densities in the sample were by no means normally distributed around some expected global average. In 1990, for example, the global average was 144 persons per hectare while the median was 103 persons per hectare, and densities in two-thirds of the cities had lower densities than the global average. A similar pattern prevailed in the year 2000 (figure 11.6). The global average was 112 persons per hectare, the global median was 86 persons per hectare, and again two-thirds of the cities had lower densities than the global average.

Third, and related to the second observation, the density of cities appeared to decrease in a systematic fashion as their density rank increased, leading to the postulation of a

FIGURE 11.6
Density Distribution in the Global Sample of 120 Cities, 1990 and 2000

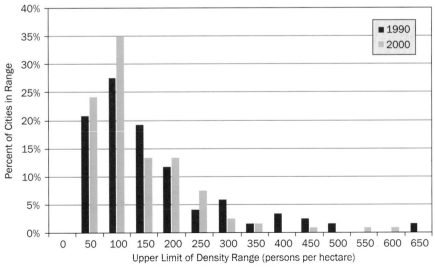

Source: Based on data from Angel et al. (2012, table 5.1, 322–345).

rank-density rule. When cities in the global sample of 120 cities were ranked in a decreasing order of their densities, those densities were proportional to the natural logarithm of their rank. The predicted value of the highest density was 634 and the predicted density value of any city was found to be proportional to the logarithm of its rank (figure 11.7), producing an almost perfect fit. The rank-density rule is different from the rank-size rule, also known as Zipf's Law (see chapter 8). That rule postulates that in large countries the city's population would be inversely proportional to its rank. The rank-density rule, on the other hand, postulates that the population density of a city is inversely proportional to the logarithm of its rank.

Fourth, densities within individual world regions were found to be similar to each other, while densities among different world regions were found to be significantly different from one another. Figure 11.8 displays the average densities in the nine world regions in 1990 and 2000, as well as their 95 percent confidence levels. Densities were significantly lower in land-rich developed countries (United States, Canada, and Australia) than in all other regions. They averaged 27 ± 4 persons per hectare and 23 ± 4 persons per hectare in 1990 and 2000 respectively. In contrast, they averaged 83 ± 17 persons per hectare and 67 ± 15 persons per hectare respectively in Europe and Japan in these two periods.

FIGURE 11.7
City Density as a Function of Its Density Rank, 1990

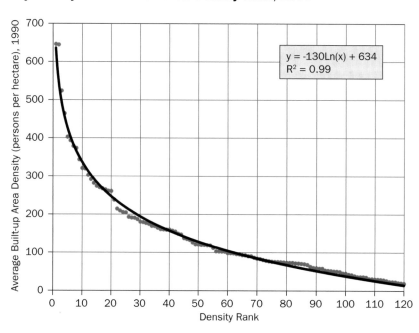

$$y = -130Ln(x) + 634$$
$$R^2 = 0.99$$

Source: Based on data from Angel et al. (2012, table 5.1, 322–345).

FIGURE 11.8
Average Built-up Area Densities in World Regions, 1990 and 2000

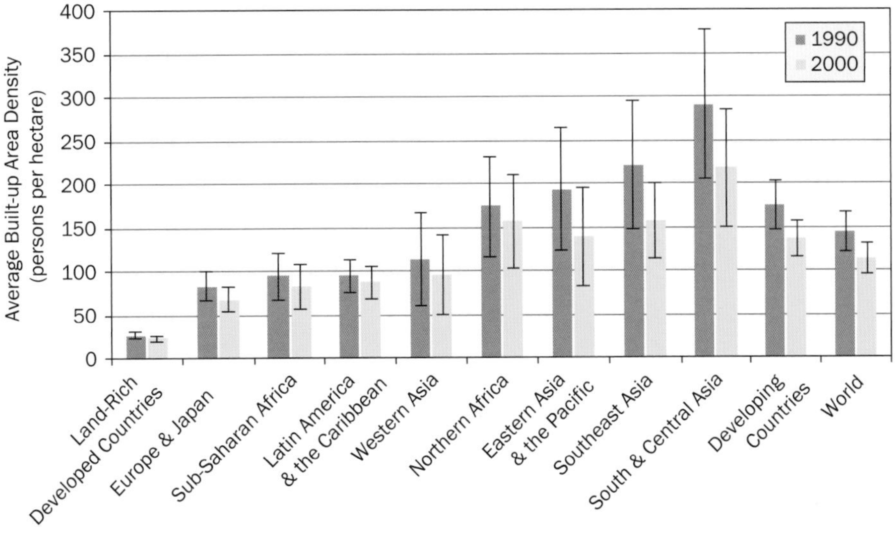

Source: Based on data from Angel et al. (2012, table 5.1, 322–345).

Average densities in developing country regions were higher than those of Europe and Japan, but not always significantly higher. Only in Eastern Asia and the Pacific, Southeast Asia, and South and Central Asia were they significantly higher than those observed in Europe and Japan in both periods. That said, densities in the developing countries as a whole were significantly higher than those of Europe and Japan, averaging 174 ± 28 persons per hectare in 1990 and 136 ± 21 persons per hectare in 2000. In general, we found that urban densities in Europe and Japan were half those of developing countries, and that urban densities in land-rich developed countries were one-third those of Europe and Japan.

Patterns of density change between 1990 and 2000, most notably its decline during this period, also showed a number of interesting regularities.

First, the average built-up area densities of cities worldwide declined significantly, from a mean of 144 persons per hectare in 1990 to a mean of 112 persons per hectare in 2000. Between 1990 and 2000, average built-up area densities declined in 72 of the 88 developing-country cities and in all 32 cities in developed countries (figure 11.9). Only 16 cities exhibited an increase in their average built-up area densities during this period, and only 5 of them increased at a rate greater than 1 percent. The highest rates of increase were observed in Pretoria and Johannesburg, South Africa, at 3.3 and 1.7 percent respectively, and these were clearly outliers associated with the densification of their city centers brought about with the abrupt end of apartheid. The city-state of Singapore, which has been following an aggressive densification policy by largely

FIGURE 11.9

A Comparison of Densities in the Global Sample of 120 Cities, 1990 and 2000

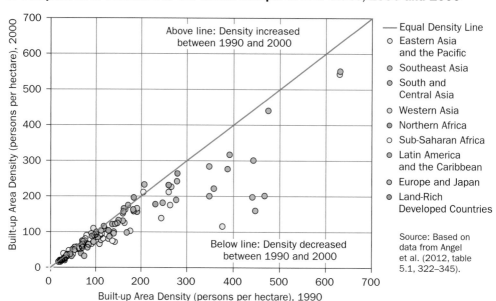

restricting residential development to dense high-rise neighborhoods, registered an increase in average density of only 0.25 percent per annum.

Second, there was no significant difference in the average rate of decline in built-up area densities in all nine regions (figure 11.10), and mean built-up area densities worldwide declined at an annual rate of 2.01 percent during this period. At this rate of density decline, the built-up area of cities in developing countries will increase no less than 3.75-fold between 2000 and 2030 to accommodate the expected doubling of their populations.

Third, although there were no significant differences in the observed rates of density decline among regions, higher densities declined faster than lower ones. The co-efficient of density as an independent variable in a linear regression model with density change as a dependent variable was found to be negative and significantly different from zero. This can be detected although not strictly observed in figures 11.9 and 11.10. Rates of density decline can be observed to be higher in those cities and regions where densities in 1990 were higher.

Fourth, density declines were strongly associated with increases in per capita income —the faster the increase in per capita income, the steeper the decline. The change in density between 1990 and 2000 as a function of income change and initial density is illustrated in figure 11.11 for a subsample of 20 cities from the global sample.

This chapter does not aim to explain all of these patterns or account for all of the observed regularities. In truth, it remains unclear why densities should obey a variation

FIGURE 11.10
Average Annual Rates of Density Decline in World Regions, 1990–2000

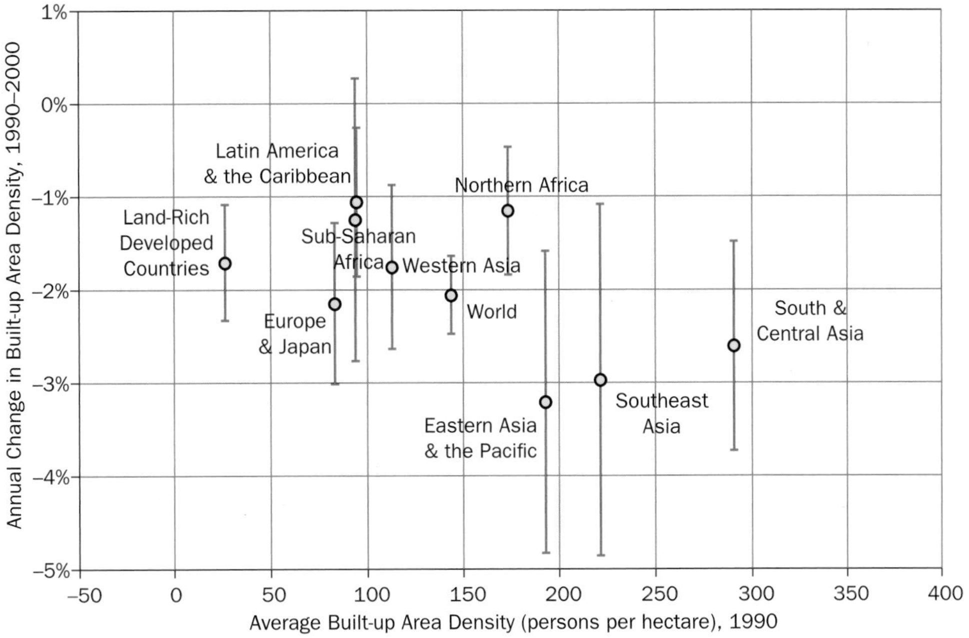

Source: Based on data from Angel et al. (2012, table 5.1, 322–345).

of Zipf's Law, or why they now appear to decline faster in higher-density cities than in lower-density ones. We have not uncovered a body of theory that postulates these regularities, and therefore leave these questions open to further research by interested scholars. We shall satisfy ourselves with the modest task of employing the well-known and now quite familiar classical economic theory of urban spatial structure to explain the observed density differences among cities with different incomes, transport costs, topographical constraints, and agricultural land prices. We can also test our conjectures that observed density differences may be affected by the size of the city population and by its prevailing income inequality. These conjectures cannot be strictly derived from the classical theory.

Multiple regression models were used to test a number of hypotheses derived from the classic economic theory of urban spatial structure (Angel et al. 2010). The models could explain as much as 75 percent of the variation in average built-up area density among the 120 cities in the sample.

- Cities in countries with higher incomes—related to higher land consumption, extensive car ownership, and lower household sizes—had lower densities. A doubling of income per capita was associated with a 40 ± 1 percent decline in average density.

FIGURE 11.11
Density Change and Income Change in a Subsample of 20 Cities, 1990–2000

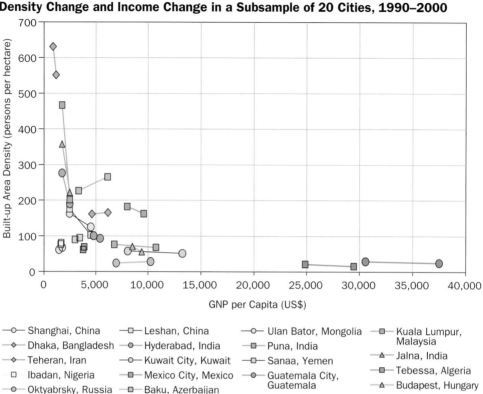

Sources: Based on density data from Angel et al. (2012, table 5.1, 322–345); and income data from World Bank (2012a).

- Large cities had much higher average densities than smaller ones. A doubling of the city population was associated with a 19 ± 1 percent increase in density.
- Cities in countries with higher gasoline prices had higher densities. A doubling of gasoline prices was associated with a 16 ± 2 percent increase in density.
- Cities in countries with extensive arable lands (a proxy variable for agricultural land prices) had lower densities. A doubling of arable land per capita was associated with a 25 ± 2 percent decline in average density.
- Cities with fewer geographical constraints on their expansion and cities in countries with higher levels of income inequality also had lower densities.

The results for built-up area densities for the global universe of 3,646 large cities (with populations of 100,000 or more in 2000) were similar to those obtained for the sample of 120 cities, but not identical. The differences in pixel size between the Landsat-based maps used for the sample of 120 cities and the Mod500-based digital maps used for the universe resulted in differences in the physical extent of cities between the two sets of maps; the Mod500 map may be somewhat less accurate in identifying the built-up areas of cities correctly.

That said, in the universe of cities as a whole, average built-up area densities in cities in land-rich developed countries in 2000 were still found to be roughly half those of cities in Europe and Japan, and the latter in turn were roughly half those of cities in developing countries. The average built-up area density in 2000 was 25 ± 1 persons per hectare in cities in land-rich developed countries; 50 ± 1 persons per hectare in cities in Europe and Japan; and 129 ± 3 persons per hectare in cities in developing countries. Again, all of these averages were significantly different from each other.

Multiple regression models based on the classic economic theory of urban spatial structure could explain only 40 percent of the variation in average built-up area density among the 3,646 large cities in the universe. A lower percent of the variation could be explained because some of the countrywide explanatory variables that proved to be significant in the statistical models in the sample (specifically gasoline prices) were found not to be significant at the 95 percent level of confidence in the universe of large cities, possibly because of the large number of cities in a few individual countries. The universe contains 830 cities in China, for example, amounting to 23 percent of the total number of cities in the universe.

In the universe of cities taken as a whole we found various results, and a map of the average density of large cities in all 158 countries that had large cities in 2000 provides visual confirmation (figure 11.12).

FIGURE 11.12
Average Density of Large Cities in All Countries, 2000 (persons per hectare)

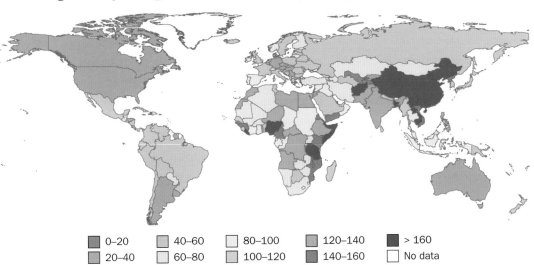

■ 0–20	■ 40–60	□ 80–100	■ 120–140	■ > 160
■ 20–40	□ 60–80	□ 100–120	■ 140–160	□ No data

Source: Angel et al. (2012 online).

- Cities in countries with higher incomes had lower densities. A doubling of income per capita was associated with a 25 ± 2 percent decline in average density.
- Large cities had much higher average densities than smaller cities. A doubling of the city population was associated with a 16 ± 0.2 percent increase in density.
- Cities in countries with extensive arable lands (a proxy variable for agricultural land prices) had lower densities. A doubling of arable land per capita was associated with a 27 ± 0.2 percent decline in average density.

DENSITY PROJECTIONS, 2000–2050

Based on these results, we project that future urban land cover in cities, countries, and regions worldwide may take place in three density change scenarios.

- High projection: Assumes a 2 percent annual rate of density decline, corresponding to the average rate of decline in the global sample of 120 cities in 1990–2000.
- Medium projection: Assumes a 1 percent annual rate of density decline, corresponding to an average rate of decline between the high and low projections.
- Low projection: Assumes constant densities, or a 0 percent annual rate of density decline, corresponding to the observed rate of urban tract density decline in the 1990s in U.S. cities.

In some countries, such as China and India, the high projections may prove to be more appropriate, while in others, including the United States, the low projection may prove to be more realistic. Low projections may also be associated with future increases in gasoline prices occasioned by monopolistic pricing practices, declining supplies, the increasing cost of production, or increased taxation. If the models discussed earlier are correct, then the doubling of gasoline prices every decade may indeed be sufficient to keep densities from declining. That said, the effect of raising gasoline prices on built-up area densities around the world could certainly benefit from further study.

The forces driving global urban expansion—population growth, urbanization, rising per capita incomes, cheap agricultural lands, efficient transport, and income inequality—are quite formidable. Accordingly, absent a highly effective policy intervention or a steep increase in travel costs in the future, there is little reason for urban expansion at declining densities to stop anytime soon.

In a survey of local consultants in each of the 120 cities in the global sample, conducted between 2006 and 2008, we were unable to identify best-practice examples of policy instruments that were associated with increasing the average density of built-up areas.

Even Portland, Oregon, which had adopted an urban growth boundary (UGB) in the mid-1970s to contain urban sprawl, did not manage to increase its built-up area density. In a recent study not yet published, we calculated the density of the built-up area in each census tract within the UGB and assigned each tract to a 10-kilometer-

FIGURE 11.13
Density Changes Within Portland, Oregon's Urban Growth Boundary, 1973–2005

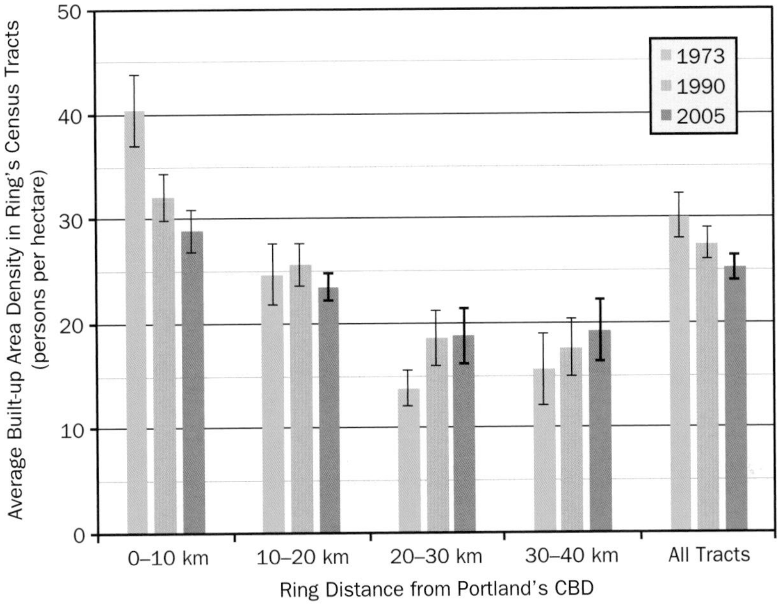

Note: The thin vertical bars are 95 percent confidence intervals.
Sources: Built-up area density data from Landsat imagery; and census tract population data from U.S. Bureau of the Census (1970–2010).

wide ring around Portland's CBD. Figure 11.13 displays the average built-up area density in census tracts in each ring as well as in all census tracts within the UGB in 1973, 1990, and 2005. We can say with a 95 percent level of confidence that the density of the built-up area of census tracts declined in the first ring and increased in the third ring between 1973 and 1990, and that overall density declined significantly between 1973 and 2005. All other density changes were found to be statistically insignificant. We can only conclude that Portland's UGB may have been successful in encouraging the infill of vacant land within it (see chapter 13). But, after being in place for some 30 years, it was still unsuccessful in increasing built-up area densities.

The search for cost-effective and politically acceptable infrastructure strategies, regulations, and tax regimes that can lead to significant overall densification in low-density cities must continue in earnest in order to make them more sustainable. At the same time, appropriate strategies for managing urban expansion at sustainable densities in rapidly growing cities in developing countries must be identified and employed effectively. No matter how we choose to act, however, we should remain aware that conscious and conscientious efforts to increase the density of our cities would require the reversal of a powerful and sustained global tendency for urban densities to decline.

The upper classes enjoy healthy country air and live in luxurious and comfortable dwellings which are linked to the center of Manchester by omnibuses which run every twenty to thirty minutes.

Friedrich Engels (1844, 54)

CHAPTER 12

From Centrality to Dispersal

How centralized are the residences and workplaces in cities, do they tend to disperse to the periphery over time, and if so, why, and why should it matter?

The pattern of centrality and dispersal in major cities around the world has undergone three important transformations over the past two centuries. The first, from the walking city to the monocentric city, began with the advent of the omnibus and the horsecar—an omnibus on rails—in the later decades of the nineteenth century. In the historic walking city, workplaces and residences were interspersed at uniformly high densities. In the monocentric city, spatial segregation of residences and workplaces began to occur. Both remained concentrated at high densities in the city center, but some residences began to disperse to the periphery at rapidly decreasing densities as distance from the center increased.

A second and less radical transformation—the decentralization of the monocentric city—began in the early years of the twentieth century with the introduction of trolleys and commuter railroads. The overall spatial structure remained the same as the city expanded outward. It was still a monocentric city, but residential densities no longer declined at a rapid pace with distance from the city center. They now declined at a slower pace, as the low-density suburban periphery was gradually filled in and rebuilt at higher densities.

A third and more radical transformation, from the monocentric to the polycentric city, began in the middle decades of the twentieth century with the rapid increase in the use of cars, buses, and trucks. Trucks, in particular, allowed for the dispersal of industrial workplaces, but commercial and service workplaces in most cities remained concentrated in central areas. At the outset, commuting patterns remained largely radial, from the periphery into the city center, except in metropolitan areas in the United States, where periphery-to-periphery travel gradually became predominant. Still, traffic congestion at the center, coupled with improved roads and bus services on the periphery, encouraged the continued yet slow dispersal of workplaces into suburban municipalities worldwide. Residential densities remained high in the central city and also increased in the periphery through infill and rebuilding.

By the end of the twentieth century, many cities had become truly polycentric, with the large majority of trips originating and terminating outside the central city area (Muller 2004). Some aspects of this global pattern of centrality and dispersal allow precise measurement, but others remain obscure because of the lack of good comparative data, especially regarding the suburbanization of workplaces. As workplaces disperse into the urban periphery, they need not necessarily be distributed uniformly. Indeed, many writers have noted that there are good reasons for workplaces to agglomerate in fewer locations where they can take advantage of common services, exchange labor and ideas, be closer to transit hubs or established towns, or create a greater pull for their services from the surrounding population (Bogart 1998; Coe, Kelly, and Yeung 2007; O'Flaherty 2005).

BUENOS AIRES, ARGENTINA

The city of Buenos Aires offers an illustrative case for explaining these transformations from centrality to dispersal in more detail. In 1810, the year Argentina gained its independence from Spain, the capital city of Buenos Aires had a population of 45,000 occupying an area of some 200 hectares on the western bank of the La Plata River at an average density of 225 persons per hectare. Its life centered on the port—its citizens are still referred to as *porteños*—and it was clearly a walking city. As Argentina's main gateway to the rest of the world, the city thrived on a combination of commerce and banking, trade with the interior, and its position as the seat of the federal government. The country gained importance as a food exporter and a major market for European goods, and between 1857 and 1865 four new railroad lines were built from the city into the interior, sealing its position as the country's main commercial center (Sargent 1974).

By 1869, the city's population increased more than threefold to 171,000, while its area also grew more than threefold to occupy a semicircle of 714 hectares, with a 4-kilometer (km) radius around the historical center. The average density in the center remained about 225 persons per hectare, but declined rapidly with distance from that center. Buenos Aires remained largely a walking city. Omnibuses—multiseat carriages pulled by horses on generally unpaved roads—were used as the major form of public transportation, but did not circulate beyond the walking city perimeter. While settlements began to develop around railway stations in the interior, steam-powered trains were infrequent and people who worked in the city typically lived in the city.

The horsecar—a carriage pulled by horses on rails and an improvement on the omnibus—was introduced to Buenos Aires in the mid-1860s at the same time it was introduced in several other Latin American cities. Horsecars were faster than omnibuses and could retain their speed in all weather conditions, thus propelling a second phase of the city's expansion and beginning its transformation into a monocentric city. Initially, services were intermittent, there were no designated stations or transfers, and "[m]ost of the lines were well within a two-kilometer radius that defined the city core" (Sargent 1974, 28). Most people did not depend on the horsecars for their journey to work, but the lines gradually expanded into residential subdivisions in concentric rings around the core. By the end of the nineteenth century, the extension of regular and reliable horsecar service helped to expand the city beyond the walking city range.

By 1895 the city's dense network of horsecar lines serviced an area of 69 square kilometers (km²) and its edges were some 5 km away from its traditional center along the river (figure 12.1). Still, densities at the historical center remained high, averaging

FIGURE 12.1
Horsecar Lines in the Built-up Area of Buenos Aires, Argentina, 1895

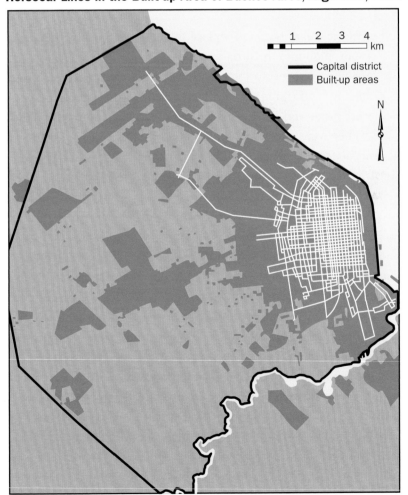

Sources: For horsecar lines, Sargent (1974, figure 13, 37); for built-up area, Vapñarsky (2000).

228 persons per hectare, but they declined appreciably as distance from the center increased. The horsecar transformed Buenos Aires from a walking city into a monocentric city by extending its perimeter while maintaining the dominance of the center.

The administrative boundaries of Buenos Aires were extended in 1888 to form an area of 207 km² fanning out of the historical center, surrounded by the wide *Avenida General Paz* as its new city limit, and forming the Federal Capital District. In 1898, the municipal authorities drew up a street grid plan for the entire district.

> The plan was published in 1904 and the private expansion process started the same year, fostered by the real estate and tram networks, and guided by a public plan of streets that not only promised each of the neighborhoods emerging from those market impulses future integration into a collective layout but also offered them the public support of potential urbanism. (Gorelik 2003, 149–150)

By 1898, the electric trolley began to replace the horsecar, greatly extending the reach of public transportation into the urban periphery (figure 12.2). The first trolleys connected the surrounding towns to the city center, while later ones both displaced the horsecars within the central area and vastly extended the area within commuting range. The trolleys were faster and more reliable than horsecars, and they could operate for longer hours. They were also more comfortable, running on heavier rails on a concrete base, and better organized, especially after the unification of all lines under the Anglo-Argentine Tramway Company in 1910 (Sargent 1974).

The railways also added momentum to the expansion of the commuting range during this period. The four main railway lines into the city were already established by 1898, and one additional line of minor importance was added in 1900. "The number of inbound daily trains to Buenos Aires increased from 306 in 1898 to 751 in 1914," and the number of passengers increased fivefold during this period (Sargent 1974, 69). Trains were powered by steam, a mode more suitable for lines with long distances between stops, but their increased frequency made land adjacent to stations more attractive for commuters, especially those coming from further destinations than the areas served only by trolleys.

By 1910, the population of Greater Buenos Aires increased to 1.41 million people and its built-up area increased to 255 km², an area already greater than that designated for the Federal Capital District. Residential densities in the historical center remained as high as before, while those in the periphery declined with distance from the city center, albeit at a slower rate.

The role of the railroads in the dispersal of Buenos Aires into a monocentric city became more pronounced with their electrification, which started in 1916 and was

FIGURE 12.2

Trolley Lines in the Built-up Area of Buenos Aires, Argentina, 1910

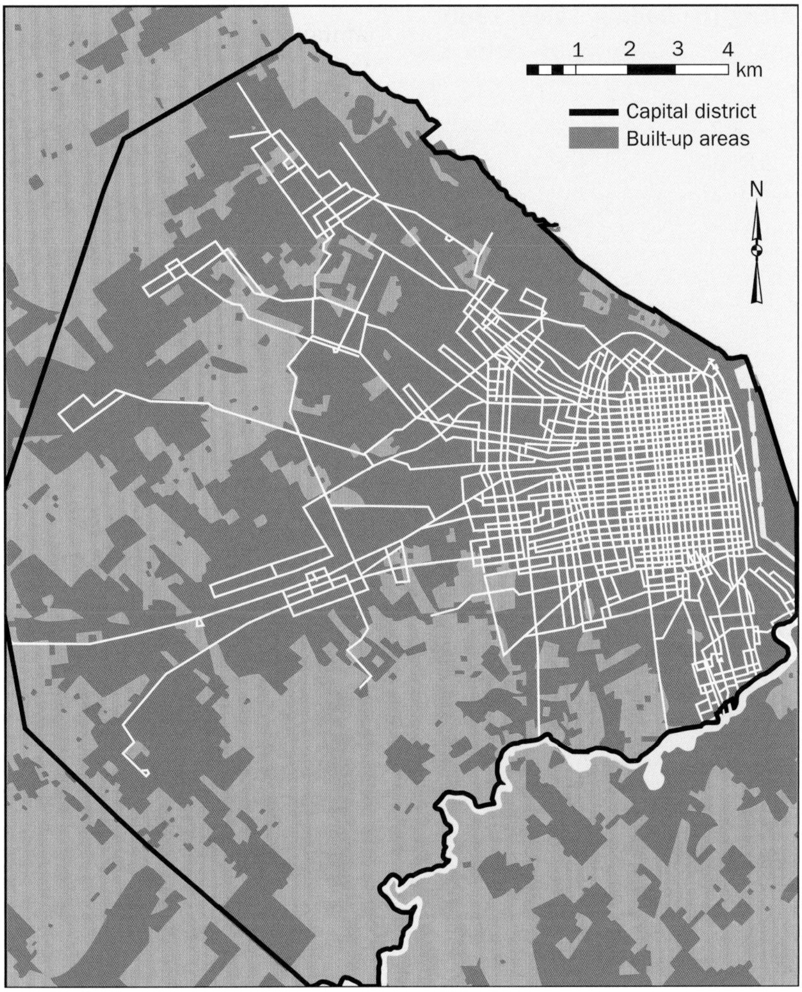

Sources: For trolley lines, Sargent (1974, figure 18, 68); for built-up area, Vapñarsky (2000).

completed by 1931 (Sargent 1974). The railroads facilitated the settlement of large areas outside the Federal Capital District, out of reach of most trolley lines. Buses, introduced in the 1920s, did not contribute much to fringe development, as most rural roads remained unpaved. The railroads thus dominated the development of the *alrededores*, the suburban municipalities outside the district. "Passenger volumes in the *alrededores* rose sharply from an estimated 6,400,000 in 1896 to 82,000,000 in 1930" (Sargent 1974, 96). By the end of the 1930s, suburban expansion, largely residential in character, followed the railway lines into the periphery (figure 12.3).

The reliance of the majority of the working population on essentially radial transportation lines for their journey to work ensured that Greater Buenos Aires remained a

FIGURE 12.3
Extension of the Built-up Area of Buenos Aires, Argentina, Along the Railway Lines, 1960

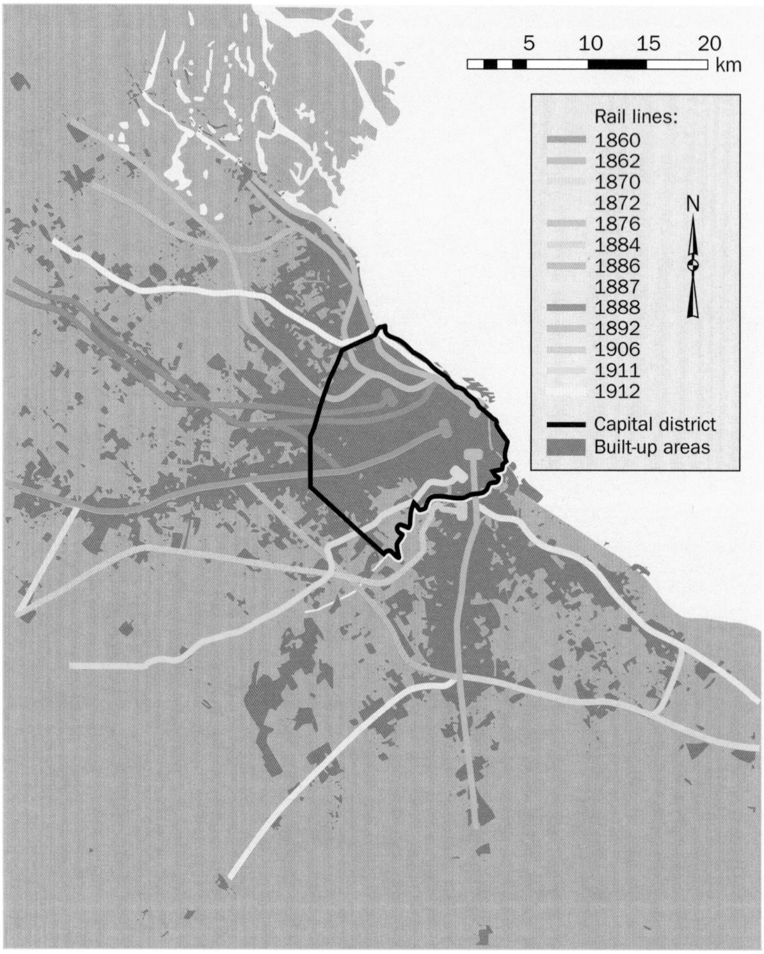

Source: For railway lines, Sargent (1974, figure 6, 8); for built-up area, Vapñarsky (2000).

monocentric city. Its spatial structure was reinforced by federal authorities who contin-ued to favor radial lines instead of ring roads and supplemented them with subway connections at their terminals. Federal officials also improved public services within the Federal Capital District, such as the pavement of roads and the provision of water and sewer mains, while neglecting to improve them in the *alrededores*.

Still, the monocentric city began to show signs of transformation into a polycentric city by the 1930s, when industrial plants began to relocate from the center into the periphery. As the use of cars and trucks became more predominant, and as congestion lengthened commuting times into the Federal Capital District, the decentralization of industrial workplaces was accelerated. Between 1935 and 1994, for example, the share of industrial jobs in the district decreased from 80 percent to 37 percent (figure 12.4). By 2001, the population of Greater Buenos Aires increased to 12 million and its built-up area increased to 2,071 km^2. The district had a population of 2.8 million and a built-up area of 165 km^2. By 2010, the share of all public transport trips in Greater Buenos Aires that had the district as their destination decreased to 18.6 percent, of which 6.6 percent originated in the district (Secretaria de Transporte 2010). In other words, more than four-fifths of all destinations by public transport were in municipalities outside the Federal Capital District. Although the district continues to provide a large number of commercial and service jobs, and although residential densities in the center remain high, we can conclude that by 2010 Buenos Aires was clearly transformed into a polycentric city.

The dispersal pattern in Greater Buenos Aires can be measured by the flattening of its residential density curve over time. Historical data on built-up area density as a

FIGURE 12.4

Share of Industrial Jobs in Buenos Aires, Argentina, Inside and Outside the Federal Capital District, 1935–1994

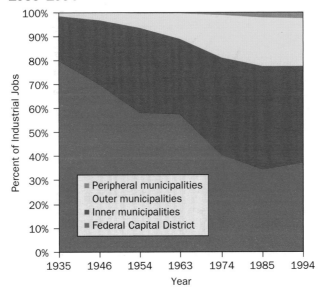

Source: Instituto Nacional de Estadistica y Censo (INDEC), various dates.

function of distance from the city center were calculated by Gonzalo Rodriguez for the period 1869–2001, using census data and maps of the built-up area in different periods originally drawn by Vapñarsky (2000). As the city became more dispersed and densities everywhere become more similar, the gradient of the density curve declined and density curves became flatter. The population and built-up area data from Rodriguez for 54 districts in Greater Buenos Aires for four time periods (1869, 1910, 1965, and 2001) were used to graph the built-up area density for each district against the distance of its centroid (its geographical center) from City Hall (figure 12.5). A negative exponential curve[1] is then fitted to the data points for each date. While densities in the center of Buenos Aires remain high—in 2001, the average density in districts within 4 km from the city center was still 245 persons per hectare—the curves definitely become flatter over time. The gradient of the density curve for Greater Buenos Aires declined from 0.36 in 1869 to 0.06 in 2001.

FIGURE 12.5
The Flattening of the Density Curve in Greater Buenos Aires, Argentina, 1869–2001

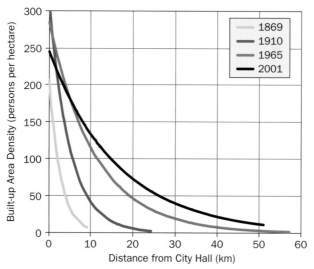

Sources: Calculated from unpublished density data obtained from Gonzalo Rodriguez, Buenos Aires, Argentina, based on INDEC census data; and Vapñarsky (2000).

U.S. CITIES

This flattening of the gradient of the density curve over time in cities worldwide has been observed by many scholars. "[V]irtually all cities in the developed world and most others elsewhere have decentralized over the last century or more—the density gradient has declined over time" (Anas, Arnott, and Small 1998, 15). Mills and Tan (1980) document this decline in a number of developing countries; Ingram and Carroll (1981) present similar evidence for Latin America; and Mills and Ohta (1976) present evidence for Japan. The classical economic model of the monocentric city, in fact, predicts that increases in income and reductions in the cost of transport will result in flatter density curve gradients (Anas, Arnott, and Small 1998).

---

1 See footnote 2 on page 150.

The measurement of this decline in a global sample of cities requires density data for small administrative districts for several decades, which are not readily available for most countries. In the United States, the declines in the values of both the density curve gradient and the density curve intercept in 20 U.S. cities during the twentieth century are displayed in figure 12.6. During this period, the average value of the gradient declined fourfold, from 0.22 in 1910 to 0.05 in 2000 and at a rate similar to that in Greater Buenos Aires. At the same time, the average value of the density curve intercept declined sixfold, from 325 to 50 persons per hectare between 1910 and 2000, as American cities suburbanized and as densities at different distances from the city center became more and more similar. Thus, while in Buenos Aires, central city residential densities remained high at 245 persons per hectare in 2001, in the United States they declined to one-fifth that value as central cities lost a large share of their population to the suburbs.

The decline in the gradient of the density curve in and of itself does not necessarily imply the transformation of urban areas from a monocentric to a polycenteric spatial structure, and may or may not be associated with such a transformation. The shift to a polycentric spatial structure involves the dispersal of workplaces as well as residences, which may accelerate the decline in the value of the residential density gradient, but is not required for the gradient to decline.

The emergence of polycentric cities with dispersed workplaces in the twentieth century was largely facilitated by the introduction of cars and trucks (Glaeser and Kahn 2004). The former reduced the dependence of commuters on radial public transportation lines, while the latter reduced the dependence of firms on ready access to central rail depots for the delivery of raw materials and finished products. Firms

FIGURE 12.6
Decline in the Average Value of the Density Curve Gradient and Density Curve Intercept in 20 U.S. Cities, 1910–2000

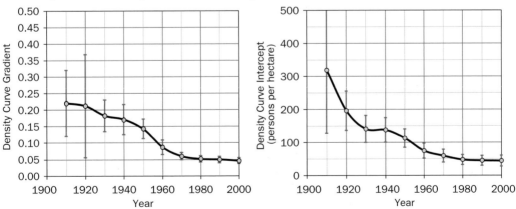

Note: Vertical bars are 95 percent confidence intervals.
Source: Census data from National Historical Geographic Information System (2012).

could now move to the suburbs to locate in larger and more spacious facilities with ample parking on cheaper land and be more accessible to their workers by eliminating travel along congested streets in the city center. The dispersal of workplaces away from the central business district (CBD) has reduced the explanatory power of the classical monocentric model that assumed at the outset that all workplaces were concentrated in the CBD. This has led urban economists to search for more complex models of urban spatial structure that could account for the simultaneous location of both firms and residences in an economic equilibrium that maximized both the utility of households and the profits of firms (Anas, Arnott, and Small 1998).

The dispersal of jobs away from the CBD in recent decades is confirmed by limited global comparative data on major metropolitan areas as reported by Kenworthy and Laube (1999). The authors collected data on commuting patterns in 47 cities, 40 of which had 1 million people or more in 1990—13 cities in the United States, 7 in Canada, 6 in Australia, 11 in Europe, 10 in Asia, and none in Latin America or Africa. They defined the CBD in each city as "the area with the most significant employment concentration in the metropolitan area and was generally decided in consultation with authorities in each city" (Kenworthy and Laube 1999, 35). They also defined the urbanized area of each city using land use maps and seeking to ensure "that all land that is predominantly urban in its use was included" (Kenworthy and Laube 1999, 38). On average, the area of the CBD in 1990 constituted only 1.8 ± 0.8 percent of the

Century City is a large concentration of workplaces in the Los Angeles metropolitan area outside its central business district, which can be seen in the distance.

Chicago's central business district accommodated less than one-sixth of the total number of workplaces in the metropolitan area in the year 2000.

urbanized area of 39 cities in their study for which data were available (in the 13 U.S. cities in the study, it was only 0.26 ± 0.08 percent).

The share of jobs in the CBD (in a subset of 29 of these cities where data were available) declined significantly from 25.4 percent in 1960 to 21.2 percent in 1970; it declined significantly again (in a subset of 38 cities where data were available) from 21.5 percent in 1970 to 18.1 percent in 1980; and it declined significantly yet again (in a subset of 41 cities where data were available) from 18.0 percent in 1980 to 16.2 percent in 1990. The only city in the sample in which the share of jobs in the CBD increased during this period was Tokyo, Japan, where it increased from 25.8 percent in 1960 to 26.1 percent in 1970, to 26.6 percent in 1980, and to 27.7 percent in 1990. On the whole, CBDs—loosely defined as the largest concentrations of workplaces in cities and metropolitan areas worldwide—may now contain fewer than one-fifth of the total jobs in these cities and metropolitan areas.

Commuting data for the year 2000 for a sample of 40 U.S. metropolitan areas show them to be quite different from Buenos Aires, because commuting by private automobile started earlier and remains much more prevalent in the United States. In 1960, there were 411 cars per 1,000 people in the United States compared with 55 cars in

Argentina. By 2002, the comparable results were 812 versus 186 cars. In 2009, only 5 percent of U.S. workers commuted to work by public transport (U.S. Bureau of Transportation Statistics 2010). Only a few cities—New York, Boston, Washington, DC, and Chicago, for example—had a significant share of commuter trips on public transport, largely on radial routes into the CBD (figure 12.7).

By the year 2000, all U.S. cities had made the transformation into a polycentric spatial structure, with the majority of workplaces firmly outside their central cores.

FIGURE 12.7
Commuter Rail Lines in the Chicago Metropolitan Area, 2012

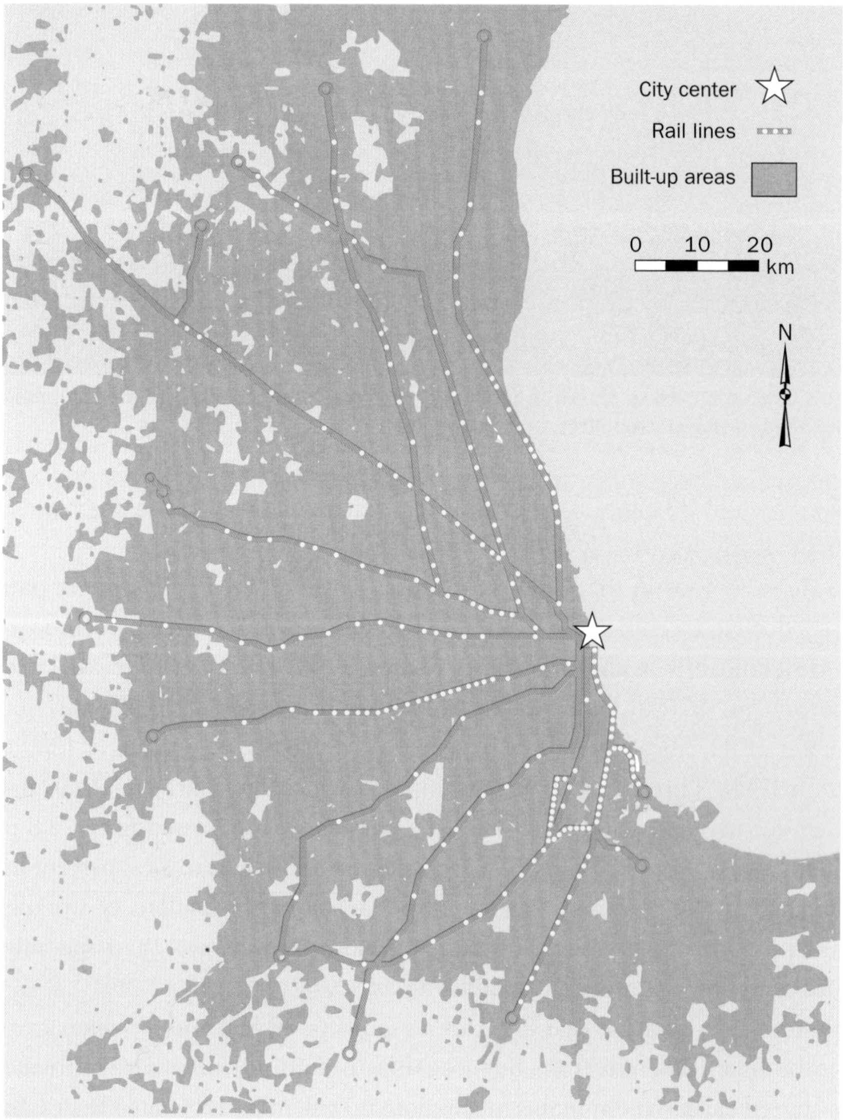

Sources: Commuter rail lines from Chicago Metrarail (2012); and built-up area for 2000 adapted from Angel et al. (2012, 66).

FIGURE 12.8

Shares of Circular Cordon Crossings in Chicago, Illinois, and Los Angeles, California, for Four Types of Commuter Trips

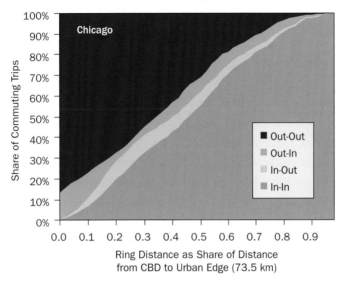

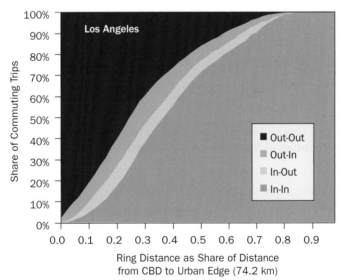

Source: Drawn from unpublished data obtained from Alejandro M. Blei, University of Illinois at Chicago.

Figure 12.8 shows the share of commuter trips in Chicago and Los Angeles in every circular cordon around their city centers. In the case of Chicago, the *x* axis shows the distance of the cordon as a percentage of the circular cordon with a radius of 73.5 km that encircles the entire metropolitan area. The *y* axis shows the share of trips that remain within the cordon (In-In), the share crossing it inward (Out-In), the share crossing it outward (In-Out), and the share remaining outside the cordon altogether (Out-Out).

The total number of commuter destinations within a circle with a radius equal to 6 percent of the maximum extent of Chicago (4.4 km) amounts to 15.8 percent of all commuter trip destinations in the metropolitan area. Thus, more than five in six destinations in the Chicago area remain outside that circle, and Chicago has a higher-than-average value with respect to other U.S. cities. The corresponding value for Los Angeles, for example, is only 6.2 percent.

A second interesting feature of polycentric U.S. cities is that workplaces farther away from the CBD now require a shorter rather than a longer time for the journey to work. Figure 12.9 shows the average travel time of all workers to their workplaces in a given census tract in Atlanta, Georgia, as a function of its distance from the CBD in the year 2000. Travel time to workplaces in Atlanta declined significantly as the distances increased. Workers commuted, on average, for 34 minutes to workplaces in the CBD, 28 minutes to workplaces 30 km from the CBD, and only 22 minutes to workplaces 60 km from the CBD.

In the sample of 40 U.S. metropolitan areas, average travel time to workplaces in 2000 decreased significantly as the distance of the workplace from the CBD increased in 20 metropolitan areas, including the 15 largest ones. In an additional 19 cities, mostly midsize ones, average travel time to workplaces was essentially the same regardless of the distance between the workplace and the CBD. Only in Pueblo, Colorado—the second-smallest city in the sample with a population of 123,000 in 2000—did travel time to workplaces increase significantly as the distance of the workplace from

FIGURE 12.9

Average Travel Time to Workplaces in Atlanta, Georgia, as a Function of Their Distance from the CBD, 2000

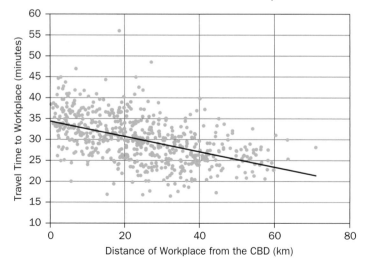

Source: Drawn from unpublished data obtained from Alejandro M. Blei, University of Illinois at Chicago.

the CBD increased. If U.S. cities are harbingers of our common urban future, which they may or may not be, then the polycentric spatial structure is indeed our future. At present, while comparative data for a global sample of cities are sorely lacking, this polycentric destiny must remain only a conjecture.

SUMMARY AND CONCLUSIONS

The possibility that cities worldwide are now in a process of transformation from a monocentric to a polycentric spatial structure poses an interesting challenge. It suggests that if public transport is to be a viable option in areas of expansion to economize on the energy expended and to limit greenhouse gas emissions, then it cannot be limited to continued reliance on radial routes to the city center. The transport network must be two-dimensional, providing frequent and reliable service among suburban destinations over the entire metropolitan area, rather than a one-dimensional network of radial routes into the center. Some public transport systems that already provide such service are the bus lines of Edmonton and Toronto in Canada.

To provide reliable point-to-point service throughout metropolitan areas and to function effectively, bus lines or new transportation technologies will need to operate on a grid of arterial roads. Thus, making the essential preparations for urban expansion on the metropolitan periphery of rapidly growing cities should involve acquiring the rights-of-way for an arterial road grid spaced not more than 1 km apart, within ready walking distance of all residences and workplaces throughout the urban periphery. The grid need not necessarily be orthogonal with all roads running north-south or east-west. It can be constructed from closely spaced radial and ring roads as well, as long as it facilitates movement in all directions, not only in the direction of the urban core. Urban expansion in China, for example, has embraced the ring road rather than the grid as a tool for facilitating lateral movement in cities that are fast becoming poly-centric. Beijing, for example, completed its sixth ring road in 2009 and now is in the process of planning a seventh (figure 12.10). These ring roads facilitate peripheral movement and can form a critical part of a dense network of arterial roads throughout the urban area. By themselves, however, they do not create an effective road network for public transport because they are more than 1 km apart and beyond a 10-minute walk from most locations.

To conclude, three transformations can be identified in the spatial structure of cities during the past two centuries. The first transformation, from the walking city to the monocentric city, involved the introduction of reliable public transportation, primarily in the form of omnibuses, horsecars, electric trolleys, commuter rail lines, and subways, that gradually enlarged the commuting range beyond walking distance. The introduction of these new technologies in the late nineteenth and early twentieth centuries led to the low-density suburbanization of residences away from the crowded city centers,

FIGURE 12.10
**Ring Roads in Beijing, China, in 2009 Superimposed
on Its Built-up Area in 2000**

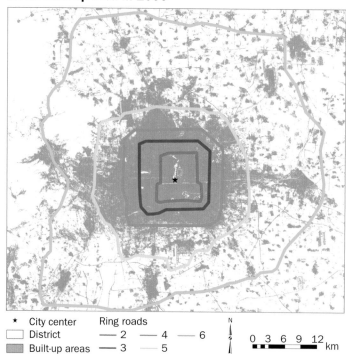

★	City center	Ring roads			
☐	District	— 2	— 4	— 6	
▨	Built-up areas	— 3	— 5		

0 3 6 9 12 km

Sources: Location of ring roads based on Google Maps; built-up area
redrawn from Angel et al. (2012, 48).

while workplaces remained within the urban core. The dispersal of residences resulted in a monocentric city, where population densities were high near the city center and declined with distance from that center.

As incomes increased and transport costs declined, suburbanization at higher densities accelerated, resulting in the decline of the gradient of the density curve and often in the decline in density in the city center as well. Then, as cars and trucks became more pervasive, as better roads made faster gasoline-powered travel possible throughout the urban area, as traffic congestion and shortage of parking choked CBDs, and as land values in central locations soared, workplaces decentralized to the urban periphery as well. These changes signaled a third transformation in the spatial structure to a polycentric city in which workplaces are distributed throughout the metropolitan area, drawing their workers from the entire metropolitan labor market.

Why does all this matter? It matters because in preparing for the coming urban expansion, we should take into account, at the very minimum, that the cities of the future will most likely be polycentric. This realization requires, first of all, planning for mixed residential, productive, and commercial land use throughout the metropolitan fringe. We cannot and need not decide in advance where specific uses should be or at what densities different areas must be developed. These decisions are best left to the interactions of supply and demand for land on the urban periphery. Such interactions are likely to generate construction at a higher density of office, residential, and commercial developments—near existing towns, in emerging new concentrations, or along arterial corridors—that involve high levels of risk that are better left for the marketplace to decide. For the public good, it is important to formulate and employ land use regulations that maximize the creative possibilities inherent in cities, while ensuring that nuisances among adjacent uses are minimized.

Second, rather than limit transportation investments to the radial routes to the CBD as required during the days of the monocentric city, we now have to ensure efficient movement by public transport, as well as trucks and cars, on an arterial road and infrastructure grid that connects all suburbs to one another. Such a grid, to be of optimal use for public transport, must be spaced within walking distance of all residences and workplaces, approximately 1 km apart. This can be an orthogonal grid, like the one employed by Romans in their *centuriation* or like the one employed by the United States in its Land Ordinance of 1785. Or, it can be a network of closely spaced ring roads and radials, a combination of both, or a grid of meandering roads. The most important feature is that it could be developed over time into a dense network of arterial roads throughout the urban periphery that could facilitate maximum connectivity among all locations. For such a grid to develop over time, we must acquire the rights-of-way and plan it now, before land on the periphery is subdivided and converted to urban use. Market forces, effective as they are in determining land uses and densities, cannot and will not bring such a transportation grid into being.

Breaking out of the old bounds, walls, boulevards, or administrative limits which set it apart, the city has massively invaded the open country, though parts of the countryside may have kept their rural appearance.

Gottmann and Harper (1990, 101)

CHAPTER 13

The Fragmentation
of Urban Landscapes

*How fragmented are the built-up areas of cities, how are levels
of fragmentation changing over time, why, and why should it matter?*

Most cities and metropolitan areas are highly fragmented, typically consisting of disconnected patches of urban fabric broken up by swaths of open space including a variety of green, barren, unbuilt, and unpaved areas. Some open spaces are in permanent public or private use, but most are vacant lands, possibly used for occasional recreation or under cultivation, that may or may not be built upon through a gradual process of infill. As we build cities at declining densities, we are also creating urban environments that are fragmented and disconnected.

The traditional image of the fully built-out city of old—with buildings and impervious surfaces, surrounded by a wall, and situated in the green countryside—is of a city that neither fragments nor is fragmented by the countryside. Whether such a strict division of city and countryside ever existed remains an open question. While, as we saw in chapter 6, historic walled cities typically had some fragmented suburban fringe areas, the modern urban landscape is quantitatively different. Both city and countryside now interpenetrate and fragment each other on a vast scale.

A key question that has confronted urban planners, policy makers, and concerned environmentalists worldwide for some time is whether the fragmentation of the urban landscape is an inherent feature of contemporary cities that must be taken into account in planning for and managing urban expansion, or a disorderly, wasteful, and undesirable form of sprawl that must be brought under control through regulations. Sprawl was defined 50 years ago as "lack of continuity in expansion" (Clawson 1962, 99). Since then many writers have bemoaned the ill effects of scattered or leapfrogging development and the costs it imposes on both the built environment and the rural

Fragmentation on the urban fringe: Where does the city end and the countryside begin?

fringe of cities (Carruthers and Ulfarsson 2001; Heim 2001). "[P]arcelization of farm-lands leads to a checkerboard distribution of farmlands, i.e., many noncontiguous fields. Farming such scattered plots is problematic" (Pfeffer and Lapping 1995, 85).

Landscape ecology studies also maintain that settlements developed near a forest or prairie affect vegetation and wildlife along their edges, often in a belt up to 100 meters in width (Brand and George 2001; Chen, Franklin, and Spies 1992; Winter, Johnson, and Faaborg 2000). More fragmented urban areas cause more disturbance to vegetation and wildlife along the adjoining countryside. The fragmentation of urban footprints is an important concern in terms of both inefficiency in the built environment and its adverse effects on the ecology of the countryside.

Urban economists have explained discontinuous development as the natural result of the operation of market forces. Ewing (1994, 2), for example, paraphrasing Lessinger (1962) and Ottensman (1977), explains: "Expectations of land appreciation on the urban fringe cause some landowners to withhold land from the market. . . . The result is a discontinuous pattern of development." Some economists have observed that while fragmentation may be inefficient in the short term, it leads to more efficient development patterns in the long term: "[C]ontrary to conventional wisdom, a freely function-ing land market with discontinuous patterns of development inherently promotes higher density development" (Peiser 1989, 193). Such views suggest that fragmentation is an inherent feature of the urban expansion process, not the result of the failure of land mar-kets on the urban fringe that should be addressed by ameliorative action by the state.

While it would be difficult to dispute that some fragmentation on the urban fringe is necessary for the proper functioning of land markets and is an inherent feature of the urban landscape, there is a quantitative aspect to this assertion that is left unexplored: How much fragmentation would be necessary and sufficient for the smooth functioning of the urban development process, and when can we determine that fragmentation is excessive and requires ameliorative action to reduce it? We can also ask how much fragmentation is minimally necessary to ensure that enough rainwater is percolated to replenish groundwater aquifers or that enough food is grown for local consumption.

More specific empirical questions can address levels of fragmentation in particular countries and cities: Are Chinese metropolitan areas more fragmented than other metropolitan areas, as a few observers have suspected (Webster et al. 2010)? If so, why? Has urban containment in Portland, Oregon, reduced fragmentation within its strictly enforced urban growth boundary (UGB) over time? And, if so, has Portland reduced fragmentation at a more rapid rate than Houston, Texas, a city that does not practice any form of urban containment? These empirical questions have not been properly addressed in the literature of landscape ecology or urban studies, and it is precisely those questions that are addressed here.

Analyzing satellite images for 1990 and 2000 for a global sample of 120 cities, my colleagues and I found that cities typically contain or disturb vast quantities of open spaces equal in area, on average, to their built-up areas (Angel, Parent, and Civco 2012). We also found that fragmentation, simply defined as the relative share of open space in the urban footprint, is now in decline. Using multiple regression models, we found that larger cities are less fragmented; high levels of car ownership tended to reduce fragmentation rather than to increase it; cities that constrained urban development were slightly less fragmented; and there were parallel declines in average built-up area densities and in levels of fragmentation during the 1990s.

Given that cities contain vast amounts of open space, we recommend that plans make room for urban expansion in rapidly growing cities and take the expected fragmentation levels into account. Assuming that all vacant lands within the urbanized area will be developed before new lands on the fringe are encroached upon may be unrealistic. No city in our global sample was fully built out, and urbanized open spaces added at least one-third to its built-up area. On average, for the sample as a whole, open space added an area equivalent in size to the built-up area.

FRAGMENTATION IN THE GLOBAL SAMPLE OF CITIES, 1990–2000

The excessive fragmentation of urban landscapes has often been associated with the pejorative term *sprawl*. Burchfield et al. (2006) follow Clawson (1962) in defining urban sprawl as the fragmentation of the urban landscape, choosing to ignore low density altogether as one of its essential attributes. They specifically define fragmentation as the average share of an urban neighborhood (1 square kilometer [km²] in area) that is taken up by open space. My colleagues and I measured fragmentation with two complementary metrics: the openness index and the city footprint ratio (Angel, Parent, and Civco 2012). The first metric, following Burchfield et al. (2006), measures the average share of open pixels within the walking distance circle (a circle of 1 km² in area) around every built-up pixel in the city. It is a neighborhood-scale measure of fragmentation. The second is the ratio of the total area of the city, including its urbanized open space, and its built-up area. It is a citywide measure of fragmentation.

Both the openness index and the city footprint ratio are area metrics that do not measure open space per person. Metrics that do so are affected by the density of the built-up areas of the city. Other things being equal, the denser the built-up area, the less the amount of open space per person. Opting for area metrics ensured that fragmentation and density remain as two independent measures of urban spatial structure. Indeed, the correlation between the two fragmentation metrics and the density of the built-up area in the global sample of 120 cities was not significantly different from 0 in both time periods for which we have data. In fact, cities can be less sprawled in terms of built-up area density and more sprawled in terms of fragmentation at the same time. In 2000, for example, Kolkata, India, ranked seventh in built-up area density in the global sample of 120 cities. It was one of the least sprawled cities in terms of density, but it had the sixth-highest city footprint ratio, so was one of the most sprawled cities in terms of fragmentation. In contrast, Los Angeles ranked 103rd in built-up area density while its city footprint ratio ranked 117th. Los Angeles was one of the most sprawled cities in terms of density and one of the least sprawled in terms of fragmentation.

What is the share of urbanized open space—the sum of all areas that are not covered by impervious surfaces—in a typical city neighborhood? Our key findings regarding fragmentation in the 1990s show that the average value of the openness index in the global sample of 120 cities was almost one-half. That is, typical neighborhoods contained as much open space as their built-up areas. Similarly, city footprints, on average, were double the built-up areas of cities. That is, on average, urbanized open spaces added an area to the city equivalent to its built-up area and, at a minimum, added 36 percent to the built-up areas.

City footprints circa 2000 added no less than 93 percent, on average, to the built-up areas of cities, ranging from only 40 percent to the built-up area of Los Angeles (the fourth-lowest value), to nearly 90 percent in Ho Chi Minh City, Vietnam (the median value), and 180 percent in Zhengzhou, China (the second-highest value) (figure 13.1). Despite these considerable variations, cities around the world now typically contain urbanized open space equivalent in area to their built-up areas, a surprisingly high figure with few references to this trend in the literature.

The mean value of the openness index for a typical city was 0.47 in 1990 and 0.42 in 2000. These values for all cities in the global sample in 1990 and 2000 were very similar to the values of 0.43 in 1976 and 0.42 in 1992 for the United States found by Burchfield et al. (2006). Unlike density values, the openness index values appear to be distributed normally about their mean (figure 13.2 top), and the median value is almost equal to the mean value. Two cities in the global sample had values lower than 0.2 in 2000: São Paulo in Brazil and Accra in Ghana. Four cities had values in excess of 0.7 in 2000: Rajshahi and Saidpur in Bangladesh, Yulin in China, and Ilheus in Brazil. Cities in developing countries had average values of 0.48 in 1990 and 0.43 in 2000. These values were significantly higher, at the 95 percent confidence level, than those in developed countries: 0.44 in 1990 and 0.39 in 2000. Cities in developing countries thus were found to be more fragmented, on average, than cities in developed ones.

The findings for the city footprint ratios parallel those for the openness index with minor differences, and their

FIGURE 13.1
City Footprints of Los Angeles, California (2000), Ho Chi Minh City, Vietnam (1999), and Zhengzhou, China (2001)

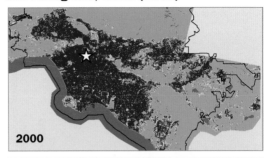
2000

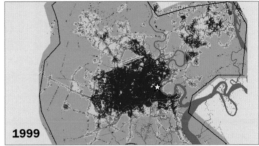
1999

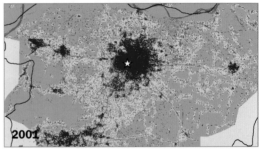
2001

Urban built-up area — Rural open space
Suburban built-up area — Study area
Rural built-up area — Water
Urbanized open space — No data — CBD

Sources: Angel et al. (2012, 138; 92; and 252).

distribution also appears to be normal (figure 13.2 bottom)—the median value was equal to the mean in both periods. The mean value of the city footprint ratio for a typical city was 2.01 in 1990 and 1.93 in 2000, and there were no significant differences in this ratio between developed and developing countries or among Europe and Japan and land-rich developed countries. There were no values below 1.36 in both periods, no values below 1.4 in 1990, and only three values below 1.4 in 2000. In other words, open spaces added at least 36 percent to the built-up areas of cities in the sample.

Satellite images of the global sample of 120 cities also provide evidence that fragmentation is an inherent feature of the urban development process insofar as it is a

FIGURE 13.2

**Frequency Distribution of the Openness Index (top) and
Footprint Ratio (bottom) for 120 Cities, 1990 and 2000**

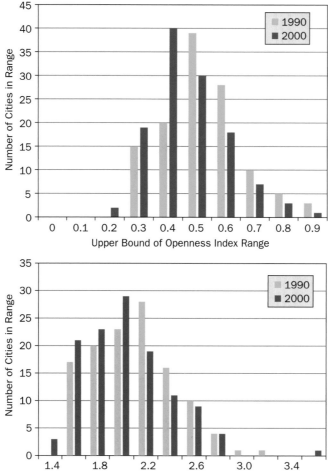

Source: Based on data from Angel et al. (2012, table 5.1, 322–345).

fringe area phenomenon. Vacant open spaces near the center of the city are filled in, while new vacant areas on the periphery become part of the city footprint, so the overall share of open space in the city remains largely unchanged. When we measured the average distance to open space pixels from the city center (the location of city hall) in 1990 and 2000, we found it to be significantly longer than the average distance to built-up pixels: 10.4 compared to 8.3 kilometers in 1990 and 12.1 compared to 9.5 kilometers in 2000. Urbanized open space was further out from the center, on average, than the built-up area, yet the ratio between the average distances from the center to open space pixels and to built-up pixels remained similar—1.31 in 1990 and 1.34 in 2000—

and this small difference was not statistically significant. Thus, as cities expanded, urbanized open spaces remained approximately one-third of the distance further away, on average, from the centers of cities than their built-up areas.

The average value of the openness index increases systematically as distance from the city center increases. In a subgroup of 25 cities (forming 20 percent of the global sample of 120 cities for which we had data on the distribution of population and open space at the census tract level), we measured the average value of the openness index in 10 rings, each containing one-tenth of the city population around each city center. Figure 13.3 demonstrates that the average value of the index in each ring for this subgroup of cities increases monotonically as the distance from the city center increases. It ranges from as low as 0.15 in the inner ring to 0.55 in the outer ring, suggesting again that the openness of urban footprints is primarily a fringe phenomenon.

FIGURE 13.3

The Openness Index as a Function of Distance from the City Center in a Subgroup of 25 Cities in 2000

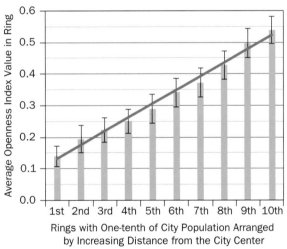

Rings with One-tenth of City Population Arranged by Increasing Distance from the City Center

Sources: Based on census tract data available for 25 cities from the global sample of 120 cities circa 2000; and openness index values from Angel et al. (2012, table 5.1, 322–345).

Why are some cities more fragmented than others? Multiple regression models can explain 30 to 50 percent of the variation in levels of fragmentation among cities in the global sample (Angel, Parent, and Civco 2012). The fragmentation of city footprints can be explained by variations in such factors as city population size, income, levels of car ownership, topographical restrictions on expansion, the availability of well water, the preponderance of informal settlements, and to a smaller extent by the presence of regulatory restrictions on expansion as well. The following conclusions are based on data for the year 2000.

- Large cities had significantly lower levels of fragmentation than smaller cities: A doubling of the city population was associated with an 11 percent decline in the openness index.
- Cities with more buildable land in and around them were more fragmented: A doubling of the share of buildable land was associated with a 12 percent increase in the openness index.
- Cities in countries with higher incomes also had higher levels of fragmentation: A doubling of income per capita was associated with a 12 percent increase in the openness index.
- That said, cities in countries with higher levels of car ownership per capita were less fragmented: A doubling of the level of car ownership per capita was associated with an 8 percent decline in the openness index.
- Access to well water also increased fragmentation, as already noted by Burchfield et al. (2006) in U.S. cities: A doubling of the share of the population that obtained its water from wells was associated with a 12 percent increase in the openness index.
- The density of built-up areas did not affect the spatial fragmentation of cities.
- Informal settlements acted as infill and they were associated with a decline in fragmentation: A doubling of the share of the population in informal settlements was associated with an 8 percent decline in the openness index.
- The importance of agriculture to the country's economy was also associated with higher levels of fragmentation: A doubling of the share of the country's GDP from agriculture, a proxy for the value of agricultural land on the urban fringe, was associated with an 8 percent increase in the openness index.
- The availability of large quantities of agricultural lands per person in the country did not lead to the increased fragmentation of its urban areas.
- Finally, planning restrictions were associated with a decline in fragmentation: A doubling of the area of the metropolitan plan where no development was allowed was associated with a 6 percent decline in the openness index.

THE DECLINE IN FRAGMENTATION, 1990–2000

Levels of fragmentation measured by both the openness index and the city footprint ratio declined significantly between 1990 and 2000 in the global sample of 120 cities. More than two-thirds of these cities experienced a decline in the city footprint ratio, compared to less than one-third that experienced an increase. On average, the infill of urbanized open spaces within city footprints constituted 50.9 percent of all new development between the two periods. The immediate extension of built-up areas into the periphery constituted 26.0 percent, and leapfrogging beyond the edge of city footprints constituted 23.1 percent of all new development.

The 10-year decline in the openness index between 1990 and 2000 was –0.05, representing a decline from 0.47 to 0.42. There was a parallel decline in the city footprint ratio of –0.08, from 2.01 to 1.93. The rate of change of the openness index was –1.2 percent per year, and that of the city footprint ratio was –0.04 percent per year. Both rates were significantly different from zero and did not vary among the three regional groups or among developing and developed countries. To put the latter rate in perspective, it was one-third the rate of decline in the city footprint ratio within Portland, Oregon's UGB between 1973 and 2005, which was –1.2 percent per annum. Other findings are noted as well.

Informal settlements in Caracas, Venezuela, cover an entire hillside with no fragmentation.

- Multiple regression models could explain 14 to 43 percent of the variation in the annual rate of change of the openness index in the sample of 120 cities.
- The models show that the faster the rate of population growth in the city, the faster the rate of decline in the openness index: A 10 percent increase in the population growth rate was associated with a 2.7 decline in the rate of change in the index. Rapidly growing cities, in other words, resorted to infill more readily than to scattered development.
- Rapid economic growth, in contrast to rapid population growth, led to increased fragmentation: A 10 percent increase in the rate of growth of GDP per capita was associated with a 1 percent increase in the rate of growth of the openness index.
- The higher the level of car ownership in the country, the faster the rate of decline in the openness index, but that effect, while significant, was minimal.
- Finally, the rate of inflation or the restrictions on the conversion of land from rural to urban use could not be said to affect significant changes in the rate of change of the openness index.

To conclude, the fragmentation of city footprints declined in the 1990s as cities became less sprawled, if sprawl is defined as scattered development. This finding contrasts other evidence that built-up area density declined during the 1990s as cities became more sprawled, if sprawl is defined as low-density development. Yet, despite the decline in fragmentation observed in the 1990s, city footprints still contained urbanized open space that was roughly equal in area to their built-up areas.

CASE STUDIES

While it has been difficult to obtain comparative data that could be used to test the effects of policy on urban fragmentation at a global scale, it was possible to begin to examine these effects in the two case studies presented below.

Excessive Fragmentation in Chinese Cities

Although not well documented, fragmentation in Chinese cities is excessive and most likely the result of state policies. The mean value of the city footprint ratio for nine Chinese cities (not including Hong Kong) in our global sample of 120 cities in the year 2000 was 2.40. For all other cities in the sample it was 1.89, and the two values were significantly different at the 99 percent confidence level. All the Chinese cities in the sample had city footprint ratios that ranged from 2.1 in Shanghai and Beijing to 2.8 in Zhengzhou. In other words, in 2000 the built-up area of Chinese cities fragmented and

Urban villagers on the fringe of Zhengzhou, China, engage in subsistence agriculture, but it is no longer their main source of income.

Dense affordable housing in urban villages was demolished to make way for urban expansion while cultivated land remains vacant in Tianjin, China, as shown in 2004 and 2009.

disturbed open space in and around them equivalent to 110–180 percent of their built-up areas, and these values were significantly higher than those of other countries. Why?

The academic literature has noted a broad rural-yet-urban fringe in Chinese cities, a zone termed *desakota* by urban geographers in the early 1990s (Ginsburg 1990; McGee 1991). In this zone, there is a dense scattering of villages with a high share of nonagricultural activities and a large number of workers who commute to urban jobs in the city proper. Chinese cities are often located on once densely settled agricultural lands. As they grow and expand outward, they enclose and incorporate many villages. More distant villages also become more urban in character. "The urbanization process unfolding is thus caused not only by a stream of rural-to-urban migrants but also by urbanization in place; that is, entire districts becoming more urbanized at all levels of the rural-urban continuum" (Guldin 1996, 278).

This dense pattern of urban villages on the periphery of Chinese cities does not explain the proliferation of cultivated lands within Chinese cities, however. Indeed, as Webster et al. (2010, 17) noted, "[t]he result of sample land use surveys conducted in suburban areas in Chengdu, Tianjin, and Zhengzhou shows that on average about 34% of the land within existing ring roads remain under agricultural use while urban development expands much farther away from the city center." Angel, Valdivia, and Lutzy (2011), following Webster et al., attributed this persistence of largely subsistence agriculture to central government policies that limit the conversion of cultivated land to urban use in line with China's food security policies. "The Chinese government has given a high priority to agricultural land preservation in its food security policies, among them the Basic Farmland Protection Regulation of 1994, the 1998 Land

Management Law, and the New Land Administration Act of 1999 [Lichtenberg and Ding, 2007]" (Angel, Valdivia, and Lutzy 2011, 145).

Fragmented cultivated land in Zhengzhou, for example, is only half as productive as land in larger fields in the surrounding Henan Province, as most farming families have other sources of income. Angel, Valdivia, and Lutzy (2011) observed that strict central government limitations on land conversion have forced the municipality of Zhengzhou to appropriate the built-up areas of several of its surrounding villages while leaving their cultivated lands intact, to often demolish extensive affordable bedroom communities there, and to redevelop them for urban use. These policies exacerbate the fragmentation of Chinese cities, resulting in inefficient infrastructure networks, longer commutes, urban land supply bottlenecks that make housing unaffordable, and unproductive agriculture.

More than 100 such villages were incorporated within the urbanized area of Zheng-zhou by 2005. In these residential areas, villagers have a small plot, typically some 200 square meters (m^2) in area. Many villagers have chosen to build walk-up apartment buildings on their plots, where they rent rooms for some $8–$40 per month to rural migrants working in the city. These 10–14 m^2 rooms in dense neighborhoods constitute the affordable housing stock in China today. Because of these urban villages, Chinese cities have no shantytowns or slums—an extraordinary feature of contemporary Chinese cities considering their rapid rate of urbanization, the limited incomes of the

Dense affordable housing in an urban village in Shenzhen, China, is being demolished, to be replaced by less dense and less affordable housing.

urban work force, and the total absence of a social safety net for the tens and now hundreds of millions of rural migrants who have come to work in cities and do not have the required residence permits (*hukous*). The United Nations' claim that 37.8 percent of China's urban population of some 178 million in 2001 lived in slums is quite misleading (United Nations Human Settlements Programme 2003). If China's urban villages are omitted from the data, as they should be, the United Nations' global estimate of 1 billion people living in slums circa 2000 may be too large by that amount.

In an important sense, China has inadvertently solved its affordable housing problem by allowing low-cost housing in its urban villages to flourish. Apparently oblivious to this astonishing development, Chinese municipalities are engaged in the wanton destruction of this affordable, yet invisible, housing stock to make way for what government officials consider affordable housing: 70–90 m^2 apartments in high-rise buildings, typically affordable only by the highest quintile of the income distribution. Not surprisingly, because of strict municipal building regulations, these high-rise buildings are often built at lower densities than the walk-up apartment buildings in urban villages, thus increasing the consumption of land per person in the city.

Declines in Fragmentation in Portland, Oregon, and Houston, Texas

In 1973 the State of Oregon enacted Senate Bill 100, which mandated that every urban area in the state, including Portland, create an urban growth boundary (UGB). Metro, a regional government, was created by Portland voters in 1979 to manage the UGB in a three-county metropolitan area. Metro was charged with enforcing the boundary and extending it every 5 years to ensure a 20-year supply of residential land. It is not clear from the available documentation whether this 20-year supply includes all vacant land within the boundary, or whether it assumes that a significant share of urbanized open space, on the order of at least one-third of the built-up area, is meant to remain vacant at all times. If Metro does not extend the UGB outward in a timely manner to allow for an adequate amount of land to remain vacant, as Cox (2004) and others suspect, there is a good reason to expect that land supply in Portland will be further constrained with concomitant effects on housing affordability.

The chief aim of the UGB was to contain urban sprawl and preserve the natural beauty of the surrounding countryside within reach of city residents. Sprawl was not defined precisely, but presumably it included both low-density development and fragmentation. After examining the change in built-up area density within the UGB between 1973 and 2005, we found that densities decreased rather than increased (see figure 11.13). That said, the creation of Portland's UGB was associated with a rapid decline in fragmentation. Figure 13.4 shows the increase in the built-up area within Portland's UGB between 1973 and 2005. During this period, Portland's city footprint ratio declined from 2.20 to 1.51, at an average rate of −1.2 percent per annum.

FIGURE 13.4

Decline in Fragmentation Within Portland, Oregon's Urban Growth Boundary, 1973 and 2005

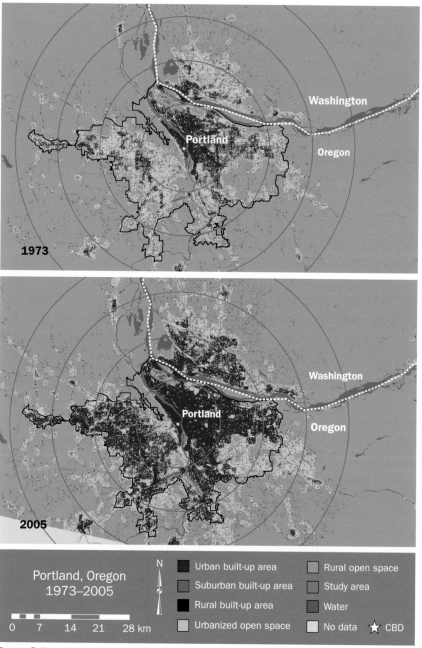

Source: Built-up area maps prepared from Landsat data in NASA (multiple dates).

By comparison, Houston's city footprint ratio declined from 2.13 to 1.75 between 1990 and 2000 at an annual rate of −1.9 percent. This finding is surprising because Houston, which does not have a zoning law, let alone a containment policy, has a very open housing market, and housing there is considerably more affordable than in Portland. In the third quarter of 2009, for example, 4.2 median household incomes were required to purchase a median-priced house in Portland, but only 2.9 incomes were needed in Houston (Demographia 2010).

Recent research has allowed us to compare the average decline in fragmentation in the census tracts within Portland's UGB with the average decline in Washington State census tracts across the Columbia River that are within Portland's metropolitan area but not subject to Oregon's land use regulations. We looked at the decline in fragmentation in four 10-kilometer-wide rings encircling Portland's central business district. The first ring was entirely within the UGB. In the other three rings there was no significant difference in the average openness index between the regions within the UGB and across the river in 1973, 1990, or 2005 (figure 13.5). The openness index declined in both regions, but it did not decline any faster within the UGB than in the unregulated region across the Columbia River. We must conclude, therefore, that the UGB did not have a statistically significant effect on fragmentation in the Portland metropolitan area during this period. Accelerated infill and the concomitant decline in overall fragmentation do

FIGURE 13.5
Average Openness Index Values in Rings Around the Portland, Oregon, CBD Within the Urban Growth Boundary and Outside It in Washington State

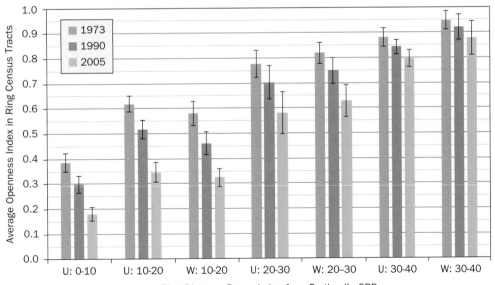

Ring Distance Range in km from Portland's CBD
(U = within UGB; W = Outside UGB in Washington State)

Source: Calculated from built-up area maps prepared from Landsat data (multiple dates).

occur naturally in open markets that are not subject to regulatory restrictions. We therefore urge caution in concluding that rigorous containment is a necessary policy tool for accelerating infill and reducing fragmentation.

CONCLUSION

On average, the inclusion of urbanized open space in the city footprint doubles the area of that footprint. If that average were considered a global norm, we would advise urban planners and policy makers not to be surprised to find half of their city's footprint occupied by urbanized open space. They should be surprised if it varies substantially from that norm. In planning and preparing for urban expansion, and in the absence of active intervention, future city footprints can be expected to continue to be half empty as well. As a minimum global norm, planners and other officials should expect urbanized open space to add no less than one-third to the built-up area of their city, except in highly atypical situations.

The Columbia River separates Portland, Oregon, inside the urban growth boundary, from Vancouver, Washington, outside it, shown across the river in 2011.

Urbanized open space is a fringe phenomenon. We may safely assume that as some vacant spaces closer to the city center are filled in, new urbanized open space will be incorporated into the city footprint on the periphery and add at least one-third to the built-up area of the city at any one time. Without additional information, however, we cannot say whether this would be sufficient to ensure the smooth functioning of land markets.

Data are not available to determine what range of city footprint ratios is common to cities with an unconstrained and responsive supply of urban land, adequate to ensure that housing remains affordable over time. It stands to reason that projected city footprint ratios in a city with unconstrained land supply should be higher than the minimum ratios observed in the global sample of cities (1.4) and in Portland (1.5). If this were the case, then the areas planned for 20 to 30 years of urban expansion must be at least 50 percent larger than the areas obtained by simply projecting populations and built-up area densities. We cannot apply such an estimate to individual cities with different topographies (e.g., steep slopes and floodplains), different rates of rainwater percolation and runoff, different historical levels of density and fragmentation, different amounts of open space in permanent use, and different food-growing cultures within cities. While we know that expected fragmentation levels are in global decline, we can only urge planners to take fragmentation into account and to prepare substantially larger areas for expansion than those usually contemplated.

Should cities employ rigorous containment measures to bring excessive fragmentation under control? There may be sufficient cause for reining in excessive fragmentation where it is the result of misguided land policies. And a case can be made for reducing exurban fragmentation through policy intervention in areas that are expected to remain outside city footprints projected 20 to 30 years into the future, such as by postponing the official designation of lands as urban or by delaying the extension of urban infrastructure networks into these exurban areas. As a rule of thumb, however, city planners should be willing to prepare an area for expansion over a projected 20 to 30 years that is one-third to one-half as large as the land required for the built-up area of their city.

When trams and railways revolutionized transport, enabling people to move further, faster and more comfortably, they changed the shape of cities from cuddly and roundish to leggy and spread out.

Paul Downton (2001, n. p.)

CHAPTER 14

The Pulsating Compactness of Urban Footprints

How compact are the shapes of urban footprints, how are their levels of compactness changing over time, why, and why should it matter?

Dictionaries typically define a compact object as one closely and firmly packed, or as having component parts closely crowded together. The area occupied by a city or metropolitan region has a geographical shape whose compactness, as a two-dimensional form rather than as a three-dimensional object, can also be defined. We can examine and measure a city's shape compactness in various ways, as geographers have done for almost two centuries (Ritter 1822 in Frolov 1975). Yet, this investigation is quite independent of the "compact city" debate (see Jenks, Burton, and Williams 1996), which is a debate about the density of urban areas rather than about their footprints.

The city footprint maps in the *Atlas of Urban Expansion* (Angel et al. 2012), the companion volume to this book, illustrate how compactness varies among cities, and how it changes over time in individual cities as well. The aim of this chapter is to explore these variations and changes in the compactness of cities, to begin to understand why they occur, and to explain why such an understanding is crucial for guiding and managing urban expansion.

The shape compactness in city footprints can be compared to organisms such as a jellyfish, which is more compact than a starfish, which is more compact than a sea snake. In the global sample of 120 cities in the year 2000, for example, the city footprint of Ibadan, Nigeria, had a high degree of compactness—not quite like that of a jellyfish but close to it. The city footprint of Warsaw, Poland, had a considerably lower level of compactness, resembling that of the starfish, with long extensions along transportation corridors emanating from its center. The city footprint of Alexandria, Egypt, had an even lower level of compactness, snaking in a linear fashion along its shorelines (figure 14.1).

In studying and preparing for urban expansion, it is important to come to terms with the relative compactness of cities and its changes over time. Expansion inevitably takes place on the urban edge; hence the shape of this edge matters.

There may be good reasons for making cities more compact. In purely geometric terms, for example, if two cities have the same area, then residents in the more compact city will have to travel a shorter distance, on average, to the city center or to any other location in their city. Overall access in the more compact city will be greater than in the less compact one, and public infrastructure lines will be shorter on average. In identifying areas for urban expansion, the public sector may seek to direct new urban development to the vacant areas between built-up tentacles of the city or vacant areas closer to the city core to increase overall accessibility.

Conversely, the public sector may prefer plans to make the city less compact, such as by providing residents with easier access to open space. Policies to protect open space may prevent development in some areas closer to the city center in order to maintain access to parks, forcing new development into more peripheral locations. Other factors that may make cities less compact are the continued ownership of large tracts of land by powerful government agencies that resist any change in their use; concerns with protecting environmentally sensitive habitats or reservoir watersheds; or food security issues that prevent lands under cultivation from being converted to urban use.

Regardless of any public-sector actions designed to favor or inhibit compactness, however, private-sector development may take place in any and all locations on the urban periphery if it cannot be prevented by stringent and enforceable regulations. The private sector—both formal and informal—has its own concerns for access or profitability and does not necessarily share the rationales underlying any particular public policy. In general, the overall shape of a city comes about only partially as a result of decisions taken by public officials. More often than not it evolves as a result of an interaction of various recognizable public and private forces acting on that shape. These may include the introduction of new transport technologies; the development of new intercity transport corridors; freeway congestion; the decay of public transit companies that reduces the advantages that transportation corridors may have conferred in the past; geographical constraints on development such as steep slopes, bodies of water, or wetlands; broad public support for and successful enforcement of open space policies; or the preferences of residents for a view of the sunset over the blue sea instead of access to the urban core. The compactness of real cities is usually the result of the interplay of these forces. Unless we—as professionals, as policy makers, as activists, or as a concerned public—understand them better, we can never hope to participate in, let alone guide, urban expansion in any meaningful way.

FIGURE 14.1
High, Medium, and Low Compactness of Marine Organisms Compared to the Compactness of City Footprints in Ibadan, Nigeria (2000), Warsaw, Poland (2002), and Alexandria, Egypt (1999)

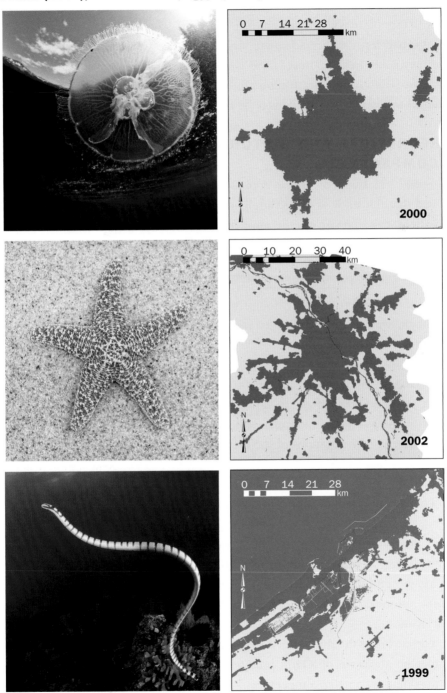

Sources: City footprint maps redrawn from Angel et al. (2012, 100; 242; and 24).

For viable urban expansion to occur, advance planning for the location of public works and public open spaces must be attuned to the advance acquisition and development of lands by market actors in both the formal and informal sectors. This may be a tall order, but the absence of a shared understanding about where urban expansion is likely to take place will not prevent it. Uncoordinated expansion will result in a disorganized urban form with inadequate lands for public works and public open spaces where they could have mattered, and where the later provision of public services—arterial roads and trunk infrastructure lines, for example, as well as public open spaces and neighborhood streets—will likely be far more expensive and far less adequate.

A THEORETICAL AND HISTORICAL PERSPECTIVE ON COMPACTNESS

In a theoretical study of shape compactness in geography, my colleagues and I proposed that the study and measurement of shape compactness rest on two simple observations: first, the circle is the most compact of shapes; and second, there are 10, and possibly more, distinct geometrical properties of the circle that make it compact (Angel, Parent, and Civco 2010). Understanding that there were different types of compactness, shaped by distinct forces, was a necessary precondition for deciding how to look at the compactness of city footprints and, more important, how to measure it in a meaningful way. As Louis Sullivan, one of the founders of the Modern Movement in architecture noted (1896, 409):

> It is the pervading law of all things organic and inorganic,
> Of all things physical and metaphysical,
> Of all things human and things super-human,
> Of all true manifestations of the head,
> Of the heart, of the soul,
> That the life is recognizable in its expression,
> That form ever follows function. This is the law.

Four of the compactness properties we have identified are quite relevant for examining the shapes of cities, not least because the rationales and the forces underlying them are recognizable. Furthermore, their relevance to cities has flowed and ebbed in different historical periods. Among all shapes with a given area, the circle has these characteristics.

- The circle has the minimum perimeter, as in the shape of a string tying together the stems of a large bouquet of flowers. We can say that it has maximum perimeter compactness.

- The circle has the shortest average distance from all points within it to its center, as in the shape of a circus tent where everyone wants to be as close to the action as possible. We can say that it has maximum proximity compactness.
- The circle has the shortest average distance-squared from all points to all points within it, as in the shape of a spherical star where its plasma particles are all as close to each other as possible.[1] We can say that it has maximum cohesion compactness.
- The circle has the longest average distance from its interior points to its periphery, as in the shape of a circular dance pavilion that poses a greater difficulty for dancers to escape it when fire breaks out. We can say that it has maximum depth compactness.

The first rationale that has forced city footprints to be more compact pertains to their walls. When cities required protective walls for their defense, there were very strong grounds for their footprints to have high perimeter compactness. City walls were by far the most expensive of public works for a city administration. To enclose a city of a given area with the shortest length of wall, and to minimize the total cost of the wall, required that area to have a shape as close to a circle as possible. The circular wall of Palmanova, Italy, designed and built between 1593 and 1623 is a prime example of a conscious effort to maximize its perimeter compactness (figure 14.2).

By the end of the Napoleonic Wars at the beginning of the nineteenth century, cities relinquished their responsibility to defend themselves. The construction of city walls, except in cities along national borders, essentially came to an end, as did the importance of perimeter compactness. The perimeter of a city without a wall has lost its meaning altogether. The built-up areas of contemporary cities do not have a well-defined perimeter. Their perimeter depends on the scale at which it is measured, as noted by Mendelbrot (1967) in his famous essay, "How Long is the Coast of Britain?" Intuitively, one may suspect that an urban periphery with a more meandering perimeter may indicate a greater degree of fragmentation of the built-up area by open space. But, since the perimeter of a city is no longer well defined, we would do better to measure the fragmentation of city footprints with the openness index or the city footprint ratio, as described in chapter 13, rather than seek to determine its perimeter compactness.

The second, and altogether different, rationale for city footprints to be compact came to the fore with the emergence of monocentric cities of the late nineteenth and

---

1 My colleague Geoffrey M. Hyman has written formal proofs for all these propositions in unpublished private correspondence. It stands to reason that among all shapes of a given area, the circle also has the shortest average distance, rather than distance-squared, among all its points, but a rigorous proof of this proposition has so far eluded him.

FIGURE 14.2

The Walled City of Palmanova, Italy, Designed and Built Between 1593 and 1623 to Maximize Perimeter Compactness

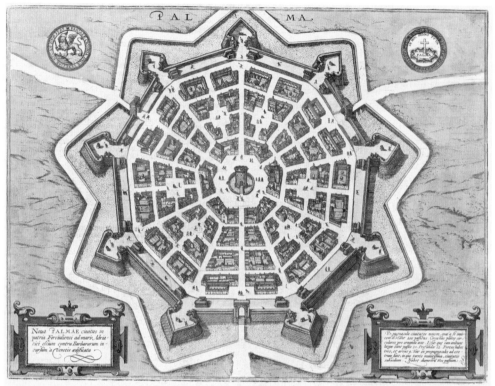

Source: Braun and Hogenberg (1572–1617), courtesy of the Hebrew University of Jerusalem Historic Cities Research Project and Ozgur Tufekci.

early twentieth centuries, when most workplaces were concentrated in city centers and travel from home to work took place along radial routes. In abstract terms, if all workplaces are centered at a point, if travel to work can take place from all directions with equal ease, and if workers seek to minimize the length of their journeys, then they will arrange their homes in a circle around that point. The circle, as noted earlier, maximizes proximity compactness. It ensures that everyone within it is as close to its center as possible. The actual formation of a circular footprint in a monocentric city is a cumulative process. A new arrival seeks to locate on the urban periphery as close to the center as possible and locates along that periphery in a place that is closest to the center. This process is repeated again and again with later arrivals.

At some point, there are no locations on the periphery that are any closer to the center than any other locations, and the shape of the periphery will have become a circle. Additional newcomers then locate their homes in concentric rings around the periphery and the overall shape of the city footprint will remain a circle. This realization is at the core of the classical economic model of the monocentric city proposed by Alonso

(1960; 1964), Mills (1967), and Muth (1961; 1969). They assumed *a priori* that when all jobs in their abstract city are concentrated at a point in a central business district (CBD), then the shape of the footprint of that city will be circular. Tokyo, Japan, for example, was largely a monocentric city in the late nineteenth and early twentieth centuries. By 1930 it had a nearly circular city footprint (figure 14.3).

A third and quite different rationale is needed to understand why the polycentric cities that emerged in the second half of the twentieth century would seek to be compact as well. In these cities, most travel is not on radial routes to the city center, but among locations distributed throughout the metropolitan area. The earlier forces that compelled monocentric city footprints to become more compact—the desires of workers to locate in close proximity to the CBD—no longer generate a circular urban form because workplaces have dispersed throughout the urban area. Polycentric cities tend to be circular because they seek to maximize a third compactness property, cohesion

FIGURE 14.3
High Proximity Compactness in the Built-up Area of Tokyo, Japan, 1930

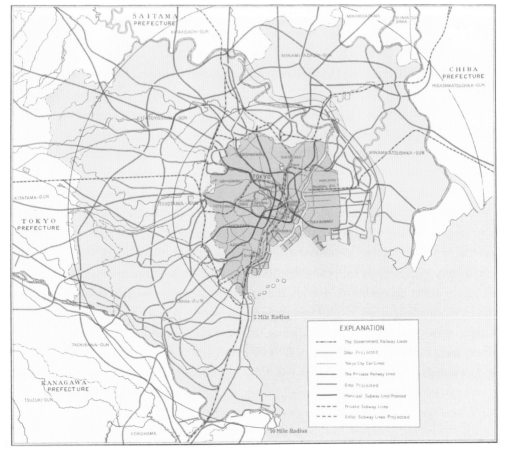

Source: Tokyo Shiyakusho (1930, 52).

compactness, ensuring that all locations within their footprints are as close as possible to each other. In abstract terms, if homes and workplaces are distributed evenly throughout the urban area, if travel can take place in all directions with equal ease, and if the length of the journey to work from all homes to all workplaces is minimized, then the city will take the form of a circle. In other words, the higher the cohesion of polycentric cities, the closer everyone is to everyone else, contacts and interactions among urban residents are then maximized, and distances to desirable destinations everywhere are minimized.

As we saw in chapter 12, the cohesion compactness of Buenos Aires was high even before its emergence as a monocentric city. It was already high in the walking city period, when residences and workplaces were distributed throughout the city, and it remained high when horsecars became ubiquitous, allowing the city to expand beyond its walking city limits while keeping all locations as close as possible to all others. More generally, we can surmise that cities were compelled to have a high level of cohesion compactness before the emergence of the monocentric city, when they still entertained high levels of mixed use.

In sum we can identify at least three distinct sets of forces acting on city footprints to make them more compact: forces seeking to minimize the costs of their walls that lead to high perimeter compactness; forces seeking to minimize the length of the journey to work in the CBD that lead to high proximity compactness; and forces seeking to minimize the length of the journey to work in the mixed-use city—be it the walking city, the horsecar city predating the monocentric city, or the polycentric city postdating it— that lead to high cohesion compactness.

Given the compelling nature of these forces, why are the city footprints of places like Warsaw, Poland, not more compact? The general answer is that other forces must be acting on those city footprints to make them less compact. One of the major reasons is the distortion of simple distances between locations caused by the uneven distribution of transport facilities. In theory, the perfect compactness of circular cities is predicated on the highly simplified assumption that travel can take place in all directions with equal ease. When travel in some directions can take workers further for the same cost or for the same expenditure of time, then some workers can locate further away from the city center than others and still expend the same cost or time on travel to work. Under these conditions, city footprints that minimize travel cost or travel time to work, rather than travel distance, will no longer be circular in shape. In other words, monocentric and polycentric cities will have a tendency to become more compact if travel can take place in all directions with equal ease and less compact if travel in some directions takes place with greater ease than in others.

This may be illustrated with a simple geometrical example that simulates the introduction of new transport technologies into an abstract monocentric city where all

FIGURE 14.4

The Effects of New Transport Technologies on the Proximity Compactness of a Monocentric City with Streets Spaced 500 Meters Apart

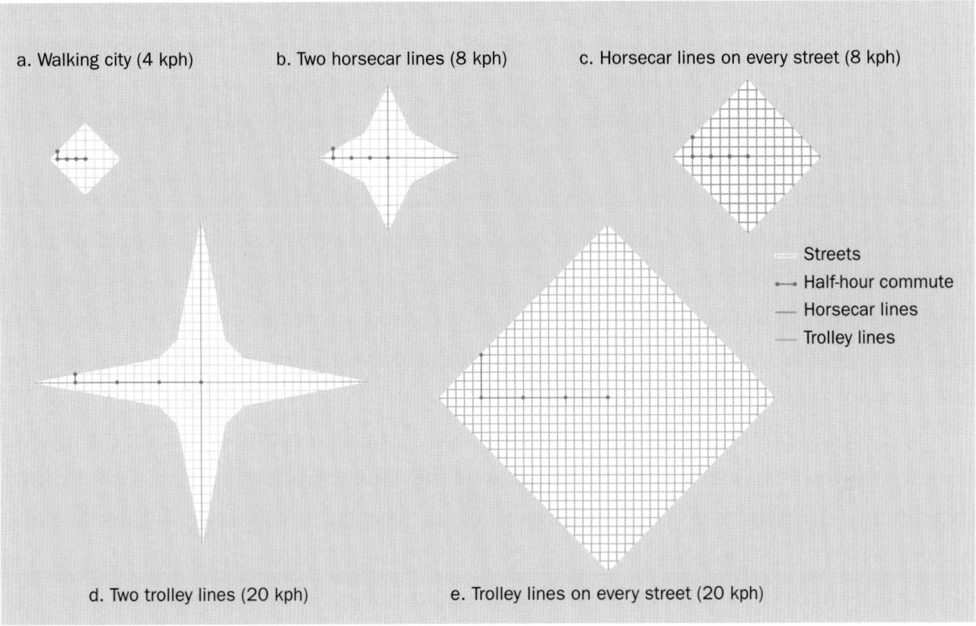

a. Walking city (4 kph)   b. Two horsecar lines (8 kph)   c. Horsecar lines on every street (8 kph)

Streets
Half-hour commute
Horsecar lines
Trolley lines

d. Two trolley lines (20 kph)   e. Trolley lines on every street (20 kph)

Source: Drawn by the author.

travel takes place along a street grid, streets are spaced a half-kilometer apart, all workplaces are concentrated in the city center, and workers are willing to expend a maximum of a half-hour on their journey to work.

We first consider the case of the walking city, where travel along streets can proceed with equal speed in north-south and east-west directions. The average walking speed is about 4 kilometers per hour (kph), so people walking to work can locate as far as 2 kilometers (km), or 4 blocks, from the city center (figure 14.4a). This assumption leads to a city footprint where all residences on the city perimeter are not more than 4 blocks away from the city center in a square shape with high proximity compactness.

Two horsecar lines are then introduced, crossing the center in the north-south and east-west directions with travel speeds of 8 kph, or 8 blocks in a half-hour. The speed on other streets remains 4 kph, or 4 blocks in a half-hour. The city can now extend up to 8 blocks along the horsecar lines, but not nearly as far in other directions, creating a star shape with lower proximity compactness (figure 14.4b)

As horsecars become ubiquitous throughout the city, people can again travel on all streets at equal speeds. They can travel to work by horsecar from all directions as far as 8 blocks away, and the shape of the city footprint again becomes a square with high proximity compactness (figure 14.4c). The availability of horsecars everywhere enlarges the city considerably, but does not render it less compact.

Two trolley lines are then introduced, crossing the center in the same north-south and east-west directions, with travel speeds of 20 kph, or 20 blocks in a half-hour. The walking speed on other streets remains 4 kph, or 4 blocks in a half-hour, and, to keep things simple, horsecars have now become extinct. The city can now extend up to 20 blocks along the trolley lines, but not nearly as far in other directions, creating a star shape with still lower proximity compactness than that created at the onset of the horsecar period (figure 14.4d).

Trolleys then become ubiquitous and there is a trolley line on every street in the city. People can again travel on all streets at equal speed. Workers can travel to work by trolley from all directions as far as 20 blocks away, and the shape of the city footprint again becomes a square with high proximity compactness (figure 14.4e). The availability of trolleys everywhere enlarges the city far beyond its size in the horsecar era, but does not render it less compact.

The introduction of commuter railroads along a limited number of radial routes to the city center has an effect similar to that of the initial trolley lines on radial routes in reducing the proximity compactness of cities, as seen in the case of Buenos Aires between 1930 and 1960 (see figure 12.3). The difference between commuter rail and the earlier transport technologies is that it could never become ubiquitous throughout the city because of the great expense involved in railway rights-of-way, stations, tracks, and rolling stock. In Buenos Aires, for example, it meant that the spaces between city fingers created by the extension of the built-up area along railway lines were not filled in easily by later development. This pattern only changed with the introduction of cars and buses that could travel on a dense network of paved roads in these areas because both vehicles and roads required considerably lower levels of capital investment.

In general, we should expect road-based, gasoline-powered vehicles to facilitate infill and increase the compactness of either monocentric or polycentric cities. The persistence of city fingers in Warsaw can be explained in part by the late introduction of private automobiles. Before the fall of Poland's communist government in 1990, the country had relatively low levels of car ownership: 138 cars per thousand in 1990, for example, compared to 480 in West Germany, 448 in France, and 403 in the United Kingdom in that year (Euromonitor 1995). Intercity railways and roads connected Warsaw to the rest of the country, but there was a shortage of roads in the urban periphery and no ring roads. Both factors contributed to the reduced supply of urbanized land in the interstices between the fingers of urban development. Some lands remained in agricultural use, although not always in cultivation, while other large tracts of land were designated for conservation. Several public parks—Kampinoski National Park and the Mazovia and Chojnów Landscape Parks, for example—reduced the supply of lands for urban development in these areas.

Freeways and expressways have had similar effects on the compactness of city footprints in the age of the automobile as railroads had previously. Freeway networks, like the U.S. Interstate Highway System built in the 1950s and 1960s, were typically financed by central governments, and their primary purpose was to connect cities to each other across national space. Their effect on the shape of city footprints was largely unintended, but, as in the case of commuter railroads, these roadways reduced compactness by allowing commuters to travel further from the city center in some directions but not in others.

FIGURE 14.5
The City Footprint of Buenos Aires, Argentina, 2000

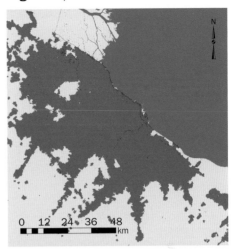

Source: Redrawn from Angel et al. (2012, 52).

In many cases, however, the impact of freeways on the compactness of city footprints appears to have been short-lived. Freeways require massive investments, create massive dislocations that disturb the fabric of cities, and generate stiff local resistance to new construction. When freeways are in limited supply, they soon become congested and traffic is diverted to alternate routes, until travel speed on all routes becomes constant. This phenomenon is an extension of Wardrop's First Principle of traffic assignment, which can be restated simply as follows: Informed drivers will choose their routes so that travel costs on two competing routes are equal when both are in use (Wardrop 1952). We can conjecture that in the longer run, cities dominated by automobile or bus travel on a dense network of arterial roads—even those lined with freeways—will become more compact as freeways become congested and as more travel shifts to alternative routes. The city footprint of Buenos Aires in 2000 already illustrates this effect (figure 14.5). Regardless of whether its metropolitan area has completed its transition from a monocentric to a polycentric city or not, its city footprint in 2000 exhibited a high level of proximity compactness.

A discussion of the forces acting to make city footprints more or less compact would be incomplete without reference to geographical features that prevent cities from expanding in one direction but not in others, as well as to regulatory policies that reserve large tracts of land near city centers. Features such as green wedges, linear parks, greenbelts, army training grounds, urban agriculture areas, and other forms of nonurban land uses force urban development to extend further out and lead to less compact city footprints and lower levels of accessibility among urban locations.

Water bodies also exert powerful deterrents to urban expansion. Mumbai, India, San Francisco, California, and parts of Alexandria, Egypt, are located on thin peninsulas

A large part of Alexandria, Egypt, is located on a narrow peninsula with the Mediterranean Sea on both sides, making its footprint less compact.

that allow them to expand in only one direction. Cebu City in the Philippines is constrained by both water and a steep mountain slope. The built-up areas of cities typically are limited to slopes of 15 degrees or less, so it stands to reason that cities located on relatively flat terrains will be more compact. But topographical constraints are not the only reasons why cities become less compact. Kuwait City, like many coastal or riverfront cities, has expanded linearly along the Persian Gulf over many years due to a combination of geography and the preferences of its inhabitants to be close to the water for both commercial and personal reasons.

COPENHAGEN, DENMARK, AND CHANDIGARH, INDIA

In terms of public policy, the 1947 Finger Plan for Copenhagen and the 1952 Le Corbusier plan for Chandigarh provide interesting examples of planned reductions in compactness. Both regional development plans sought to keep built-up areas within reach of open spaces, such as the agricultural areas within green wedges emanating from the city center in the Copenhagen plan, or the linear public parks meandering through built-up areas in the Chandigarh plan.

The 1947 Finger Plan for Copenhagen, which has never become law, has nevertheless guided the regulation of the development of the metropolitan area for several decades (figure 14.6). It envisioned the expansion of the built-up area along five fingers, each served by a commuter rail line. The plan was quite successful and all five of the green wedges envisioned in the plan are still recognizable. Two were partly filled in, succumbing to the pressure to make the city more compact and improve overall access while increasing the distance to peripheral open space for many residents. This finger plan, allowing for its noncompactness, does not constrain urban expansion as a greenbelt would, while preserving access to ample open space.

Le Corbusier's 1952 plan for Chandigarh, the capital of the State of Punjab in India, suffered a more severe fate than that for Copenhagen. It sought to keep built-up areas no further than a 10-minute walk from linear green parks running through the middle of its 1.2-by-1.8 km superblocks. The built-up area as a whole remained relatively compact from the perspective of access, keeping all locations in quite close

FIGURE 14.6
The Finger Plan for Copenhagen, Denmark, 1947–2010

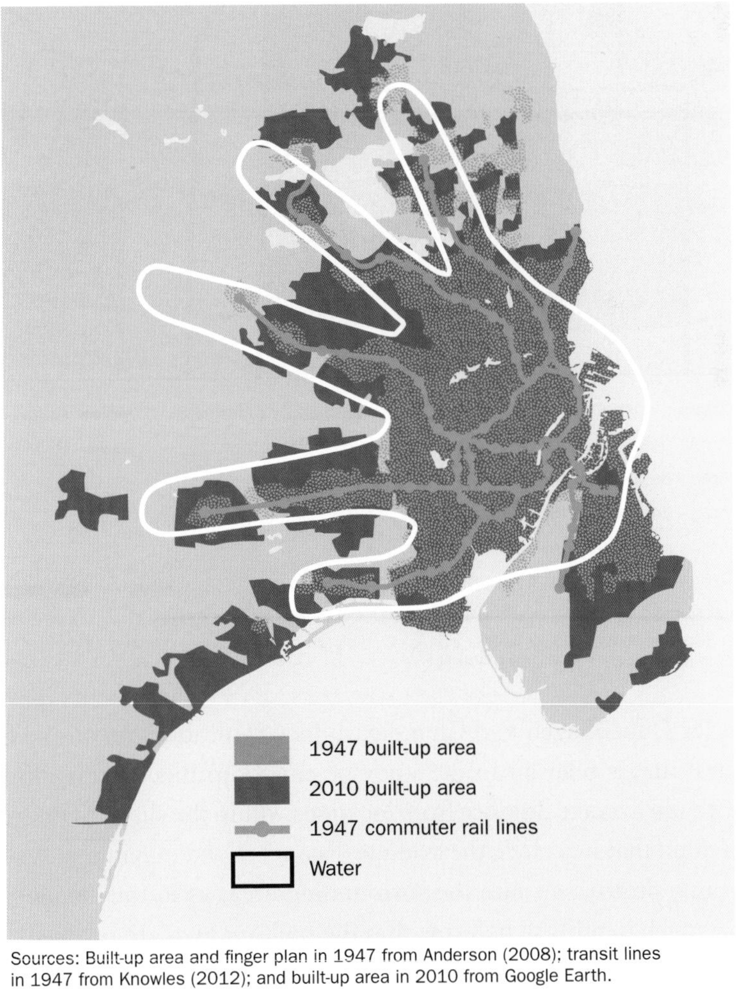

Sources: Built-up area and finger plan in 1947 from Anderson (2008); transit lines in 1947 from Knowles (2012); and built-up area in 2010 from Google Earth.

proximity to the city center and to each other. In contrast to a greenbelt plan, this plan—like the Copenhagen Finger Plan—also allowed for the expansion of the built-up area of the city within the superblock grid while maintaining ample access to open space within the grid. Attractive as it was, however, municipal authorities were unable to resist the infill of most of the planned green parks within the superblocks. By 2002, only a few public parks remained while most of the planned green areas and all linear parks were fully built-up (figure 14.7).

FIGURE 14.7
The Loss of Planned Open Space in Le Corbusier's 1952 Master Plan for Chandigarh, India, 2010

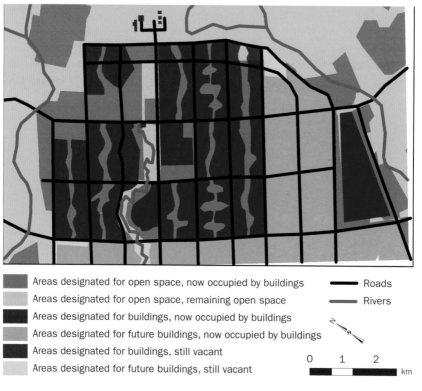

▓ Areas designated for open space, now occupied by buildings	▬ Roads
░ Areas designated for open space, remaining open space	▬ Rivers
■ Areas designated for buildings, now occupied by buildings	
▨ Areas designated for future buildings, now occupied by buildings	N
■ Areas designated for buildings, still vacant	
░ Areas designated for future buildings, still vacant	0 1 2 km

Sources: Redrawn from the 1952 master plan for Chandigarh in Le Corbusier (1960, 187); and built-up area in 2010 from Google Earth.

The plans for Copenhagen and Chandigarh focus our attention on the fourth type of compactness that is relevant to the study of city footprints. Depth compactness is concerned with the average distance from locations within the shape to the area outside it, bearing in mind that in a circle the average distance is at a maximum. A shape made up of many long protrusions into the surrounding area, as in the Copenhagen plan, does not have much depth. All points within the built-up area are relatively close to its periphery. An analogy is the floor plan of a sprawling college dormitory that allows the

Le Corbusier holds up the master plan for Chandigarh, circa 1950.

structures and the open space around them to interpenetrate each other and provides natural light and air in all rooms.

COMPACTNESS METRICS

We developed metrics to measure the compactness of cities that essentially compare them to a circle of the same area (Angel, Parent, and Civco 2010). We introduce three of the metrics here, ignoring the perimeter compactness of cities since they are no longer surrounded by walls. The metrics vary between 1 for a full circle and 0 for the least compact shape.

- The proximity index is the ratio of the average distance of all points in a circle of the same area to its center and the average distance from all points in the city to its city hall.
- The cohesion index is the ratio of the average distance between all pairs of points in a circle of the same area and the average distance between all pairs of points in the city.
- The depth index is the ratio of the average distance from points in the city (including all fully contained open spaces) to its outer periphery and the average distance to the periphery in a circle of the same area.

FIGURE 14.8
Changing Compactness in Buenos Aires, Argentina, 1800–2000

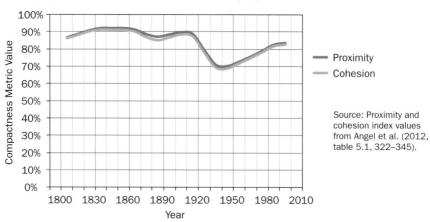

Source: Proximity and cohesion index values from Angel et al. (2012, table 5.1, 322–345).

The changing values of the proximity and cohesion indices for the urbanized area of Buenos Aires during the past two centuries are shown in figure 14.8. Values for these indices did not vary appreciably from each other over the years. This suggests that one can be the proxy of the other, and the proximity index is used here as a representative compactness index for the empirical data. The figure also shows that during its walking city period and up to the introduction of horsecars in the mid-1860s, Buenos Aires was very compact. Its compactness declined with the introduction of the first horsecars, but soon increased again as both horsecars and then trolleys became ubiquitous. Its compactness declined precipitously in the 1920s as commuter railways became the most important transport mode from the expanding suburbs into the central city. Compactness reached an all-time low value after the end of World War II and then began to climb slowly as cars and buses became more ubiquitous and as more roads on the periphery were paved. By 2000, Greater Buenos Aires reached the same levels of proximity and cohesion compactness as during its walking city era in the early decades of the nineteenth century.

The changing values of depth compactness in Buenos Aires follow similar trends as the other two compactness indices. The depth values are not shown in figure 14.8, however, because our analysis is not sufficiently sensitive to measure what constitutes fully contained open spaces in a city. In estimating city footprints, we considered large enough open spaces (more than 200 hectares in area) to be part of the open periphery (see figure 14.5), so as to leave out open fields surrounded by strip developments lining the roads along their perimeter. But this allowance distorts the measure of depth compactness proposed here, which should refer only to the average distance to what A. A. Milne referred to in his poem *Disobedience* as "the end of the town": "I can get right down to the end of the town and be back in time for tea" (1924, 30).

In conclusion, this theoretical and historical overview of the compactness of urban footprints has documented the powerful forces acting on urban footprints to make them more or less compact. To get a better sense of whether the procompactness forces tend overwhelm the anticompactness ones or vice versa—or alternatively whether cities worldwide tend to become more or less compact over time—we turn to the empirical evidence.

OBSERVED COMPACTNESS IN 120 CITY FOOTPRINTS, 1990–2000

We calculated the proximity index and the cohesion index for the city footprints of the global sample of 120 cities for 1990 and 2000. The correlation between the two indices in each period was above 0.995, so this analysis focuses only on the proximity index, which is also a proxy for the cohesion index.

For the cities in the global sample as a whole, the compactness of city footprints measured with the proximity index did not change significantly between 1990 and 2000. Approximately half the cities became more compact and half became less compact. The three cities that made the most gains in compactness were Ahvaz in Iran, Puna in India, and Zhengzhou in China. The three cities that lost the most in compactness were St. Catharines in Canada, Leshan in China, and Leipzig in Germany. We could not detect significant changes in compactness in the span of one decade, and compactness did not vary significantly among geographic regions. Only cities in East Asia and the Pacific were found to be significantly less compact than cities in Sub-Saharan Africa and land-rich developed countries at the 95 percent confidence levels, and we have no ready explanation for that finding.

There is no accepted economic theory that predicts why cities should be more or less compact or could explain the variations in compactness among cities in the global sample. The classical model of the monocentric city simply assumes that cities are circular and leaves it at that. The previous sections suggested a number of possible hypotheses that could be tested using the data on the proximity index for the global sample of 120 cities, together with additional data on these cities, in a similar fashion to the analysis of variations in density and fragmentation in previous chapters. Some of these additional data were obtained from secondary sources, while others were obtained from a survey of local consultants in these cities. The survey included responses that were sometimes fragmentary or variable in quality, so some results (hypotheses 3, 5, and 6 below) must remain tentative at best. Six such hypotheses were proposed and then tested using statistical regression models.

1. Cities built on flatter terrains with no natural obstacles, such as water or steep slopes, will tend to be more compact. This is one of only two hypotheses that could be confirmed at the 95 percent level of confidence.

2. Larger cities, which are likely to be more polycentric than smaller ones with travel flowing in all directions, can be expected to be more compact. This hypothesis was also confirmed at the 95 percent level of confidence: the larger the city, the more compact it tends to be.

3. Cities with more rail stations per person should be expected to be less compact, assuming that commuter rail lines that are largely along radial lines tend to create long tentacles of built-up areas along their routes. This hypothesis was not confirmed by the data.

4. Cities in countries with higher levels of car ownership should be expected to be more compact, because the preponderance of cars makes travel on many alternative routes possible and tends to equalize travel time on all roads, eliminating the built-in advantages of radial routes and thus making cities more compact. This hypothesis could not be confirmed by the available evidence from the global sample.

5. Cities with dense bus networks and a shorter average time of travel to bus stations should be more compact, but this hypothesis also could not be confirmed by the data.

6. Cities that reserve large areas for open space where development is not allowed should be less compact because new development must be located further from the city center than it would be otherwise. This hypothesis also could not be confirmed by the available evidence.

OBSERVED COMPACTNESS IN U.S. CITIES, 1910–2000

The expansion of the U.S. Interstate Highway System, authorized by the Federal Aid Highway Act of 1956, is assumed to be the leading cause of the significant decline in the compactness of U.S. cities during the 1950s and the 1960s, when suburbanization was at its peak. The freeways emanating out of major cities made it possible to locate new residential areas further away from CBDs, while still making it possible to commute to work in less than 30 minutes. An analysis of maps of the urban tract areas of U.S. cities between 1910 and 2000 lends empirical support to this assumption. Maps were drawn for two sets of cities: one set for which digital census tract maps were available from 1910 (for 7 cities in 1910, 3 in 1920, 19 in 1930, and 20 thereafter); and another set for which digital census tract maps were available for 65 cities with populations of 50,000 people or more in 1950, for the period 1950–2000. The average proximity index values for these two sets of cities are shown in figure 14.9.

Data from the set of 20 cities suggest that the decline in the average compactness of U.S. cities started in 1940 and reached its nadir between 1960 and 1970, when it started to rise slowly. Data from the set of 65 cities show average compactness values to be in decline throughout the 1950s and 1960s, reaching their nadir in 1970, after which

FIGURE 14.9

**Compactness Values for Two Sets of U.S. Cities,
1910–2000**

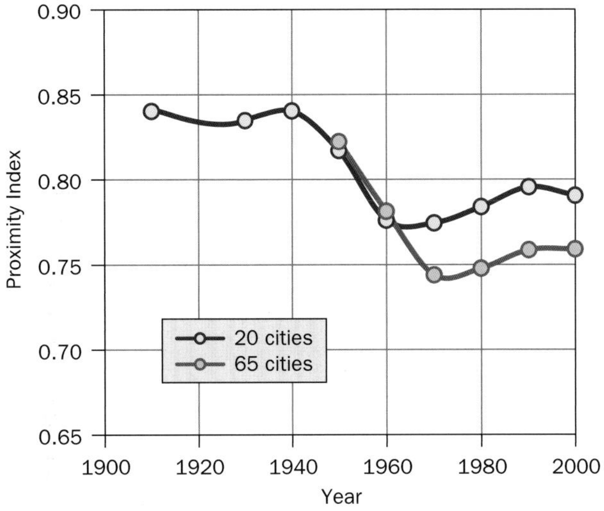

Source: Calculated from census data in National Historical Geographic
Information System (2012).

they began to climb slowly. The results from the two data sets are consistent, except that the decline in compactness in the set of 65 cities appears to be considerably steeper. By 1990 the increase in average compactness values in both data sets stopped and a slight decline was registered between 1990 and 2000. In 2000 the most compact urban areas in the United States were Greensboro, North Carolina; Toledo and Columbus, Ohio; and Minneapolis–St. Paul, Minnesota. The least compact cities were Atlantic City, New Jersey; Duluth, Minnesota; Bridgeport, Connecticut; and Miami, Florida.

Average values of the proximity index from 1970 onward in the set of 65 cities were found to be significantly lower than the initial values observed in 1950. The construction of new freeways within metropolitan areas has now largely come to an end and in many places they have become quite congested. Nevertheless, city footprints have not returned to their earlier compactness levels, as they did in Buenos Aires.

Developments in transportation may not have been the only cause for changes in compactness. Beginning in the 1970s, stricter zoning regulations aimed at protecting large tracts of land on the urban periphery from conversion to urban use (Fischel 1995) have likely prevented cities from becoming more compact. Hence, while the decline in the average compactness of U.S. cities between 1940 and 1970 and its gradual increase since then are clearly observable (albeit to lower levels than those of 1940), convincing explanations as to why these shifts have occurred must await a more rigorous analysis.

OBSERVED COMPACTNESS IN 30 CITY FOOTPRINTS, 1800–2000

The *Atlas of Urban Expansion* contains maps of the urbanized areas of 30 representative world cities for the period 1800–2000 (Angel et al. 2012). The maps show the urbanized area in each city at 20- to 25-year intervals, so we can measure the changes in the values of the proximity index and compare them to other cities to discern common patterns. Comparing the changes requires a note of caution, however, given that these 30 cities developed their transportation and regulatory systems at different time periods.

We begin by exploring whether the compactness of cities has increased or decreased in one common time frame, roughly from 1820 to 2000 (there were fewer than 16 observations in 1800 and 1810). Figure 14.10 shows that, on average, the compactness of cities remained relatively high and relatively stable throughout the nineteenth century, declined significantly in the first decades of the twentieth century, and stabilized at a lower level of compactness from 1940 to 1980. In recent decades, the average compactness of cities has increased again, but that increase has not been statistically significant. By the end of the twentieth century, average compactness levels were lower (but not significantly lower in a statistical sense) than those prevailing in the nineteenth century.

The general pattern shown in figure 14.10 is an average of the fluctuations in the compactness of the 30 individual cities in this sample. But each city has followed a

FIGURE 14.10
Average Compactness in the Global Representative Sample of 30 Cities, 1820–2000

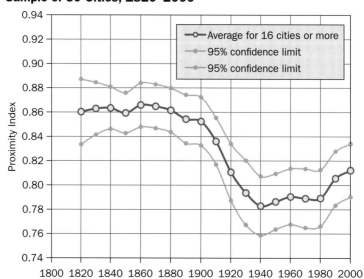

Source: Calculated from maps in Angel et al. (2012, 260–319).

unique path that is quite different from the global average. Five groups of cities each had similar patterns of changes in their proximity indices over time, as shown in the graphs in figure 14.11. Each graph also contains the average for the group and the average for all 30 cities in the sample. The first group contains five cities where compactness has been relatively high and stable for a long time: London, Paris, Moscow,

FIGURE 14.11
Proximity Index Trajectories in Five Groups of Cities, 1800–2000

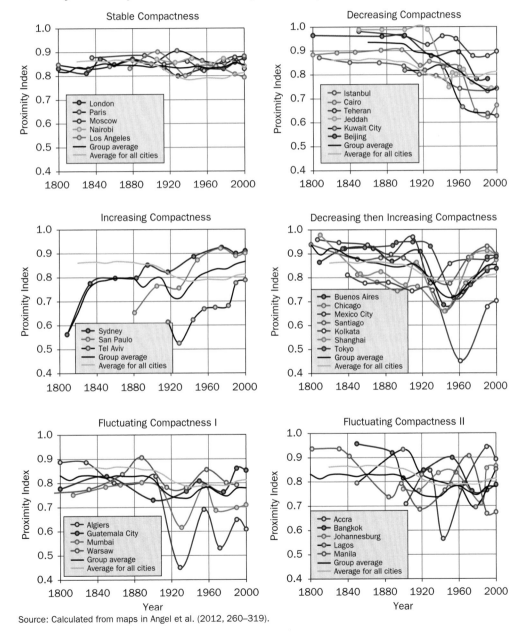

Source: Calculated from maps in Angel et al. (2012, 260–319).

Nairobi, and Los Angeles. The second group contains six cities where compactness levels were generally high in the nineteenth century and declined in the twentieth century: Istanbul, Cairo, Teheran, Kuwait City, Jeddah, and Beijing. The third group contains three cities that registered increasing compactness over time: Sydney, São Paulo, and Tel Aviv. The fourth group contains seven cities that experienced decreasing compactness followed by increasing compactness to previous levels: Buenos Aires, Chicago, Mexico City, Santiago, Kolkata, Shanghai, and Tokyo. The fifth group contains nine cities (split into two graphs) that have experienced several fluctuations in their levels of compactness over time: Algiers, Guatemala City, Mumbai, Warsaw, Accra, Bangkok, Johannesburg, Lagos, and Manila.

We do not have enough information at the present time to be able to explain why a particular city would fall into one or another of these five groups. It is clear that a complex set of forces are acting to make cities more or less compact, and the relative import or effect of any one of these forces changes over time.

COMPACTNESS AND PLANNING FOR URBAN EXPANSION

When making preparations for expansion in any particular city in the coming decades, we need to develop a deeper understanding of these forces and come to terms with their real potential to subvert our best intentions. This is particularly crucial if planning for expansion by public authorities aims to guide growth into particular lands while seeking to prevent the conversion of other lands to urban use. There is a natural and perfectly understandable desire on the part of public officials to guide built-up areas away from open spaces that need special protection. These areas may include lands needed to ensure access to public open space within a reasonable distance from built-up areas, as those envisioned in the Copenhagen and Chandigarh plans; lands with steep slopes that should be left unoccupied because of landslides or other dangers, like the canyons of Guatemala City; lands that form watersheds of reservoirs; wetlands containing sensitive fauna and flora that should be left undisturbed; or farmlands on rich soils that need to be preserved to protect food supplies.

Most, if not all, of these considerations can make urban footprints less compact and decrease overall access in the urban area, while increasing the length of infrastructure lines into the periphery. When making plans for expansion, such trade-offs need to be properly considered. We must also keep in mind that the forces acting to negate and compromise such plans, as lofty as their goals may be, may result in unplanned consequences, as the disappearance of the linear parks in Chandigarh clearly demonstrates.

The open space plans for Guatemala City, to take another example, not only were compromised, but were based on a nonexistent reality from the very start. Land use in the metropolitan area of Guatemala City is divided into two broad types: the relatively flat land on the plateaus where the formal city is located, and the steep land in the

The Colonia Buena Vista in Guatemala City, like most other squatter settlements in the city, is located on steep slopes designated as green areas in city plans.

canyons (*barrancos*) where the informal city is located. Some 40 to 50 percent of the city population lives in informal settlements on the canyon slopes, but this population remains largely unrecognized by official planners (Angel 2000a, 20).

The 2010 development plan for the metropolitan area recommended declaring these settlements as areas of high landslide risk endangering their inhabitants, clearing them, and transferring their inhabitants to dormitory communities outside the metropolitan area. In the process, planning officials promised to increase the amount of land in the metropolitan area devoted to green areas, forests, and protected areas to 46.1 percent of the total area. Canyon slopes were to be transformed into forested areas that would have created ecological greenbelts throughout the city footprint. Not surprisingly, the plan omitted any mention of how such an enormous undertaking would ever take place in practice (Municipality of Guatemala 1995). Impractical as it was, official insistence on the preservation of large green areas and on "exclusion zones," where no construction was allowed because of the risk of landslides, limited the land available for residential development in accessible locations and prevented (or postponed) the legalization of squatter settlements that had been in existence for decades.

The metropolitan population that was in serious danger of landslides like the one that devastated the metropolitan area in 1976 was located on only about 5 percent of the total area (International Land Systems 1997). The risks to the other 95 percent of

The overall shape of the built-up area of São Paulo, Brazil, remains very compact as it stretches in all directions with no large open spaces penetrating it.

the areas in danger of landslides could be mitigated with low levels of infrastructure improvements, such as drainage canals and retaining walls. Yet, there was a general reluctance among planning officials to move decisively to upgrade settlements on canyon slopes. Their favored green-city policies postponed the improvement of infra-structure services in these residential communities and delayed both the mitigation of environmental risks and opportunity for families to invest in transforming their homes into dignified dwellings. Planning authorities were too weak to carry out their radical plans, which would have required relocating hundreds of thousands of people now close to the center of the city to distant locations, so the plan was never implemented.

CONCLUSION

Plans for guiding urban expansion cannot and should not be based on wishful thinking but instead on a full recognition of the forces seeking to make city footprints more compact, that is, the desires of households and businesses to be as close as possible to the city center and to each other. It should be no surprise that the pursuit of urban locations with easy access to jobs, markets, and other people fulfills a more basic need in the hierarchy of needs than access to open space. It is a legitimate preference of many families—especially low-income ones—that should be given its due weight in the planning calculus. In general, open spaces are difficult to protect when household and corporate preferences result in strong political and economic pressures to occupy them.

We must keep in mind that the economic and political costs of effectively protecting open spaces are limited and must be marshaled judiciously. Trying to protect too much open space with too few resources may result in failure to protect any open space at all. As the Talmud says, "If you have seized a lot, you have not seized; if you have seized a little, you have seized."

The effects on urban expansion of radial intercity commuter rail lines or freeways that allow for higher travel speeds should also be taken into account when seeking to guide expansion, because their construction tends to make city footprints less compact over time. From a public policy perspective, that may sometimes be undesirable. In that case, guiding urban development into the interstices between the tentacles of urban development along these lines will require the planning and construction of a dense network of arterial roads that can carry public as well as private transport, that allow for the movement of traffic in all directions, and that can help equalize travel times along alternate routes so as to compromise the advantage of radial travel on intercity lines. Simply marking these areas on land use plans as available for urban use may not be sufficient to direct development there. Guiding urban expansion in a realistic fashion, in other words, cannot take place in a vacuum. It must be planned and executed in full recognition of the complex interplay of forces now acting to make cities more or less compact.

[Zhengzhou's] 2010 plan, submitted in 1998, grossly underestimated both population growth and urban expansion: It estimated its 2010 population at 2.3 million and its area at 189 square kilometers. Both were surpassed by 2003.

Angel, Valdivia, and Lutzy (2011, 141)

CHAPTER 15

Urban Land Cover Projections, 2000–2050

How much land will urban areas require in the future, why, and why should it matter?

BARCELONA, SPAIN

The city council of Barcelona, Spain, organized a competition in 1859 for a plan to expand the city and selected the visionary plan submitted by Ildefons Cerdá as the winning entry (Soria y Puig 1999). Like the three commissioners who approved the iconic grid plan for New York City in 1811, Cerdá envisioned a massive, ninefold expansion of the area of the existing city that then had a population of 150,000 (figure 15.1). Like the commissioners, Cerdá also focused on a practical vision and was intimately involved in devising the legal, administrative, and financial instruments necessary to execute the plan and follow it through to its implementation. Being a realist, he was very critical of utopian dreams.

> In our times we have seen some dazzlingly brilliant utopias appear, and they really have shown and dazzled, but simply in the manner of a fleeting bolt of lightening, and they have left no trace behind. Some hard and rather costly lessons brought skepticism to seep into the hearts of our societies, and now only patent proofs of non-remote possibilities can sweep away the doubts, distrust, and lack of confidence. (Soria y Puig 1999, 375)

Cerdá's plan for Barcelona, the New York City Commissioners' Plan of 1811, the Topographical Bureau's 1900 plan for New York, and the 1904 plan for Buenos Aires were not utopian dreams. They were pragmatic plans that were implemented quickly, and all three cities soon outgrew them. These cities show that there is nothing new in

FIGURE 15.1
Ildefons Cerdá's Ensanche Plan for Barcelona, Spain, 1859

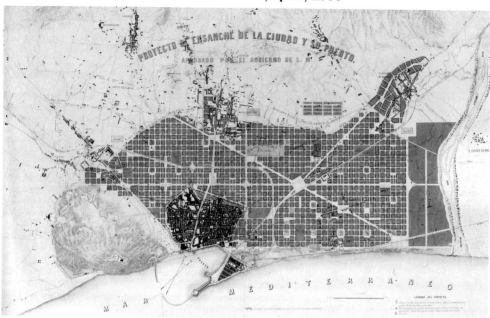

Source: Soria y Puig (1999, figure 19, 279).

making generous plans for urban expansion, yet it is difficult to identify one urban plan that has allowed for such generous expansion of a metropolitan area in recent decades. The need exists, however, since the 30 cities in our global representative sample expanded sixteenfold in a matter of 70 years, on average, during the twentieth century. We can subscribe the absence of such plans to a failure of imagination or a failure of nerve. But it is exactly this kind of imagination and nerve that must be rekindled to realistically project the expansion of many cities in urbanizing countries in the coming decades.

FORECASTING URBAN LAND COVER IN INDIVIDUAL CITIES

If we are to prepare cities for their expansion, we need to know how much land on the fringe of a given city will need to be converted to urban use in the next 20 to 30 years. Better yet, we also need to forecast in what parts of the urban fringe expansion is likely to take place so we can secure the necessary lands for public use in advance of their subdivision and development. These are not simple problems, and the answers involve considerable speculation. Still, we will be better off trying to provide thoughtful answers, allowing for contingencies, and accommodating adequate margins of error than giving up on preparing for expansion altogether or simply making convenient assumptions about the expected amount and location of future urban expansion based on wishful thinking.

Forecasting urban land cover involves a combination of several independent projections: We need to forecast the city population, its built-up area density, and its level of fragmentation. To forecast where expansion will likely take place, we also need to forecast and plan for possible changes in its compactness. Disregarding changes in compactness for now, if we measure fragmentation by the city footprint ratio, we can find the city's projected urban land cover from the following simple formulas.

1. Built-up area density = Population ÷ Built-up area. Therefore,
2. Built-up area = Population ÷ Built-up area density.
3. Urban land cover = Built-up area × City footprint ratio. Therefore,
4. Urban land cover = (Population ÷ Built-up area density) × City footprint ratio.

In other words, if we have forecasts for the population, the built-up area density, and the city footprint ratio, then we can forecast the urban land cover of the city. For example, if the projected population in 20 years is 500,000 and the projected built-up area density is 200 persons per hectare, then the projected built-up area will be 2,500 hectares or 25 square kilometers (km^2). If the projected city footprint ratio is 1.6 (i.e., open space is expected to add 60 percent to the built-up area), then the projected urban land cover of the city (including its open spaces) will be 2,500 x 1.6 = 4,000 hectares or 40 km^2.

In this connection, the State of Oregon requires all cities to adopt urban growth boundaries (UGBs) that contain sufficient lands within them for 20 years of projected population growth. To estimate the amount of land needed for expansion,

> [c]ities must adopt a 20-year population forecast for the urban area. . . . The forecast must be developed using commonly accepted practices and standards for population forecasting used by professional practitioners in the field of demography or economics, and must be based on current, reliable and objective sources and verifiable factual information. . . . The forecast must take into account documented long-term demographic trends as well as recent events that have a reasonable likelihood of changing historical trends. (State of Oregon 2012, 660-024-0030)

Not surprisingly, the population forecast is the most basic building block in planning and preparing for urban expansion. To estimate a city's population 20 years hence, this forecast involves finding out the annual rate at which its population is likely to grow in the foreseeable future.

In chapter 8, we observed that the growth rate of the population of individual cities in most countries does not vary with the city population size. On average, cities of all population sizes grow at the same rate. It stands to reason, therefore, that the default

The projected amount of land needed for urban expansion will depend on expected densities and levels of fragmentation. Recent development in Beijing, China (top) and in Quito, Ecuador (bottom) highlights stark contrasts in both density and fragmentation.

growth rate of the population of any individual city will be the average urban population growth rate of the country as a whole. But we also observed that city populations are not distributed around a mean in a bell-shaped curve. Their distribution obeys a power law, consisting of a large number of small cities, a smaller number of larger ones, and a few that are very large. When forecasting the population of an individual city, there is a small probability that it could become very large, for example, if its growth rate becomes much higher than average for the country as a whole. Taleb (2007, 208–211), who has studied the impact of small-probability events, notes that the appropriate strategy to confront this uncertainty is to focus on its consequences rather than its likelihood.

> Invest in preparedness, not in prediction. . . . The probabilities of very rare events are not computable. . . . We can have a clear idea of the consequences of an event, even if we do not know how likely it is to occur. . . . All you have to do is mitigate the consequences.

This suggests that erring on the high side of projecting urban land cover in a particular city expansion plan may be the correct strategy for reducing the risk of laissez-faire expansion, as long as the cost of putting adequate preparations in place is kept at a minimum. The main risk of laissez-faire expansion is the undersupply of public goods, the most important of which are lands for arterial roads—including those required for the main infrastructure lines—and lands for public open spaces, both of which will not be supplied adequately by the ordinary operations of land markets (see chapter 5).

Securing the lands required for public goods in advance of development, and securing them in ample supply in all directions where development can be expected to occur, may be the most appropriate strategy for confronting the uncertainty of correctly projecting city populations. This, in itself, does not require massive investments in the actual construction of roads or in the development of public parks. That implementation can come later in response to actual population growth and actual construction on the urban fringe. What needs to be done in advance is to secure the lands for these public works—the rights-of-way for arterial roads and the open spaces for a hierarchy of public parks—throughout the urban fringe.

Still, the question remains that if we are to err on the high side of population projections, how can we estimate what erring on the high side means? A starting point for projecting the population of individual cities could be the rate of urban population growth in the country as a whole, a rate for which relatively good short-term and long-term projections are available from national census bureaus and the United Nations Population Division. Individual cities can also base their projections on their own historical growth trajectories. If those trajectories change unexpectedly due to some cataclysmic event, such as the influx of war refugees, an environmental catastrophe, or rapid economic growth, they can be adjusted in time.

GLOBAL AND REGIONAL URBAN LAND COVER PROJECTIONS

The United Nations provides forecasts of the urban populations of all countries for every decade up to 2050. These projections are adjusted every two years and can be considered reliable and consistent, keeping in mind, of course, that longer-term forecasts are less reliable than shorter-term ones. The latest projections are used here to discuss the main characteristics of projected urban population growth in different world regions (United Nations Population Division 2012).

- The world urban population is expected to double between 2010 and 2050, from 2.6 billion to 5.2 billion.
- The rate of increase of the world urban population is expected to slow from 2 percent per annum in 2000 to 1.65 in 2030 and to 1.14 percent in 2050.
- The urban population in developing countries will grow at a rate five times faster than the urban population in developed countries.
- The urban population of developed countries will increase by 160 million between 2010 and 2050 and will stabilize at around 1 billion people.
- The urban population of developing countries will increase by 2.4 billion between 2010 and 2050, or 15 times that of developed countries.
- Among countries in the developing regions, the fastest growth in the urban population will occur in Sub-Saharan Africa and in the Indian Subcontinent, followed by China and Southeast Asia.

A large number of countries will experience massive increases in their urban populations in the coming decades: 26 are expected to double their urban populations between 2010 and 2030, and 55 will double them between 2010 and 2050. Urban land cover in these countries will increase by considerably larger factors than their urban populations because built-up area densities can be expected to decline (see chapter 11). Given the long history and the pervasiveness of density decline, as well as the persistence of the causes of that decline—economic development coupled with increases in household incomes and low transportation costs, and the general absence of effective policy instruments for increasing densities—we can expect densities to decline in future decades as well. This expectation must be qualified, however. If economic development slows to a crawl, if transport costs double or triple, if housing and travel preferences change, and if effective densification policies that draw broad public support can be found, density decline may come to a halt and worldwide increases in urban densities may occur.

The fastest growth in the population and built-up area of cities in coming decades will occur in Sub-Saharan Africa: Children in a squatter settlement on the garbage dump of Freetown, Sierra Leone.

Barring such major changes, assuming that densities will continue to decline as they have in the past may be appropriate in estimating future urban land needs. Three realistic density scenarios are used to project urban land cover into the future:

1. A high projection, assuming a projected density decline of 2 percent per annum;
2. A medium projection, assuming a projected density decline of 1 percent per annum; and
3. A low projection, assuming that densities remain unchanged.

Projected urban expansion between 2000 and 2050 will mainly be a function of urban population growth and density change, assuming that levels of fragmentation do not decline substantially during the coming decades.[1] Figure 15.2 and Table 15.1 show the increases in urban land cover in different world regions under these three density scenarios (for country projections, see Angel et al. 2012, table 5.4).

---

1 The land cover estimates used in our projections were obtained from our Mod500 global map of large cities, at 463x463–meter pixel resolution. These larger pixels contain significant amounts of urbanized open space. In the global sample of 120 cities, they included urbanized open space that amounted to 55 percent, on average, of the built-up area calculated from the Landsat 30x30–meter pixel imagery. The Mod500 estimates are therefore not unrealistic estimates of the land needed to accommodate the projected fragmentation in city footprints.

In the year 2000, global urban land cover amounted to 0.47 percent of the land area of countries. At constant densities, the world's urban land cover will increase to 0.73 percent of the land area of countries by 2030 and to 0.88 percent by 2050. In other words, it will less than double between 2000 and 2050 as the world's urban population doubles. At a 1 percent annual rate of density decline, the world's urban land cover will

FIGURE 15.2
Projections of Urban Land Cover for World Regions Under Three Density Change Scenarios, 2000–2050

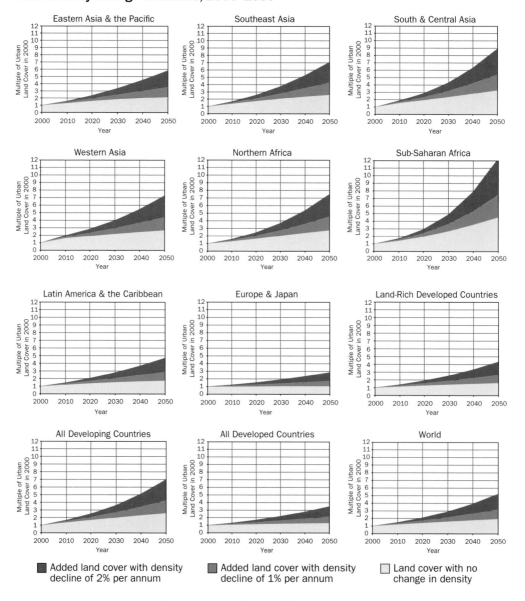

Source: Calculations based on United Nations Population Division (2010, file 2) and the author's density projections.

TABLE 15.1
Projections of Urban Land Cover for World Regions Under Three Density Change Scenarios, 2000–2050

Region	Urban Land Cover, 2000 (km²)	Annual Density Decline (%)	Urban Land Cover Projections (km²)				
			2010	2020	2030	2040	2050
Eastern Asia & the Pacific	52,978	0	69,225	85,086	98,329	107,916	114,154
		1	76,505	103,925	132,730	160,991	188,208
		2	84,552	126,934	179,167	240,170	310,302
Southeast Asia	34,448	0	47,520	60,166	71,641	81,848	89,952
		1	52,518	73,487	96,705	122,103	148,306
		2	58,041	89,758	130,538	182,156	244,516
South & Central Asia	59,872	0	93,434	116,653	143,282	171,123	197,324
		1	103,261	142,480	193,410	255,286	325,332
		2	114,121	174,026	261,076	380,842	536,382
Western Asia	22,714	0	37,127	43,418	49,931	55,933	61,041
		1	41,032	53,031	67,400	83,442	100,639
		2	45,347	64,772	90,981	124,480	165,926
Northern Africa	12,104	0	15,782	20,093	24,676	29,277	33,519
		1	17,441	24,542	33,309	43,677	55,263
		2	19,276	29,975	44,962	65,158	91,113
Sub-Saharan Africa	26,500	0	37,568	52,304	71,375	94,325	120,182
		1	41,519	63,884	96,347	140,716	198,147
		2	45,886	78,028	130,054	209,924	326,689
Latin America & the Caribbean	91,300	0	109,552	126,218	140,209	151,227	158,925
		1	121,074	154,164	189,262	225,605	262,023
		2	133,807	188,296	255,477	336,563	432,002
Europe & Japan	174,514	0	177,635	180,569	183,661	185,162	184,439
		1	196,318	220,547	247,917	276,230	304,089
		2	216,964	269,377	334,653	412,086	501,358
Land-Rich Developed Countries	131,447	0	150,691	168,848	184,906	198,850	211,039
		1	166,539	206,232	249,597	296,649	347,944
		2	184,054	251,892	336,920	442,549	573,663
All Developing Countries	299,915	0	410,208	503,939	599,442	691,649	775,096
		1	453,350	615,512	809,163	1,031,819	1,277,918
		2	501,029	751,788	1,092,255	1,539,294	2,106,931
All Developed Countries	305,961	0	328,326	349,417	368,567	384,012	395,478
		1	362,856	426,779	497,513	572,879	652,033
		2	401,018	521,269	671,573	854,635	1,075,021
World Total	605,875	0	738,534	853,355	968,009	1,075,661	1,170,575
		1	816,206	1,042,291	1,306,676	1,604,698	1,929,951
		2	902,048	1,273,057	1,763,828	2,393,929	3,181,952

Source: Calculations based on United Nations Population Division (2010, file 2) and the author's density projections.

increase to 0.99 percent of the land area of countries by 2030 and to 1.21 percent by 2050. In other words, it will double by 2030 and not quite triple by 2050. At a 2 percent annual rate of decline, the world's urban land cover will increase to 1.34 percent of the land area of countries by 2030 and to 2.44 percent by 2050. In other words, it will triple by 2030 and increase fivefold by 2050. According to our high projection, at a 2 percent annual rate of density decline, urban land cover in Sub-Saharan Africa will expand at the fastest rate—more than twelvefold between 2000 and 2050.

If average urban densities in developed countries remain unchanged (low projection), then their urban land cover will grow by only 20 percent between 2000 and 2030 and by 29 percent between 2000 and 2050—from 300,000 km² in 2000 to 370,000 km² in 2030 and to 400,000 km² in 2050. Assuming that densities in the developed countries decline, on average, by only 1 percent per annum (medium projection), urban land cover will grow by 63 percent between 2000 and 2030 and by 113 percent between 2000 and 2050—from 300,000 km² in 2000 to 500,000 km² in 2030 and to 650,000 km² in 2050. In other words, at a 1 percent annual decline in average densities, urban land cover in developed countries will double in 50 years. If incomes continue to increase relative to gasoline prices and densities continue to decline at the rate of the 1990s (high projection), then urban land cover in developed countries will more than double between 2000 and 2030, and will triple between 2000 and 2050.

The situation is likely to be more critical in developing countries, where most urban population growth will take place. Assuming that their densities decline, on average, by only 1 percent per annum (medium projection), urban land cover will grow by 170 percent between 2000 and 2030 and by 326 percent between 2000 and 2050—from 300,000 km² in 2000 to 800,000 km² in 2030 and to 1,300,000 km² in 2050. Assuming that densities in developing countries decline, on average, by 2 percent per annum (high projection), urban land cover will grow by 264 percent between 2000 and 2030 and by 603 percent between 2000 and 2050—from 300,000 km² in 2000 to 1,100,000 km² in 2030 and to 2,100,000 km² in 2050. These numbers begin to require the kind of foresight shown by Cerdá in his plan for Barcelona.

Figures 15.3 and 15.4 show two global maps of projected urban land cover as a share of total land area in all countries, for 2030 and 2050, both assuming a 1 percent annual density decline. In general, the larger area of the country, the smaller is the share of its land in urban use. The Russian Federation, for example, will have only 0.2 percent of its land area in urban use by 2030; China, 1.3 percent; the United States, 2.4 percent; Canada, 0.2 percent; Brazil, 1 percent; Australia, 0.3 percent; Argentina, 0.3 percent; and India, 3.0 percent. By the year 2030 some 17 countries will have more than 10 percent of their land in urban use. Most of these countries are small island countries, but Belgium and the Netherlands, two highly urbanized countries, are on that list. By 2050 the number of countries that will have more than 10 percent of their land in urban use will increase to 29, including the United Kingdom, the Czech Republic, Italy, and Lebanon. By that year, an additional 34 countries will have more than 5 percent of their land in urban use, including Japan, the Republic of Korea, Bangladesh, the Philippines, Germany, France, Hungary, and Ghana.

FIGURE 15.3

Urban Land Cover as the Share of Total Land in All Countries: 2030 Projections at a 1 Percent Annual Density Decline

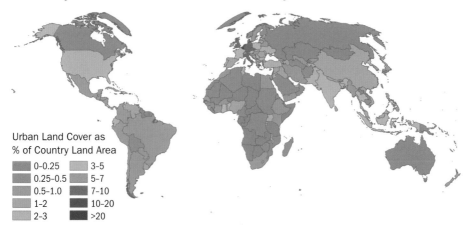

Sources: Land cover calculations based on United Nations Population Division (2010) and the author's density projections; country land area data from World Bank (2012a).

FIGURE 15.4

Urban Land Cover as the Share of Total Land in All Countries: 2050 Projections at a 1 Percent Annual Density Decline

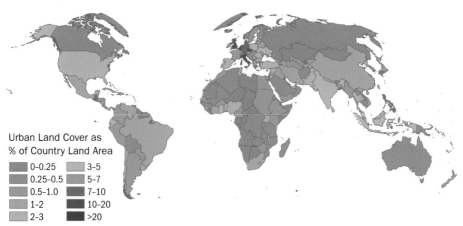

Sources: Land cover calculations based on United Nations Population Division (2010) and the author's density projections; country land area data from World Bank (2012a).

ZHENGZHOU, CHINA

Realistic projections of urban land cover are critical for keeping housing affordable, in line with the Decent Housing Proposition introduced in chapter 4. Strict containment of urban expansion destroys the homes of the poor and puts new housing out of reach for most people. Decent housing for all can be ensured only if urban land is in ample supply.

This proposition is illustrated clearly in the current efforts by the government of China to contain urban expansion, in this case in the name of food security. The State Council of the People's Republic of China is the chief administrative authority in the country and is headed by its Premier. To protect China's food security, the council retains the power to approve any and all urban expansion plans, typically refusing to approve plans that require the conversion of large amounts of cultivated land to urban use, regardless of the deleterious effects of such refusal on urban land supply, and thus on housing affordability. In the case of contemporary China, it also has serious negative effects on local economic growth, the rate of inflation, and the health of the financial system.

The State Council's position on containing urban expansion in the name of food security, as well as its insistence that the total amount of cultivated land within each province must not decline, may be due for reassessment. In 2007, for example, it cost $2.40 to prepare 1 square meter (m^2) of land for cultivation in Xinyan Province. In comparison, 1 m^2 of urban land served by infrastructure was auctioned in Zhengzhou and in several other Chinese cities for $890 that year, or 375 times the cost of adding 1 m^2 to the total amount of cultivated land in China in another province (Angel, Valdivia, and Lutzy 2011). Diverting a significant share of this surplus value of urban land to rural development—to increase agricultural productivity and the amount of land in cultivation—or, for that matter, investing in agricultural development in other countries with a view to securing its food imports in times of need, may be more sensible for China than artificially restricting its urban land supply.

The 2010 master plan for Zhengzhou projected the city's population to increase to 2.3 million by 2010, its density to remain at 110 persons per hectare, and its land area to increase to 189 km^2. By 2010, the population of Zhengzhou was already 3.8 million (United Nations Population Division 2012) and its built-up area occupied 293 km^2 (Gong 2012). In other words, Zhengzhou's 2010 population was two-thirds larger than the master plan's projections, and its built-up area was two-thirds larger than the master plan's projections.

The municipality of Zhengzhou, aware of its error, seemed to have learned its lesson. Its 2020 master plan, approved by the Henan Provincial Government, projected the population of the city to increase to 5.5 million, its density to remain at 110 persons per hectare, and its land area to increase to 500 km^2 (Angel, Valdivia, and Lutzy 2011).

Policy-driven land supply bottlenecks in Chinese cities have resulted in massive land and housing price inflation: Real estate fair in Zhengzhou in 2010.

These were conservative, yet possibly realistic, estimates. If densities continue to decline at the same rate as in recent decades—at more than 3 percent per annum between 1992 and 2006, for example—its area may reach 630–750 km^2 by 2020. Admittedly, this possibility was ignored, thus increasing the plan's risk of failure.

In August 2010, the State Council approved Zhengzhou's 2020 plan, provided its area does not exceed 400 km^2 by 2020 (China Daily 2010). While falling short of allowing for the conversion of adequate lands for urban expansion, the decision of the State Council may be seen as a pragmatic compromise between its concerns for the city's land needs and its overarching concerns for food security. Still, this decision, like similar ones concerning other cities before it, is fraught with undesirable consequences as it continues to perpetuate an artificial shortage of urban land in China.

Recent evidence from a study of the 220 largest Chinese cities in the period 1996 to 2003 confirms that land shortages have a strong and significant negative effect on local economic development. For Chinese cities as a whole, a 1 percent increase in the availability of land increased the gross domestic product (GDP) in cities by more than 3 times as much as a 1 percent increase in domestic investment, more than 6 times as much as a 1 percent increase in foreign direct investment (FDI), and more than 10 times as much as a 1 percent increase in government expenditures. In coastal China, the harmful effects of land shortages on local economic development are much more severe. A 1 percent increase in the availability of land "increases urban GDP by more than eight times as much as a 1 percent increase in domestic investment, more than 14 times as much as a 1 percent increase in FDI, almost 27 times as much as a 1 percent increase in government expenditures, and 1.6 times as much as a 1 percent increase in the labor supply" (Ding and Lichtenberg 2011, 312).

The high levels of inflation in China in recent years are due in no small part to the skyrocketing housing (and land) prices in its rapidly growing cities (Barboza 2011). At present, most corrective measures seek to restrict the flow of money to developers and potential buyers and to make bank lending more secure. They are, so to speak, demand-side measures. No parallel measures seek to mend the supply side—the artificial shortages in the supply of land for urban and particularly for residential use.

Real (not nominal) housing prices in 35 Chinese cities increased by 225 percent during the past decade with over 60 percent of that rise occurring since 2007 (Wu, Gyourko, and Deng 2010). Buying an average apartment in Beijing in 2010, for example, required more than 20 years of average household income in the city. It required more than 10 years of household income in many other cities, including Zhengzhou. Land price inflation has been even more spectacular. Land prices in Beijing, for example, increased no less than eightfold since 2003, and land prices now form no less than 60 percent of the price of housing there (Wu, Gyourko, and Deng, 2010). In comparison, between 1975 and 2006, the share of the price of land in the total price of a housing unit in the United States averaged 36 percent (Davis and Heathcote 2007). There is also little doubt that Chinese development companies— the largest among them belonging to state-owned enterprises that are "too big to fail"— are hoarding land in expectation of future shortages.

Land shortages for urban development in China's cities are endemic, and it is quite clear that, other than easy access to money, they are the main reason for its housing affordability crisis. Two principal policies inadvertently create these shortages. The first, already mentioned, is limitations on urban expansion imposed by the State Coun- cil because of its concern with food security. The second has to do with the strict legal distinction between urban and rural land in China. For any plot of land to be available for urban development, it has to be owned by a municipality, which in turn has to purchase the land from rural communes, pay compensation, install infrastructure, and then lease it to developers through land auctions. This is a rather tedious process and many municipalities fail to respond to the demand for land in a timely fashion.

Municipalities have no particular incentive to ensure an ample supply of land to keep it affordable because they rely on the control of the conversion process for gen- erating income. In 2005, for example, local government revenue from this process in China's 220 largest cities amounted to no less than 40 percent of their budgetary incomes from all sources, down from 55 percent in 2003 (Ding and Lichtenberg 2011). In the absence of other sources of income, such as a property tax, municipalities appear to have become addicted to this land development process and thus have a built-in interest in keeping land prices high. There is little hope for their support in needed reforms that will open up the rural land surrounding cities for urban development and eliminate the land supply bottlenecks that the present process entails. This will also necessitate giving farmers some property rights in land, a highly controversial issue that eventually will need to be addressed by the State Council.

To conclude, incorrect projections of the amount of land required for urban expansion are fraught with undesirable consequences. We can only hope that in preparing plans for urban expansion, more urban and national authorities will follow the example of Cerdá and the Barcelona he helped shape with his generous vision than the strict containment policy of the State Council of the People's Republic of China.

[California's Central] valley supplies half of the fruits and vegetables of the United States. . . . We saw this fruit bowl of America become planted with its final crop of ticky-tacky cookie-cutter houses and gated communities with homes overlooking artificial lakes.

Light and Light (2012, 7)

Overall, however, it is fair to say that, although there is a number of countries (in particular in the Near East/ North Africa and South Asia) that have reached or are about to reach the limits of land available, on a global scale there are still sufficient land resources to feed the world population for the foreseeable future.

United Nations Food and Agriculture Organization (2009)

CHAPTER 16

Urban Expansion and the Loss of Cultivated Lands

How much cultivated land will be consumed by expanding urban areas, why, and why should it matter?

Global data on the expansion of cities into cultivated lands are only starting to become available, so the answer to this question at the planetary scale must be exploratory and tentative. This chapter explains why urban expansion necessarily entails the loss of cultivated lands. It also estimates the share of the projected areas of urban expansion that will displace land currently under cultivation and the share of the total amount of cultivated land that will be lost to urban expansion in countries, regions, and the world. It further explores the implications of the magnitude of these projected losses of cultivated land on global food security.

CITIES AND CULTIVATED LANDS IN HISTORICAL PERSPECTIVE

During the first period of urbanization, until approximately 1800, the vast majority of cities relied on the food surpluses produced in their immediate vicinity to feed their inhabitants (figure 16.1).

> Engendered by agriculture, the city has remained completely tributary to it. The proportion of city residents among the total population is determined by the relative size of the food surplus that country people, voluntarily or not, are able to allocate them. This fact is obvious, but it should not be forgotten. That surplus was never truly substantial until the Industrial Revolution. (Bairoch 1988, 497)

FIGURE 16.1
Cultivated Lands Surrounding Berlin, Germany, 1798

Source: Schneider (1798), courtesy of the Hebrew University of Jerusalem Historic Cities Research Project.

Until the advent of the Industrial Revolution in the late eighteenth century, when agricultural innovations vastly increased productivity and transportation innovations greatly reduced the cost of shipping foodstuffs, the population of a city was limited by the amount of surplus food that could be grown nearby and transported to local markets. All cities thus required an extensive agricultural hinterland that produced an adequate and accessible food surplus. Early urban civilizations flourished in the most fertile regions—soil-rich riverbeds and river deltas in temperate climates efficiently served by riverboat transport. Only a very small number of early cities, such as Athens, Rome, and Constantinople, could rely on food imports from distant shores. The vast majority of cities had to obtain their food locally, and the cost of transporting it put serious limits on how far it could be carried.

Clark and Haswell (1970, quoted in Bairoch 1988, 12), analyzed a large body of data and estimated that transporting 1 ton (1,000 kilograms [kg]) of grain for a distance of 1 kilometer (km) before the advent of mechanized transport required an equivalent of 8.8 kg of grain for human portage, 4.8 kg for animal portage, and 3.9 kg for portage by cart. This implies that the grain would be fully consumed if it were carried by humans for 114 km, by beasts of burden for 208 km, and by carts for 256 km. Clearly, then, most cities had no choice as to their location. They needed to be surrounded by cultivated lands to ensure their survival, and the closer and more productive these lands were, the more beneficial they were to the city.

Johann Heinrich von Thünen, a German landowner and economist, published *The Isolated State* in 1826, before the Industrial Revolution began in Germany. Given a few simplifying assumptions—no spatial variations in topography, climate, transport cost, or soil fertility—he showed that cultivated lands would arrange themselves in concentric rings around a city. More intensive agricultural land users would be willing to pay

Agricultural activities on the fringe of Paris, France, illustrate potential competition with urban land uses that can afford much higher rents for the lands they occupy.

a higher land rent to reduce their transport costs, and would outbid less intensive ones in order to occupy lands closer to the city. Dairy products, vegetables, and fruit, which are perishable and need to reach markets quickly, would bring the highest rents in the inner ring. Forests supplying firewood and building materials would occupy the second ring. Grains, which are less perishable than vegetables and fruit and lighter than wood, would occupy the third ring. Pastures would occupy the fourth ring, since the animals grazing there could transport themselves to market to be sold or butchered. Beyond the fourth ring, land would remain in uncultivated wilderness. Von Thünen (1826) thus provided a ready explanation as to why we should expect to find the lands at the edge of the city in intense agricultural cultivation. Indirectly, he also provided the explanation for why we should expect a growing city to expand into the most productive cultivated lands that commanded the highest agricultural land rent.

The intimate relationship between cities and their agricultural hinterlands was weakened with the advent of the Industrial Revolution. Mechanized agriculture led to a massive increase in food production, while mechanized transport, via railroads, steamships, and later trucks, greatly reduced the cost of delivering foodstuffs and thus increased long-distance trade in agricultural commodities. Cities were freed from the harsh constraints of foraging for food nearby, and their populations and built-up areas could grow without limit as long as they could trade their manufactures and services for food produced elsewhere or obtain it through conquest and coersion.

This freedom also allowed cities to locate and thrive in places that had little, if any, agricultural lands in their vicinity. These places provided other advantages, such as location on major shipping routes (e.g., Singapore); access to exploitable natural resources (e.g., Kuwait City); tourist attractions (e.g., Las Vegas); places of pilgrimage (e.g., Mecca); or political control over large territories (e.g., Brasilia). But these types of cities remain the exception rather than the rule.

Christaller's (1966) central place theory predicts that most cities form elements of a national, regional, or global spatial hierarchy and, as such, are located to maximize access to the rural population that still forms half of the total world population today (see chapter 8). This theory suggests that most cities will be distributed near cultivated areas, with the smallest cities being closest to the villages they serve and the larger ones interspersed among the smaller cities. To the extent that cities still form local rather than global central places, we would expect them to be located among villages and surrounded by cultivated lands. We would also expect the largest cities in the country to be a part of a global network of cities, functioning as centers of global trade and commerce rather than as market centers for their surrounding countryside, a function better performed by the smaller cities. Larger cities would convert a smaller share of cultivated land to urban use as they expand than would smaller cities, a proposition confirmed by the empirical evidence introduced later in this chapter.

URBAN LAND COVER AND LAND UNDER CULTIVATION

To get a sense of how much land is taken up for urban versus agricultural purposes, it is useful to start with global magnitudes. In the world at large, one-third of the land area of countries is in agriculture, one-third is forested, and one-third is in other land uses. Of the land in agriculture, one-third is under cultivation and two-thirds are in meadows and pastures. Urban land cover takes up a much smaller share of the area of countries, and in 2000 it was less than one-half of 1 percent of the area of all countries. In that year, urban land cover amounted to some 4 percent of cultivated land.

The total area of all countries on the planet is 134.5 million square kilometers (km^2). The total land area amounts to 130 million km^2 (96.8 percent), while inland water bodies comprise the balance of 4.3 million km^2 (3.2 percent). In the year 2000, 15.2 million km^2—11.7 percent of the total land area of countries—were in arable land and permanent crops, most of it under cultivation; 40.9 million km^2 (31.5 percent) were forested; 33.4 million km^2 (25.7 percent) were in permanent meadows and pastures; and 40 million km^2 (30.8 percent) were in other land uses (including deserts and tree-less tundra) (FAO Statistics Division 2012). According to our own calculations, an estimated 600,000 km^2 (0.47 percent) were in urban use in 2000 (figure 16.2).

The ratio between urban land cover and the cultivated land area varied widely among different countries. Figure 16.3 shows urban land cover as a share of arable land and land in permanent crops in all countries that had large cities in 2000.

- Five countries had more land in urban use than arable land: Singapore, Bahrain, Kuwait, Djibouti, and Qatar.
- Three countries had more land in urban use than half the arable land cover: Puerto Rico, Iceland, and Belgium.
- In 12 countries, urban land cover comprised 20 to 50 percent of arable land cover, among them the Netherlands, Japan, and the United Kingdom.

FIGURE 16.2
Relative Shares of the Land Area of Countries in Major Land Uses, 2000

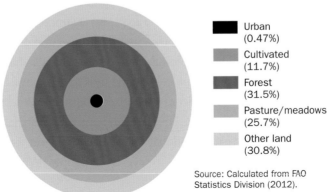

Urban
(0.47%)

Cultivated
(11.7%)

Forest
(31.5%)

Pasture/meadows
(25.7%)

Other land
(30.8%)

Source: Calculated from FAO
Statistics Division (2012).

FIGURE 16.3
Urban Land Cover as a Share of Arable Land in All Countries, 2000

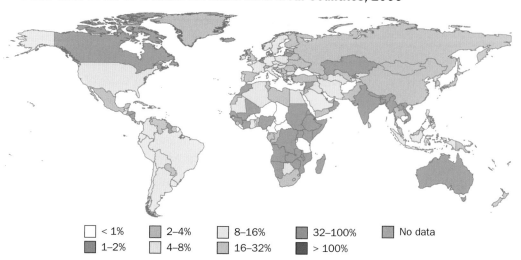

☐ < 1%	■ 2–4%	☐ 8–16%	■ 32–100%	■ No data
■ 1–2%	☐ 4–8%	■ 16–32%	■ > 100%	

Sources: Country arable land data from World Bank (2012a); and urban land cover data from Angel et al. (2012, table 5.4, 362–380).

- In 14 more countries, urban land cover comprised 10 to 20 percent of arable land cover, among them the Republic of Korea, Venezuela, and Germany.
- In 29 additional countries, urban land cover comprised 5 to 10 percent of arable land cover, among them Egypt, the United States, and Brazil.
- In 45 more countries, urban land cover comprised 2 to 5 percent of arable land cover, among them Iran, Argentina, China, and the Russian Federation.
- In 35 more countries, urban land cover comprised 1 to 2 percent of arable land cover, among them India and Canada.
- The 12 remaining countries had urban land cover that comprised less than 1 percent of arable land cover, among them Tanzania and Afghanistan.

LAND UNDER CULTIVATION: PAST, PRESENT, AND FUTURE

Uncertainty about food security fuels both global and national concerns about the encroachment of cities into cultivated lands. Egypt, for example, has adopted a series of laws and decrees dating back to 1966 forbidding the conversion of agricultural lands to urban use (see chapter 10). The People's Republic of China also has numerous laws and decrees regulating the conversion of cultivated lands to urban use (see chapter 15). Since all or nearly all countries trade in globalized markets, where foods are sold as commodities, global food security has become an issue of immediate local concern as well. When food is in short supply, global food prices rise and tend to be volatile, making it harder for individual countries to feed their people. When enough food is produced, food prices remain low and stable.

Even if enough food can be produced globally in a typical year, a national gov-ernment may have several reasons to be concerned with its ability to feed its own population. First, it may not have the foreign currency required to purchase food in global markets. Second, in times of shortage, foreign countries may ban or restrict exports to avoid food shortages and possibly food riots at home. Between 2007 and 2011, one-third of 107 countries surveyed had imposed food export restrictions, such as taxes, quotas, and bans (Sharma 2011). For example, strict export bans were imposed by India on wheat (2007), by Pakistan on wheat (2009), by Russia on wheat (2010), by Egypt and Vietnam on rice (2007), and by Ethiopia and Tanzania on cereals (2008).

Motivated by food security concerns and unable to expand lands for cultivation within their own boundaries, a number of governments have empowered their state trading corporations or other national corporations to buy or lease large tracts of land for cultivation in other countries, with the view to investing in agricultural development elsewhere and importing the harvests for domestic use. Such land deals, typically encouraged by host governments, could generate much-needed foreign exchange and foster orderly investment and development in poor rural areas. But such agreements can also create pressures to dislocate and impoverish those now tilling the land or grazing their herds on it. This tension between the interests of small, local farmers and those of transnational corporations is already felt in countries with land available for cultivation, mostly in Sub-Saharan Africa and to a lesser extent in Latin America and Southeast Asia, where corporations from food-importing countries are now buying or leasing vast areas of land for agricultural development.

> Researchers estimate that more than 200m hectares (495m acres) of land—roughly eight times the size of the UK—were sold or leased between 2000 and 2010. Details of 1,006 deals covering 70.2m hectares mostly in Africa, Asia and Latin America were published by the Land Matrix project, an international partnership involving five major European research centres and 40 civil society and research groups from around the world. (Provost 2012, n.p.)

It is not yet clear how these lands were bought or leased because their ownership is often of a customary or tribal nature and may be disputed. It is also not clear that these lands are indeed vacant.

> The supposed existence of this spare land is widely quoted in forecasts of capacity to meet the food requirements for future population increase. It is argued here that these estimates greatly exaggerate the land available. (Young 1999, 3)

If these estimates are correct, even within a wide margin of error, recent international land deals will increase the amount of land under cultivation by some 200 million hectares (2 million km^2). This is 13 percent of the land under cultivation in 2000 and more than three times the total amount of land in urban use in that year. This new development brings into focus the continuing globalization of our food supply, as individual countries seek to increase their food security by growing food in other countries.

Has the global amount of land under cultivation been increasing or decreasing over the last 50 years? How much additional land will be needed by 2050 to ensure our global food supply? The United Nations Food and Agriculture Organization (FAO) publishes annual data on harvests of major crop groups on arable land. The total harvested area is typically smaller than the available arable area, partly because some land is not cultivated or lies fallow, and partly because of different methods of data collection. Figure 16.4 shows the increase in the area harvested in major crop groups during the past 50 years—cereals; vegetables, pulses, roots, and tubers; fruits and nuts; and fibers and oil crops. The total area harvested increased during this period from 9.4 to 12.2 million km^2, at an average annual rate of 0.5 percent, adding some 56,000 km^2 per year, on average, to the total, despite losses due to soil erosion, desertification, abandonment, or urban expansion.

To determine whether lands that were brought into cultivation were more or less productive than those that were lost, we need to look at the change in overall food production in the major crop groups during the past 50 years (figure 16.5). Food production almost tripled during this period, from 1.7 to 5.0 billion tons per annum, because lands were used more efficiently. Yields more than doubled, on average, from

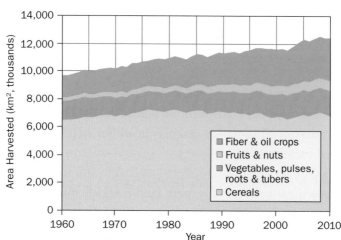

FIGURE 16.4
Land Area Harvested in Major Crop Groups, 1960–2010

Source: Calculated from FAO Statistics Division (2012).

FIGURE 16.5

Total Annual Production of Major Crop Groups, 1960–2010

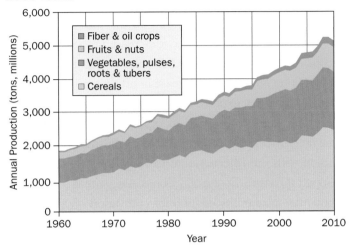

Source: Calculated from FAO Statistics Division (2012).

FIGURE 16.6

Annual Production per Capita of Major Crop Groups, 1960–2010

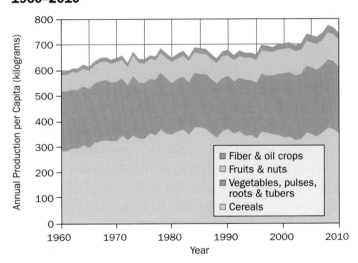

Source: Calculated from FAO Statistics Division (2012).

1.8 to 4.1 tons per hectare. As a result, food production kept up with population growth. Figure 16.6 shows the change in per capita food production, which increased from 580 to 720 kg per year between 1960 and 2010.

In summary, harvested lands worldwide increased by 2.8 million km² during the last 50 years, adding some 30 percent to the total harvested land. Yields per unit of land area have more than doubled. As a result, overall production has tripled during this period, keeping up with global population growth and ensuring an increase in global per capita food production.

The FAO has estimated that annual food production will need to increase by 70 percent by 2050 "to cope with a 40 percent increase in world population and to raise average food consumption to 3,130 kcal (kilocalories) per person per day" (Bruinsma 2009, 2). It expects 90 percent of the increase in production to come from higher yields and only 10 percent from the expansion of land under cultivation. According to these FAO estimates, arable land would need to expand by 700,000 km^2 by 2050, less than 5 percent of the land under cultivation in 2000 (Bruinsma 2009).

In collaboration with the International Institute for Applied Systems Analysis, the FAO has developed the Agro-Ecological Zones Assessment (AEZ), a methodology for assessing the potential availability of land for cultivation on a global scale, taking into account climate, soil, and terrain conditions relevant to agricultural production. The results indicate that,

> at the global level, Earth's land, climate, and biological resources are ample to meet food and fiber needs of future generations, in particular, for a world population of 9.3 billion, as projected in the United Nations medium variant for the year 2050. (Fischer et al. 2006, n.p.)

There is very little room for extending the land under cultivation in Europe, Russia, or Asia, where 90 percent of cultivable land is already cultivated. In North America, some three-quarters of lands considered very suitable and suitable are already under cultivation, making some extension of cultivated land possible. Africa and Latin America and the Caribbean are estimated to have some 11.4 million km^2 of land that is very suitable or suitable for cultivation, approximately one-third of which is forested—in addition to 3.3 million km^2 in land that is moderately suitable. About half of this land is concentrated in just seven countries—Angola, Democratic Republic of Congo, Sudan, Argentina, Bolivia, Brazil, and Colombia.

Cultivatable land that is very suitable, suitable, or moderately suitable for rain-fed crop production constitutes one-quarter of the total land area of the planet, or 33.3 million km^2, of which 7.4 million km^2 (or 22 percent) are in forest ecosystems and only 15.2 million km^2 were under cultivation in the year 2000. Despite underreporting of land under cultivation, estimated by Fischer et al. (2006) to be on the order of 10 to 20 percent, substantial amounts of land are available for the expansion of food production in future decades. Without encroaching on forests, land under cultivation can increase by 70 percent, although the estimated area for cultivation only needs to expand by 5 percent to reach 2050 food production goals.

Expanding areas under cultivation will not be simple, however. It will require major capital, social, and political investments in agricultural research and development, preparing areas for cultivation, machinery, infrastructure, transport, and appropriate institutional arrangements that will promote local agricultural development, avoid forced evictions, and minimize land disputes while supporting a reliable system for international trade in foodstuffs. This is a tall order, and it must go hand-in-hand with preparing land for urban uses to ensure that both agricultural and urban expansion are efficient, equitable, and sustainable.

THE SHARE OF GLOBAL URBAN EXPANSION ON CULTIVATED LAND

In chapter 15, we estimated the additional area that will be required for the expansion of cities in coming decades given three density change scenarios: no change in density, a 1 percent annual decline, and a 2 percent annual decline. At constant densities, 0.6 million km^2 will be required for global urban expansion by 2050; at a 1 percent annual decline, 1.3 million km^2; and at a 2 percent annual decline, 2.6 million km^2. How much of that expansion will encroach on land now under cultivation?

My colleague Jason Parent and I simulated the expansion of the universe of 3,646 cities that had 100,000 or more people in 2000 for the decades 2010 to 2050. We assumed that the populations of cities of all sizes in any given country will grow at the same rate (see chapter 8), and we used the United Nations urban population projections for 2010–2050 to determine the population growth rate of each of that country's cities. The Mod500 global land cover map for the year 2000 provides information on 16 land use classes for each 463x463–meter pixel for the planet as a whole (see chapter 9). We simplified this map to three land use categories: urban land cover, cultivated land, and other land uses. We assumed that every city would expand in all directions at an equal rate and mapped the future built-up area in every decade as a set of expansion bands. The projected area of the city in any time period was simply a function of its projected population and its projected density. Given these assumptions, it was then possible to obtain gross preliminary estimates of the amount of cultivated land that would be lost in every decade as a result of urban expansion.

Figures 16.7 and 16.8 show the projected expansion bands of Ankara and Adana in Turkey in every decade between 2010 and 2050, given a 1 percent projected annual decline in density.

Ankara, the national capital, is projected to expand from a total built-up area of 405 km^2 in 2000 to 890 km^2 in 2030 and 1,257 km^2 in 2050. Only 19 percent of the projected expansion of the built-up area of the city by 2050, a total of 160 km^2, is projected to occupy land that was under cultivation in the year 2000. Most expansion will occupy land that was not under cultivation that year. In contrast, Adana is projected to

FIGURE 16.7
The Projected Loss of Cultivated Lands in Ankara, Turkey, 2000–2050

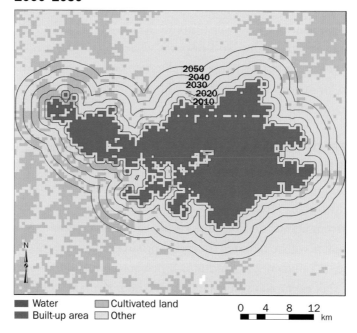

■ Water   ☐ Cultivated land   0 4 8 12
■ Built-up area   ☐ Other   km

FIGURE 16.8
The Projected Loss of Cultivated Lands in Adana, Turkey, 2000–2050

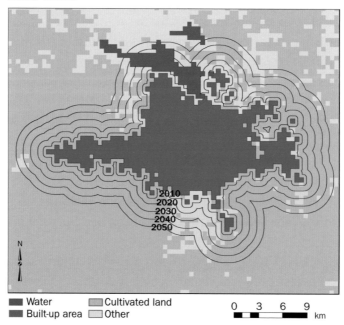

■ Water   ☐ Cultivated land   0 3 6 9
■ Built-up area   ☐ Other   km

Sources (for both figures): Urban land cover data from Angel et al. (2012 online); cultivated land map based on MODIS data in Friedl et al. (2002); and urban expansion estimates based on United Nations Population Division (2010) and the author's density projections.

expand from a total built-up area of 153 km^2 in 2000 to 337 km^2 in 2030 and 476 km^2 in 2050. Nearly 85 percent of the projected built-up area of the city in 2050, a total of 275 km^2, is likely to occupy land that was under cultivation in the year 2000. The difference between the two cities is striking. Ankara will expand into a dry area that is largely uncultivated, while Adana will expand into a rich and fertile plain to its west, south, and east that is almost fully cultivated. As a result, less than one-fifth of the projected area of urban expansion in the former, but as much as five-sixths in the latter, are projected to displace cultivated lands.

The same calculations were repeated for all 3,646 cities in the universe of large cities. The cities were then divided into 10 groups (deciles), so there was an equal population in each group. Because city population sizes obey a power law (see chapter 8), the average city population in each group was a fixed multiple of the average city population in the preceding group. Figure 16.9 demonstrates that the larger the average city population in each group, the smaller the share of its expansion was likely to involve the loss of cultivated lands. In fact, in the group of smallest cities, 60 percent of the area of expansion, on average, will occupy cultivated land. In the group of largest cities only 25 percent of the area of expansion, on average, will occupy cultivated land, and the two averages are significantly different from each other at the 95 percent confidence level.

FIGURE 16.9

Share of Cultivated Land Estimated to Be Lost to Urban Expansion in 2000–2050 as a Function of City Population Size in 2000

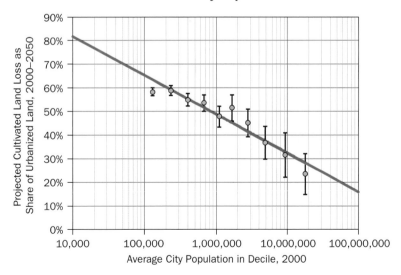

Notes: Estimates assume a 1 percent annual density decline. Vertical error bars denote 95 percent confidence intervals.
Sources: Urban land cover data from Angel et al. (2012 online); cultivated land map based on MODIS data in Friedl et al. (2002); and urban expansion estimates based on United Nations Population Division (2010) and the author's density projections.

Global urban expansion must go hand-in-hand with the expansion of lands under cultivation: A tea estate near Lake Kivu, Democratic Republic of Congo.

This is an important observation when it comes to calculating the total loss of agricultural land to urban expansion for cities of all sizes. Smaller cities with fewer than 100,000 people in the year 2000 occupied some 266,000 km^2, or some 44 percent of the estimated total land in urban use in the year 2000 (see chapter 10). To calculate the loss of agricultural land in these cities, we applied a country correction factor to the estimates for large cities in every country and a regional correction factor in countries that had no large cities. We used these individual country results to calculate regional totals.

We then estimated the loss of cultivated lands in different world regions and in the world as a whole by 2050, assuming a 2 percent average annual decline in urban densities—the worst-case scenario in terms of estimating the potential loss of cultivated lands due to urban expansion. Given these assumptions, urban areas worldwide—including smaller cities and towns—are expected to expand by 2.4 million km^2, from 0.6 million km^2 in 2000 to 3 million km^2 in 2050. This fivefold expansion will entail the loss of 1.2 million km^2 of land that was cultivated in the year 2000. In other words, expansion by 1 km^2 will involve the loss of one-half of 1 km^2 of cultivated land. Cities in developing countries will account for two-thirds of global urban expansion, half of which, or 0.8 million km^2, will occupy cultivated lands. Cities in developed countries will account for one-third of global urban expansion, half of which or 0.4 million km^2 will occupy cultivated lands.

Figure 16.10 shows the amount of land that will be converted to urban use in nine world regions, as well as the share of that land that was cultivated in the year 2000. In the more arid zones of Western Asia, Northern Africa, and Sub-Saharan Africa, the share of land area for urban expansion that will encroach on cultivated lands is less than 33 percent, considerably lower than the world average. The share is expected to be considerably higher in the more intensively cultivated zones in East, Southeast, and South Asia (56–66 percent) and in Europe and Japan (62 percent). While these shares vary among regions and even more among countries, on average, half of the land that will be needed for urban expansion in coming decades will be land that was under cultivation in 2000.

How large a share of the total land under cultivation in 2000 is likely to be lost to urban expansion? The burden of loss of cultivated lands will not be distributed evenly among countries in the same region or among countries in different regions. Countries now undergoing massive urban expansion are likely to lose more cultivated lands than

FIGURE 16.10

Shares of Expected Areas of Urban Expansion on Cultivated Land in World Regions, 2000–2050

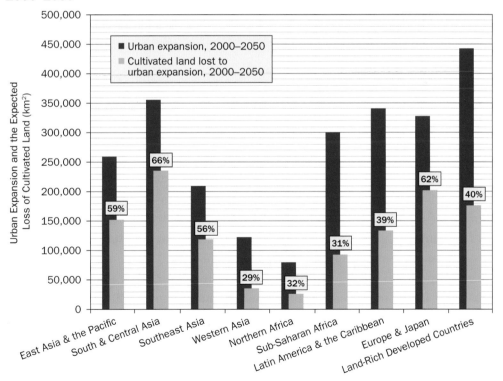

Note: Estimates assume a 2 percent annual density decline.
Sources: Urban land cover data from Angel et al. (2012 online); cultivated land map based on MODIS data in Friedl et al. (2002); and urban expansion estimates based on United Nations Population Division (2010) and the author's density projections.

FIGURE 16.11

Twenty Countries with Expected Losses of Cultivated Land of 10,000 km² or More Due to Urban Expansion, 2000–2050

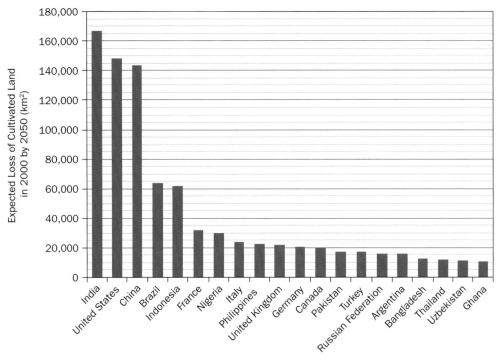

Note: Estimates assume a 2 percent annual density decline.
Sources: Urban land cover data from Angel et al. (2012 online); cultivated land map based on MODIS data in Friedl et al. (2002); and urban expansion estimates based on United Nations Population Division (2010) and the author's density projections.

countries that will add fewer people to their urban populations. Figure 16.11 shows the loss of cultivated lands in 20 countries, each of which is expected to lose 10,000 km² (similar to the land area of Lebanon) or more of land that was in cultivation in 2000 to urban expansion by 2050, assuming a 2 percent annual density decline. These countries account for three-quarters of all cultivated lands that are expected to be lost to urban expansion, with the highest losses in India, the United States, and China, each of which is expected to lose more than 140,000 km²—roughly the land area of Bangladesh. Brazil and Indonesia are each expected to lose more than 60,000 km² of cultivated land—roughly the land area of Sri Lanka.

Finally, figure 16.12 presents estimates of the expected loss of cultivated lands to urban expansion by 2050 as a share of the total amount of land under cultivation in 2000 for all world regions, assuming a 2 percent annual density decline. As noted earlier, in the world at large, 1.2 million km² of land cultivated in 2000 can be expected to be lost to urban expansion by 2050, of which two-thirds will be lost in developing

FIGURE 16.12

Expected Loss of Cultivated Land Due to Urban Expansion in World Regions, 2000–2050

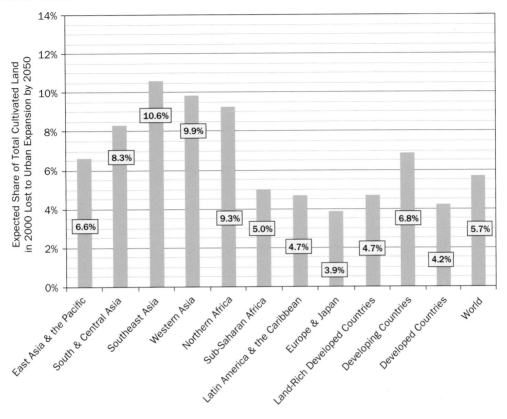

Note: Estimates assume a 2 percent annual density decline.
Sources: Urban land cover data from Angel et al. (2012 online); cultivated land map based on MODIS data in Friedl et al. (2002); and urban expansion estimates based on United Nations Population Division (2010) and the author's density projections.

countries and one-third in developed ones. These losses will amount to 5.7 percent of the total land under cultivation in the world in 2000. Some regions can be expected to lose higher shares: Southeast Asia may lose more than 10 percent of its cultivated lands; Western Asia and North Africa, close to 10 percent; South and Central Asia, 8 percent; and East Asia, close to 7 percent. These losses could be considered worst-case scenarios, based on density declines of 2 percent per year, but for the first time they offer quite realistic orders of magnitude of how much new land will be needed in cultivation to meet projected food needs. Thus, if the FAO projects that an additional 700,000 km^2 of land will need to be brought into cultivation by 2050 to meet world food needs, we will have to almost triple that amount to replace the expected 1.2 million km^2 that will be lost to urban expansion.

THE POLICY IMPLICATIONS

The growing urban population in our planet of cities in the coming decades will require substantial increases in global food supplies and yields, and a corresponding increase in the amount of land under cultivation. Up to 90 percent of the increase in global food production can be attained by increasing yields, while 10 percent will involve the global expansion of lands under cultivation. Both cultivated fields and cities will need to expand, but they need not come into conflict. They need each other and must be mutually supportive. Adequate reserves of cultivatable lands are sufficient to feed the planet in perpetuity, and some of these lands must now be brought into cultivation in an equitable, efficient, and sustainable manner. In parallel, a sufficient share of the wealth generated by global urban expansion will need to be invested in ensuring a plentiful and affordable global food supply.

Once the connection between growing cities and their growing food needs is recognized—or rather, given its long history, brought into focus once more—then cities can begin again to shoulder the responsibility of ensuring their food supply. Rural development in the name of increasing the global food supply can be supported and financed by a share of the surplus value generated by the more intensive use of land in expanding urban areas.

Several conclusions can be drawn from this analysis: cities should be allowed to expand into the cultivated lands on their immediate periphery, as they must if they are to accommodate their growing populations in the most accessible locations; new cultivated lands should be brought into agricultural production in areas that are still uncultivated or undercultivated; yields must be increased on lands that are already under limited cultivation; and more of the surplus generated by skyrocketing land values in cities worldwide must be captured and invested in converting new lands on the rural fringe into efficient food production.

Cities need not grow at the expense of their food supply, but as they grow they should shoulder the responsibility for their food supply rather than take it for granted. For the global food supply to remain plentiful and affordable, land for cultivation will need to expand until the global population reaches equilibrium and the urbanization project comes to an end, possibly by the end of the twenty-first century. In the same way that we cannot rely on increasing densities to contain urban expansion, we cannot rely on increasing yields to contain the expansion of fields under cultivation. We can build tall buildings in appropriate places to increase urban densities, and we can also promote intensive urban agriculture in appropriate places to increase food yields. Unfortunately, both endeavors require massive investments that cannot be replicated at the required global scale, especially in poorer countries where most urban population growth is expected. In the world at large, urban expansion will need to go hand-in-hand with the expansion of lands under cultivation.

Conclusion

For myself, I always write about Dublin, because
if I can get to the heart of Dublin I can get to the
heart of all the cities of the world. In the particular
is contained the universal.

James Joyce (Power 1949, 63–64)

CHAPTER 17

Making Room for a Planet of Cities

MILAGRO, ECUADOR

Milagro is a small city in Ecuador. In an attempt to prepare for accommodating its expected population growth, its municipal planners developed a minimalist expansion plan for the city, essentially a network of interlaced radial and ring roads on its southern periphery, away from the agricultural plantations to its north (figure 17.1). These officials joined counterparts from four other cities in Ecuador and some international and local experts in 2007 in the capital city of Quito to prepare action plans for urban expansion (Angel 2008).

Ecuador's Municipal Law provides two important legal tools that enable municipalities to acquire land for roads and other public uses without compensation. One is a regulation that allows municipalities to obtain for public use at no cost up to 35 percent of any land being urbanized, once landowners decide to develop their land (Government of Ecuador 2004, Art. 237.3.b). The second legal tool is a regulation allowing the municipality to obtain up to 10 percent of the area of any land parcel, free of

FIGURE 17.1
The Proposed Arterial Grid in the Expansion Plan for Milagro, Ecuador, 2007

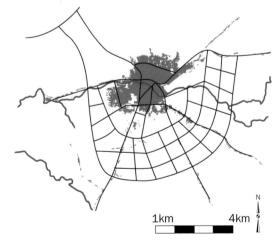

1km   4km

N

Redrawn from the plan provided to the author by the City Planning Department, Municipality of Milagro, Ecuador.

charge, for use as a right-of-way for public works (Government of Ecuador 2004, Art. 238).

In preparing a financial plan for acquiring the rights-of-way for the arterial grid, local planners in Milagro and other intermediary cities in Ecuador agreed that areas of 1 hectare would be acquired for all arterial road intersections through negotiation or marked as liens on property titles (see the plan for Manta, figure 1.2). In addition, 3-meter-wide strips along the inside edges of each road would be obtained, typically free of charge in large land parcels and at market value in smaller ones.

In mid-2006, the average size of rural properties in the county (*Canton*) of Milagro was 5.8 ± 1.2 hectares, and the price of 1 hectare of agricultural land on the rural periphery of the city was \$4,000 (Municipality of Milagro 2006). Subdivided land cost almost 10 times as much. The median price for the land at the intersections was about \$10,000 per hectare. The cost of the outright purchase of 1-hectare plots for 100 intersections may thus have been around \$1 million, but many of these areas did not need to be purchased outright since municipal law permits the government to register liens on the relevant titles. Admittedly, Milagro is a small town of some 50,000 people, and the same program in a city of 1 million people could cost 100 times more. Still, the costs involved in bringing such a project to fruition in Milagro and elsewhere are miniscule compared to its projected benefits.

Ecuadorian officials believe that the right-of-way for arterial roads should be 25–30 meters wide. They agreed that this right-of-way, once identified in a survey by road engineers, should be marked as a series of liens on all properties on its path in order to secure the land for future road building. They also agreed that 3-meter-wide strips along the inside edges of each road should be transferred to the municipality as part of its legal land allowance, cleared immediately and marked properly, allowing for inspection by officials to ensure that no construction takes place on the rights-of-way, whether by squatters or by land developers. This concern is warranted. In Quezon City, part of metropolitan Manila in the Philippines, an entire section of the right-of-way of Republic Avenue was settled by squatters, completely frustrating the city's plans for the avenue. There is no easy way to avoid this outcome, and each city that chooses to follow the path of Milagro must carefully consider this possibility of invasions and embrace effective means to guard against it.

Contemporary Milagro, like the Dublin of James Joyce, is alone in its particular predicament, yet it contains the universal. Like New York City, Barcelona, and Buenos Aires long before it, Milagro brings to light the realization that massive urban expansion is inevitable and that an actionable program for making preparations on the ground can be put in place now. Indeed, the local planners of Milagro, far away from the global centers of power and influence, have arrived independently at the central conclusion of this book. When urbanization is still in full swing, the Containment or

Squatters occupy an entire section of the right-of-way of Republic Avenue in Quezon City, in metropolitan Manila, the Philippines.

Compact City Paradigm is unworkable and unrealistic; it must be replaced by an alternative paradigm, the Making Room Paradigm.

THE FOUR PROPOSITIONS

The Making Room Paradigm is predicated on the four propositions introduced at the beginning of this book.

The Inevitable Expansion Proposition stated: first, the urbanization process, while it is still in full swing, cannot be stopped or reversed; and second, the expansion of cities that it entails cannot and will not be contained. No matter how sensible and noble the motives, rather than trying to stop people from coming to settle in cities and failing in the attempt, it makes more sense to take the necessary steps to accommodate them. In other words, when it comes to confronting the prospects of urban population growth and expansion, we would do well to heed the advice of the New York City commissioners who created the 1811 grid plan for Manhattan, rather than that of Queen Elizabeth I, who forbade any construction within three miles of the gates of London.

The Sustainable Densities Proposition sought to broaden our perspective so we can see the entire spectrum of cities—from cities that are spread out at very low densities, contribute an unfairly large share of carbon emissions, and are thus unsustainable, to cities that are so dense and overcrowded that they are unfit for dignified human habitation and are thus unsustainable in a different yet no less important sense. Selective densification is now an important agenda in low-density cities, especially in North America. But no matter how reasonable the motives for densification may be, and despite the urgency of slowing down climate change or protecting cultivated lands and precious rural landscapes, it is not the appropriate strategy for dense and overcrowded cities. On the contrary, in many cities densities need to be allowed and encouraged to decline. This can be done practically and economically by opening up new lands for expansion.

The Decent Housing Proposition is concerned with the millions of families, mostly in developing countries, who have settled in or are still migrating to cities to live and work with dignity. If we adopt urban containment as a strategy for mitigating climate change, then the protection of our planet would likely come at the expense of the poor. Strict measures to protect the natural environment by blocking urban expansion or making it difficult, as commonly advocated in the United States and readily exported to developing countries, could choke the supplies of affordable lands on the fringes of cities and limit the abilities of ordinary people to house themselves. We would be better off employing other strategies for mitigating climate change, and we can draw inspiration from key advocates for keeping global warming at bay—like Gore (2006) and Stern (2008) for example—that do not include urban containment in their comprehensive kits of tools for mitigating climate change.

The Public Works Proposition required that an adequate amount—on the order of one-third—of land on the urban fringe be allocated for public works before urban development takes place there. A share of about 5 percent of that land should consist of the rights-of-way for a grid of arterial roads to carry public transport and trunk infrastructure as well as facilitate drainage—preferably spaced 1 kilometer (km) apart within walking distance from the interior of the areas they enclose. Another share of a similar size should contain a protected hierarchy of public open spaces where development—whether by formal developers, informal developers, or squatters—can be repulsed.

The laissez-faire operations of the urban land market may be relied upon in most places to allocate adequate lands for public works at the subdivision level, when land is converted from fields to urban plots. But they cannot be relied upon to allocate sufficient lands for two essential forms of public works—arterial roads and a hierarchy of public open spaces. This is a serious market failure with serious consequences for the environmental sustainability of cities. The allocation of lands for public works at the municipal and metropolitan levels calls for organized public action that cannot come about simply by individuals and firms acting in their own self-interest in the marketplace. It is our public works that indeed enable the free market in urban land to work in an efficient, equitable, and sustainable manner.

TOWARD A SCIENCE OF CITIES

The body of this book has examined many particular instances that illustrate these four propositions in cities in different parts of the world and at different points in time. Its main contribution, however, is its pioneering attempt to look at the 3,646 large cities across the planet that had more than 100,000 people in the year 2000, and to examine their commonalities and differences as they pertain to the key attributes and characteristics of urban spatial structure and its change over time, and as they pertain to these four propositions.

I have sought to present the evidence in as scientific a manner as possible, without using esoteric jargon, complex formulae, and sophisticated statistics. More technical presentations of this material have been and are being published in peer-reviewed journals. This book has focused instead on making the science of cities more accessible to the many of us who care about cities but do not necessarily want to immerse ourselves in the complicated notations and impenetrable theorizing of technical papers.

This scientific approach to the urban expansion problem has been enabled by recent advances in satellite imagery and its quantification in simple metrics, which now make it possible to study cities on a global scale in a rigorous comparative framework. Available theoretical approaches to urban spatial structure, coupled with emerging global data sets on the geographic, economic, social, and political contexts in which urban expansion takes place, also made it possible to construct and test numerous hypotheses that can explain the variations in different spatial attributes of cities. These important advances put the field of urban studies on a new footing, possibly hailing an era of more rigorous scientific research that can focus on the urgent policy questions now facing cities the world over, grounding them in perceived and measurable realities rather than allowing them to continue to float in a sea of fussy ideologies or recurrent dreams of utopia and dystopia.

THE URBANIZATION PROJECT

My central intellectual challenge was to broaden our perspective on cities into a global one that looks at all cities as a single set of connected large and small places that together form a planet of cities. In particular, I wanted to bring cities in both developing and developed countries into one common analytical framework and to help us understand that the prescriptions for cities in developing countries are not necessarily the same as those for cities in developed ones, especially when focusing on actionable programs for urban expansion. While containment of one kind or another may be suitable for some cities—where population growth has ebbed, densities are already low, public transit use is low, carbon emissions are high, and land use regulations are strictly followed—it may not be at all suitable in other cities—where population growth is still in full swing, densities are high, public transit use is high, carbon emissions are low, and land use regulations are largely ignored.

The first part of the book explored planetary urbanization in an historical and geographic perspective and showed that we are in the midst of an urbanization project that started in earnest at the beginning of the nineteenth century, has now reached its peak annual growth rate with half the world population residing in urban areas, and will come to an end, possibly by the end of this century, when most people who want to live in cities will have moved there. This realization lends urgency to my call for preparing for urban expansion now, when the urbanization project is still in full swing, rather than later, when it would be too late to make a difference.

The study of the geography of world urbanization revealed that countries where urbanization is still occurring have quite different characteristics from those that are almost fully urbanized. In particular, their cities have higher densities and lower carbon emissions, but they also suffer from weak public sectors, weak regulatory regimes, and weak rule of law. This distinction strengthens the realization that growing cities need to employ quite different strategies for confronting their expansion than those championed in North America and Europe.

The study of the global hierarchy of cities revealed that cities do not have an optimal size. Rather cities are small, large, or very large for a reason, and they have different roles in the global hierarchy of cities. Smaller cities have closer relations to their rural hinterlands, while larger ones have closer relations to the global centers of commerce, finance, and innovation. This study also revealed that the average growth rates of cities of all population sizes tend to be the same, suggesting that our attention should shift away from the few megacities that seem to receive the bulk of attention from policy makers and the media to focus instead on the entire system of cities. Megacities are not growing any faster than their smaller counterparts and are likely to house only a relatively small share of the planet's urban population in the decades to come.

THE SEVEN QUESTIONS

The second part of the book sought to deepen our understanding and thus calm our fears of urban expansion by providing detailed quantitative answers to seven questions or sets of questions regarding the dimensions and attributes of urban expansion.

Question 1: Extent of Urban Areas

The first question focused on the extent of urban areas worldwide and its growth over time. During the past two centuries, urban land cover has been growing very rapidly compared to earlier periods. Yet by the year 2000—when half of the world's population lived in cities—urban areas worldwide occupied only some 600,000 km², less than one-half of 1 percent of the total land area of countries. In a global representative sample of 30 cities, urban land cover grew sixteenfold, on average, between 1930 and 2000—a global average rate of more than 3 percent per year. In a global sample of 120 cities, urban land cover expanded at a rate of 3.7 percent per year in the final decade of the twentieth century, while the population of cities only grew at less than half that rate. At these growth rates, global urban land cover will double in some 20 years.

Urban expansion is driven by urban population growth; increasing household incomes leading to higher land consumption by households, which also become smaller while occupying larger homes; the expansion of businesses and public facilities that accompanies economic development; and inexpensive transport. The projected urban expansion in all regions, especially the developing countries, should give pause to advocates of urban containment. It is said that King Canute (1015–1035), annoyed by courtiers who told him he was an all powerful king who could even hold back the tide, had his throne placed on the beach and ordered back the tide, only to get his feet wet. As heroic and justified as it may be, containing the oncoming global urban expansion is much the same as holding back the tide.

Question 2: Urban Population Densities

The second question focused on urban population densities and their change over time. New empirical evidence on the average population density of cities across space and time confirms that these densities have been in decline almost everywhere for a century or more. The new evidence is counterintuitive, since numerous academic researchers believe that urban densities have been on the increase. Were that true, it would lend encouragement and support to those favoring densification. However, urban density decline has been persistent and global in scope, and it predated the automobile. It is not restricted to the United States or other industrialized countries, but is pervasive in developing countries as well.

Based on the empirical evidence, we may project that future urban land cover in cities, countries, and global regions may take place under three density change scenarios: a high projection assuming a 2 percent annual rate of density decline, a medium projection assuming a 1 percent annual rate of density decline, and a low projection assuming constant densities, or a 0 percent annual rate of density decline. The forces driving density decline—rising per capita incomes, cheap agricultural lands, efficient transport, and income inequality—are quite formidable. Accordingly, absent a highly effective policy intervention or a steep increase in travel costs in the future, there is little reason for the global decline in densities to slow down anytime soon.

Best-practice examples of policy instruments for increasing the average density of built-up areas are exceedingly rare. Even Portland, Oregon, which had adopted an urban growth boundary (UGB) in the late 1970s to contain urban sprawl, did not manage to increase its built-up area density. The search for cost-effective and politically acceptable infrastructure strategies, regulations, and tax regimes that can lead to significant overall densification in low-density cities must continue in earnest in order to make them more sustainable. At the same time, appropriate strategies for managing urban expansion at declining yet sustainable densities in rapidly growing cities in developing countries must be identified and employed effectively. No matter how we choose to act, however, we should remain aware that conscious and conscientious efforts to densify our cities would require the reversal of a very powerful and sustained global tendency for urban densities to decline.

Question 3: Centrality and Dispersal

The third question focused on the centrality and dispersal of residences and jobs in cities over time. We detected two transformations in the spatial structure of cities during the past two centuries. The first, from the walking city to the monocentric city, led to the suburbanization of residences away from the crowded city centers at lower densities, but kept workplaces within the urban core. Then, as cars and trucks became more pervasive, workplaces started to decentralize to the urban periphery, signaling a second transformation in the spatial structure of urban areas from the monocentric city to the polycentric one, where workplaces are distributed throughout the metropolitan area and draw their workers from the broader labor market.

These transformations have two important policy implications. First, in preparing for the coming urban expansion we should take into account that the cities of the future will most likely be polycentric. This realization requires planning for mixed residential, productive, and commercial land use throughout the metropolitan fringe. We cannot and need not decide in advance where specific uses should be or at what densities different areas must be developed. These decisions are best left to the interactions of supply and demand for land on the urban periphery. What we can do for the public good is to formulate and employ land use regulations that maximize the creative possibilities inherent in cities while insuring that nuisances between adjacent uses are minimized. Second, rather than limiting transportation investments to the radial routes to the central business district (CBD) that were required during the heyday of the monocentric city, we now have to ensure efficient movement by public transport, as well as by trucks and cars, on a dense arterial road and infrastructure grid connecting every suburb to every other suburb.

Question 4: Fragmentation of Urban Landscapes

The fourth question focused on the fragmentation of the built-up areas of cities by open space, the corresponding fragmentation of open space by built-up areas, and changes in these processes over time. On average, the inclusion of urbanized open space in the city footprint doubles the area of that footprint. If that average were considered a global norm, urban planners and policy makers should not be surprised to find half of their city's footprint occupied by urbanized open space, and they should be surprised if it varied substantially from that norm.

Fragmentation is a fringe phenomenon that accompanies the regular operation of urban land markets. As open spaces closer to the city are filled in, new urbanized open spaces are created by noncontiguous building activity on the urban periphery. In planning and preparing for urban expansion, we may therefore assume that in the absence of active intervention, future city footprints can be expected to continue to be half empty as well. While we cannot apply such an estimate to individual cities that have different topographies and different historical patterns of fragmentation, we can urge planners to take fragmentation into account and to prepare substantially larger areas for expansion than might be contemplated otherwise. As a rule of thumb, we should be willing to prepare an area of expansion for a city that is at least one-and-one-half times as large as the land required for the projected built-up area of that city.

Question 5: Compactness of Urban Footprints

The fifth question focused on the shape compactness of urban footprints and its change over time. In the absence of topographic or regulatory barriers, monocentric cities will tend to become more compact—resembling a circle—to maximize access to their CBDs. Polycentric cities will also tend to become more compact to maximize the accessibility of every location within them to every other location. Planned open spaces that render the built-up areas of cities less compact will be difficult to protect when household and corporate preferences for greater accessibility result in strong political and economic pressures to occupy them. We must keep in mind, therefore, that the economic and political costs of effectively protecting open spaces are limited and must be marshaled judiciously. Trying to protect too much open space with too few resources may result in failure to protect any open space at all.

Radial intercity commuter rail lines or freeways that allow for faster travel speeds in some directions but not in others make urban footprints less compact, rendering the open spaces between them easier to protect. Guiding urban development into the interstices between the tentacles of urban development along these lines, in order to make cities more compact, requires the planning and construction of a dense network of arterial roads. Simply marking these areas on land use plans as available for urban use may not be sufficient to direct development there. In short, guiding urban expansion in a realistic fashion cannot take place in a vacuum. It must be planned and executed in full recognition of the complex interplay of forces now acting to make cities more compact or less compact.

Question 6: Future Land Needs of Expanding Cities

The sixth question focused on estimating the future land needs of expanding cities in the decades to come. If we are to prepare cities for their expansion, we need to know how much land on the fringe of a given city will need to be converted to urban use in the next 20 to 30 years. This is not a simple question, and the answers will necessarily involve considerable speculation. Still, we will be better off trying to provide thoughtful answers, allowing for contingencies, and accommodating adequate margins of error than giving up on preparing for expansion altogether or simply making convenient assumptions about the expected amount of land needed for future urban expansion based on wishful thinking.

We can estimate the areas needed for urban expansion given population and density projections. At a 1 percent annual decline in average densities, for example, urban land cover in developed countries will double between 2000 and 2050. At a 2 percent annual density decline, urban land cover in these countries will more than double between 2000 and 2030, and will triple between 2000 and 2050. The situation is likely to be more critical in developing countries, where most urban population growth will take place. At a 1 percent annual decline in average densities in cities in developing countries, urban land cover will almost triple between 2000 and 2030, and more than quadruple between 2000 and 2050. At a 2 percent annual decline in densities, urban land cover will almost quadruple between 2000 and 2030, and increase sevenfold between 2000 and 2050. While conditions in individual cities may vary greatly, realistic planning for urban expansion must take place with these orders of magnitude in mind.

Question 7: Loss of Cultivated Lands to Urban Expansion

The seventh and last question focused on the share of cultivated lands that will be lost to urban expansion in coming decades. In the year 2000, urban land cover amounted to some 4 percent of cultivated land. Historically, lands under cultivation were always in close proximity to cities to minimize the cost of shipping produce to market. As cities began to expand, they consumed nearby cultivated lands. On average, preliminary estimates suggest that in the world at large, one-half of the area of projected urban expansion in coming decades is likely to occupy land now under cultivation. In a worst-case scenario, assuming a 2 percent annual decline in density, some 6 percent of the land now under cultivation in the world at large will be lost to urban expansion between 2000 and 2050. The growing urban population will require substantial increases in the global food supply, entailing mostly improved yields and, to a lesser extent, the expansion of lands under cultivation.

Both cultivated lands and cities will need to expand, but they need not come into conflict. There are adequate reserves of cultivatable lands on the planet sufficient to feed the world population in perpetuity, and some of these lands must now be brought into cultivation in an equitable, efficient, and sustainable manner. There are also adequate reserves of wealth in our emerging planet of cities sufficient to ensure that resources are invested in a plentiful and affordable global food supply. In other words, urban expansion that proceeds hand in hand with urban research and investment aimed at increasing agricultural yields, as well as at the responsible expansion of lands under cultivation, need not compromise our food supply.

AN ACTIONABLE PROGRAM FOR GUIDING URBAN EXPANSION

The Making Room Paradigm can be readily transformed into an actionable program to help prepare individual cities for their expansion. Such a program, to be realistic, would require an understanding of the city's present legal, political, economic, and cultural context. It will also benefit from the accumulated experience of cities that have embarked on such ventures, successful or unsuccessful as they may have been. At the conceptual level it may contain, at the very minimum, variations on four key components: a realistic projection of urban land needs; generous metropolitan limits; selective protection of open space; and an arterial grid of dirt roads.

A Realistic Projection of Urban Land Needs

Forecasting urban land cover involves a combination of several independent forecasts: the city population, its built-up area density, and its level of fragmentation as measured by the city footprint ratio (see chapter 13). To forecast where expansion will likely to take place, we would also need to forecast and plan for possible changes in its compactness. We noted that the rate of urban population growth in a country as a whole, a rate for which there are relatively good short-term and long-term projections by national census bureaus and by the United Nations Population Division, could be a starting point for population projections in individual cities. They can also base their projections on their own historical growth trajectories and adjust them if a change is caused unexpectedly by some cataclysmic event, such as the influx of war refugees, an environmental catastrophe, or rapid economic growth.

The New York City commissioners' 1811 projections for Manhattan and Cerdá's 1859 projections for Barcelona both made room for more than a sevenfold increase of the areas of their cities at the time, and proved to be entirely realistic. The absence of similar examples today may be a failure of imagination or a failure of nerve, but such visions are exactly what will be required to make realistic projections for the expansion of many cities in urbanizing countries in the coming decades.

Figure 17.2 graphs our estimates of the amount of increase of the 2000 urban land cover in all countries by 2050 under three scenarios of annual density decline. Under the 1 percent scenario, 22 countries will have their urban land cover multiplied tenfold or more between 2000 and 2050. Under the 2 percent scenario, 47 countries will be in this situation. The New York and Barcelona projections of a sevenfold increase or more may not be unrealistic after all for cities in many urbanizing countries.

Generous Metropolitan Limits

A realistic projection of urban land needs for future expansion must go hand in hand with policy reforms that abandon artificial limits on population growth and urban

FIGURE 17.2
Number of Countries with Various Multiples of Their 2000 Urban Land Cover by 2050

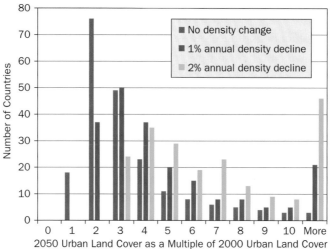

Source: Urban expansion estimates based on the author's density calculations and United Nations Population Division (2010, file 2).

expansion in favor of urban economic development and improvements in the quality of urban life. The Regional Plan for the Mumbai Metropolitan Region, 1996–2011, has undergone this transformation. It acknowledged the failure of earlier plans and promoted a new strategy based on an accelerated rate of urban expansion that far exceeds its population projections.

> The Regional Plan of 1973 primarily aimed at containing Mumbai's growth . . . the outcome has been far from intended. . . . Although Mumbai's popu-lation growth was expected to stabilize around 70 lakhs (7 million) by 1991, it has reached 99 lakhs (9.9 million). (MMRDA 1996, 330)

The Mumbai Metropolitan Region Development Authority (MMRDA) projected the population of the region to grow from 14.5 million in 1991 to 23.5 million in 2011 and to 25.8 million in 2031 (MMRDA 1996, 42). In other words, the population of the region was expected to grow by three-quarters between 1991 and 2031. In contrast, the built-up area in the region was allowed to more than triple. "[A]s against 418 sq.km. of existing built-up area the revised plan allocates 1194 sq.km. area for future urbaniza-tion" (MMRDA 1996, 356). A simplified map of the regional expansion plan shows that Mumbai is no longer pursuing a policy of containment and is instead projecting its population and its area for expansion more realistically than before (figure 17.3). This makes complete sense given that the average population density of the built-up area of

FIGURE 17.3
**Generous Areas for Urban Expansion in the Mumbai
Metropolitan Region Land Use Plan, 1996–2011**

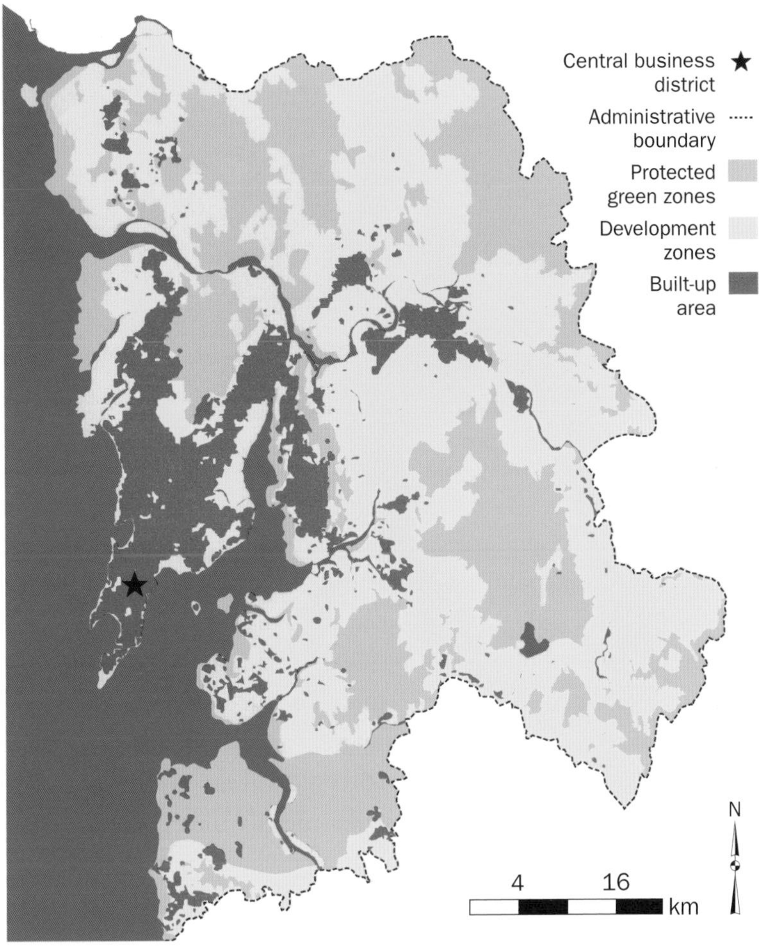

Source: Redrawn from a land use map in MMRDA (1996, figure 13.8, 354).

Mumbai in 2000, at 440 persons per hectare, was the third highest in the global sample of 120 cities after Dhaka, Bangladesh, and Hong Kong, China,

Urban land cover projections by sophisticated demographers, even those willing to err on the high side, will be of little use unless they are put into practice by designating expanded urban administrative areas and enshrining them in law. The boundaries of these areas cannot be instituted by municipalities. They need to be created by state, provincial, or national legislation. Just as the New York City plan was authorized by the State of New York, and Portland's UGB was authorized by the State of Oregon, new metropolitan administrative boundaries are a concern and a responsibility of higher levels of government. Cities are powerless to plan for their expansion outside their

The free market cannot be relied upon to create a hierarchy of public open spaces in cities, such as an urban forest park in Singapore.

municipal administrative boundaries, as are metropolitan areas containing large numbers of independent municipalities.

The main and crucial difference between Portland's UGB and the designation of appropriate administrative boundaries for making room is simply a matter of generosity. Metropolitan limits have to be large enough to accommodate 30 years of urban expansion given realistic projections of population growth, density decline, and changes in fragmentation levels. If they are to err, they should err on the side of more rather than less to allow for the small probability that the city may become very large. Once they are put into law, these metropolitan limits—designating areas where orderly urban development is allowed and encouraged—should be subject to study and review, and changed regularly, preferably every decade, as population, density, and fragmentation trends become better understood. Only the creation of generous administrative boundaries for metropolitan expansion and enshrining them in state, provincial, or national law can create the necessary legal framework for orderly urban expansion.

Selective Protection of Open Space

There is no question that urban dwellers put a value on proximity to open spaces of all sizes; that homes adjacent or within walking distance to parks and playgrounds command higher prices; and that people who move to the outer suburbs often cite their desire to be closer to the open countryside as a reason for their move. Singapore, for example, has an enviable hierarchy of urban parks distributed throughout the city-state. It includes 6 nature parks, 8 riverine parks, 11 city and heritage parks, 11 community parks, 6 coastal parks, 5 horticultural parks, and 2 botanic gardens within a land area of 710 km². These parks are clearly in permanent use as publicly accessible open space, the most useful type of open space for urban dwellers. Not every city can institute an open space hierarchy within its city footprint comparable to that of Singapore, but city officials should advocate for the creation of such a hierarchy of areas that can remain open in perpetuity in areas of expansion, and they should advocate for it now, when land on the urban periphery is still inexpensive and in ample supply.

This selective protection of open spaces involves four key steps: (1) the creation of a metropolitan open space plan that contains a hierarchy of open spaces of all sizes and types—from football fields and playgrounds to wetlands, reservoir watersheds, farms, and nature parks—in areas of expansion; (2) the passage of new regulations or the enforcement of existing regulations that mandate the allocation of a certain share of private lands for public use; (3) the purchase of private lands for use as public open space on the urban periphery while land prices are low, the registration of liens on private lands designated for future use as open space, or the acquisition of the development rights to land through purchase or exchange of land rights; and (4) the creation of an institutional framework comprising public, private, and civic organizations for the aggressive protection of these open spaces from invasion by formal and informal developers.

The most important aspect of this element of the Making Room Paradigm is that its actual extent will be limited by the private, public, and civic resources—both financial and human—that can be made available for its implementation. That is why it must be selective. Instead of protecting too much land from development at no cost to the public and ending up with no open space at all, this strategy aims to protect some land at a minimal cost to the public so it remains open in perpetuity.

It is a strategy that does not rely on a regulatory regime that penalizes some landowners on the urban fringe by prohibiting them from developing their land for urban use, in order to provide an entire urban population the free benefit of enjoying the view of their open lands without having to compensate them. Instead, it takes as a given that owners of land on the urban fringe in areas designated for urban expansion have the right to use their land in accordance with the laws governing urban development, subject to their willingness—enshrined in enforceable regulations—to forgo a part of their land for public use, already a common practice in many countries from Israel to Ecuador. In addition, the Making Room Paradigm—by opening up large areas for urban development—aims to reduce the premium typically associated with the conversion of land from rural to urban use. This is likely to keep land prices on the urban fringe low, enabling the purchase of land for public use as well as the purchase of development rights from landowners by land conservancies to ensure that their lands remain open in perpetuity.

In short, instead of a greenbelt on the periphery of the city, the Making Room Paradigm opts for a green city full of open spaces large and small, far and close, designated for intensive use and protected from overuse. Instead of surrounding the city with a greenbelt that aims to contain its inevitable expansion and likely failing in the attempt, this element of the paradigm calls for built-up areas and open spaces to interpenetrate each other as the city expands outward.

An Arterial Grid of Dirt Roads

Assuming that the various objections to expansion can be overcome, that the obstacles to creating new administrative limits for planned urban expansion can be surmounted, and that designated green areas can be protected from urban encroachment, a further question arises: What needs to be done, at the very minimum, to prepare new lands for urban use? In urbanizing countries the answer is straightforward: Secure the rights-of-way now for an entire arterial road and infrastructure grid within these new administrative boundaries.

The arterial grid pertains to the network of major arterial roads that typically carry intra-urban traffic, public transport, and trunk infrastructure, especially water and sewer lines. The main difference between an arterial grid and the local street grid can be seen in Detroit, where the arterial grid encompasses 1.6-km-wide urban super-blocks with local streets arranged in various ways within them to provide access to all plots (figure 17.4).

FIGURE 17.4
The Arterial Grid and Pattern of Local Roads in a Section of Detroit, Michigan

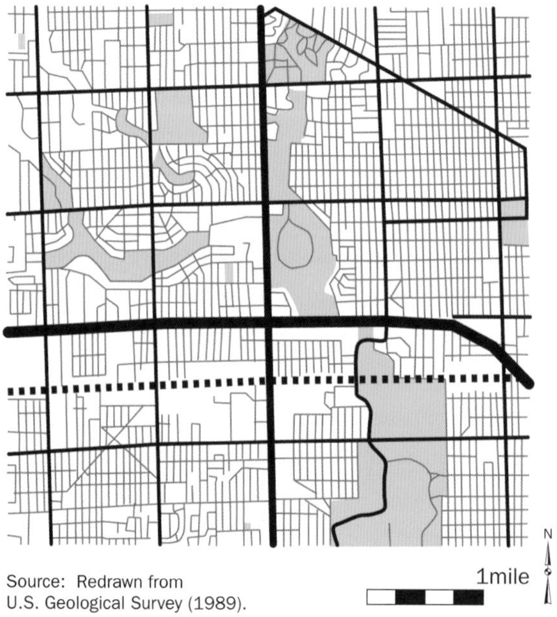

Source: Redrawn from
U.S. Geological Survey (1989).

1mile

N

To accommodate urban expansion, an arterial grid on the urban fringe must have five essential properties:

- Total coverage: The grid must cover the entire area designated for expansion in the next 20 to 30 years, not just a segment of that area.
- Connectivity: The arterial grid should be a mesh of long, continuous roads that crisscross the expansion area and connect it to the existing road network.
- One-kilometer spacing: To ensure that public transportation is within a 10-minute walk, these roads should be spaced no more than 1 km apart.
- Wide right-of-way: The width of the roads should be 20–30 meters, so they can have designated bus lanes, bike paths, a median, and several lanes to carry intracity traffic, while remaining easy to cross.
- Progressive improvement: Initially, the rights-of-way for the entire grid should be acquired by municipal authorities. Dirt roads can then be opened up in portions of the grid, and selected segments can be paved and improved over the years as demand builds up and as budgets become available.

An early introduction of an arterial grid into expansion areas would help attain five important objectives.

An antipoverty objective. The proposed arterial grid is meant to open up sufficiently large areas for urban expansion to ensure that land supply is not constricted, and that large numbers of residential plots remain affordable. In contrast to earlier affordable housing strategies in developing countries that focused on the provision of a limited supply of individual plots—commonly referred to as sites-and-services projects—the proposed strategy aims to provide a large number of superblocks that can be subdivided by formal and informal developers into individual plots. To create the desired impact of the proposed arterial grid on the urban land market, the entire network should be initiated now, and individual road segments can be improved to higher standards as demand for travel along them increases.

This strategy minimizes the risk of land speculation that typically occurs when only a few fully paved roads are put in place, as well as the risk of paving roads at the wrong time and in the wrong places. If only a portion of the rural periphery is converted to urban use and a full complement of infrastructure services is introduced immediately —in a public-private land development partnership or in a land pooling and readjustment scheme (Larsson, 1993), for example—then land prices there increase dramatically, rendering the area out of reach for the urban poor. Only a comprehensive approach to the land supply issue can keep land prices in metropolitan areas from rising steeply, especially in rapidly urbanizing cities where there is strong demand for land.

A planning objective. Urban infrastructure plans and investments in cities in urbanizing countries typically follow rather than guide urban development. Developers pressure municipalities to extend infrastructure services in piecemeal fashion to areas that the developers have chosen, often blatantly disregarding municipal plans. The arterial road grid would function as a basic framework for planning the city. Participatory planning would be considerably more effective if it focused on an individual superblock rather than on the metropolitan area as a whole. By locating the grid before land subdivision and development begin, municipalities can actively shape future growth. They will then be leading the developers into new areas rather than following them.

The arterial grid plan simply assumes that, no matter how the city develops, it will need an underlying network of arterial roads to carry its traffic and trunk infrastructure. Unlike a typical master plan, it does not designate land uses or densities, nor does it recommend strategies for the economic, social, or cultural development of the city. Its planning, design, and implementation do not require unique expertise or rare ingenuity. In most cases it can be planned and implemented by municipal planners with little or no outside help.

A transport objective. For an arterial grid to function as the road network for a public transport system, three conditions must hold: (1) residential densities must be sufficiently high to sustain public transport; (2) the width of the rights-of-way for the roads needs to be around 20–30 meters; and (3) the roads need to be spaced not more than 1 km apart so the majority of people can walk to a public transit stop from any location in less than 10 minutes. The arterial road grid of the city of Milton Keynes in England, one of the new towns on the outskirts of London, has arterial roads spaced within walking distance of the areas they enclose, and there is a bus line on each of them (figure 17.5).

While the absence of an arterial grid may prevent the introduction of an effective public transport system that extends far into the urban fringe, putting in place an arterial road grid is not a guarantee, in and of itself, that the grid would be used effectively to carry public transport. Unless strong and enduring political alliances in cities take steps to introduce and strengthen public transport alternatives to individual automobile travel, the appropriation of the arterial grid by cars and trucks—to the exclusion of buses, bicycles, or other environmentally friendly forms of transport—should come as no surprise. Toronto is one city that has been able to build and maintain an effective public transport system that extends along a road grid far into the suburbs and it now boasts the third-largest transit system in North America (figure 5.4).

An environmental objective. The arterial grid is an essential element of an effective public transport system, and one of the most important elements in any urban strategy that aims to reduce our carbon footprint. To the extent that a good public transport system can reduce our future reliance on private automobile travel, the arterial grid provides an essential building block. The organization of the urban periphery in a set of superblocks will increase the chances that environmental justice concerns

FIGURE 17.5
The 1-Kilometer-Wide Arterial Grid of Milton Keynes, England

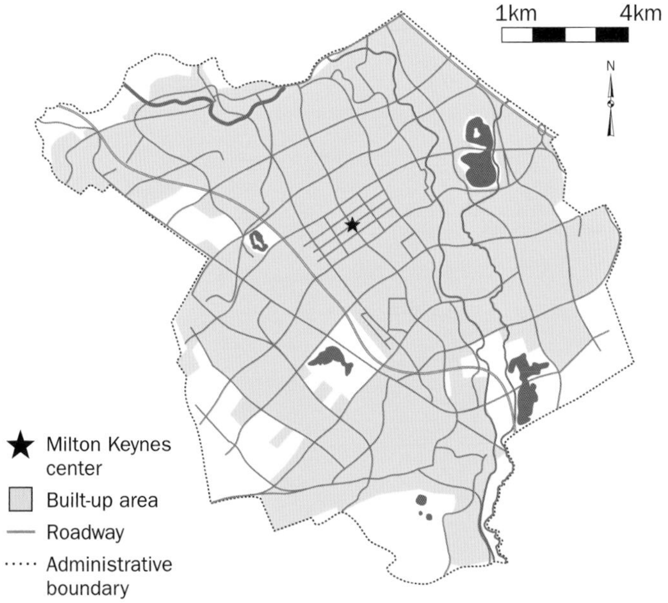

★ Milton Keynes
  center
▢ Built-up area
— Roadway
····· Administrative
  boundary

Source: Redrawn from Red-Grey.co.uk (2012).

will be addressed. The superblock system created by the arterial road network makes it possible to demand and ensure that each superblock contains an adequate amount of public open space; that environmentally unfriendly facilities are distributed evenly; and that human-scale communities and neighborhoods have a say in the planning, designing, and making of their physical environment.

Finally, to the extent that location within the planned superblocks with access to arterial roads is perceived of as an advantage by formal and informal developers alike, the arterial grid will provide planners with an effective tool for directing urban development away from low-lying areas that will be vulnerable to flooding as sea levels rise, or away from sensitive natural habitats or reservoir watersheds that are likely to be encroached upon otherwise. This objective will be particularly important in cities where the regulatory regime by itself is incapable of preventing the conversion of rural peripheral lands to urban use.

A financial objective. Budget constraints typically prevent putting in place a completed arterial road network incorporating a system of well-paved, well-drained, and well-lit and signed roads in advance of development. That said, cities in rapidly urbanizing countries can acquire the land needed for such a network now, and then improve individual road segments to higher standards as demand for travel along them increases. If demand along a particular road segment never increases, no great harm was done.

If it does increase, it can be met at a cost several decimal orders of magnitude lower than if an arterial road had to be built through an established neighborhood. This is the essence of the strategy proposed by Taleb (2007) for mitigating the uncertain consequences of unforeseen expansion at the lowest possible cost.

CONCLUSION

This book asserts that there is an efficient, equitable, and sustainable way for the public sector to engage in the urbanization project now taking place in many developing countries. It involves the abandonment of the prevailing Containment Paradigm as irrelevant and ill-fitting for cities that are scheduled to grow several-fold in coming decades. Instead, it calls for the adoption of an alternative Making Room Paradigm, an urban development strategy that aims to accommodate urban population growth rather than constrict and constrain it.

This new paradigm is not laissez-faire in the sense of allowing market forces to determine the shape of the cities of the future. It recognizes the importance of markets in the development of urban lands for residential, economic, and civic activities, but also recognizes their inability to ensure the creation of a hierarchy of public and private open spaces protected in perpetuity, or to establish an adequate network of arterial roads to make cities sustainable through the development of efficient public transport.

This research into urban expansion in a global and historical framework has helped establish the basic parameters and dimensions of the expansion process. We now know how much and how fast cities have expanded in the past, and we can project how much and how fast they are likely to expand in the future. We now know that densities have been in persistent decline for a century or more, and we can expect them to continue to decline as long as incomes increase and transport remains relatively inexpensive. We now know that the cities of the future are likely to be more polycentric than monocentric, requiring the development of transport networks that increase the connectivity of the city as a whole rather than the connectivity of the city to its center. We now know that city footprints contain open spaces in and around built-up areas that are equivalent in size to their built-up areas, requiring that expansion plans take that into account rather than assume that all vacant lands will be filled in. We now know that powerful forces acting to maximize accessibility can frustrate noble attempts to keep people and businesses from occupying planned open spaces, requiring a more nuanced approach to planning and protecting the urban hierarchy of open spaces. We can now estimate the total urban land cover in all countries and, given these estimates, together with population projections and realistic assumptions on density decline, we can begin to project the amount of land that will be needed to accommodate urban populations in all regions, countries, and cities in coming decades. And finally, we now know how much cultivated land is likely to be lost to urban expansion, and we can plan for urban expansion hand-in-hand with planning for the expansion of cultivated lands.

This book therefore provides both the conceptual framework and the basic empirical data necessary for the minimal yet meaningful management of the urban expansion process. Karl Popper (1994, xiii) reminds us that

> [t]he future is open. . . . When I say "It is our duty to remain optimists", this includes not only the openness of the future but also that which all of us can contribute to it by everything we do: we are all responsible for what the future holds in store. Thus it is our duty, not to prophesy evil but, rather, to fight for a better world.

This is especially pertinent to the future of our cities, by far our largest, most ambitious, and most complex projects. They are, at the same time, the places where most of us have chosen to come together and our most forceful signatures on the global landscape. Because cities are our common home, we need to shape and reshape them in a spirit of respect and compassion, for us, for them, and for the planet. It is my hope that the evidence, the analysis, and the conclusions presented here may lay the foundation for a fruitful discussion of the fate of our planet of cities and what we can do to make it a better place for a long time to come.

Acknowledgments

Without the valued assistance of many individuals and organizations, the creation of this book would have been an insurmountable task indeed. Their contributions to this study of global urban expansion deserve lasting acknowledgement.

My earnest thanks go to my three principal collaborators on this study: Jason Parent, Daniel L. Civco, and Alejandro M. Blei. Together we were able to collaborate over a number of years in assembling and classifying satellite data and in inventing and testing metrics for measuring this data. Jason Parent has been my principal collaborator in creating and analyzing the satellite-based maps using sophisticated geographic information system (GIS) tools. Alejandro Blei has been instrumental in collecting and analyzing historical maps, as well as collecting and analyzing large data sets involving density and travel behavior in U.S. cities. The four of us co-authored numerous publications in refereed journals, as well as the Lincoln Institute's policy focus report, *Making Room for a Planet of Cities* (2011), and the *Atlas of Urban Expansion* (2012), the companion volume to this book. *Planet of Cities* is my own work, but it relies heavily on their contributions, especially in the collection of data and its translation into measurable metrics.

This book is the result of an eight-year study of global urban expansion. The first phase of the study involved the collection and analysis of satellite imagery and census data in the global sample of 120 cities. It was supported by a grant from the Research Committee of the World Bank to the Transport and Urban Development Department of the Bank. I am grateful to Christine Kessides of the department for helping us obtain this grant. I am also grateful to Deborah Balk of the Center for International Earth Sciences Information Network (CIESIN) of Columbia University for providing us with the census data for the sample of cities. The team that worked on this phase of the study included Shlomo Angel, Stephen Sheppard, and Daniel Civco as principal investigators, assisted by Jason Parent, Anna Chabaeva, Micah Perlin, Lucy Gitlin, and Robert Buckley.

The second phase of the study involved the administration of a survey by local consultants in each of the cities in the global sample of cities. The survey included questions on the latest census; on the status of metropolitan area planning, regulation, and enforcement; on general housing market conditions; on informal settlements; and on financial institutions that provide mortgage loans. This phase was supported by a grant from the National Science Foundation. The team that worked on this phase of the study included Shlomo Angel, Stephen Sheppard, and Daniel Civco as principal investigators, assisted by Lucy Gitlin, Alison Kraley, Jason Parent, and Anna Chabaeva. The local consultants who conducted the survey in each city are listed in the working paper titled "The Persistent Decline in Urban Densities," which can be found on the website of the Lincoln Institute of Land Policy (*www.lincolninst.edu*).

In parallel with the second phase of the study, I helped design a World Bank project, under the direction of Alexandra Ortiz of the Bank, to assist five intermediate-sized municipalities in Ecuador in making minimal preparations for urban expansion. I am grateful to William Cobbett, the manager of Cities Alliance, for supporting the preparatory workshop for the project in Quito, Ecuador, in 2007.

The third phase of the study involved the creation of a set of metrics for measuring urban spatial structure and a python script for calculating these metrics with ArcGIS software. The team for this phase of the study included Shlomo Angel, Jason Parent, and Daniel Civco. Part of this research was undertaken by Jason Parent within the University of Connecticut's Center for Land Use Education and Research (CLEAR) and Department of Natural Resources and the Environment (NRE) under a grant for a project titled "Incorporating NASA's Applied Sciences Data and Technologies into Local Government Decision Support in the National Application Areas of Coastal Management, Water Management, Ecologic Forecasting and Invasive Species," financed by the National Aeronautics and Space Administration (NASA).

The fourth phase of the study involved the collection, geo-referencing, and digitizing of maps at 20- to 25-year intervals for the period 1800–2000 for a global representative sample of 30 cities; the analysis of census data for 20 U.S. cities for the 1910–2000 period and 65 cities for the 1950–2000 period; the statistical modeling of the results of all the previous phases; the preparation of three Lincoln Institute working papers; the drafting of the policy focus report, *Making Room for a Planet of Cities*; and the preparation of the *Atlas of Urban Expansion* website. Work on this phase was done by Shlomo Angel, Jason Parent, Daniel Civco, and Alejandro Blei, with statistical support from Chun Il Kim and graphic support from Craig Cook.

The fifth phase of the project involved transforming the three working papers into publishable papers in peer-reviewed journals, and the publication of *Planet of Cities* and the *Atlas of Urban Expansion* as companion volumes. Work on this phase was done by Shlomo Angel, with research support from Jason Parent and Alejandro Blei; graphic support from Mark Roland; editorial assistance in finding photographs and other images and obtaining copyright permissions from Stephanie Heimann-Roland; and editorial support from Patrick Lamson-Hall.

All the work from the third phase onward benefited from the generous support of the Lincoln Institute of Land Policy and the direct assistance of Gregory K. Ingram, president and CEO. I especially appreciate his continued attention to the project and the insightful discussions we held on the key issues pertaining to the science of cities over the years. I have learned a lot from him. Ann LeRoyer, senior editor and director of publications, managed the overall book production process with designer David Gerratt and copyeditor Jane Gebhart. I am very grateful to all of them. I am also grateful to the staff of the Institute for their active support of this study, as well as their gracious hospitality.

I would also like to thank many people who provided useful comments and suggestions as well as support and encouragement during the long years of this study: Pierre Belanger, Gershon Ben Shahar, Alain Bertaud, Andrés Borthagaray, Neil Brenner, Robert Bruegmann, Robert Buckley, Armando Carbonell, Wendell Cox, Edesio Fernandes, Anthony Flint, Brandon Fuller, Ralph Gakenheimer, Daniella Gitlin, Aharon Gluska, James Hurd, Geoffrey Hyman, Daniel Kozak, Steve Malpezzi, George Martine, Mark Montgomery, David Potere, Bertrand Renaud, Gonzalo Rodriguez, Eduardo Rojas, Paul Romer, Yvonne Rydin, David Satterthwaite, Annemarie Schneider, Karen Seto, Tsering Shawa, Martim Smolka, John Volin, and Shue Tuck Wong.

I am also grateful to Dr. Joan Clos, the executive director of the United Nations Human Settlements Programme (UN-Habitat), for inviting me to address the World Urban Forum 6 in Naples, Italy, in September 2012 on the subject matter of this book. Having the book ready in time for the Forum was a pressing and worthwhile goal.

I must not fail to take this opportunity to express my gratitude to those favorite teachers of mine who have been instrumental to my understanding of cities: Avraham Vachman, Christopher Alexander, Michael Teitz, and William Alonso.

Finally, a sincere note of heartfelt thanks to Lucy Gitlin for her unrelenting support of my work on this study over the years, for her contagious love of cities, for her warm companionship, and for her valuable help in repeatedly summoning the courage of my convictions. It is an unimaginable good fortune for me to publish this book on my seventieth birthday with her by my side, surrounded by so many wonderful people.

References

Abiko, A., L. Reynaldo de Azevedo Cardoso, R. Rinaldelli, and H. C. R. Haga. 2007. Basic costs of slum upgrading in Brazil. *Global Urban Development* 3(1): 1–23.

Acioly, C. C., Jr. 2000. Can urban management deliver the sustainable city? Guided densification in Brazil versus informal compactness in Egypt. In *Compact cities: Sustainable urban forms for developing countries*, eds. M. Jenks and R. Burgess, 127–140. London and New York: Spon Press.

Ades, A. F., and E. L. Glaeser. 2001. Trade and circuses: Explaining urban giants. *Quarterly Journal of Economics* 110(1): 195–227.

Alonso, W. 1960. A theory of the urban land market. *Papers and Proceedings of the Regional Science Association* 6: 149–157.

Alonso, W. 1964. *Location and land use*. Cambridge, MA: Harvard University Press.

Anas, A., R. Arnott, and K. Small. 1998. Urban spatial structure. *Journal of Economic Literature* 36: 1426–1464.

Andersen, H. T. 2008. Copenhagen, Denmark: Urban regeneration at economic and social sustainability. In *Sustainable city regions: Space, place and governance*, eds. T. Kidokoro, N. Harata, L. P. Subanu, J. Jessen, A. Motte, and E. P. Seltzer, 203–226. Tokyo, Japan: Springer.

Angel, S. 2000a. Housing policies and programs in Guatemala: Diagnosis, evaluation and guidelines for action. Unpublished report. Washington, DC: The Inter-American Development Bank.

Angel, S. 2000b. *Housing policy matters: A global analysis*. New York and London: Oxford University Press.

Angel, S. 2008. Preparing for urban expansion: A proposed strategy for intermediate cities in Ecuador. In *The new global frontier: Urbanization, poverty and the environment in the 21st century*, eds. G. Martine, G. McGranahan, M. Montgomery, and R. Fernandez-Castilla, 115–129. London: Earthscan.

Angel, S., R. Archer, S. Tanphiphat, and E. A. Wegelin. 1983. *Land for housing the poor*. Singapore: Select Books.

Angel, S., A. Blei, J. Parent, and D. L. Civco. 2011a. The decline in transit-sustaining densities in U.S. cities, 1910–2000. In *Climate change and land policies*, eds. G. K. Ingram and Y.-H. Hong, 191–212. Cambridge, MA: Lincoln Institute of Land Policy.

Angel, S., and S. Boonyabancha. 1988. Land sharing as an alternative to eviction. *Third World Planning Review* 10(2): 107–127.

Angel, S., and J. Parent. 2011. Non-compactness and voter exchange: Towards a constitutional cure for gerrymandering. *Northwestern Interdisciplinary Law Review* 4 (1): 89–146.

Angel, S., J. Parent, and D. L. Civco. 2010. Ten compactness properties of circles: Measuring shape in geography. *The Canadian Geographer* 54(4): 441–461.

Angel, S., J. Parent, and D. L. Civco. 2012. The fragmentation of urban landscapes: Global evidence of a key attribute of the spatial structure of cities, 1990–2000. *Environment and Urbanization* 24 (April): 249–283.

Angel S., J. Parent, D. L. Civco, and A. M. Blei. 2010. The persistent decline in urban densities: Global and historical evidence of 'sprawl'. Working paper. Cambridge MA; Lincoln Institute of Land Policy. *www.lincolninst.edu/pubs/1834_The-Persistent-Decline-in-Urban-Densities*

Angel, S., J. Parent, D. L. Civco, and A. M. Blei. 2011c. Making room for a planet of cities. Policy Focus Report. Cambridge, MA: Lincoln Institute of Land Policy. *www.lincolninst.edu/pubs/1880_Making-Room-for-a-Planet-of-Cities-urban-expansion*

Angel, S., J. Parent, D. L. Civco, and A. M. Blei. 2012. *Atlas of urban expansion.* Cambridge, MA: Lincoln Institute of Land Policy. *http://www.lincolninst.edu/subcenters/atlas-urban-expansion/google-earth-data.aspx*

Angel, S., J. Parent, D. L. Civco, A. M. Blei, and D. Potere. 2011b. The dimensions of global urban expansion: Estimates and projections for all countries, 2000–2050. *Progress in Planning* 75(3): 53–107.

Angel, S., S. C. Sheppard, and D. L. Civco, with R. Buckley, A. Chabaeva, L. Gitlin, A. Kraley, J. Parent, and M. Perlin. 2005. *The dynamics of global urban expansion.* Washington, DC: The World Bank Transport and Urban Development Department. *http://www.citiesalliance.org/doc/resources/upgrading/urban - expansion/worldbankreportsept2005.pdf*

Angel, S., M. I. Valdivia, and R. M. Lutzy. 2011. Urban expansion, land conversion, and affordable housing in China: The case of Zhengzhou. In *China's housing reform and outcomes,* ed. J. Y. Man, 137–156. Cambridge, MA: Lincoln Institute of Land Policy.

Bairoch, P. 1988. *Cities and economic development: From the dawn of history to the present.* Trans. C. Braider. Chicago: University of Chicago Press.

Barboza, D. 2011. Inflation in China poses big threat to global trade. *New York Times,* April 17: 1.

Barker, K. 2004. *Review of housing supply. Delivering stability: Securing our future housing needs. Final report—Recommendations.* Norwich, England: Her Majesty's Stationery Office. *http://image.guardian.co.uk/sys-files/Guardian/documents/2004/03/17/Barker.pdf*

Baross, P., and J. van der Linden, eds. 1990. *The transformation of land supply systems in third world cities.* Aldershot: Avebury.

Benevolo, L. 1980. *The history of the city.* Cambridge: MIT Press.

Berry, B. J. L., J. W. Simmons, and R. J. Tennant. 1963. Urban population densities: Structure and change. *Geographical Review* 53(3): 389–405.

Bertaud, A., and B. Renaud. 1995. Cities without land markets: Location and land use in the socialist city. Policy Research Working Paper 1477. Washington, DC: The World Bank. (June).

Blank, A., and S. Solomon. 2000. Power laws and cities population. *http://xxx.tau.ac.il/html/cond-mat/0003240*

Bogart, W. T. 1998. *The economics of cities and suburbs.* Upper Saddle River, NJ: Prentice Hall.

Borges, J. L. 1969. *Fervor de Buenos Aires.* Buenos Aires: Emece.

Bourguignon, F., and C. Morrison. 2002. Inequality among world citizens: 1820–1992. *The American Economic Review* 92(54): 727–744.

Brand, L. A., and T. L. George. 2001. Response of passerine birds to forest edge in coast redwood forest fragments. *The Auk* 118(3): 678–686.

Brand, S. 2010. How slums can save the planet. *Prospect* 167(January 27): n.p.

Braun, G. , and F. Hogenberg. 1572–1617. *Civitates orbis terrarium*. Köln: Hogenberg. English edition: S. Füssel, ed. 2011. *Cities of the world*. Köln: Taschen.

Bridges, W. 1811. *Map of the city of New York and island of Manhattan with explanatory remarks and references*. New York: William Bridges. *http://www.library.cornell.edu/Reps/DOCS/nyc1811.htm*

Brinkhoff, T. 2012. City population. Statistics and maps of the major cities, agglomerations, and administrative divisions. *www.citypopulation.de*

Brueckner, J. K. 1987. The structure of urban equilibria: A unified treatment of the Muth-Mills model. In *Handbook of regional and urban economics*, ed. E. S. Mills, 821–845. Amsterdam: North-Holland.

Brueckner, J. 2000. Urban sprawl: Diagnosis and remedies. *International Regional Science Review* 23(2): 160–171.

Brueckner, J., and D. Fansler. 1983. The economics of urban sprawl: Theory and evidence on the spatial sizes of cities. *Review of Economics and Statistics* 55: 479–482.

Bruegmann, R. 2005. *Sprawl: A compact history*. Chicago, IL. University of Chicago Press.

Burchell, R. W., G. Lowenstein, W. R. Dolphin, C. C. Galley, A. Downs, S. Seskin, and T. Moore. 2002. *Costs of sprawl—2000*. Washington, DC: Transportation Research Board.

Burchfield, M., H. G. Overman, D. Puga, and M. A. Turner. 2006. Causes of sprawl: A portrait from space. *Quarterly Journal of Economics* 121(2): 587–633.

Bureau of Transportation Statistics. 2010. *Transportation statistics annual report—2010*. Washington, DC: U.S. Department of Transportation. *http://www.bts.gov/publications/transportation_statistics_annual_report*

Burgess, R. 2000. The compact city debate: A global perspective. In *Compact cities: Sustainable urban forms for developing countries*, eds. M. Jenks and R. Burgess, 9–25. London and New York: Spon Press.

Burton, E. 2002. Measuring urban compactness in U.K. towns and cities. *Environment and Planning B: Planning and Design* 29(2): 219–250.

Calthorpe, P. 2011. *Urbanism in the age of climate change*. Washington, DC: Island Press.

Carroll, C. 1982. National city-size distributions: What do we know after 67 years of research? *Progress in Human Geography* 6(1): 1–43.

Carruthers, J. I., and G. F. Ulfarsson. 2001. Fragmentation and sprawl: Evidence from interregional analysis. *Growth and Change* 33(Summer): 312–340.

Center for Urban Studies (CUS). 2005. *Slums of urban Bangladesh: Mapping and census*. Dhaka, Bangladesh; Chapel Hill, NC: National Institute of Population Research and Training (NIPORT) and MEASURE Evaluation.

Chandler, T. 1987. *Four thousand years of urban growth: A historical census*. Lewiston, NY/Queenston: St. David's University Press.

Chatwin, B. 1977. *In Patagonia*. London: Jonathan Cape.

Chen, I., J. F. Franklin, and T. A. Spies. 1992. Vegetation responses to edge environments in old-growth Douglas-fir forests. *Ecological Applications* 2(4): 387–396.

Cheshire, P. 2009. Urban containment, housing affordability, price stability—Irreconcilable goals. SJ Capital Group. *http://www.sjcapitalgroup.com/publications/Urban%20containment%20housing%20 affordability%20and%20price%20stability.pdf*

Chicago Metrarail. 2012. Metra system map. Commuter Rail Division, Regional Transportation Authority. *http://metrarail.com/content/metra/en/home/maps_schedules/metra_system_map/_jcr_content/download/file.res/metrasystemmap.pdf*

China Daily. 2010. Zhengzhou city master plan approved by the State Council. *http://www.china-daily.org/China-News/Zhengzhou-city-master-plan-approved-by-the-State-Council/*.

Choi, M. J. 1993. *Spatial and temporal variations in land values: A descriptive and behavioral analysis of the Seoul metropolitan area.* Unpublished doctoral dissertation. Cambridge, MA: Harvard University.

Christaller, W. 1966 [1933]. *Central places in southern Germany.* trans. C. W. Baskin. London: Prentice Hall.

City of Toronto. 2012. Parks, forestry, and recreation. Vision, mission, values, services. *http://www.toronto.ca/divisions/parksdiv1.htm*

Civco, D. L., J. D. Hurd, C. L. Arnold, and S. Prisloe. 2000. Characterization of suburban sprawl and forest fragmentation through remote sensing application. In *Proceedings of the American Society of Photogrammetry and Remote Sensing (ASPRS) annual convention.* Washington, DC. *http://resac.uconn.edu/publications/tech_papers/index.html*

Clark, C. 1945. The economic functions of a city in relation to its size. *Econometrica* 13(2): 97–113.

Clark, C. 1951. Urban population densities. *Journal of the Royal Geographical Society* 114(4): 490–496.

Clark, C., and M. Haswell. 1970. *The economics of subsistence agriculture.* London: Macmillan.

Clawson, M. 1962. Urban sprawl and speculation in urban land. *Land Economics* 38 (May): 99–111.

Clawson, M., and P. G. Hall. 1973. *Planning and urban growth: An Anglo American comparison.* Baltimore, MD: Johns Hopkins University Press.

COBRAPE. 2000. *Relatório Urbanização de Favelas: gerenciamento da fase final do programa Guarapiranga e avaliação de seus resultados.* São Paulo: BIRD/COBRAPE, Unidade de Gerenciamento do Programa (UGP).

Coe, N. M., P. F. Kelly, and H. W. C. Yeung. 2007. *Economic geography: A contemporary introduction.* Oxford, UK: Blackwell Publishing.

Córdoba, J. C. M. 2001. Balanced city growth and Zipf's Law. Unpublished. *http://www.ruf.rice.edu/~econ/papers/2002papers/03Cordoba.pdf*

Cox, W. 2004. Portland: Economic growth noose loosened. *The Public Purpose* 74(February): 1–3.

Davis, K. 1972. *World urbanization 1950–1970, vol. II: Analysis of trends, relationships and development.* Population Monograph Series 9. Berkeley: University of California, Institute of International Studies.

Davis, M. A., and J. Heathcote. 2007. The price and quantity of residential land in the United States. *Journal of Monetary Economics* 54: 2595–2620.

DeLong, J. B. 1998. Estimating world GDP, one million B.C.–present. Unpublished. Berkeley: University of California, Department of Economics. *http://econ161.berkeley.edu/TCEH/1998_Draft/World_GDP/Estimating_World_GDP.html*

Demographia. 2008. 4th Annual Demographia international housing affordability survey: 2008 ratings for major urban markets. *http://www.demographia.com/dhi2008.pdf*

Demographia. 2010. Sixth annual Demographia international housing affordability survey: 2010. *http://www.demographia.com/dhi-ix2005q3.pdf*

De Vries, J. 2001. Economic growth before and after the industrial revolution. In *Early modern capitalism: Economic and social change in Europe, 1400–1800,* ed. M. Prak, 175–193. London: Routledge.

Ding, C., and E. Lichtenberg. 2011. Land and urban economic growth in China. *Journal of Regional Science* 51(May): 299–317.

Dittmar, J. 2011. Cities, markets, and growth: The emergence of Zipf's Law. Unpublished. *http://www.jeremiahdittmar.com/files/Zipf_Dittmar.pdf*

Dobkins, L. H., and Y. M. Ioannides. 2000. Dynamic evolution of US city size distribution. In *Economics of cities*, eds. J. M. Huriot and J. F. Thisse, 217–260. New York: Cambridge University Press.

Dolkart, A. 2007. *Biography of a tenement house in New York City: An architectural history of 97 Orchard Street*. Santa Fe and Staunton: The Center for American Places.

Downs, A. 1992. Satan or savior: Regulatory barriers to affordable housing. *Journal of the American Planning Association* 58(4): 419–422.

Downton, P. F. 2001. *Ecopolis: Towards an integrated theory for the design, development, and maintenance of ecological cities*. Adelaide, South Australia: University of Adelaide, Department of Geographical and Environmental Studies.

Duranton, G. 2002. City size distribution as a consequence of the growth process. Unpublished discussion paper. London: Centre for Economic Performance.

Eaton, J., and Z. Eckstein. 1997. Cities and growth: Theory and evidence from France and Japan. *Regional Science and Urban Economics* 27(4–5): 443–474.

Eeckhout, J. 2004. Gibrat's law for (all) cities. *American Economic Review* 94(5): 1429–1451.

Eicher, T. S. 2008a. Housing prices and land use regulations: A study of 250 major U.S. cities. Unpublished. University of Washington. *http://depts.washington.edu/teclass/landuse/Housing051608.pdf*

Eicher, T. S. 2008b. Municipal and statewide land use regulations and housing prices across 250 major U.S. cities. Unpublished. University of Washington. *http://depts.washington.edu/teclass/landuse/housing_020408.pdf*

El Nasser, H., and P. Overberg. 2001. A comprehensive look at sprawl in America. *USA Today*, February 22. *http://www.usatoday.com/news/ sprawl/main.htm*

Engels, F. 1844. *The condition of the working class in England*. trans. W. O. Henderson and W. H. Chaloner (1958). Oxford, UK: Basil Blackwell.

Euromonitor. 1995. European marketing data and statistics 1995, tables 0201 and 2108. London: Euromonitor.

European Environment Agency. 2006. *Urban sprawl in Europe: The ignored challenge*. EEA Report No. 10/2006. Copenhagen.

Ewing, R. 1994. Characteristics, causes, and effects of sprawl: A literature review. *Environmental and Urban Issues* 21(2): 1–15.

Ewing, R., R. Pendall, and D. Chen. 2002. *Measuring sprawl and its impact. Vol. 1*. Washington, DC: Smart Growth America. *www.smartgrowthamerica.com/sprawlindex/sprawlindex.html*

FAO Statistics Division. 2012. Agricultural area and permanent crops tables 2000. Food and Agriculture Organization of the United Nations. *http://faostat.fao.org/site/377/default.aspx#ancor*

Federal Reserve Bank of Dallas. 2008. Neither boom nor bust, how Houston's housing market differs from nation's. *Houston Business. http://www.dallasfed.org/research/houston/2008/hb0801.pdf*

Fernandes, E. 2011. *Regularization of informal settlements in Latin America*. Policy Focus Report. Cambridge, MA: Lincoln Institute of Land Policy.

Fischel, W. A. 1995. *Regulatory takings: Law, economics and politics*. Cambridge, MA: Harvard University Press.

Fischel, W. A. 2005. *The homevoter hypothesis: How home values influence local government taxation, school finance, and land-use policies*. Cambridge, MA: Harvard University Press.

Fischer, G., M. Shah, H. van Velthuizen, and F. Nachtergaele. 2006. Agro-ecological zone assessment. *Encyclopedia of life support ystems (EOLSS)*. Oxford, UK: EOLSS Publishers, ch. 19, n.p.

Fletcher, D. 2009. The Khmer Rouge. *Time*, February 17. *http://www.time.com/time/world/article/0,8599,1879785,00.html*

Foster, M. S. 1980. The automobile and the city. *Michigan Historical Quarterly* XIX: 459–471.

Friedl, M. A., D. K. McIver, J. C. F. Hodges, X. Y. Zhang, D. Muchoney, A. H. Strahler, C. E. Woodcock, S. Gopal, A. Schneider, A. Cooper, A. Baccini, F. Gao, and C. Schaaf. 2002. Global land cover mapping from MODIS: Algorithms and early results. *Remote Sensing of Environment* 83: 287–302.

Frolov, Y. S. 1975. Measuring of shape of geographical phenomena: A history of the issue. *Soviet Geography: Review and Translation* 16: 676–687.

Fulton, W., R. Pendall, M. Nguyen, and A. Harrison. 2001. *Who sprawls the most? How growth patterns differ across the United States.* Washington, DC: The Brookings Institution.

Gabaix, X. 1999. Zipf's Law for cities: An explanation. *The Quarterly Journal of Economics* 114(3): 739–767.

Galster, G., R. Hanson, H. Wolman, S. Coleman, and J. Freihage. 2001. Wrestling sprawl to the ground: Defining and measuring an elusive concept. *Housing Policy Debate* 12(4): 681–685.

Gibrat, R. 1931. *Les Inégalités économiques.* Paris: Librarie du Receuil Sirey.

Ginsburg, N. 1990. Extended metropolitan regions in Asia: A new spatial paradigm. In *The urban transition: Reflections on the American and Asian experiences,* ed. N. Ginsburg, 21–42. Hong Kong: Chinese University of Hong Kong Press.

Glaeser, E. L., and J. Gyourko. 2008. *Rethinking federal housing policy: How to make housing plentiful and affordable.* Washington, DC: American Enterprise Institute.

Glaeser, E. L., and M. E. Kahn. 2004. Sprawl and urban growth. In *Handbook of regional and urban economics* 4(56), eds. J. V. Henderson and J. F. Thisee, 2481–2527. Amsterdam: Elsevier.

Glaeser, E. L., and M. E. Kahn. 2010. The greenness of cities: Carbon dioxide emissions and urban development. *Journal of Urban Economics* 67: 404–418.

Gong, P. 2012. Private communication referencing Wang et al. 2012.

Gore, A. 2006. *An inconvenient truth: The planetary emergency of global warming and what we can do about it.* New York: Rodale.

Gorelik, A. 2003. A metropolis in the Pampas: Buenos Aires 1890–1940. In *Cruelty and utopia: Cities and landscapes in Latin America*, ed. J. F. Lejuene, 147–159. New York: Princeton Architectural Press.

Gottmann, J., and R. A. Harper. 1967. *Metropolis on the move: Geographers look at urban sprawl.* New York: John Wiley and Sons.

Gottmann, J., and R. A. Harper. 1990. *Since Megalopolis: The urban writings of Jean Gottman.* Baltimore, MD: Johns Hopkins University Press.

Gough, K. V., and P. W. K. Yankson. 2000. Land markets in African cities: The case of peri-urban Accra, Ghana. *Urban Studies* 37(13): 2485–2500.

Gough, K. V., and P. W. K. Yankson. 2006. Conflict and cooperation in environmental management in peri-urban Accra. In *The peri-urban interface: Approaches to sustainable natural and human resource use*, eds. D. McGregor, D. Simon, and D. Thompson, 196–210. London: Earthscan.

Government of Ecuador. 2004. *Ley orgánica de régimen Municipal.* Quito.

Grant, R. 2009. *Globalizing city: The urban and economic transformation of Accra, Ghana.* Syracuse, NY: Syracuse University Press.

Grauman, J. V. 1976. Orders of magnitude of the world's urban population in history. *Population Bulletin of the United Nations* 8: 16–33.

Guidry, K. A., J. D. Shilling, and C. F. Sirmans. 1991. An econometric analysis of variation in urban residential land prices and the adoption of land-use controls. Working Paper. Madison, WI: University of Wisconsin, Center for Urban Land Economics Research.

Guldin, G. E. 1996. Desakotas and beyond: Urbanization in southern China. *Ethnology* 35(4): 265–283.

Gyourko, J., and A. Summers. 2006. Residential land use regulation in the Philadelphia MSA. Working Paper. Philadelphia: University of Pennsylvania, Wharton School. *http://real.wharton.upenn.edu/~gyourko/ Working%20Papers/Working%20Papers%202006/Phila delphia%20paper%20revised%2012%2012%2006.pdf*

Hall, P. G. 1997. *Cities of tomorrow: An intellectual history of urban planning and design in the twentieth century.* Oxford, UK: Blackwell.

Hall, P., R. Thomas, H. Gracey, and R. Drewett. 1973. *The containment of urban England.* London: George Allen & Unwin.

Harding, V. 1990. The population of London, 1500–1700: A review of the published evidence. *London Journal* 15(2): 111–128.

Hasse, J., and R. G. Lathrop. 2003. Land resource impact indicators of urban sprawl. *Applied Geography* 23: 159–175.

Haughwout, A., D. Lee, J. Tracy, and W. van der Klaauw. 2011. Real estate investors, the leverage cycle, and the housing market crisis. Unpublished paper. Federal Reserve Bank of New York. *www.ny.frb.org/ research/staff_reports/sr514.pdf*

Hayden, D. 2004. *A field guide to sprawl.* New York and London: W. W. Norton.

Heim, C. E. 2001. Leapfrogging, urban sprawl, and growth management: Phoenix, 1950–2000. *American Journal of Economics and Sociology* 60(1): 245–283.

Henderson, J. V. 1974. The sizes and types of cities. *American Economic Review* 64(4): 640–656.

Hereher, M. E. 2009. Inventory of agricultural land area of Egypt using MODIS data. *The Egyptian Journal of Remote Sensing and Space Sciences* 12: 179–184.

Hirsch, W. Z. 1959. Expenditure implications of metropolitan growth and consolidation. *Review of Economics and Statistics* 41: 232–241.

Hojdestrand, T. 2003. *The Soviet-Russian production of homelessness.* University of Stockholm, Department of Sociology. *http://www.anthrobase.com/Txt/H/Hoejdestrand_T_01.htm*

Holtzclaw, J. 1994. *Using residential patterns and transit to decrease costs.* Washington, DC: Natural Resources Defense Council.

Howard, E. 1902. *Garden cities of tomorrow.* Preface, F. J. Osborn; introductory essay, Lewis Mumford (1946 reprint). London: Faber and Faber.

Huxley, A. 1958. *Brave new world revisited.* New York: Harper and Brothers Company.

Hvistendahl, M. 2011. China's population growing slowly, changing fast. *Science* 332(May): 650–651.

Ingram, G. K., and A. Carroll. 1981. The spatial structure of Latin American cities. *Journal of Urban Economics* 9(2): 257–273.

Institut national de la statistique et des études économiques (INSEE). 1999. *Recensement de la population 1999—Exploitation principale.* Paris. *http://www.recensement-1999.insee.fr/*

Instituto Nacional de Estadisticia y Censo (INDEC). various dates. *Censo nacional de población, hogares y viviendas.* Gobierno de Argentina. *http://www.indec.mecon.ar/*

International Land Systems Inc. (ILS). 1997. *Landslide hazard mapping for Guatemala City*. Washington, DC: Inter-American Development Bank, October.

International Standards Organization. 1974. *ISO 3166(country codes)*. London: ISO 3166 Maintainance Agency. *http://userpage.chemie.fu-berlin.de/diverse/doc/ISO_3166.html*

Ioannides, Y. M., and H. G. Overman. 2003. Zipf's Law for cities: An empirical examination. Unpublished. *http://eprints.lse.ac.uk/583/1/gabaixcm.pdf*

Jackson, K. T. 1975. Urban deconcentration in the nineteenth century: A statistical inquiry. In *The new urban history: Quantitative explorations by American historians*, ed. L. F. Schnore, 110–144. Princeton, NJ: Princeton University Press.

Jackson, K. T. 1985. *Crabgrass frontier: The suburbanization of the United States*. New York: Oxford University Press.

Jenks, M., E. Burton, and K. Williams, eds. 1996. *The compact city: A sustainable urban form?* London: E & FN Spon.

Kasarda, J. D., and G. V. Redfearn. 1975. Differential patterns of city and suburban growth in the United States. *Journal of Urban History* 2(1): 43–66.

Katz, L., and K. T. Rosen. 1987. The interjurisdictional effects of growth controls on housing prices. *Journal of Law and Economics* 30(April): 149–160.

Kenworthy, J. R., and F. B. Laube. 1999. *An international sourcebook of automobile dependence in cities, 1960–1990*. Boulder: University Press of Colorado.

Kim, J., and S. Choe. 1997. *Seoul: The making of a metropolis*. New York: John F. Wiley Press.

Kim, K. G. 1990. *Land use changes in the urban fringe: The case of the Seoul capital green belt, Republic of Korea*. Paris: UNESCO.

Knowles, R. D. 2012. Transit Oriented Development in Copenhagen, Denmark: From the Finger Plan to Ørestad. *Journal of Transport Geography* 22 (May): 251–261.

Kostof, S. 1992. *The city assembled: The elements of urban form through history*. Boston, Toronto, and London: Bulfinch Press.

Kremer, M. 1993. Population growth and technological change: One million B.C. to 1990. *Quarterly Journal of Economics* 88: 681–716.

Krugman, P. 1996. Confronting the mystery of urban hierarchy. *Journal of the Japanese and International Economies* 10(4): 399–418.

Krugman, P., and E. R. Livas. 1996. Trade policy and the third world metropolis. *Journal of Development Economics* 49(1): 137–150.

Lai, R. T. 1988. *Law in urban design and planning*. New York: Von Nostrand.

Larsson, G. 1993. *Land readjustment: A modern approach to urbanization*. Surrey, UK: Ashgate (formerly Avebury).

Le Corbusier. 1960. *Le Corbusier 1910–60*. Zurich: Editions Girsberger.

Lee, C. M. 1999. An intertemporal efficiency test of a greenbelt: Assessing the economic impacts of Seoul's greenbelt. *Journal of Planning Education and Research* 19(1): 41–52.

Lessinger, J. 1962. The case for scatteration. *Journal of the American Institute of Planners* 28(3): 159–169.

Lewis, S. M., and J. Young. 1919. How 'ya gonna keep 'em down on the farm, after they've seen Paree? New York: Waterson, Berlin & Snyder Co., Music Publishing.

Li, H., M. Rosenzweig, and J. Zhang. 2009. *Altruism, favoritism, and guilt in the allocation of family resources: Sophie's choice in Mao's mass send-down movement.* University of Wisconsin Economics Workshop. *http://www.econ.wisc.edu/workshop/Rosenzweig_paper.pdf*

Liauw, L. 1998. KWC FAR 12: Kowloon Walled City density study 1995. *FARMAX: Excursions on density,* eds. W. Maas, J. van Rijs, and R. Koek, 152–173. Rotterdam: 010 Publishers.

Lichtenberg, E., and C. Ding. 2007. Assessing farmland protection policy in China. In *Urbanization in China,* eds. Y. Song and C. Ding, 101–166. Cambridge, MA: Lincoln Institute of Land Policy.

Liddell Hart, B. H. 1967. *Strategy,* 2nd rev. ed. New York: Praeger.

Light, K., and M. Light. 2012. The vanishing valley. *New York Times,* May 20, 7.

Lowry, I. 1988. *Planning for urban sprawl.* Transportation Research Board Special Report 220: 275–312. Washington, DC: Transportation Research Board.

Mackay, D. A. 1987. *The building of Manhattan.* New York: Harper and Row.

Malpezzi, S., and S. M. Wachter. 2005. The role of speculation in real estate cycles. *Journal of Real Estate Literature* 13(2): 143–166.

Martin, G., G. McGranahan, M. Montgomery, and R. Fernandez-Casilla, eds. 2008. *The new global frontier: Urbanization, poverty and environment in the 21ˢᵗ century.* London, and Sterling, VA: Earthscan.

Mayo, S. K., and D. A. Gross. 1987. Sites and services—and subsidies: The economics of low-cost housing in developing countries. *World Bank Economic Review* 1(2): 301–335.

McGee, T. G. 1991. The emergence of desakota regions in Asia: Expanding a hypothesis. In *The extended metropolis: Settlement transition in Asia,* eds. N. Ginsburg, B. Koppel, and T. G. McGee, 3–26. Honolulu: University of Hawaii Press.

McMillan, D. P. 2006. Testing for monocentricity. In *A companion to urban economics,* eds. R. J. Arnott and D. P. McMillen, 128–140. Oxford, UK: Blackwell.

Mendelbrot, B. 1967. How long is the coast of Britain? *Science,* New Series 156(3775): 636–638.

Metro. 2012a. Population estimates inside the metro boundary. Multnomah County, OR: Metro Data Resource Center. *http://library.oregonmetro.gov/files/MetroUGBpop1980toPresent.pdf*

Metro. 2012b. UGB aerial 2. Multnomah County, OR: Metro Data Resource Center.

Miles and Co. 1878. *Illustrated historical atlas of the county of York and the township of West Gwillimbury and town of Bradford in the county of Simcoe, Ont.* Toronto: Miles and Co.

Mills, E. S. 1967. An aggregative model of resource allocation in a metropolitan area. *American Economic Review* 57: 197–210.

Mills, E. S. 1972. *Studies in the structure of the urban economy.* Baltimore, MD: Johns Hopkins Press.

Mills, E. S., and K. Ohta. 1976. Urbanization and urban problems. In *Asia's new giant: How the Japanese economy works,* eds. H. Patrick and H. Rosovsky, 673–751. Washington, DC: Brookings Institution.

Mills, E. S., and J. P. Tan. 1980. A comparison of urban population density functions in developed and developing countries. *Urban Studies* 17(3): 313–321.

Milne, A. A. 1924. *When we were very young.* London: Methuen Children's Books.

Mintzker, Y. 2006. *The defortification of the German city: 1689–1866.* Unpublished doctoral dissertation. Palo Alto, CA: Stanford University.

Moomaw, R. L. and M. A. Alwosabi. 2004. An empirical analysis of competing explanations of urban primacy evidence from Asia and the Americas. *The Annals of Regional Science* 38(1, Spring): 149–171.

Muller, P. O. 2004. Transportation and urban form: Stages in the spatial evolution of the American metropolis. In *The geography of urban transportation*, 3rd ed., eds. S. Hanson and G. Giuliani, 59–84. New York and London: The Guilford Press.

Mumbai Metropolitan Region Development Authority (MMRDA). 1996. *Regional plan for Mumbai metropolitan region 1996–2011.* Mumbai, India. *http://www.regionalplan-mmrda.org/*

Municipality of Guatemala. 1995. *Metropolis 2010: Plan de desarrollo metropolitan.* Guatemala City, November.

Municipality of Milagro. 2006. Propiedades rurales que constan en el catastro municipal del Canton Milagro. Unpublished document.

Munton, R. J. C. 1983. *London's green belt: Containment in practice.* London and Boston: Allen & Unwin.

Murphy, T. 2011. First they came for the lightbulbs. *Mother Jones*, August 4. *http://motherjones.com/politics/2011/08/michele-bachmann-light-bulbs-agenda-21*

Muth, R. 1961. The spatial structure of the housing market. *Papers and Proceedings of the Regional Science Association* 7: 207–220.

Muth, R. 1969. *Cities and housing.* Chicago: University of Chicago Press.

Nandwa, B., and L. Ogura. 2010. Do urban growth controls slow down regional economic growth? Land use prof blog. *http://lawprofessors.typepad.com/land_use/2010/05/nandwa-ogura-on-the-urbran-growth-controls-and-regional-economic-growth.html*

National Aeronautics and Space Administration (NASA). multiple dates. Landsat historical maps. *www.landsat.com*

National Historical Geographic Information System (NHGIS). 2012. Aggregate census data and GIS-compatible boundary files for the United States between 1790 and 2000. *www.nhgis.org/*

Nelson, A. C., C. J. Dawkins, and T. W. Sanchez. 2004. Urban containment and residential segregation: A preliminary investigation. *Urban Studies* 41: 423–439.

Nelson, A. C., C. J. Dawkins, and T. W. Sanchez. 2008. *The social impacts of urban containment.* Aldershot, UK: Ashgate.

Nelson, A. C., C. J. Duncan, C. Mullen, and K. Bishop. 1995. *Growth management: Principles and practices.* Chicago: APA Planners Press.

Newman, P., and J. Kenworthy. 1999. *Sustainability and cities: Overcoming automobile dependence.* Washington, DC: Island Press.

New York Times Editorial Board. 1876. Overcrowding in tenement houses. *New York Times*, December 3. *http://query.nytimes.com/mem/archive-free/pdf?res=9900EED9153FE63BBC4B53DFB467838D669FDE*

Nordhaus, W. D. 1997. Do real wages and output series capture reality? The history of lighting suggests not. In *The economics of new goods*, eds. T. Bresnahan and R. Gordon, 27–70. Chicago: University of Chicago Press.

O'Flaherty, B. 2005. *City economics.* Cambridge, MA, and London, England: Harvard University Press.

Olmsted, F. L., H. Bartholomew, and C. Cheney. 1924. *A major traffic street plan for Los Angeles.* Los Angeles: Committee on Los Angeles Plan of Major Highways of the Traffic Commission of the City and County of Los Angeles.

Omran, A. R. 2005. The epidemiologic transition: A theory of the epidemiology of population change. *Milbank Quarterly* 83(4):731–757.

Ottensman, J. R. 1977. Urban sprawl, land values, and the density of development. *Land Economics* 53(4): 389–400.

Overman, H. G., D. Puga, and M. A. Turner. 2008. Decomposing the growth in residential land in the United States. *Regional Science and Urban Economics* 38(5): 487–497.

Parr, J. 2007. Spatial definitions of the city: Four perspectives. *Urban Studies* 44(2): 381–392.

Peiser, R. B. 1989. Density and urban sprawl. *Land Economics* 65(3): 193–204.

Pereira, A. S. n.d. When did modern economic growth really start? The empirics of Malthus to Solow. Unpublished. University of British Columbia, Department of Economics. *http://www.uoguelph.ca/~cneh/pdfs/pereira.pdf*

Pfeffer, M. J., and M. B. Lapping. 1995. Prospects for a sustainable agriculture on the northeast's rural/urban fringe. *Research in Rural Sociology and Development* 6: 67–93.

Piffero, E. 2009. Beyond rules and regulations: The growth of informal Cairo. In *Cairo's informal areas— Between urban challenges and hidden potentials: Facts, voices, visions*, eds. R. Kipper and M. Fischer, 21–28. Participatory Development Programme. Cairo: GTZ.

Planning and Development Collaborative International (PADCO). 1987. *The land and housing markets of Bangkok: Strategies for public sector participation*, Vol. 2: Technical Reports. Prepared for the National Housing Authority of Thailand (NHA) and the Asian Development Bank (ADB). Bangkok: Planning and Development Collaborative International.

Popper, K. R. 1994. *The myth of the framework: In defence of science and rationality*, ed. M. A. Notturno. London: Routledge.

Potere, D., A. Schneider, S. Angel, and D. L. Civco. 2009. Mapping urban areas on a global scale: Which of the eight maps now available is more accurate? *International Journal of Remote Sensing* 30(24): 6531–6558.

Power, A. 1949. *From the old Waterford house*. London: Mellifont Press.

Provost, C. 2012. New international land deals database reveals rush to buy up Africa: World's largest public database lifts lid on the extent and secretive nature of the global demand for land. *The Guardian*, April 27. *http://www.guardian.co.uk/global-development/2012/apr/27/international-land-deals-database-africa*

Pushkarev, B., and J. Zupan. 1977. *Public transportation and land use policy*. Bloomington: Indiana University Press.

Quigley, J. M., and L. Rosenthal. 2005. The effects of land use regulation on the price of housing: What do we know? What can we learn? *Cityscape* 8: 69–138.

Redcliffe-Maud, L. 1969. *Royal commission on local government in England*. Command Paper 4040. London: H. M. S .O.

Red-Grey.co.uk. 2012. Milton Keynes road map views. *http://www.red-grey.co.uk/general/milton-keynes-road-map.html*

Richardson, H. W. 1972. Optimality in city size, systems of cities and urban policy: A skeptic's view. *Urban Studies* 9(1): 29–47.

Richardson, H. W., C. C. Bae, and M. H. Baxamusa. 2000. Compact cities in developing countries: Assessment and implications. In *Compact cities: Sustainable urban forms for developing countries*, eds. M. Jenks and R. Burgess, 25–36. London and New York: Spon Press.

Riis, J. 1890. *How the other half lives*. Mineola, NY: Dover Publications. (Reprinted 1971).

Risse, A. L. 1900. General map of the City of New York. Topographical Bureau, Board of Public Improvements. New York: Robert A. Welcke.

Ritter, C. 1822. *Die erdkunde im verhältniss zur natur und geschichte des menschen, oder allgemeine vergleichende geographie*, 2nd ed., Part I, Book 1. Berlin: Georg Friedrich Hermann Müller.

Robbs, D. 2009. District energy for Helsinki—A highly efficient heating and cooling model. *Cogeneration and Onsite Power Production* 10(3): n.p. *http://www.cospp.com/articles/print/volume-10/issue-3/project-profile/district-energy-for-helsinki-a-highly-efficient-heating-and-cooling-model.html*

Rosen, K., and M. Resnick. 1980. The size distribution of cities: An examination of the Pareto law and primacy. *Journal of Urban Economics* 8: 165–186.

Roses, D. F. 1996. Vaccination's bicentennial: A surgical landmark. *Bulletin of the American College of Surgeons* 81: 28–35.

Russell, J. C. 1948. *British medieval population*. Albuquerque: The University of New Mexico Press.

Saks, R. 2005. *Job creation and housing construction: Constraints on employment growth in metropolitan areas.* Cambridge, MA: Harvard University, Joint Center for Housing Studies. *http://www.jchs.harvard.edu/publications/markets/w04-10_saks.pdf*

Sargent, C. S. 1974. *The spatial evolution of greater Buenos Aires, Argentina, 1870–1930.* Tempe: Arizona State University, Center for Latin American Studies.

Saunders, D. 2011. *Arrival cities: The final migration and our next world.* New York: Pantheon.

Schneider, A., M. A. Friedl, and D. Potere. 2009. A new map of global urban extent from MODIS data. *Environmental Research Letters* 4: 1–11.

Schneider, J. F. von. 1798. Plan von Berlin nebst denen umliegenden Gegenden im Jahr 1798. Engraver: von Ludewig Schmidt.

Secretaria de Transporte. 2010. *INTRUPUBA: Investigación de transporte urbano público de Buenos Aires.* Buenos Aires: Ministerio de Planificacion Federal.

Séjourné, M. 2006. *Les politiques récentes de traitement des quartiers illégaux au Caire.* Unpublished doctoral dissertation. Tours, France: Université de Tours.

Séjourné, M. 2009. The history of informal settlements. In *Cairo's informal areas between urban challenges and hidden potential: Facts, voices, visions*, eds. R. Kipper and M. Fischer, 17–19. Cairo: GTZ.

Self, P. 1961. *Cities in flood: The problems of urban growth.* London: Faber and Faber.

Seoul Metropolis. 1991. Reports on establishment census, vol. 2: Region. Seoul, Korea: City of Seoul.

Sharma, R. 2011. Food export restrictions: Review of the 2007–2010 experience and considerations for disciplining restrictive measures. FAO Commodity and Trade Policy Research Working Paper No. 32. Rome: U.N. FAO. *http://www.fao.org/fileadmin/templates/est/PUBLICATIONS/Comm_Working_Papers/EST-WP32.pdf*

Simon, H. A. 1955. On a class of skew distribution functions. *Biometrica* 42(3–4): 425–440.

Sims, D. 2000. *Residential informality in greater Cairo: Typologies, representative areas, quantification, valuation and causal factors.* Cairo: ECES, ILD.

Sims, D., and M. Séjourné. 2008. The dynamics of peri-urban areas around greater Cairo. Concept note, Egypt Urban Sector update. Washington, DC: World Bank.

Sinclair, R. 1967. Von Thünen and urban sprawl. *Annals of the Association of American Geographers* 57: 72–87.

Society for the Diffusion of Useful Knowledge. 1844. *Maps of the society for the diffusion of useful knowledge.* Engraved by B. R. Davies. London: Chapman and Hall.

Socioeconomic and Data Applications Center (SEDAC). 2011. *Gridded population of the world and the global rural-urban mapping project.* Center for International Earth Science Information Network (CIESIN). New York: Columbia University, Earth Institute. *http://sedac.ciesin.columbia.edu/gpw/global.jsp*

Soria y Puig, A. 1999. *Cerdá: The five bases of the general theory of urbanization.* Madrid: Electa.

State of Oregon. 2012. Oregon administrative rule 660-024. Archives of Oregon. Salem, Oregon: Secretary of State. *http://arcweb.sos.state.or.us/pages/rules/oars_600/oar_660/660_024.html*

Stern, N. 2008. The economics of climate change. *American Economic Review* 98(2): 1–37.

Strype, J. 1720. *A survey of London brought from the year 1633.* London: John Strype Publisher.

Sullivan, L. 1896. The tall office building artistically considered. *Lippincott's Magazine* 57: 403–409.

Taleb, N. N. 2007. *The black swan: The impact of the highly improbable.* New York: Random House.

Thomson, W. 1883. Lecture on electrical units of measurement. *Popular Lectures* 1(May): 73.

Tianjin Municipal Statistical Bureau. 2006. *Tianjin 2006 basic facts.* Tianjin, China.

Tokyo Shiyakusho. 1930. Old Tokyo 1930. In *Tokyo, capital of Japan reconstruction work.* English ed. Tokyo Municipal Office.

Toronto Transit Commission. 2012. System map. Toronto, Ontario. *http://www3.ttc.ca/Routes/General_Information/Maps/System.jsp*

Torrens, P. M., and M. Alberti. 2000. Measuring sprawl. Working Paper 27. London: Center for Advanced Spatial Analysis (CASA).

Turner, J. F. C. 1967. Barriers and channels for housing development in modernizing countries. *Journal of the American Institute of Planners* 32(3): 167–181.

United Nations. 1948. *Universal declaration of human rights.* New York: United Nations. *http://www.hrweb.org/legal/udhr.html*

United Nations Food and Agriculture Organization (FAO). 2009. *High level expert forum—How to feed the world in 2050.* Office of the Director, Agricultural Development Economics Division. Rome: United Nations. *http://www.fao.org/fileadmin/templates/wsfs/docs/Issues_papers/HLEF2050_Global_Agriculture.pdf*

United Nations Human Settlements Programme. 2003. *The challenge of slums.* New York: United Nations.

United Nations Population Division. 2005. *World urbanization prospects—The 2003 revision.* New York: United Nations Department of Economic and Social Affairs.

United Nations Population Division. 2008. *World urbanization prospects: The 2007 revision.* New York: United Nations Department of Economic and Social Affairs.

United Nations Population Division. 2010. *World urbanization prospects: The 2009 revision.* New York: United Nations Department of Economic and Social Affairs.

United Nations Population Division. 2012. *World urbanization prospects: The 2011 revision.* New York: United Nations Department of Economic and Social Affairs.

United States Geological Survey (USGS). 1989. Map of Detroit, Michigan. National aerial photography program. Washington, DC: U.S. Department of the Interior.

U.S. Bureau of the Census. 1970–2010. *Statistical abstracts.* Washington, DC: Bureau of the Census, Department of Commerce. *www.census.gov/prod/www/abs/statab.html*

U.S. Bureau of the Census. 2002. Urban area criteria for census 2000. Washington, DC: Bureau of the Census, Department of Commerce. *http://www.census.gov/geo/www/ua/uafedreg031502.txt*

U.S. Bureau of Transportation Statistics. 2010. *Transportation statistics annual report—2010.* Washington, DC: U.S. Department of Transportation. *http://www.bts.gov/publications/transportation_statistics_annual_report*

Vallance, S., H. C. Perkins, and K. Moore. 2005. The results of making a city more compact: Neighbours' interpretation of urban infill. *Environment and Planning B: Planning and Design* 32(5): 715–733.

Van Tilburg Clark, W. 1940. *The ox-bow incident.* New York: Random House.

Vapñarsky, C. 1975. The Argentine system of cities: Primacy and rank-size rule. In *Urbanization in Latin America*, ed. J. Hardoy, 369–390. Garden City, NY: Anchor Books.

Vapñarsky, C. 2000. *La aglomeración Gran Buenos Aires: expansión espacial y crecimiento demográfico entre 1869 y 1991*. Buenos Aires: Eudeba.

Vermeulen, W., and J. V. Ommeren. 2008. Does land use planning shape regional economies? Tinbergen Institute Discussion Paper. Rotterdam, The Netherlands: Erasmus University. *http://www.tinbergen.nl/discussionpapers/08004.pdf*

Von der Dollen, B. 1990. An historico-geographical perspective on urban fringe-belt phenomena. In *The built form of western cities*, ed. T. R. Slater, 319–345. Leicester: Leicester University Press.

Von Thünen, J. H. 1826. *Der isolierte staat in beziehung auf landwirtschaft und nationalölkonomie, oder untersuchungen über den einfluß, den die getreidepreise, der reichtum des bodens und die abgaben auf den ackerbau ausüben*. English ed. (1966) trans. C. M. Wartenberg as *Von Thünen's Isolated State*, ed. P. Hall. London and New York: Pergamon Press.

Wang, L., C. C. Li, Q. Ying, X. Cheng, X. Y. Wang, X. Y. Li, L. Y. Hu, L. Liang, L. Yu, H. B. Huang, and P. Gong. 2012. China's urban expansion from 1990 to 2010 determined with satellite remote sensing. *China Science Bulletin* 57: 1–11.

Wardrop, J. G. 1952. Some theoretical aspects of road traffic research. *Proceedings, Institute of Civil Engineers*. part II, vol. 1, 325–378.

Weber, A. F. 1899. *The growth of cities in the nineteenth century*. New York: Macmillan Company for Columbia University.

Webster, D., A. Bertaud, C. Jianming, and Y. Zhenshan. 2010. *Toward efficient urban form in China*. Working Paper No. 2010/97. New York: World Institute for Development Economics Research (WIDER).

Weitz, J., and T. Moore. 1998. Development inside urban growth boundaries: Oregon's empirical evidence of contiguous urban form. *Journal of the American Planning Association* 64(4): 424–440.

Wheaton, W. C. 1974. A comparative static analysis of urban spatial structure. *Journal of Economic Theory* 9(2): 223–237.

Wheaton, W. C. 1976. On the optimal distribution of income among cities. *Journal of Urban Economics* 3: 31–44.

Wheaton, W. C., and H. Shishido. 1981. Urban concentration, agglomeration economies and the level of economic development. *Economic Development and Cultural Change* 30: 17–30.

Winter, M., D. H. Johnson, and J. Faaborg. 2000. Evidence for edge effects on multiple levels in tallgrass prairie. *Condor* 102(2): 256–266. *http://www.npwrc.usgs.gov/resource/birds/edgeffct/index.htm*

Wolman, H., G. Galster, H. Hanson, M. N. Ratcliffe, K. Furdell, and A. Sarzynski. 2005. The fundamental challenge in measuring sprawl: Which land should be considered? *Professional Geographer* 57(1): 94–105.

World Bank. 2012a. *World development indicators*. New York: World Bank Group. Digital Data. *http://data.worldbank.org/data-catalog/world-development-indicators*

World Bank. 2012b. *Worldwide governance indicators—The 2011 revision*. New York: World Bank Group. Digital Data. *http://info.worldbank.org/governance/wgi/sc_country.asp*

World Resources Institute. 2012. *Earth trends: Environmental information*. Washington, DC: World Resources Institute. *http://www.wri.org/project/earthtrends/*

Wu, J., J. Gyourko, and Y. Deng. 2010. Evaluating conditions in major Chinese housing markets. NBER Working Paper 16189. New York: National Bureau of Economic Research.

Yankson, P. W., R. Y. Kofie, and L. Moller-Jensen. 2004. Monitoring urban growth: Urbanization of the fringe areas of Accra. *Bulletin of the Ghana Geographical Association* 24: 1–13.

Yehboah, I. E. A. 2000. Structural adjustment and emerging urban form in Accra, Ghana. *Africa Today* 47(2): 61–89.

Young, A. 1999. Is there really spare land? A critique of estimates of available cultivable land in developing countries. *Environment, Development and Sustainability* 1: 3–18.

Zhao, P., B. Lu, and G. Roo. 2010. Performance and dilemmas of urban containment strategies in the transformation context of Beijing. *Journal of Environmental Planning and Management* 53(2): 143–161.

Zheng, S., R. Wang, E. L. Glaeser, and M. E. Kahn. 2011. The greenness of China: Household carbon dioxide emissions and urban development. *Journal of Economic Geography* 11(5): 761–792.

Zheng, X. 2007. Measure of optimal city sizes in Japan: A surplus function approach. *Urban Studies* 44(5/6): 939–951.

Zipf, G. K. 1949. *Human behavior and the principle of least effort.* Cambridge, MA: Addison-Wesley.

Photograph Credits

64   A *tuk-tuk* in Bangkok, Thailand: *Shutterstock*

66   The El Carmen settlement, Comas district, Lima, Peru: © *Google Earth 2012/GeoEye 2012*

67   House in the Comas district, Lima, Peru: *Courtesy of Inmobiliaria MantyObras*

78   "Fight Between Carnival and Lent" by Pieter Breugel the Elder, 1559: *Courtesy of the Kunsthistorisches Museum*

79   Copper works in Swansea Harbor, Wales: *CMSP Education/Newscom*

84   "Marketplace in Naples During the Plague of 1656," by Carlo Coppola: © *Roger-Viollet/The Image Works*

88   The city walls of Xian, China: © *Maros Mraz, Creative Commons*

92   Omnibus service in Paris, France: © *Musee Carnavalet/ Roger-Viollet / The Image Works*

93   Horsecar on rails in New York City: *Courtesy of New York Transit Museum*

99   (top): Amsterdam Harbor, the Netherlands: *INTERFOTO / A. Koch / Mary Evans Picture Library*

99   (left): A silk factory in Japan: © *Enami-Suito/Rob Oechsle Collection*

99   (right): An electronics factory in Cicarang, Indonesia: *iStockphoto*

108   An arterial road in Lagos, Nigeria: *AFP PHOTO / PIUS UTOMI EKPEI /Newscom*

109   (top): Low-density sprawl in the United States: *Creative Commons*

109   (bottom): A bridge approach in Shanghai, China: *iStockphoto*

112   Greater Tokyo, Japan: *Creative Commons*

130   Bangkok, Thailand: *iStockphoto*

144   (left): Lakewood suburb of Los Angeles, California: *Courtesy of Security Pacific National Bank Collection/Los Angeles Public Library*

144   (right): Franklin Township, New Jersey: © *Anton Nelessen*

146   (left): The medinah in Fez, Morocco: *Creative Commons*

146   (right): Le Corbusier's *Plan Voisin*, Paris, France, 1925: © *Fondation Le Corbusier*

159   Low-density development on the fringe of Accra, Ghana: © *Google Earth 2012/DigitalGlobe 2012*

163   (top): The expansion of informal settlements in Cairo, Egypt, 2002: © *Google Earth 2012/DigitalGlobe 2012/ORION-ME 2012; U.S. Geological Survey*

163   (bottom): The expansion of informal settlements in Cairo, Egypt, 2010: © *Google Earth 2012/DigitalGlobe 2012/ORION-ME 2012*

177   (left): Downtown Hong Kong, China: *iStockphoto*

177   (right): Tacoma, Washington: © *Ron Reiring*

196   Century City, Los Angeles, California: *iStockphoto*

197   Chicago, Illinois: © *James Grumme/Above All Photo*

206   Wildlife on the urban fringe: *iStockphoto*

213   Informal settlements in Caracas, Venezuela: © *José Miguel Menendez*

214   Subsistence farming in Zhengzhou, China: © *Aritesoma Ukueberuwa, Princeton University*

215   (left): Tianjin, China, 2004: © *Google Earth 2010/DigitalGlobe 2010*

215   (right): Tianjin, China, 2009: © *Google Earth 2010/GeoEye 2010*

216   Shenzhen, China: © *Ross Renjilian*

220   The Columbia River in Portland, Oregon: © *Rick Bowmer / AP Photos*

225   (top): Jellyfish: © *Paul Souders / The Image Bank / Getty*

225   (middle): Starfish: © *Lilli Day / Photodisk / Getty*

225   (bottom): Sea Snake: © *Borut Furlan / WaterFrame / Getty*

234   Alexandria, Egypt: *iStockphoto*

237   Le Corbusier with plan for Chandigarh, India: © *FLC / ADAGP 2012*

245   The Colonia Buena Vista, Guatemala City, Guatemala: © *Alvaro Uribe*

246   São Paulo, Brazil: *iStockphoto*

252   (top): Beijing, China: *iStockphoto*

252   (bottom): Quito, Ecuador: © *Alvaro Uribe*

255   Children in Freetown, Sierra Leone: *iStockphoto*

261   A real estate fair in Zhengzhou, China: *Imaginechina / AP Images*

267   Suburban fringe of Paris, France: *iStockphoto*

278   Tea estate near Lake Kivu, Democratic Republic of the Congo: *iStockphoto*

287   Republic Avenue in Quezon City, Metro Manila, the Philippines: © *Google Earth 2010 / Digital Globe 2010 / Mapabc.com 2010 / Kingway 2010*

298   An urban park in Singapore: *Creative Commons*

Index

Numbers in italics indicate pages with illustrations and photographs.

233; geographical constraints on, 233–234, 239; in global samples of cities, 239–240, 242–244; historical perspective on, 227–230; land cover and, 251; metrics for, 142–143, 145, 146, 151, 237–239; monocentric cities and, 227–228; planning for expansion and, 224–226, 244–246, 293; polycentric cities and, 229–230; private-sector development and, 224; shape of cities and, 145; spatial structure of cities and, 145; theoretical study of, 226–227; transport changes and, 230–232, 247, 293; in U.S. cities, 240–241; variations in, 223–224, 242–244; walled cities and, 227

Congo, Democratic Republic of, 168, 274, *278*

Constantinople, 90–91, 266

Containment Paradigm: background of, 18, 42; expansion and development viewed in, 18, 42, 73, 286–287; housing policy and, 41–42, 53; land use planning with, 41, 73; Making Room Paradigm as an alternative to, 18, 73, 287, 304; Seoul's greenbelt as example of, 42–45

containment strategies: China's policies using, 14, 260–263; fragmentation and, 207, 220; suitability of, 289; U.S. urban expansion and, 108; urban growth boundary for, 184–185, 207, 213, 217, 219, 251, 291, 297–298; urban sprawl and, 13–14, 41–42

Copenhagen, Denmark, 234–236, 244

Cordoba, Rodolfo, 14

corruption, 60, 105

cultivated lands, 265–282; central place theory on, 118; in China, 215, 260–262, 263, 270; city populations and, 277–278, 294; compactness and, 233, 244; density changes and, 182, 184, 275–277; in Egypt, 160–161, 162, 270; expanding areas of, 275–277; food security policies and, 215, 260–262, 263, 270–271; fragmentation of, 206; global amount of land as, 272–274; government regulation of leasing of, 271; growth of cities and, 282; historical perspective on, 265–268; land cover and, 168, 169, 260, 269–270; loss of, 278–281; major crop groups and, 272; maps showing location of, 140, 146; planning and, 282, 294; potential availability of, 274; productivity and yields from, 272–274, 282; urban expansion and, 9. *See also* agriculture

Curitiba, Brazil, 34, *35*

Czech Republic, 125, 259

Dar es Salaam, Tanzania, 15

Darwin, Charles, 55

Davis, Kingsley, 114–115, 123

Decent Housing Proposition, 41–55; Bangkok's affordable housing policies and, 45–52; basic policy framework using, 73; Containment Paradigm and, 41–42; environmental policies and, 54–55; improving living conditions in informal settlements and, 52–53; infrastructure needs and, 53–54; land rental slums and, 47–50; land supply and affordable housing in, 52, 53;

Seoul's greenbelt and limits in, 42–45; statement of, 19, 73, 288

Delhi, India, 111

Democratic Republic of Congo, *278*

densities: in ancient Rome, 92; in Bangkok slums, 47–48; in Buenos Aires, 188, 189–194; carbon emissions and, 31–33, 290; census track data on, 37, 138, 139, 148, 149, 172, 185; centrality changes and, 194–201; change over time of, 291–292; Chinese cities' overcrowding and, 38–39; classical economic theory of urban spatial structure on differences in, 181–182, 183; compactness and, 145; comparison of United States and Bangladesh for, 30–31; containment strategies and, 41, 289; expansion of cities and, 29, 294; fragmentation and, 146, 208; in global samples of cities, 139, 176–179; Goldilocks Principle and, 30; land cover maps of large cities and, 140; metrics for, 145, 146, 148–149; Moscow's land use policy and, 58; in New York City, 30–31, 35–37; primacy level of countries related to, 129, 131; public transit and, 33–35, 36; Seoul's redevelopment policy and, 44–45; spatial structure of cities and, 144–145; sprawl and, 97, 145, 171, 184–185, 208, 214, 217; Sustainable Densities Proposition on, 29–39, 287–288; urbanization and population growth and, 105, 108

density decline, 171–185; in Baltimore, 172–173; change over time in, 291–292; classical economic theory of urban spatial structure on, 181–182; cultivated land and, 275–277; in developed countries, 172; in developing countries, 171–172, 180; global nature of, 171; in global samples of cities, 174, 175–184; historical evidence of, 172–176; in Mexico City, 174–175; per capita income and, 180; population growth and, 172, 176, 180, 254; projections of, 254–255; projections (2000–2050) for, 184–195; sprawl and, 171; in the United States, 171, 172–174

depth compactness, 227, 236, 238

depth index, 151, 237

Detroit, Michigan, 300

developed countries: city footprint ratios in, 209; compactness of cities in, 239; cultivated land in, 137, 278; decentralization in, 194; densities of cities in, 178, 179, 183, 194; land cover in, 258; openness index in, 209; population growth in, 104, 172, 254; urban expansion issues and, 12–16; urbanization in, 97–100

developing countries: containment strategies in, 13; cultivated land in, 278; densities of cities in, 179, 183, 194; density decline in, 171–172, 180; land cover in, 176, 258, 294; openness index in, 209; population growth in, 172, 176, 180, 254; urban expansion issues and, 12–16; urbanization in, 100–105, 109

DeWitt, Simeon, 24

Dhaka, Bangladesh, 30, 38, 48, 120, 297

Djibouti, 269

Duluth, Minnesota, 241

About the Author

Shlomo Angel is a visiting fellow of the Lincoln Institute of Land Policy. He is an adjunct professor of urban planning at the Robert F. Wagner School of Public Service of New York University, and lecturer in public and international affairs at the Woodrow Wilson School of Princeton University. As of 2012, he is also a senior research scholar at the Urbanization Project at the Stern School of Business of New York University.

Dr. Angel earned a bachelor's degree in architecture and a doctorate in city and regional planning at the University of California, Berkeley. While at Berkeley, he collaborated with colleagues on two books on architecture, planning, and building: *A Pattern Language: Town, Buildings, Construction;* and *The Oregon Experiment*. In 1973, he started a program in Human Settlements Planning and Development at the Asian Institute of Technology in Bangkok, Thailand. As a professor of human settlements planning, he taught at the Institute from 1973 to 1983, while undertaking research on housing and urban development in the cities of East, South, and Southeast Asia. He also organized and managed the Building Together Project, a self-help and mutual-aid housing project for 200 Bangkok slum families. At the end of his tenure at the Institute, he co-edited and published *Land for Housing the Poor*.

From the mid-1980s to the mid-1990s, he worked as a housing and urban development consultant to the United Nations Centre of Human Settlements (UN-Habitat), the Asian Development Bank, and the Government of Thailand. He also co-drafted the United Nations' *Global Strategy for Shelter for the Year 2000* in 1988, and the World Bank's housing policy paper, *Housing: Enabling Markets to Work*, in 1992. From the mid- to late-1990s, he worked as a consultant to the World Bank on urban and housing indicators and on housing sector reforms in Eastern Europe. In 2000, he published *Housing Policy Matters: A Global Analysis*, a comparative study of housing conditions and housing policies in 53 cities in 53 countries. From 2000 onward, he prepared housing sector assessments of 11 Latin America and Caribbean countries for the Inter-American Development Bank and the World Bank. In 2003, he published *The Tale of the Scale: An Odyssey of Invention*, which focuses on the teaching of design through narrative. He has visited cities in 40 countries in connection with research and professional work on housing and urban development.

About the Lincoln Institute of Land Policy

The Lincoln Institute of Land Policy is a private operating foundation whose mission is to improve the quality of public debate and decisions in the areas of land policy and land-related taxation in the United States and around the world. The Institute's goals are to integrate theory and practice to better shape land policy and to provide a nonpartisan forum for discussion of the multidisciplinary forces that influence public policy. This focus on land derives from the Institute's founding objective—to address the links between land policy and social and economic progress—which was identified and analyzed by political economist and author Henry George.

The work of the Institute is organized in three departments: Valuation and Taxation, Planning and Urban Form, and International Studies, which includes programs on Latin America and China. We seek to inform decision making through education, research, policy evaluation, demonstration projects, and the dissemination of information through our publications, website, and other media. Our programs bring together scholars, practitioners, public officials, policy makers, journalists, and citizens in a collegial learning environment. The Institute does not take a particular point of view, but rather serves as a catalyst to facilitate analysis and discussion of land use and taxation issues—to make a difference today and to help policy makers plan for tomorrow. The Lincoln Institute of Land Policy is an equal opportunity institution.

LINCOLN INSTITUTE
OF LAND POLICY

113 Brattle Street
Cambridge, MA 02138-3400 USA

Phone: 1-617-661-3016 or 1-800-526-3873
Fax: 1-617-661-7235 or 1-800-526-3944
E-mail: *help@lincolninst.edu*
Web: *www.lincolninst.edu*